1495

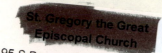

# THE HUMILIATION OF THE WORD

## Jacques Ellul

*TRANSLATED BY*
Joyce Main Hanks

WILLIAM B. EERDMANS PUBLISHING COMPANY
GRAND RAPIDS, MICHIGAN

Copyright ©1985 by William B. Eerdmans Publishing Co.
255 Jefferson Ave. S.E., Grand Rapids, Mich. 49503

Translated from the French *La parole humiliée*,
©*Éditions du Seuil, Paris, 1981*

**Library of Congress Cataloging in Publication Data**
Ellul, Jacques.
   The humiliation of the word.

   Translation of: La parole humiliée.
   1. Christianity—20th century. 2. Word of God
(Theology) 3. Image (Theology) 4. Idolatry. I. Title.
BR479.E4813   1985        230'.42        85-10121
ISBN 0-8028-0069-6

# CONTENTS

*Preface*     **vii**

*Introduction: Back to Basics*     **1**

CHAPTER I. SEEING AND HEARING: PROLEGOMENA     **5**

1. Seeing     5
2. Hearing     13
3. Seeing and Hearing     27
4. What about the Philosopher?     37
5. Writing     42

CHAPTER II. IDOLS AND THE WORD     **48**

1. God Speaks     48
2. Visions and Idols     71
3. The Theology of the Icon     102
4. The Word of the Witness     106

CHAPTER III. SIGHT TRIUMPHANT     **112**

1. The Invasion of Images     114
2. Utility     127
3. Television     139
4. Technique     148

CHAPTER IV. THE WORD HUMILIATED     **155**

1. De Facto Devaluation     155
2. Contempt for Language     162
3. Hatred of the Word     172

CHAPTER V. THE RELIGIOUS CONFLICT
BETWEEN IMAGE AND WORD                                 183

1. The Church Invaded by Images                        183
2. Ultimate Value and the Captive Word                 192
3. The Exclusion of What Is Hidden                     198

CHAPTER VI. THE IMAGE–ORIENTED PERSON                  204

1. The Consumer of Images                              205
2. The Intellectual Process                            210
3. Space and Visualization in Modern Art               221

CHAPTER VII. RECONCILIATION                            228

1. Light                                               231
2. Reconciliation                                      237
3. The Rediscovery of Icons                            241
4. The Gospel of John                                  242
5. Change                                              254
6. The Freedom of the Word                             268

*Works by the Same Author*                             271

*Index of Names and Subjects*                          274

*Index of Scripture References*                        284

# PREFACE

For years, Jacques Ellul has warned repeatedly that our modern addiction to images is a kind of terrorist time bomb ominously ticking away in the comfortable hotel of free democratic society. *The Humiliation of the Word* powerfully and convincingly demonstrates the wholesale abuse of language and this dangerous addiction to images characteristic of modern society. Public officials are "electable" in the United States today only if they project an attractive television image. Reaction to presidential "debates," for example, depends almost entirely on image, not substance, truth, or coherent rational argument.

Similarly, the Church indulges our desire to "feel good" instead of responding to our need to be spiritually challenged and fed through solid exposition of the Scriptures. The electronic Church in particular panders to our appetite for entertainment rather than authentic discipleship and maturity.

Ellul's response to such incoherent flabbiness is spelled out in this book, and can be summed up in his words: "Anyone wishing to save humanity today must first of all save the word." Like most of Ellul's themes, his view of the problems of language and image stems from ideas already present in his seminal *The Presence of the Kingdom* (1948). One of the key problems for modern thinking Christians at that time, in Ellul's view, was the problem of communication, to which he devoted one of the book's chapters. There he confronts his reader with the technically determined choice of facts made available through the mass media, the distortion of language by the media (with which dialogue is impossible), and their tendency to distract and entertain rather than to stimulate reflection. Propaganda has replaced the commonly held ideas made communication between persons possible. Films' destructive power relates in part to language.

Ellul's proposed solution to the complex of problems presented in *The Presence of the Kingdom* is the discovery of a new language. This is the only way understanding can begin to flow again, so that we can communicate the gospel in such a way that it "penetrates."

Except for certain changes of emphasis and the addition of technical and sociological developments since 1948, *The Humiliation of the Word* can be viewed as the development of Ellul's early concerns about language in *The Presence of the Kingdom*. He cannot be accused of having "mellowed with age," however. This volume's sharp attacks on audiovisual methods, television, souvenir photography, structuralism, and modern art will strike some readers as overdone. But those familiar with the author's previous works will recognize in his polemic an effort to arouse our image-lulled consciousness and move us to do battle.

In the interim since *The Presence of the Kingdom*, Ellul has, of course, written often about language before finally dedicating an entire book to the theme. The select subject index in my *Jacques Ellul: A Comprehensive Bibliography* (Greenwich, CT: JAI Press, 1984) lists major references to *speech* or the *word* in nine of Ellul's forty books (others could have been added), as well as in ten of his six-hundred-odd articles.

In *Prayer and Modern Man* (1970), for example, Ellul examines the difficulties we experience in prayer stemming from our present "tragic crisis of language, in which words can no longer attain the level of speech." The failure of language produces a lack of personal relationships and a feeling that words are not only inadequate (Rom. 8:26) but pointless.

In *Hope in Time of Abandonment* (1972), Ellul devotes a section to the "Death of the Word," in which he examines briefly the phenomenon he calls "the disintegration of language." Propaganda, the meaningless multiplication of words, the disassociation of the word from the person speaking it, and society's increasing dependence on images—all contribute to the picture Ellul draws of a world with no solution and no future. These same aspects of the problem of language in our day become major sections of *The Humiliation of the Word*.

Before writing his books on prayer and hope, Ellul had already published *Propaganda* (1962), which the present volume complements and updates in several respects. *Propaganda* was the first of Ellul's books to isolate one element of *The Technological Society* (1954) for in-depth study. Later he devoted several volumes to the impact of Technique on different aspects of modern society. *The Humiliation of the Word* marks his latest contribution to this series.

In the theological sphere, Ellul deals with the relationship of language and faith in his *Living Faith* (1980), where he emphasizes the need for confidence in the words of those who witness to salvation history if we are to believe. He also mentions the confidence in Jesus which enables us to believe his words, and the danger of separating the words from the person of Jesus. These themes undergird the fundamental argument of the present volume.

Just a year before *The Humiliation of the Word* Ellul published his work on art and Technique, *L'Empire du non-sens* (1981). This art book refers with extraordinary frequency to language, and the present book on language often calls on art to illustrate a point. In fact, the two works overlap considerably, especially in the chapter entitled "Message and Compensation" in *L'Empire du non-sens*. Ellul's difficult book on art is best read in conjunction with the present volume, since they often deal with common problems of communication and meaning.

Ellul also previously expressed some of the basic arguments of *The Humiliation of the Word* in "Notes innocentes sur la 'question herméneutique'" (published in *L'Evangile hier et aujourd'hui: Mélanges offerts au Professeur Franz J. Leenhardt* [Geneva: Labor et Fides,1968]). But now at last he has considered the question of the modern crisis in language at length, and we can follow his thinking in ordered steps rather than in scattered, specialized bits.

Besides the spirited attacks already mentioned, in this book Ellul also criticizes icons and images as idols, along with computers, comic strips, slogans, technical efficiency, the death-of-God theology, and political and liturgical spectacle. Although Ellul himself responds in his last chapter to the potential criticism of this book as sheer negativism, the fundamental positive thrust here should not be overlooked. He has not written an essentially negative book, criticizing the preponderance of images. His basic aim is not to denigrate images but to liberate language as the fundamental weapon in the struggle for human freedom. Only as it relates to language does he deal with the problem of images. Ellul deals positively with language: its essence, its value, and its relationship to freedom. In this sense *The Humiliation of the Word* is a continuation of the author's *The Ethics of Freedom* (1973–1984).

Many of Ellul's books can be viewed primarily as efforts to attack or even demolish something. But *The Humiliation of the Word* belongs with Ellul's more constructive books, most of which are theological. Like many of his more positive studies, the present book devotes a heavy proportion of its space to exploring oppressive factors and forces in the area under investigation, but its main thrust is not negative.

We have heedlessly capitulated to the allure of images, and thus language has been dethroned from its proper preeminence in human affairs. Our preference for images has corrupted and distorted language, which has become sound without sense. In a similar manner, Ellul has shown earlier that we have preferred the wrong sort of revolution (*Autopsy of Revolution, Changer de révolution*), given ourselves to the wrong sort of prayer (*Prayer and Modern Man*), allowed the idolatrous city to dominate our affections (*The Meaning of the City*), and substituted facile belief for vital faith (*Living Faith*).

In most of these situations something good and necessary has been either corrupted or blown up out of proportion, so that it dominates what it should be subject to. Such lack of proportion involves the dialectic between reality and truth, in the case of images and language. Our attention has focused on the tangible to such an extent that we no longer consider truth to carry any serious weight.

Reality deals with fixed things not open to discussion, things which one can only observe. It forces us to conform. Truth, like the word, is infinitely open-ended and invites reflection, response, relationship, and dialogue. Reality refuses to allow us the distance necessary so that we can be critical of what we are considering. In modern society we tend to accept truth only if it bears on reality—specifically scientific reality—which has become our ultimate "truth."

In the same vein, we tend to believe words only if they have some visual evidence supporting them. Whatever cannot be expressed through images seems to us to have no genuine importance, or even existence.

Another reason for maintaining that *The Humiliation of the Word* is not primarily a negative book is Ellul's repeated effort at synthesis. The dichotomy between word and image and between truth and reality is a temporary effect of the Fall, and contrary to

God's ultimate purpose for humankind. In the Incarnation and the consummation of God's Kingdom, word and image are reconciled.

In what sense is language "humiliated," according to Ellul? His title alludes to a book written during 1939 and 1940 by the novelist and polemist Georges Bernanos, but not published until 1949: *Les Enfants humiliés* (Paris: Gallimard). Bernanos deplores the fact that promises made to those involved in World War I were broken, leading to a second conflagration. In Ellul's book the problem is not broken promises but rather a broken humanity. He does not attack images in themselves so much as the imperialism of images and our idolatrous prostration before them.

For several years Ellul led public discussions of significant films in his native Bordeaux. Such activity makes it clear that he is not flatly opposed to proper use of images. But images tend to neutralize the effects of the word, which becomes a sort of optional "footnote" to the dominant images. In this sense the word is continually humiliated in our society.

Never have I seen such a strange tragedy as Jean Racine's *Phèdre* (1677), performed by a French troupe in 1975 for an American audience. I was astounded at how the words seemed to have lost all value and meaning. The actions dominated utterly, usually having no relationship whatever with the words, which were mouthed quickly, without expression. I was stunned. The play's meaning was utterly distorted, not to say lost. A professor friend's response to my distress was: "This is the only way Racine can be presented in our day."

In the book you are holding, Jacques Ellul has enabled me to understand the enigma of *Phèdre* divorced from its text. In the process, Ellul clarifies many other puzzling tendencies in modern society. Until I read *The Humiliation of the Word*, for instance, I could not understand why my students in French literature classes had so much to say and ask about the texts they read but never had any verbal response whatever when I showed them a film.

Language is further humiliated by intellectuals, especially certain structuralists, whose attacks on language that communicates meaning and whose preference for the "pure" language of the insane appear to have triggered the writing of this book.

Most of us now think essentially by association of images, Ellul believes, and can no longer construct or follow a rigorous logical demonstration, unless this is supported by charts and diagrams. As schools increase their reliance on images, educational levels decrease, indicating that images are not the panacea we presume them to be.

In theological terms, God's choice of language as the basis of his contact with humanity signifies that we are free to respond—or to ignore him if we choose. Reliance on images eliminates the freedom that is essential to us if we are to respond to God.

Some of Ellul's sociological books include brief but clear statements of his Christian hope (*Changer de révolution*) or veiled references to the Christian faith as the only conceivable way out of the tunnel his books describe (*Autopsy of Revolution, The New Demons*). But *The Humiliation of the Word* is the first book in which Ellul has intertwined major theological sections with his sociological analysis.

It is impossible to say whether this book is predominantly theological or sociological. In Ellul's latest list of books (at the end of *La Subversion du christianisme*), *The Humiliation of the Word* appears in the sociological category, presumably at Ellul's request. But the work is filled with theological reflection and exegesis of biblical texts (Ex. 32, Isa. 6, John's Gospel, etc.). In a thematic study, Ellul tries to show that there are no genuine theophanies in the Bible. According to the author, the modern world's preference for images stems from the fourteenth century, when the Church chose to favor them in preference to the word.

The combination of sociological and theological reflections in this book enables each discipline to hammer away at and refine the other. Thus rejection of words in favor of action on the sociological plane is related to the Hebrew concept (*dabar*), which combines words and action.

Ellul returns repeatedly to the theme of language as our human distinctive. If we use it thoughtlessly or devaluate it in any way, we also devaluate God, who chose it for his communication with us, and ourselves. We become less human when we opt for images rather than the word. The theological implications of Ellul's sociological arguments are manifold. Clearly, the Church must not lean toward visual methods or attractions. Over-reliance on lavish liturgy or spectacle (common both to liturgical churches and modern evangelistic campaigns) constitutes a radical distortion of the Christian message.

Ellul could have chosen to write a sociological treatise on language and paired it with a later theological work, as he has previously done (*The Meaning of the City* explores the theological implications of *The Technological Society; The Politics of God and*

*the Politics of Man* is the biblical and theological counterpart of
*The Political Illusion*). But in *The Humiliation of the Word* the
author has preferred to integrate sociology and theology into a
single whole, for reasons he has not yet explained in print.

I believe it is because of the confrontation of the two disciplines in this work that Costa Rican graduate students have re-
sponded to it more thoughtfully than to some of Ellul's other
books. Seeing the sociological realities that motivate the author's
theology helps us grasp his emphases. And understanding how
theology can respond to sociological problems enables us to view
the future with hope, as Ellul does. As always, however, in Ellul's
thought, this hope is coupled with realism and a spur to thoughtful
action.

For twenty years I have worked in the Third World, where
the problems Ellul presents in this book have even graver consequences than in North America. Here we are daily bombarded
with foreign images that crowd out local, "inferior," images and
trample on local culture. Even worse, what you merely see on your
television screen is reality here. You can cheer or be indifferent
when you see the bullet hit its target, but for us the pain and death
are not "pretend." If Christian churches are ever to become a
prophetic voice they must give serious attention to the fundamental issues Ellul raises in this book as well as in his previous works
on propaganda in technological societies. We realize that "the eyes
of the world are upon us," but is anybody really listening?

Joyce Main Hanks
University of Costa Rica

Note: Except where otherwise indicated, the Revised Standard
Version is the basis for biblical quotations when accompanied by
a concrete reference to book, chapter, and verse. The major exceptions to this are indicated by the letters "JE," which signify my
own translation of Ellul's biblical quotation. He uses various
French Bibles and sometimes his own translations and paraphrases. I have made no attempt to distinguish his source.

Publication dates above refer to the first edition of Ellul's
books, usually in French.

# THE HUMILIATION
# OF THE WORD

# INTRODUCTION:
# BACK TO BASICS

Do not look here for some scholarly study on iconic expression or syntagmatics or metalanguage. I am not pretending to push forward scientific frontiers. Rather, I try to do here the same thing I do in all my books: face, alone, this world I live in, try to understand it, and confront it with another reality I live in, but which is utterly unverifiable. Taking my place at the level of the simplest of daily experiences, I make my way without critical weapons. Not as a scientist, but as an ordinary person, without scientific pretensions, talking about what we all experience, I feel, listen, and look.

Images today are the daily nutrient of our sensory experience, our thought processes, our feelings, and our ideology. When we say "image," the word immediately breaks up into its different meanings: verbal images (why shouldn't they be considered images as well as the ones I see?); mental images, which can exist only when I am using language to think; and images that feed the imagination or are produced by it, and are therefore inseparable from it.

In this book I will retain the oversimplified distinction between seeing and hearing, between showing and speaking. I am well aware that organized images also constitute a language, and that this distinction is not restricted to speech. Despite all modern advances, however, in this book I will reserve the use of "language" for speech, ignoring the language of gestures, mime, and film. A biased approach? Certainly! At the same time, my desire is to reestablish a measure of clarity in an area filled with confusion, complexity, and misunderstandings.

There is also cinematic language—I'm well aware! But too often people forget that this sequence of images is not the same thing as the organization of sentences. Defining language by talking about codes, signifiers, the syntagma, semiotics, and semiology does not solve the problem. Always we must come back to simple facts, common sense, and commonplaces as our starting point. Because, whether we know it or not, and whether we like it or not, "everybody grinds his grain and bakes his bread according to everyday truths and constraints."

"But," you say, "why connect hearing and speaking? I hear lots of things besides speech: music, noise, and the crucial noise that interferes with communication. Noise sometimes gives birth to order, and is sometimes silenced for the sake of meaning. Music can be an image or suggest images to us, just as, on the other hand, the word can be written, and writing is something visual: you can read words. No necessary and exclusive relationship exists between hearing and speaking, or between seeing and image." I'm well aware of what you say, and still I stick with my misleading simplification. I continue to relate hearing and speaking, and oppose them to seeing and image, not in an exclusive sense, but fundamentally. I'm aware that fringes exist, that there is no unmistakable cleavage, and that the visual interpenetrates the auditory. But even admitting all this, we must come back to two dissimilar domains: what I hear constitutes a special universe, different from that other universe composed of what I see.

Far from being a superficial proposal, this distinction corresponds to everyone's experience, in spite of excessive challenges based on scientific foundations. These scientific studies are undoubtedly useful for the purposes of the research scientist, but my aim is different. And the conclusions we come to will compensate for the oversimplification inherent in this fundamental experience.

I refuse, then, to transform the Word into an image or a sequence of images. I refuse to transform Images into a word, or to consider their sequence a language. I do this even though I understand the relationships between word and image, and the scientific reasons for considering them to be identical. But in reality, we are not suggesting an absolute discontinuity between seeing and hearing. I have spoken of two universes based on the distinction between them, but most of the time, at least, they are not separate universes.

In our common experience seeing and hearing are related, and the proper equilibrium between the two produces the equilibrium of the person, so it is dangerous to favor one, in triumphant fashion, to the detriment of the other. Yet this is exactly what is happening today, as we witness the unconditional victory of the visual and images. Furthermore, the above-mentioned ideas concerning (visual) images as constituting a language, the (printed) word as being reduced to visual images, and the word as evoking only images, are hardly innocent and objectively scientific. These assertions are really simply an indication of the triumphant march of the Visual and (visual) Images in our society and thought.

We should not, however, sever the relationship between seeing and hearing. Each person is made up of the confrontation of what he sees and hears, of what he shows and speaks. These are two different senses, each the door to different universes that perpetually encounter and confront each other. These two universes meet at every level of existence.

Nevertheless, I refuse to follow Oswald Spengler, who considers sight to be the decisive sense. He believes that our two eyes in the forefront of the face, with focused binocular vision, constitute human specificity in relation to the animal world, which has one eye on each side of the face. This arrangement produces two separate views of the world, one right and one left. Spengler considers this disposition of the eyes to be the origin of humanity's conquering power and its upright position, which places the eyes at the top of our bodies.

In a more basic way I side with the entire current of thought that makes *spoken* language the basis of human specificity, and here again I relate language and word. I accept, of course, that ants have a tactile "language," and that bees have a visual "language," that is to say, a method of designation, communication, and transmission of information. Their "language" is both codified and learned. But however subtle it may be, it has nothing in common with spoken human language. The only way to identify these methods of communication as languages is by presupposing that language can be reduced to factual information. Speech, however, is not essentially transmission of information. It is much more than that. The word has another domain, another sphere of action. The spoken relationship involves receiving messages other than information; it involves emotions that transcend reflexes.

I am not saying that human spoken language is more complex, perfected, or evolved than bees' language. I say it is not comparable, because its nature is different. In order to compare them, you would have to begin by eliminating from human language everything that goes beyond visual information, everything that is inaccessible to the code. The result would be not just an amputation, which is the traditional reductionist method of all the sciences, but a surgical excision of language's very heart.

Human spoken language is characterized precisely by these elements we have mentioned: overflowing of limits, going beyond, and destructuring what can be conveyed in tactile or visual language. Its essential aspects are breadth of meaning, ambiguity, and variation in interpretation. A sign in human language does not correspond to a thing. A word calls up echoes, feelings intertwined with thoughts, reasons mingled with irrationality, motives that lead nowhere, and uncoordinated urges. This specificity is what matters, it seems to me, rather than the common denominator. Taking all that can communicate information and calling that human language seems to me biased (in that same way the social sciences, especially, have made us too accustomed to bias!).

"Difference is what matters." Surely we have heard this formula often enough in linguistics and other disciplines. Well then, let's apply it! Let's concentrate most of all on the differentiating factors that distinguish human language: the play between the signifier and the signified. "Play" in this sense can be understood in all three of its meanings! It concerns the changeableness and flexibility of the word in its relationship with meaning.

For me, then, human spoken language cannot be reduced to any coherent collection of signs made understandable through use of a code. The logical sequence of visual images and the coherence of spoken language are the starting point of this study. I realize there are other alternatives. But I consider them to be choices (involving pre-suppositions also) related to other concerns and other methods of research that are not the same as mine. I do not despise or evade them; they are simply different, and belong to a different area of truth.

# Chapter I

# SEEING AND HEARING: PROLEGOMENA

## 1. SEEING

Forget about origins and history. Let's deal with our simplest, most direct experiences. I look out in front of me, and perceive the sea lit up out to the horizon. I look around me: to my left and right, I see the limitless straight line of the beach, and behind it, the dunes—all in space. With my gaze I make the space my own. The objects are clear and plain. I see the wind bend over to the ground the reeds that keep the dunes in place.

I record these images one by one, and their juxtaposition shows me the real world in which I live, the world around me. I am at the center of this universe by means of my gaze, which sweeps across this space and lets me know everything in it. By combining these images of reality, I grasp it as a whole, and become a part of it as a result of my looking. I am the point of departure from which the universe and space are ordered: my vision situates me and every other component, placing each where it belongs. As I look I discover order. My looking is in itself what constitutes this order, by means of its sequence, which provides me with a progressive discovery of everything around me.

The very fact that I express myself in this way shows how inevitably my sight makes me the center of the world.[1] It lets me know what is to the left and right of me, what is near and what is far away. All of reality unfolds itself to me little by little. Without sight,

---

1. This is true in all societies, although it is denied by the extremely peculiar and dogmatic notion which considers perspective to be a Renaissance invention that expresses the bourgeois universe: separation between values and facts, between subject and object. Of course, these dichotomies are seen as results of the class struggle. Although this idea is partly correct, it has become an extremely trite commonplace because it has been expressed so dogmatically. See for example Jean-Joseph Goux, *Les Iconoclastes* (Paris: Seuil, 1978).

I would be suddenly deprived of the very possibility of grasping reality and of situating myself in space.

My sight constructs a universe for me. It reveals to me a directly perceivable reality composed of colorful, simple, harmonious images. But it also furnishes me with more subtle materials. I learn to read my brother's or my enemy's face. Transmitted images are superimposed on one another, and as a result, I now know that a given image belongs within a particular context of reality. It conjures up another image; I anticipate what I am going to see, but what is coming will in any case be located in space and will constitute part of reality—deeper and hidden, in a sense, but still reality.

By looking I learn the signs in the sky that indicate what the weather will be. But in itself, my gaze shows me only heavily laden clouds coming from the northwest, with ambiguous round shapes rising high in a gray sky. I deduce a rainstorm, but my sight has shown me only a group of images.

Vision also furnishes me with information. I need to know what action to take and where to place myself; my sight enables me to know the reality in which my action will take place, and whether my action is possible. Sight gives me information concerning the world around me. It permits me to accumulate pieces of information, each of which is an image, in space, of reality. How could I possibly take part in this reality without such an unfailing source of information? Such information is precise and pinpointed, and deals only with reality. Nothing else, no other dimension, is ever involved. A different activity allows me to understand and associate, to see beyond, in the distance, the thing I cannot physically see.

Vision works exactly like a camera, which provides me with dozens or hundreds of snapshots that are connected only if my mind relates them. And because of this information, I can take part and involve myself in this reality by means other than sight. Sight has made me the center of the world because it situates me at the point from which I see everything, and causes me to see things relative to this point. My vision makes a circular sweep of space, working from this point: my point of view.

But now I am tempted, as the center of the world, to act on this spectacle and transform this setting. What was missing in my vision was someone to act, and I am available. Sight moves to action at the same time that it serves as the means of action. Again, without it, how could I act, since I wouldn't even know what my hand was touching or what was within my reach? Sight previously showed me reality as a thing present to my consciousness; now it urges me to be a presence myself, in relation to this reality. I will use all the information that sight has conveyed to me, as I change this universe of images by creating new ones. I am a subject, not separated from what I look at. Rather, what I see becomes part of me, as my action involves me in what I see.

Images both permit and condition my action; they are always imperative. I lean out the window and look searchingly into the emptiness. Images of distance and depth thrust themselves on my consciousness. I know I mustn't lean out any further. The image defines and marks the boundaries of my action. The image does not induce my action, but establishes its conditions and possibilities.

Without visual images my action is definitely blind, incoherent, and uncertain. Sight conveys certainties and pieces of information to me, as we have said. Such information is reliable. I perceive a gray ocean and an overcast skyline. This is unquestionable. The reality around me is a certainty in which I can be confident. It is neither incoherent nor deformed.

I know, of course, that this is also something learned; there are no data coming directly from the senses, and the shapes and colors and distances I apprehend are perceptible to me because I learned them. My culture has furnished me with the very images I see. But however important this may be (and we must not push this idea too far!), it is still true that I see. I see images which are reliable. In order to change the shape of this reality, I must intervene or change my viewpoint, by putting on glasses or distorting it as I draw it. But in this case, I see my drawing rather than the reality of the universe.

What a dreadful uneasiness takes hold of us when reality becomes uncertain because it is submerged in fog. Then sight fails to furnish me with reliable, clear, guaranteed images, and I cannot act because I no longer have unquestionable sources of information—visual images. Fear of the dark is a consequence of the same uncertainty. The world loses its midpoint. It is off center because I cannot see it anymore. The center could be anywhere, but it is no longer located where I am. It could be anywhere, or nowhere. I am not situated anymore. Things are no longer situated in relation to me. Dimension and colors have disappeared. I remain immobilized and wait, incapable of intervention and unable to change the situation. I am suddenly paralyzed without images.

Sight offers me the whole realm of reality, space, and concrete objects, thus allowing me to act.[2] Without space, no action is possible. Without a known, constructed, coherent space, no action is possible. But on the other hand, action is called forth and induced by the very existence of this reality, in which everything beckons to me.

---

2. But we will see later on that this relationship between sight and action is profoundly changed when sight is based on projected images.

My outstretched hand is also an image of this reality; how can I avoid extending it toward this fruit ready to be picked?

The visual image of the fruit ready for picking is not ambiguous. The image furnishes me reliably with precisely what I need to know in order to act. It is neither deceptive nor hypocritical, and does not mislead me. In order for my sight to mislead me concerning reality, there must be some unusual phenomenon, like a mirage. The image is not ambiguous. This peach I am looking at is red and weighs heavily on the bending branch. This is absolutely certain. But the image is insignificant. It has no meaning in itself and must be interpreted. In the case of a fruit ripe for picking, the visual image gives me indisputable information, but if I stop there, nothing will happen—my action will not be set in motion. I see clearly that the peach is beautifully red. I see clearly that it is round and heavy. But so what? The image does not provide me with any meaning for this reality which it so faithfully conveys to me. It must therefore be interpreted. In order to move from the vision of the fruit to "I should pick it" or "It can be picked," there must be an interpretation: an attribution of meaning to these real images of reality. Another dimension must be added to sight: interpretation will come through speech.

Thus the image contains within itself a deep contradiction. It is not ambiguous: it is coherent, reliable, and inclusive; but it is insignificant. It can have innumerable meanings, depending on culture, learning, or the intervention of some other dimension. For this reason I must learn to see, before looking at the image. After seeing it, I must learn to interpret it. The image is clear, but this clarity does not imply certainty or comprehension. My certainty is limited to this directly perceived reality that my sight reveals to me. Nothing beyond that. Next I must decide what I am going to do about it. Nevertheless, what I perceive in this limited manner is the reality in which I must live.

The image furnished by sight is neither dream nor vision. Certainly visions are not the same thing as sight. On the contrary, I compare them with what I see. I recount what I see; it is as if I were seeing, but I see nothing. These visual images owe nothing to sight. Instead, they are the product of nerves excited in a different manner. I call them "vision," but only by extension—by projecting onto this phenomenon the guaranteed reliability of my good, solid sight, in which I can have confidence. I call these images "vision" because they are connected with the other images I am accustomed to. I would be tempted to say in this case that the order is reversed. The visual image exists, and then I attribute a meaning to it; but the vision appears only as the illustration of a previously established meaning.

No matter how insignificant it may be, the visual image is always rigorous, imperative, and irreversible. I saw what I saw. I cannot change this image. I cannot change the reality which is conveyed to me in this way, except through my action. There is no ambiguity at this point. Nor is there reversibility. As irreversible, an image indicates the orientation for my action. This involves a kind of "meaning," but it is like a circular drive with only two possible directions: one prohibited and the other obligatory! By virtue of the image I am situated in this reality which is neither polyvalent nor polynuclear. It is ordered in such a way that it is irreversible and invariable. It is an order of permanence; each image could be, and is in fact, eternal.

This reality is directly perceived, directly present, and permanent. Duration has no effect on this image which is conveyed to me by my sight. It is always an instantaneous matter. No duration is included in an image. As we have said, there is a sequence of instantaneous images which are connected and which can be coordinated or not: instantaneous "takes" of a single image that are superimposed on each other.

My sight is not really continuous, even when I fix my gaze on the same broom plant. I do not see it change. I see it; then an instant later I see it again, and the image is imperceptibly different. The same thing applies to different instantaneous images in space. My view covers only a limited field. I change my angle of vision and join together the instantaneous views of the different fields which I have recorded. This way the visual image, the images I have grasped and accumulated, produces a world made up of small dots, as in a pointillist painting.

The visual world is pointillist. Images are points which take on value only when reassembled, so that they acquire an identity as part of a total picture. If I had only one "view" of my universe, I would be a participant in a totality which would be both terribly coherent and yet at the same time composed of fragments without any necessary relationship. The totality would be like a cloud of irrational dots which can form only the framework of an action, a change in the relationships between the points. But the cloud of dots cannot be used for understanding anything, because this pointillism of images is space but not duration.

The image is present. It is only a presence. It bears witness to something "already there": the object I see was there before I opened my eyes. The image exists in the present and conveys to me only a present. For this reason it seems permanent to me, as a thing with duration because of the passage of time. The image conveys to me objects that do not change—truly unchanging objects.

The visual image constitutes the object—*ob-jactus*: that which is thrown before me. The word "before" implies in itself this visualization, which makes something an object. But I exist in this world of seen objects that are objects because they are seen. I belong, inseparably, to this observed setting. I am continually involved in it. I am continually refashioned within myself by what I see, and I cannot take my distance from it. I have a point of view, a location from which I see things, but it is situated within what I see and inseparable from it. Wherever I place myself, however I shift my position, I remain in the field of vision. I remain in the middle of what I see. I can never take my distance, act as if I were not present, or even begin to think independently of what I see.

At night, when I cannot see, a certain distance is established. This explains why the day's events become so painful at night: the distance between me and the world around me allows for reflection and meditation. A flood of images overwhelms me, beckons me, and carries me along: an image I have seen follows immediately after the one I have just dismissed from my mind. I can never stop this movement of reality in space. I can never consider a given image like a diamond or a painting from which I can take my distance in order to be "myself," instead of being overwhelmed by the images composed of dots.

The image prevents me from taking my distance. And if I cannot establish a certain distance, I can neither judge nor criticize. Of course, I also feel pleasure or displeasure in what I see. I can find it beautiful or ugly. But this is not a critical process. No judgment is involved. Furthermore, what possible criticism or judgment can we make with respect to space and reality? In spite of the frailty we have all observed in a person's testimony about what he has seen, everyone has the same certainty about anything he has seen. He has seen reality. And this leads to the widely held opinion: seeing the same images results in an identical viewpoint! When we describe in this manner the characteristics of the visual image as pointillistic, permanent, and irreversible, and as eliminating distance and criticism, we are only pointing out the characteristics of the reality which we perceive in this manner.

*   *   *   *   *   *

It happens, however, that we have started down a more perilous path than we thought. Sight guarantees my possession of the world and makes it into a "universe-for-me." Seeing gives me the possibility of action. The apprehension which sight gives me of reality commits me to action. I see objects and am tempted to place my hand on them. Isn't an object made to be used once it has been seen? Sight is the basis of my mastery.[3] Deprived of vision, I find myself in the paralysis of darkness where nothing seems right.

---

3. Reality is what is seen, counted, and quantified, and is located in space. But reality is at the same time what is *definite* (Axel Hägerström). This

In connection with mastery I am led to a technical process. Sight alone is not sufficient to accomplish it, but without sight no technique is possible. Sight is not sufficient, but at this point Spengler may well be right. A *human being's* sight commits him to technique. The visual image points out the totality of my possible life in a world where I am both master and subject. All techniques are based on visualization and involve visualization. If a phenomenon cannot be transformed into something visual, it cannot be the object of a technique.

The correlation is even more marked with respect to efficiency. Sight is the organ of efficiency. Conversely, making use of images is efficient. Images sell things in advertising. Images ensure a pedagogical efficiency unknown before our time, and science now depends on visual representation. We will return to this matter. The correlation between "visual" and "technique" is one of the first facts to note. The visual image potentially contains within itself all the traits and characteristics of what later becomes the experience, experimentation, and organization of technique.

At this point we are on the threshold of a new dimension in sight. Up until now we have remained on the most elementary level of direct apprehension as the response of sight when brought to bear on things in nature, in the human environment, or in the cultural sphere. But now we are beginning to see that sight is a great deal more than this. We have already alluded to its larger role. What is seen is constructed. We have said that an image depends on the individual's cultural background. We must go farther on this point. Sight refers to and proceeds from a specific notion of humanity, from a previously established image, an *eidolon*, which we already have in mind. Sight places us in the most direct and natural relationship possible with the environment, but at the same time it involves the artifice of a given

---

corresponds clearly to the visual universe. The indefinite is the domain of the word. Thus visual reality is clearly noncontradictory. You can *say* that a piece of paper is both red and blue. But you cannot *see* it as both red and blue at the same time. It is either one or the other. The famous principle of noncontradiction is based on visual experience of the world, just as the principle of identity is. Declaring that two opinions cannot both be true, when one denies what the other affirms, has to do with vision, which involves instantaneousness. But language involves duration. Consequently what is visual cannot be dialectical. Knowledge based on sight is of necessity linear and logical. Only thought based on language can be dialectical, taking into account contradictory aspects of reality, which are possible because they are located in time. This is basic for understanding the opposition between the two methods of thought we will be discussing in Chapter VI. But this distinction also teaches us that language grants us access to knowledge of a plurality of aspects in a reality that sight cannot grasp. In other words, truth includes reality and permits a deeper knowledge of reality. But this knowledge is not based on evidence or immediacy.

element. This artificial element, as we have seen, causes a direct division between subject and object. Then it transforms nature into something outside the human environment and changes the human observer into someone outside his own milieu.

Sight leads us simultaneously along the paths of separation and division, of intervention and efficiency, and of artificiality. It has been said, quite accurately, that the urban milieu is a visual world where sight finds its satisfaction. The city allows humanity to see its mirror image in the sense of contemplating itself as it contemplates the product of its own work.

\* \* \* \* \* \*

Sight involves a relationship with reality as established in space. It is an artificial construction. Medusa's head transfixes whoever gazes at her. Whoever looks at the scenes on the shields of the *Iliad* is terror stricken. Sight introduces us to an unbearable shock. Reality when seen inspires horror. Terror is always visual. Horror stories play only on our visual sense and suggest representation.

In contrast, the spoken word can involve us in mystery or drama. It places us in situations of conflict and makes us conscious of tragedy. But it is never on its own terrifying or stupefying. We are dazed by sight—by an image or a vision. The word takes us to the edge of terror only when descriptive and painting extremely precise images. Edgar Allan Poe's short stories are an example.

All the descriptions we have heard of Nazi death camps move us to revulsion and to a judgment that may be based more on strong feelings than anything else. The image of bulldozers pushing along mounds of skeletal corpses, which shortly before had been living beings, faces teetering from the machine's pushing—this image drawn from *Night and Fog*[4] moves us to abject horror. It terrifies us, because we see. Such terror results from the horror of reality.

Reality apprehended by sight is always unbearable, even when that reality is beauty. We have a horror of reality, perhaps because we depend on it so. Language, even when it is realistic, allows us to escape from this terrible reality. Sight locks us up with it and obliges us to look at it. There is no way out—except by controlling and mastering the reality. I think that through technical process I can claim to be master of what I see. But this process in turn breeds stupefaction and misgivings when we see its results. All at once technique does not belong to us any more. We see it in these reflected images that both excite and terrify us. It is a vision of apocalypse.

---

4. A film by Alain Resnais (1956).—TRANS.

## 2. HEARING

I hear noises. The wind is blowing through these pine trees. In the distance the sea roars. I can judge its force and its condition. The pine cones crackle. I hear their bursting. Their sound reminds me how hot it is. The sequence of sounds sometimes forms a symphony. Noises come to me. I do not turn my ears toward a certain spot where I suspect there might be something to hear. I direct my gaze, turning it spontaneously toward a certain face, toward a landscape which awaits me. I am the subject. I act and decide what I want to see.

Sounds come to me, and I receive them when they are produced. They form a sequence of impressions that carves up time. A baby's cry drowns out everything else. Instead of a symphony, now I hear an outburst. The noise assails and haunts me. I cannot close anything, as I would my eyes, to shut it out.

Images fall into a pattern with respect to each other, but sounds do not. Instead, sounds contradict each other and cancel each other out. I am listening to a Mozart concerto, and suddenly near me someone speaks. Or a visitor knocks at my door. Or someone starts noisily putting away dishes and silverware. Sounds produce incoherence. The noises I hear form no panorama of the world.

Apparently a dog's panorama of the world is basically olfactory. Using various odors, dogs create a coherent whole. For us as human beings, on the contrary, an odor is only an incidental sign. Our coherent and unbroken panorama of the world is visual (it is an unbroken panorama even though it is pointillistic, just as the impressionist painters saw it!). It is not auditory. The sequence of noises I perceive does not constitute a universe. They cannot be compared with the sequence of images resulting from the movement of my eyes.

Noise overwhelms me with uncertainty, because of the very fact of its sequence. Where is it coming from? What does it herald? I cannot avoid asking these temporal questions. A sound is never clear and plain by itself. It always brings questions with it. What is going to happen? It may be that this uncertainty is really a cultural matter, if we have learned to decode shapes and colors accurately but not sounds. But whatever its origin, this uncertainty is part of us.

I am much more concerned with the temporal origin of sound. Sight is spatial. Sound's domain is temporal, and it inserts us within a duration rather than an expanse. Sound generates an immediate, unconscious interrogation: What now? What sound will come next? Naturally, sight also can, on second or third thought, give rise to the question: What is beyond? I see the horizon; what is beyond it? But anyone can see the difference between the two. The question "What lies beyond?" is secondary and indirect; it is based on thought. The question about the sound I hear—What next?—is immediate and primary, arising in the same instant I perceive the sound. What will the next sound be? And this brings us to the highest order of sounds.

Alone among all other sounds there is one that is particularly important for us: the spoken word. It ushers us into another dimension: relationship with other living beings, with persons. The Word is the particularly human sound which differentiates us from everything else. In this connection a fundamental difference between seeing and hearing is immediately apparent. In seeing, the living being is one form among many. A human being has a special shape and color, but he is included with all the rest as part of the landscape: a discrete, moving speck. When I hear speech, however, the human being becomes qualitatively different from everything else.

Right at the beginning of this issue, we find ourselves in the presence of a gripping question. We have just seen that our auditory sense is probably less culturally sharpened than the visual, since auditory education is less complete, complex, and distinctive. This is true for all cultures, including musical families and "primitive" societies that are much more skilled in interpreting the noises of the forest or of the savanna. In all societies, the auditory sense does not permit us to construct a universe. And yet language, which is related to it, is the most culturally elaborated, the richest, the most "universalizing," and the most significant aspect of a culture, as well as the sign of human specificity.

This contradiction gives us a profound insight into the complex nature of speech and hearing. Speech always depends on hearing. It engulfs us in temporality, because of the unfolding of discourse, if for no other reason. A sentence has a certain rhythm, and I must wait for the end of it to know what is being said to me. Some languages accentuate even more strongly this suspense over meaning during the development of the sentence. When German places the verb at the end of the sentence, I must listen to the entire sentence before I can understand it, and that occurs in a temporal sequence.

Sight, however, can give me an image not limited by time because it is instantaneous and inclusive. I need not wait in order to grasp the meaning of what I see. But I must always wait in order to grasp the exact meaning of the sentence which has just begun. I am suspended between two points in time. The beginning of the sentence has already been pronounced, and has already faded away; the end has not yet been spoken, but it is coming, and it will give meaning to what was said at the beginning. Let's not deal yet with writing, and certainly not with tape recording; these involve a forcing of speech into space, in which it ceases to be speech. We will return to this matter, but for now let's limit ourselves to spoken language.

The spoken word, even if it involves an essential proclamation or the thought of a genius, falls into the void, passes, and disappears, if it is not heard and recovered by someone. The ocean over there, even if no one contemplates it, remains what it is and what it was. I see it, and it produces a flurry of emotions in me. I leave. I go away, but it does not. The spoken sentence has sunk into nothingness; time has gone by, and there are no "frozen words" which can make themselves heard again later.[5] Time does not return, and speech has no permanence.

When I hear a sentence, I am in the present with it. I have grabbed hold of and memorized its beginning, which is now past, and it plunges me into the past with it. I am also listening carefully for the end of the sentence; I am waiting for the direct object which will clarify the meaning of the whole sentence. I am straining toward this future implied by speech.

For the word to exist, then, we must have several elements present at the same time: duration, two people (the speaker and the listener, who are living in the same moment of time), and concentration on the fact that the past is abolished. Thus speech is basically presence. It is something alive and is never an object. It cannot be thrown before me and remain there. Once spoken, the word ceases to exist, unless I have recovered it. Before it is spoken, the word places me in an expectant situation, in a future I await eagerly. The word does not exist on its own. It continues to exist only in its effect on the one who spoke it and on the one who recovered it. The word is never an object you can turn this way and that, grasp, and preserve for tomorrow or some distant day when you may have time to deal with it.

The word exists now. It is something immediate and can never be manipulated. Either it exists or it doesn't. It makes me what I am, establishes the speaking me and the listening me, so that my role is determined by the word itself rather than by its content. For the word to become an object, someone must transform it into writing. But then it is no longer speech. Yet even in that form, it requires time. My glance must scan the line, then the page, moving downward, and this movement of the eyes takes time. The image I see changes: an overall glance is not enough. There is no possible instantaneous approach to the written page; seeing takes time when it is applied to the word. The word remains sovereign even when transformed into writing and visualized.

---

5. An allusion to François Rabelais's *Quart Livre* (1548), in which words spoken long ago were "frozen" and could be heard later by those traveling to the spot where they had been spoken.—TRANS.

*   *   *   *   *   *

The word is, of necessity, spoken to someone. If no one is present, it is spoken to oneself or to God. It presupposes an ear; the Great Ear, if necessary. It calls for a response. Every word, even a swearword, an insult, an exclamation, or a soliloquy, begins a dialogue. The monologue is a dialogue in the future or the past, or else it is a dialogue incorporated into a monologue. Here again, time is involved. Dialogue develops according to a variable timetable, but dialogue cannot exist unless those engaging in it are inserted into time.

Language is a call, an exchange. I avoid using the threadbare term "communication." It is not true that language exists only to communicate information. This concept is superficial and holds little interest for us. Obviously, language is *also* communication. It communicates information *also*. But if we spoke only to convey information our relationships would be greatly impoverished. To verify this you have only to listen to the "information" given on television, in spite of the speakers' talent and the surprising and varied way things are presented.

Language is uncertain, communicating information but also a whole universe that is fluid, without content or framework, unpretentious, and filled with the rich complexity of things left unexpressed in a relationship. What is not said also plays a role in language. More accurately, what is said sometimes hides what could be said, and on the other hand sometimes it reveals what is not said. Language never belongs to the order of evident things. It is a continuous movement between hiding and revealing. It makes of the play in human relationships something even more fine and complex than it would be without language. Language exists only for, in, and by virtue of this relationship. Dialogue involves the astonishing discovery of the other person who is like me, and the person like me who is different. We need both similarity and difference at the same time. I speak the same language that you do; we use the same code. But what I have to say is different from what you have to say. Without this difference there would be neither language nor dialogue.

Do we have something to say? In spite of the condemnation of this concept by linguists and modern artists, I insist that I speak because I have something to say. If this pressure were absent, I would not speak. Speech is not born of nothing. It does not itself give birth to the signified that it points to. In spite of the extravagant modern ideas we will examine later, it is still true that when I speak to another person, it is because I have a desire to convey to him something I have that he does not have—or that I think he does not have. And based on this situation, I find the words and phrases that correspond to what I indeed have to say. There is something that precedes speech.

Speech does not take its pattern directly from what there is "to say"; it creates in addition a sphere of unexpectedness, a wonderful flowering which adorns, enriches, and ennobles what I have to say, instead of expressing it directly, flatly, and exactly. I have an idea in mind—or a fact, an outline. I begin to write, and if I reread what I have written a few days later, I am amazed by what I have written. It tallies, to be sure, with what I had to say, up to a point, but it overflows this, and I realize that I have written a different text. What I have written conjures up ideas, images, and shapes which I did not expect, which I have forgotten.

Dialogue involves a certain distance. We must be separated as well as different. I do not speak to a person identical to me. I must have something to say which the other lacks, but he must also be different from me. Yet similarity is required as well. When Adam sees Eve he bursts into speech. He speaks because of her and for her. She was flesh of his flesh, bone of his bone; and yet different: a dissimilar similar person.

Speech fills the infinite gap that separates us. But the difference is never removed. Discourse begins again and again because the distance between us remains. I find I must repeatedly begin speaking again to restate what I have said. The result is an inevitable, yet rich and blessed, redundancy. The word is resumed and repeated because it is never fully explicit or an exact translation of what I have to say. It is never precisely received, never precisely understood. Language is Word. The Word contains fuzziness, a halo that is richer and less precise than information.

Even the simplest word—*bread*, for instance—involves all sorts of connotations. In a mysterious way, it calls up many images which form a dazzling rainbow, a multitude of echoes. When the word *bread* is pronounced, I cannot help but think of the millions of people who have none. I cannot avoid the image of a certain baker friend of mine, and of the time during the Nazi occupation when bread was so scarce and of such poor quality. The communion service comes to me: the breaking of bread at the Last Supper and the image of Jesus, both present and unknown.

I pass quickly to the moral lessons I learned as a child: that it is a crime to throw away a piece of bread, since it is a sacred substance. And from there, of course, I arrive at the enormous, incredible amount of wastefulness in our society. We waste many things besides bread, but it remains the negative symbol of our squandering ways. Memories come back to me: the warm, crusty bread of my childhood. The promised bread of life that will satisfy all hunger. And not living by bread alone. What ever happened to this Word of the Father which is proclaimed without being understood?

Not all of these memories are conjured up every time I hear the word, and they do not all come at once, but it is a rarity when none of them follows the oft-repeated request: "pass me the bread."

Language deals with connotations and overtones. It takes its place in the center of an infinitely delicate spider's web, whose central structure is fine, rigorous, and dense. As you move away from the center, the web becomes larger and distended, until it reaches incoherence, at its edge, where it sends off threads in every direction. Some of these threads go a great distance, until they arrive at the invisible spots where the web is anchored. This complex web is a marvel which is never the same, not for me at different points in time nor for another person.

The spoken Word puts the web in motion so that waves sweep through it and cause lights to flicker. The waves induce vibrations that are different for the other person and for me. The word is uncertain. Discourse is ambiguous and often ambivalent. Some foolishly try to reduce language to something like algebra, in which each word would have a mathematically precise meaning, and only one meaning. Each word would be put in a straitjacket, having only one meaning, so that we would know with scientific precision what we were saying. And the receiver of our message would always know exactly what we meant.

But the blessed uncertainty of language is the source of all its richness. I do not know exactly how much of my message the other person hears, how he interprets it, or what he will retain of it. I know that a kind of electric current is established between us; words penetrate him, and I have the feeling that he either reacts positively or else rejects what I have said. I can interpret his reaction, and then the relationship will rebound, accompanied by a rich halo of overtones. He does not understand, and I see that. So I speak again, weaving another piece of cloth, but this time with a different design. I come up with what I think will reach him and be perceived by him. The uncertainty of meaning and the ambiguity of language inspire creativity. It is a matter of poetics, but not just the esthetics of poetry. There is a poetics of language and of relationships also. We must not limit this poetics to language, which must be constantly rewoven, but remember that the relationship is *also* involved. Language requires that we recommence this relationship, which is always uncertain. I must disavow it over and over again, through sharp questioning, explanation, and verbal interchange.

Discourse is ambiguous; it is never clear. It arrives from one person's unconscious aggregate of experiences, desires, skills, and knowledge, only to fall into another person's, thus producing a different meaning. Because of these continual misunderstandings, new life is breathed into the relationship. We must constantly begin all over again, and as a result the relationship becomes a rich, complex landscape, with unexpected mountain passes and inaccessible peaks. By all means let's not turn language into something mathematical, nor reduce the rich complexity of human relationships to identical formulas.

Meaning is uncertain; therefore I must constantly fine-tune my language and work at reinterpreting the words I hear. I try to understand what the other person says to me. All language is more or less a riddle to be figured out; it is like interpreting a text that has many possible meanings. In my effort at understanding and interpretation, I establish definitions, and finally, a meaning. The thick haze of discourse produces meaning.

All of intellectual life (and I use the word "all" advisedly), even that of specialists in the most exact sciences, is based on these instabilities, failures to understand, and errors in interpretation, which we must find a way to go beyond and overcome. Mistaking a person's language keeps me from "taking" the person—from taking him prisoner.

We are in the presence of an infinitely and unexpectedly rich tool, so that the tiniest phrase unleashes an entire polyphonic gamut of meaning. The ambiguity of language, and even its ambivalence and its contradiction, between the moment it is spoken and the moment it is received produce extremely intense activities. Without such activities, we would be ants or bees, and our drama and tragedy would quickly be dried up and empty. Between the moment of speech and the moment of reception are born symbol, metaphor, and analogy.

Through language I lay hold of two completely different objects. I bring them together, establishing between them a relationship of similarity or even identity. In this manner I come to know this distant, unknown object, through its resemblance. It becomes intelligible to me, because through language I have brought it near this other one that I know well. This is an astonishing process, and logically a foolish one. It is obviously an indefensible operation, yet there it is, utterly successful, utterly enlightening. The uncertainty and the ambiguity of language have permitted it to function. I have access to the unknown through verbal identification, as well as through symbolic language that allows me to express the inexpressible.

As a result of this alchemy, after many efforts, the nugget of pure gold appears: we are in agreement. This is completely unexpected, and always a miracle. Through metaphors and syllogisms, analogies and myths, in the tangles of uncertainties and misunderstandings, agreement crops up. In the middle of so much "noise" (in the sense of interference), word and meaning come to the surface and permit an unclouded agreement, a conformity, in which heart meets heart. The innermost being of one person has reached the innermost of another through the mediation and ambassadorship of this language go-between. Overloaded with meaning, it has now been stripped of all excess and reduced to its essence. Now we can engage in common action without fear of error. Our life together can continue on the basis of a renewed authenticity.

But we must be careful: this happy result is achieved only to the degree that—exactly to the degree that—we have experienced all the "interference" of meaning: the rich connotations, the polyphony, and the overtones produced. In the middle of all this, and because of it, a common understanding springs forth and is formulated. It is not exactly what I said (fortunately!). Rather, it is more than that. Nor is it exactly what a tape recorder could have taken down. Instead, it is a symphony of echoes that have reverberated in me. Our agreement commits us to a renewed relationship that will be more profound and genuine. We will be continually reinventing this relationship, just as our speaking must continually recommence.

The word reduced to the value of an algebraic formula with only one possible meaning would be useful for us in carrying out an identical superficial activity. But such language could never create meaning, and would never produce agreement and communication with another person. "Algebraic" language could never produce or suggest a story. Bees communicate pieces of information to each other, but do not produce anything like history.

History is produced by the tangle of our misunderstandings and interpretations. Something unexpected is continually cropping up even in the simplest of our relationships. This unexpected element involves us in some action, explanation, or procedure that will constitute the history of our relationship. History is a product of language and the word. This applies not only to something memorized so that we can tell it later. The historian, even if his field is the history of science, is always limited to telling stories—sometimes his own. This is not only true of the history that is distant from us, which only language can evoke and make new again, since it is told in the present. It is also true of the history we are making, which has yet to be invented: history in process, whether mine or the story of my society or of humanity in general. In every case, language alone sets history in motion, defines it, and makes it possible or necessary. This can be a word from the politician or from the masses.

The word can also obstruct and impede history, when mythical language immerses us in an ahistorical time that is repetitive and continually reduced to myth. Language is either historical or ahistorical, either a discourse on action to be undertaken or of myth to listen to. According to the sort of language used, human history either arises and becomes a significant aspect of humanity's existence, or else it remains on the level of everyday incoherence.

As in the case of human agreement, history is born and organized, continues, and takes on meaning as a result of the innumerable sounds arising from the Word. Finally the moment comes when understanding takes place, when language is understood after so many setbacks. From the level of being and of the heart, language proceeds to the level of intelligence, and finally it is understood, beyond and because of the repeated misunderstandings which have been progressively eliminated. All this takes place without losing any part of the symphony of meaning.

The instant when language is understood seems like a genuine illumination. It is not the sum of the understood fragments, not the slow and tortuous march of a gradual and complicated unfolding, nor is it the triumphant QED of a solved algebra problem. Instead, this moment of insight is an inspiration which reveals in an instant the meaning of the entire message the other person was trying to give me. Everything is reduced to this sparkling moment which makes order out of the rest of the imbroglio and finds the way out of the maze. In a single instant the entire idea becomes clear: the other person's argument ceases being mere rhetoric, and his symbols and metaphors are no longer pointless. In a flash that some have compared to a kind of vision, communication between two intelligent beings has taken place.

Have I really "seen" what the other person said? Sudden insight has nothing in common with sight but its instantaneousness. Insight is not a kind of vision, but rather a light. The difference between the two will become clear in a later section. With insight, meaning becomes perfectly transparent. The other person's words become mine; I receive them in my own mind. I experience utter intellectual delight, but a delight in my whole being as well, when I understand and am understood.

\*　　\*　　\*　　\*　　\*　　\*

The Word ushers us into time.[6] It makes us live with endless misunderstandings, interpretations, and overtones. Language does not enlighten me concerning the reality around me. I have no need for someone beside me to describe what I can see as well as he can. I have no need for spoken information about the reality I can verify directly. In this situation no ambiguity or distance is involved. Instead, based on my own experience of reality, I could establish the unreliability of the other person's useless words. This is what happens when someone testifies to what he has seen.

In this reality, language naturally also has its uses. It can command an action. It gives birth to institutions. But reality is not where its specificity lies. We have mentioned myths and symbols, allegories and metaphors, analogies and history, as spheres in which language moves about easily. In these contexts it takes on its full stature and becomes truly the word. In other words, it is true to itself when it refers to Truth instead of Reality.

Of course, I do not presume to deal with Truth here, nor do I intend to define it. When I say that language normally deals with Truth rather than Reality, I only mean that there are two orders of knowledge, two kinds of references we use as human beings. There are references to the concrete, experienced reality around us, and others that come from the spoken universe. The spoken universe is our invention—something we establish and originate by our words. We derive meaning and understanding from language, and it permits us to go beyond the reality of our lives to enter another universe, which we may call phantasmic, schizophrenic, imaginary, or any other name we choose. I am certain that since the beginning, human beings have felt a pressing need to frame for themselves something different from the verifiable universe, and we have formed it through language. This universe is what we call truth.

Lewis Mumford can dream all he wants to of another world; Cornelius Castoriadis can make up imaginary things; and Roger Caillois can say that myth constitutes our human specificity, our only singularity, but these ideas do not matter much to me. The important thing is that the unique value of language lies in truth. Language is not bound to reality, but to its capacity to create this different universe, which you can call surreal, meta-real, or metaphysical. For the

---

6. I will not deal here with the question of language learning or of whether genetic programming is open to more than one language or oriented toward a single tongue. These matters go beyond my purpose. See the conflict between Noam Chomsky and Jean Piaget, *Théories du langage, théories de l'apprentissage*, Centre Royaumont pour une Science de l'Homme (Paris: Seuil, 1979).

sake of convenience we will call it the order of truth. The word is the creator, founder, and producer of truth.

Note carefully that I am not establishing any hierarchy in this connection, from a mediocre reality with no value, ascending toward a transcendent truth. I merely establish two different orders. Rather than speaking of Truth, at this point I am still dealing just with the order of truth (which is also, to be sure, the order of untruth, error, and falsehood!). Nor am I saying that language has nothing to do with reality. We will examine this relationship later. I am, instead, looking for specificity, and in this case it resides in the fact that nothing besides language can reach or establish the order of truth.

This brings us to the distinctives that characterize only the word: discussion, paradox, and mystery. Language is always unobtrusive, even when it tries to be demonstrative. It includes an unknown aspect in the background that makes it something secret and revealed. Language is unobtrusive in that it never asserts itself on its own. When it uses a loudspeaker and crushes others with its powerful equipment, when the television set speaks, the word is no longer involved, since no dialogue is possible. What we have in these cases is machines that use language as a way of asserting themselves. Their power is magnified, but language is reduced to a useless series of sounds which inspire only reflexes and animal instincts.

Authentic language is of necessity debatable, and therefore unobtrusive, even when a person is speaking from extremely strong conviction. However forceful the arguments may be, however close the reasoning or ardent the speaker, we all know how possible it is to protect ourselves from such outpourings. How often we have come up against a blank wall instead of a face, when the other person did not want to understand! How can we make him understand as long as he persists in that attitude?

In reality, language is an extraordinary occurrence in which each person's liberty is respected. I can oppose my word to the other person's. Or I can turn a deaf ear. I remain free as I face someone who tries to define me, encircle me, or convince me. Nothing is more absurd than the argument we hear over and over again these days (we will come back to it later), where someone pompously labels the word and language "terrorist"! I would say that language is the only nonterrorist form of expression! People who use labels so loosely have not experienced the difference between the violence of words and a whip with braided thongs—or between a human mouth, even if it is shrieking, and the silent muzzle of a revolver.

By its very ambiguity, which is a fundamental and essential part of it, language leaves the listener with a whole margin of freedom. As the speaker, I actually invite my listener to exercise his liberty in two ways. First, every act of speech supposes either assent or rejection. In other words, of necessity I give my listener a choice to make. A situation where there is choice is a situation where there is freedom. But at the same time, I invite him to use the gift of liberty inherent in language, just as I have. He must speak in turn, consciously making use of his freedom. I invite him to start down the difficult road of self-knowledge and self-expression, of choice, self-exposure, and unveiling.

Language always involves the exercise of freedom. It is never mechanical, just as it is not an object! Subtle structural linguistic analyses are of course limited to texts; that is, to finite, fixed words rather than open-ended ones. Such analyses seem to account for everything: codes, units of meaning, morphemes, etc. But they overlook one thing. Once the languages and lexicons, rhetorics, discourses, and narratives have been stripped of their mystery, one thing is left: language itself. It remains because it is history, and such linguistic analysis excludes history. The word remains because it is a call to freedom, and in such analysis structures and systems are closed. Language is an affirmation of my person, since I am the one speaking, and it is born at the same time as the faint belief, aspiration, or conviction of liberty. The two are born together, and language is a sign bearing witness to my freedom and calling the other person to freedom as well.

This is so true that the word is always paradoxical. This is its second characteristic. The paradox, let us remember, is something situated beside or outside the *doxa* (opinion). The paradox is free of all *doxa*, but at the same time calls the *doxa* into question. Roland Barthes is right in showing that "the real instrument of censorship is the *endoxa* rather than the police." "Just as a language is better defined by what it requires (its obligatory rules) than by what it prohibits (its theoretical rules), in the same way social censorship is present not when one is prevented from speaking, but rather when one is obliged to speak. The deepest subversion (countercensorship) does not consist so much in saying something to shock opinion, morals, the law, or the police, but in inventing paradoxical speech."[7]

Whereas rules of language can be the *doxa*, the word is always paradoxical. Enrico Castelli was right again in reminding us that paradox *exists*, and that there is no need to emphasize it in a heavy-handed manner. The absence of paradox would be the unusual situation, since it is not a profound and subtle invention of the philosopher

---

7. Etienne Dagut, *Etude sur Baudrillard* (Mémoire de l'Institut d'Etudes Politiques de Bordeaux, 1978).

or intellectual revolutionary, but something that proceeds from common sense.

Common sense defies organized thought. Common sense escapes
from any sort of integrating doctrine, and, after half a century of
oppression, it springs up strangely unharmed and expresses itself in
paradoxes. Common sense is not an inferior stage of thought: it is
paradox standing up to structured, logical, organized thought, which
follows the rules (of logic, dialectic, etc.). Paradox, always related to
the word springing up as something new, prevents thought from
closing up and reaching completion. Paradox prevents the system
from accounting for everything, and does not allow a structure to
mold everything.

The poetic word contains paradox within it. You believe poetic
language to be insignificant, a side issue in comparison with political
and scientific talk? You are right, but poetry continually brings the
uncertainty of ambiguity to our attention, along with double meanings, manifold interpretations, false bottoms, and multiple facets. The
word is always paradoxical because it corresponds directly to our
ambiguity as persons.

Now we are coming to the last characteristic to keep in mind
about the word: it is mystery. The most explicit and the best-explained
word still brings me inevitably back to mystery. This mystery has to
do with the other person, whom I cannot fathom, and whose word
provides me with an echo of his person, but only an echo. I perceive
this echo, knowing that there is something more. This is the mystery
I feel as I recognize spontaneously that I do not understand well or
completely what the other person says. There is a mystery for me in
my own lack of comprehension, as I become aware of it. How am I
going to react? How can I respond? I sense a whole area of mystery in
the fact that I am not very sure I understood correctly. I am not very
sure about answering. I am not very sure of what I am saying.

There is always a margin around our conversation. More precisely, conversation is like this printed page, framed on all sides by
white margins, without words, but which can be filled in with any
word at all. The margins situate a conversation and give it the possibility of rebounding and beginning again. They allow the other person
to participate with his marginal comments. I am aware of this possibility, but I do not know what marginal comments are going to appear
beside what I say, changing it. Here again we are dealing with the
unexpected. And we come up against the mystery of silence.

The mystery is silence as a break in discourse, not silence in the
sense of something that discourse fills up! The enigmatic, disturbing,
saddening silence of the other person is an inconvenience as I wait. I
expect a response, an explanation, or a statement from him. He falls

silent, and I no longer know where or how to take my place in relation to him. More precisely, I no longer know how to *be* as I face him. I find myself faced with a mystery which eludes me when there is a lull in the conversation. I expect words, but this silence constitutes a chasm in the word, which continues unspoken. It is unheard, but it cannot be eliminated. Thus in all sorts of ways the word is related to mystery. It expresses and engulfs us in mystery. There is a reason why mythos and logos go together.

The image, however, is never mysterious. We have seen that it can be terrifying. Mystery does not terrify. It is an existential questioning. The image is nonparadoxical, since it is always in conformity with the *doxa* (opinion). As we will see, it is especially an influence toward conformity. Thus cultural revolutionaries succumb to a childish illusion when they believe that films or posters can promote revolutionary ideas. Images never reinforce anything but conformity to the dominant *doxa*. Only the word troubles the waters. Images contain neither blank spaces nor margins. They refer to reality and give a direct account of it, without mystery, since reality has none. Images can include unresolved *problems* or paralyze me with horror, but they contain no mystery. What paralyzes me is the manifestation of horror. There are no false bottoms, no echoes in the reality I perceive through sight. But truth presents neither problems to resolve nor dreadful hallucinations. It is made up of sympathetic vibrations and vibrations of reason, discreet insights and interruptions, just like the word. Truth assails me and circumvents me with mystery. Everything seems to depend on evidence; reality is evident; sight, naturally, gives me evidence. But the truth is never evident.[8]

---

8. It is clear that I am utterly at odds with Marshall McLuhan on this point. When he tries to show that the visual world is continuous and homogeneous, I agree. But when he expounds this by saying that the visual world is a universe of continuity and development, whereas the acoustical world is a universe of simultaneousness, because we hear from all directions at the same time, but do not see everywhere at once, this seems very weak to me. We hear the noises of the area around us, just as we see everywhere within our visual range.

Amazingly, McLuhan considers the visual to be the origin of the linear and the sequential, and therefore of the temporal, whereas he related the acoustical world to what is spatial and global. I have wondered what the source of his error could be, and it seems to stem from the fact that when he speaks of the visual universe, he considers the visual only in terms of alphabetical writing, related, of course, to rationality. But in order to do this, he severs the relationship between Writing and the Word. And when he speaks of the acoustical universe, he considers only music, which can of course be called spatial, global, etc., as well as simultaneous. But here he excludes language.

The same thing occurs when he says that the visual universe furnishes us with classifications, whereas the acoustical provides immediate recognition. But

## 3. SEEING AND HEARING

It stands to reason that seeing and hearing are inseparable and complementary. Nothing in human affairs can be done without their joint involvement. I have considered them separately only for the sake of convenience. Their difference is fundamental, however, and it is probably out of their confrontation and opposition that human uniqueness is born. To show how they differ, I have exaggerated their characteristics, distinguished them by isolating them, and thus made their contrast more startling. Their difference is of fundamental importance, but rarely understood.

Now let us try to confront seeing and hearing. Their main antithesis concerns, as we have seen, the distinction between Space and Time, on the one hand, and Reality and Truth on the other. Our civilization's major temptation (a problem that comes from technique's preponderant influence) is to confuse reality with truth. We are made to believe that reality is truth: the only truth. At the time of the controversy over universals, the realists believed that only truth is real. We have inverted the terms, believing that everything is limited to reality.

We think that truth is contained within reality and expressed by it. Nothing more. Moreover, there is nothing left beyond reality any more. Nothing is Other; the Wholly Other no longer exists. Everything is reduced to this verifiable reality which is scientifically measurable and pragmatically modifiable. Praxis becomes the measure of all truth. Truth becomes limited to something that falls short of real truth. It is something that can be acted upon.

The Word is related only to Truth. The image is related only to reality. Of course, the word can also refer to reality! It can be perfectly pragmatic, used to command an action or to describe a factual situa-

---

it is evident that we recognize a person's face much more quickly than the sound of his disembodied voice. Immediate recognition is related to sight! In order to arrive at his conclusion, McLuhan must exclude the universe of noises. Whereas sight allows me to distinguish shape and color, which tell me immediately what something is, hearing may allow me to classify the sound or noise, but I do not discern immediately what it is.

Thus McLuhan's definition deals exclusively with the sight of written language and with hearing music. Having said this, I hasten to add that I find myself agreeing with many of his characterizations of both universes: the visual universe has to do with the quantitative, active sphere, and perceives clearly expressed outlines; the acoustical universe is emotional, intuitive, and qualitative, having to do with abstract perceptions. But how can he miss that these attributes are precisely what contradicts the sequential and therefore temporal characteristic of the one universe, and the spatial characteristic of the other?

tion. The word enters the world of concrete objects and refers to experiences of reality. It is the means of communication in everyday life, and as a result it fits precisely with all of reality. It conveys information about reality and takes part in the understanding of it. It can even create reality, producing effects that will become part of reality. Thus the word is ambivalent. But its specificity lies in the domain of truth, since this domain is not shared with anything else. On the contrary, the image cannot leave the domain of reality. It is not ambivalent.

At this point I can hear someone tempted to ask: "What is Truth?" I will carefully avoid answering by suggesting some specific content for the word. Such an answer would be challenged immediately, involving us in a long digression which would exceed my capacity. Without attempting this sort of definition, I can show what the object of truth can be, and this will serve to distinguish it clearly from reality. The very questions asked about truth can indicate its nature, replacing the answer that cannot be given.

We can grant, then, that anything concerned with the ultimate destination of a human being belongs to the domain of Truth. "Destination" in this sense is the same as "meaning and direction in life." We can add to this everything that refers to the establishment of a scale of values which allows a person to make significant personal decisions, and everything related to the debate over Justice and Love and their definition.

These considerations allow us to become conscious of what we call truth. There is nothing original in this idea. But when we say that everything related to these considerations belongs to the domain of Truth, we do not mean at all that every answer to these questions has the same value and is therefore true; we are not advocating syncretism. We only mean that none of these matters belongs to the sphere of reality. They can only belong to the domain of reality if truth and reality are decisively merged with each other, in which case the entire group of questions we have mentioned above simply disappears.

By saying these questions belong to the order of Truth, we imply that the answers given will be either truth itself, a reflection of this truth, error, or falsehood. It is important to note that falsehood and error belong to the domain of truth. If there is no truth, neither falsehood nor error exists. They are indissolubly linked, since they belong to the same order.

There is another important matter: the *question* of Truth is not the same thing as truth. I am not entering into metaphysics here. The question is not truth, because it is not the question that a person asks himself about his own life. This sort of question is just another intellectual game and a way of remaining outside truth. After all, it does not matter if one can answer or not, nor does it matter whether the answer is personal or is objectified as philosophy or revelation. But when a person asks about his *own* life (consciously or unconsciously), then the real *question* of truth has been asked. And when anyone claims to have resolved it, he is lying. When he tries to answer this question within the framework of reality alone, he has no answer to offer. The question which his life puts to him in all its aspects and its expressions remains an open question. It is continually being put to him, and this is truth itself.

Therefore, affirming the value of material happiness and the irreplaceable value of happiness as a response to being is simply giving a final answer to the permanently open question of truth. Nothing is resolved or achieved in this manner. Such an answer leaves a person faced with the same uncertainty, immersed in the same adventure as before. A civilization based on happiness becomes a civilization of consumerism, or else the gloomy gray paradise of Sweden. Swedish-type "paradises" finally produce either rebels without a cause (such as the 1953 New Year's Eve youthful rampage in Stockholm), or strikers who strike for no reason, since they are not revolting against anything. Certainly people who have testified to the eminent value of material happiness have not attempted to answer any other question, or even tried to ask this one in the face of men and women thirsting for the unusual.

The opposition between word and image is therefore not the same as the opposition between idealism and materialism. The assertion that praxis is the solution to human problems is words, as long as it remains an assertion. The entire relationship between praxis and truth as established by Karl Marx is words. Praxis, which appears to be an action for the purpose of changing reality, an action that constitutes the only measure and limit of truth, is of necessity initiated and produced by language. And language is also the means of describing and justifying praxis. Thus even in Marx the word is prior to all praxis. The word belongs to the order of the *question of truth*. An individual can *ask* the question of truth and attempt to *answer* it *only through language*.

The image, on the other hand, belongs to the domain of reality. It can in no way convey anything at all about the order of truth. It never grasps anything but an appearance or outward behavior. It is unable to convey a spiritual experience, a requirement of justice, a testimony to the deepest feelings of a person, or to bear witness to the truth. In all these areas the image will rely on a form.

Images can convey a rite, and thus people have a tendency to confuse religious truth with religious rites. In a world obsessed with images and where statistics are necessary, people feel a need to grasp "religion" by its rites, since it cannot be understood any other way. In this manner people get the impression that they have at least grasped the expressions of faith, whereas they have grasped only some aspects of a reality which of necessity clashes with the truth.

An image can catch a psychological expression on someone's face: ecstasy, for example. People will believe that they are seeing authentic faith, whereas all they have is a psychological state that can be utterly unrelated to faith. Such a state can be induced by a drug, for example. Faced with such a problem, those who identify reality with truth are so monumentally confused that they deny faith because a psychological state can be artificially induced! An image can show a body's position, as in a photograph of clasped hands and bowed head, seeming to say that this *is* prayer. But in reality, no prayer is involved in this image; it could be only a joke. Even when no one is joking, an image is incapable of expressing the seriousness of truth. I remember a photograph of Pope Pius XII in prayer, on the cover of the magazine *Paris Match*. It was an image that reeked of inauthenticity, utterly lacking in seriousness. It made you wonder how the Pope could have agreed to pose as if he were praying!

An image can properly be used to illustrate the history of the Church for us, but it will never tell us what the Church is. Even by allusion an image cannot enable us to grasp the deep and true life of the Church—the body of Christ, for example. The image cannot even express the visible Church, except for outward acts and stereotyped forms, which are always false expressions of the visible Church. An image can report miracles, but only recorded miracles—after they have taken place and grace has departed. The image can never penetrate as far as the holy place where the Word proclaims that an individual has become a new creation. The miracle is an expression of this new creation.

No image is able to convey any truth at all. This explains in part why all "spiritual" films are failures. When we insist on expressing spiritual matters this way through images, something other than truth is always perceived. Even more serious and alarming, truth tends to disappear behind all the lighting and makeup. It tends to vanish when squelched by images. The spectator of such films finds his attention diverted from what the film should be making him feel. The better the quality of the film the more insensitive the spectator becomes to the truth which the reality should be expressing.

Given this exclusive relationship between image and reality, one can easily understand why images have expanded so much in recent times. Our generation is characterized by the exclusive preeminence of reality, both at the factual level and in our preoccupations. We are moved in this direction by the marvels of technique, the prevailing tone of our time, the great concern about economic matters, etc. Our era is further characterized by an absolute identification of reality with truth. Marxism has prevailed absolutely in this matter, and science has finally convinced people that the only possible truth consists in knowing reality, and that the proof of truth is success relative to reality.

Thus in the thinking of modern individuals the image is the means par excellence which communicates reality and truth at the same time. This attitude concerning images can be held only if one confuses reality and truth to begin with, believing that a scientific hypothesis is *true* when it is confirmed by experiments. Such a hypothesis has nothing to do with truth, and is merely *accurate*. Of course, this preeminence of reality and this confusion coincide with the universal belief in the "fact," taken to be of ultimate value.

In all this, I am not trying to minimize the importance of the image. I mean only to specify its domain and understand its limits. The image is an admirable tool for understanding reality. In the social or political world, it can even be explosive and terribly efficacious. *Land without Bread* by Luis Buñuel and *Our Daily Bread* by King Vidor are admirable films for their ability to convict and to unsettle people's good conscience. They are genuinely revolutionary. A documentary film of a riot enables us to penetrate the world of anger better than any speech could. But an image is explosive only if the spectator knows what it represents and if it is taken for what it is: a faithful representation of reality.

An image becomes falsehood and illusion as soon as a person tries to see truth in it. At that moment, by means of an amazing reversal, the image loses all its explosive power. For example, a person who finds truth in the films we just mentioned walks away from them with a perfectly good conscience. All techniques of justification stem from the confusion of truth with reality. The spectator of one of these films may believe, for instance, that any movement capable of showing such truth is itself truthful: "Since I adhere to this movement and am sensitive to the scandal portrayed in this film, I possess the truth." So when we believe that an image expresses truth, the image gives us a good conscience and a peaceful spirit. When the image is understood to speak only of reality, however, it is explosive and terrible.

At this point we discover a new problem: images in our society are always the product of a mechanical technique. Technique is truly an intermediary, since the universe of images is established for us by technique. But this is the equivalent of saying that we find ourselves in the presence of an artificial world, made by an outside force with artificial means. Therefore it is important to realize that stark reality is never conveyed to us in this universe of images. Instead we find a more or less arbitrary construction or reconstruction, with the result that we must constantly remind ourselves of the ambiguity behind the apparent objectivity of the image: it expresses a reality, but of necessity it presents us with an artifice. In this sense the image is deceptive: it passes itself off as reality when it is artifice; it pretends to be unilateral truth when it is a reflection of something that cannot be truth.

*   *   *   *   *   *

When we say that only the word is related to truth, we are not saying that the word is necessarily true. We are stating that only the word *can* be truth, as, consequently, only the word can be falsehood. An image can be inaccurate with respect to reality, but it is never false because it cannot deceive us about the truth. Images have nothing to do with truth, except for the confusion established in the modern mind between reality and truth. Only the word can be false, since it is destined to express truth and because it occupies the central position.

The word is lying when it gives a lying answer to a question concerning the truth. This has always been an open debate in human history. We will not dwell on this, since it would involve us in a discussion concerning the content of truth, which is not possible in these pages. Let us just note that this permanent debate is always situated at the level of the word, and that it has always been conducted by this means.

But we will dwell on another aspect of this falsehood of the word which is less known and more relevant: the word becomes falsehood when it denies its relationship with truth. This happens when the word claims to be nothing more than an evocation of reality, as if it were an image; when it turns aside from its vocation in order to serve only vested interests, practices, and efficaciousness, whatever their spheres: economic, political, or scientific. Not that the word should refuse to serve in these areas; but it should not enclose itself in them so decisively. Even in its pragmatic uses, the word must always remain a door opening to the Wholly Other, a question concerning ultimate causes, and an indicator of ultimate answers.

The Bible provides us with a remarkable model of this, since it recounts all sorts of concrete and practical stories, factual adventures, politics, and psychologies. Yet in its concrete use of the word, the Bible seizes ultimate mystery from all angles, and in so doing, reveals truth itself. When the word denies its dual use, it becomes of necessity a lie and a counterfeit.

In such a situation, when the word claims to speak only of reality, it is so rapidly outdistanced by the image that the word loses its vitality and its gravity. The image is ever so much more efficacious, and the word is stripped of its authenticity; people stop committing themselves to what it says because it has become merely a practical thing. Under these circumstances, the word no longer deserves to be believed. This is our present situation. The Word is devaluated in our day because it has come to be used only to express reality. Thus no one puts his whole weight behind what he says, and such a word appears useless. Indeed, it is useless, partly because it is a falsehood; it is completely useless because its only true value has been repudiated.

In this state of affairs, people no longer have any means of approaching, discerning, and grasping truth. Thus we can understand the seriousness of the warnings against vain speech, words said "in the air," which are neither yes nor no, committing us neither to anything nor to any person.

Purely doctrinal or doctrinaire language is no more closely related to truth than words said in vain. We are still influenced by this strange movement in which the preeminence of reality has attempted to restrict the word to pure objectivity. The nineteenth century, under the influence of science that dealt with reality, wanted nothing but objective language, separated from the person using it. This transformed the word into something false. If the word of the Gospels is separated from Jesus Christ, the person who says and fulfills it, it is mere vanity. All human speech is intrinsically connected to a person. Not only in theology and from God's point of view is the word the equivalent of the person. The objective word, left to itself, and in itself, loses all its weight, because of its very inability to be an object. Since someone has tried to separate it from the person who speaks it, it has lost its relationship with truth and has become a lie.

Let us be clear that this is not the same as saying that the word becomes true simply because the person who says it commits himself to it and does what he has said. Even if we can believe only the words people would die for, that still does not guarantee their veracity. It simply means that only these words have *something to do with truth.* Only these are worthy of entering the great debate, the great human quest. The word detached from the person speaking can never fulfill this minimal condition, because it is a dead word. Who would die for an objective word? Galileo answered the question well: you do not become a martyr in order to insist on the earth's turning!

Reference to reality situates me in a universe of precision and imprecision, exactitude and inexactitude. I see either a red or a green light. I act in such a way as to find the right answer, the precise solution. The visual is the royal road to discerning what is correct and incorrect, and it gives me direct experience. I have no need for reflection; I know immediately what is accurate or correct in my gesture as it relates to the situation I have seen. Hearing involves me with speech, and places me in the universe of truth, and therefore of falsehood or error. The questions are no longer the same. There is never any direct experience of truth, falsehood, or error. Truth and error dazzle equally: since speech is of necessity paradoxical, it presupposes a long effort at discernment, choice, and experimentation. What comes from the word is never obvious. Reality can be obvious, but truth never is.

*     *     *     *     *     *

In this study we are not attempting to make a radical separation between image and word, reality and truth, but rather to recall the distinction between them and the place of each. It is good for language to accompany images, to add another dimension to them and give them meaning, as long as the image is clearly subordinate to the word. For the image, like reality itself, can never be anything but the raw material for a human decision. In itself the image supplies no fundamental basis for judgment, decision, or commitment. Only the word (since it is at the same time instrument, agent, and locus of confrontation between truth and falsehood) can be also the agent and the locus of differentiation and criticism, thus leading to a judgment.

Criticism is the preferred domain of the word. In its relations with images, the word is called on to criticize the image, not in the sense of accusing it, but in the more basic sense of separation and discernment of true and false. This is one of the noblest functions of the word, and discourse should relate to it.

We realize, of course, how this mission of the word aggravates people in our day. They need prefabricated certainties (stereotypes that are not subject to criticism, images without words). They need monolithic attitudes, behavior guaranteed not to require choices. Criticism seems completely sterile to them because it impedes action. They find it negative because everything is not accepted in advance— and pessimistic because it does not automatically give its stamp of approval to all of reality.

For this reason the most distinguished use one can make of his language is the most hated one in our day. This is just one more facet of the devaluation of the word. What is at stake here is a conceivable expression of the truth within reality itself, but which must be uprooted by force, in the midst of the pain of affirming that it is falsehood. If language is not useful for this, what else could allow us to accomplish this task without which human beings do not have much significance?

Today, of course, this task seems negligible, compared to the importance of making refrigerators or refining oil. Anyone who tries to interfere with such efforts by means of the word is considered to be nothing but a conjurer. To that extent our contemporaries have lost the sense of their language and their life.

As means and locus of criticism, the word permits judgment— not the judgment of practical matters and experience, which are the only judgments we are willing to submit to in the modern world, but the laughable judgment that involves ethical values. Only through the use of language can one learn to make ethical decisions. These are a result of the choices we make in critical thinking, as we criticize situations and ourselves.

As a product of criticism, the ethical decision operates in the domain of the word because it is utterly personal. It expresses the person; it can in no way be simply the act of participating in some group activity (if the ethical decision is genuine and not simply a matter of moral conformity). This is absolutely opposed to the guidance which an image can give someone. The image tends, on the contrary, to produce conformity, to make us join a collective tendency.

Indeed, images create certain kinds of human behavior, but these are always in harmony with the societies expressed through the image. This is true even when the image tries to be nonconformist. In such cases there is always a degree of ambiguity confusing what is possible with what is good. The decision an image would lead us to make can never be an all-or-nothing decision. But the word does constrain us in this sense, probably because of its very nature. For when the word is not authentic, it is absolutely nothing. All that remains is air. On the contrary, the image and action, however inaccurate they may be, always remain and give the illusion of reality and effectiveness.

\* \* \* \* \* \*

In these times we know only too well to what extent people's psychology depends on the language they were taught. Their reactions, their relationships, and their manner of understanding and being, in the cultural sphere, depend on language. Feminists are right in claiming that the very structure of a language places women on an inferior level. Saying *man* to indicate both masculine and feminine, deriving the feminine grammatical form from the masculine, and a hundred other examples in vocabulary and syntax cause the masculine attitude to predominate. The effect of language in this area is much greater than the games which are said to orient girls toward the kitchen and men toward war! Language determines our psychology as well as our mode of reasoning. My intention here is not to emphasize cultural factors over natural ones, but to show the uniqueness of the mechanism of the spoken and heard word. It determines us as both psychic and knowing beings. It is as if everything on this level depended on verbal expression.

Furthermore, sight and language determine two different kinds of thinking.[9] Language, which is written, involves a long, careful process. My eyes follow the words one after the other, and thus a sequence of understandings are connected to each other. Thought develops according to the axis of this sequence of words. I receive knowledge progressively as the elements of what I am trying to understand link up in succession. Ideas are gradually laid bare as I follow the sentence. The sentence unfolds within a given time span, so that my knowledge necessarily takes the form of step-by-step reasoning. My knowledge progresses by following the curves of this language, assuming a certain continuity in the sentence and rationality in the relationship between words.

Finally, knowledge always involves consciousness. Language is endowed with rationality; I need to understand what the other person says to me, and I can do so only if there is rationality in the very structure of what he says (rationality by itself is not sufficient for this, but it is necessary). Thus language calls me to a conscious operation that leads me not only to new knowledge but to a broadened and developed consciousness.

The visual world with its signals based on images belongs to another order altogether. The image immediately conveys to us a totality. It gives us in a glance all the information which we could possibly need. It dispenses a reserve of knowledge I need not itemize or coordinate differently than the image itself does: that is, spatially. The transmission takes place instantaneously so long as I am located in the same space as the image. The image conveys to me information belonging to the category of evidence, which convinces me without any prior criticism. It is strange that so often a photograph is considered proof whereas there is hesitation about accepting the testimony of a witness (testimony lacks "credibility"!) or a reasoned demonstration.

Whenever something visible is involved, we are sure of our information. This certainty is direct and does not move gradually from unknown to uncertain and then from uncertain to known. But such certainty is based on absence of awareness. The sort of knowledge produced by an image is by nature unconscious. Only rarely do I remember all the elements of an image or a spectacle, but it has made a strong impression on my entire personality and has produced

---

9. Here I limit myself to a brief reference to a theme we will consider more thoroughly later.

a change in me that is based in the subconscious. This overall and unconscious perception of a whole "package" of information which does not follow the slow and arduous path of language also explains why we are naturally, through laziness, inclined to watch images rather than to read a long book or listen to a demonstration. Intellectual laziness causes the image to win out over the word automatically, and we observe its victory on every hand.

Finally, the way of thinking changes: images link themselves up to each other in a manner that is neither logical nor reasonable. We proceed by association of images and their successive changes. The aspects of an image that change in this process have to do exclusively with the spectacle in its present moment. They are never a logical sequence. In this respect Marshall McLuhan's analysis is correct. As he says, it is not the characteristics of electronic signals which have made the difference, but the manner in which images follow each other. When we think by means of images (as in typical comic strip "logic"), each image is a totality, and the sequence progresses by fits and starts.

## 4. WHAT ABOUT THE PHILOSOPHER?

As far as philosophy is concerned, the first to raise the question of sight and hearing, showing and speaking was apparently Søren Kierkegaard, in his attack on the philosophers who had preceded him.[10] Kierkegaard mounts an astounding attack on the privileged position of sight in Western philosophy, where the philosopher is a spectator and philosophy is thought of as speculation.

Platonism establishes the philosophical sovereignty of sight and G. Hegel follows it closely. Plato defines the essence of things on the basis of their perception. True knowledge is knowledge of ideas and of *form*; but idea, *eidos*, comes from the verb *eidō*, which means *to see*. René Descartes also places sight in an absolute and privileged position, as the model of intuition. *Intueri* also means *to see*. What a constant repetition of error!

Kierkegaard breaks the pattern: "The speculative individual wants to touch everything he sees. . . . Why doesn't he respect the distance imposed by Being? Why doesn't he deal carefully with the difference between himself and the other person, in order to understand who he is? In order to understand, he must give ear: hasten to listen. You must learn to listen." For language and hearing are at the

---

10. In this section I limit myself to summarizing a chapter of the remarkable book by Nelly Viallaneix, *Kierkegaard et la Parole de Dieu* (Paris: Champion, 1977), to which we will refer often!

center of being. "Everything leads to the ear. Grammatical rules lead to the ear; so does the message of the law. Jean-Philippe Rameau's unwritten base line leads to the ear, as does the system of philosophy. The afterlife is also presented as pure and simple music, like a vast harmony. If only the dissonance of my life could soon be resolved into that harmony" (cited by Nelly Viallaneix).

Phenomenology should not only cause things to *appear* as they are, but make them *sound* as they are! Classical philosophy does not know how to listen to or hear truth. Kierkegaard listens to Mozart: "The careful listener, when hearing *A Little Night Music*, will always set the speculative (visual) spectacle over against the silent 'I know'— that silent situation in which we enable ourselves to hear the melody of the world as we listen, and as we wait for God's call."

The philosopher who refuses to listen also refuses both truth and reality. He lives within one set of categories and thinks with others. He is "like a man who builds an enormous castle, but lives beside it in a hut." These philosophers may not listen to anything, but of course they talk! They do nothing else! But they use words not even "to hide their thoughts, but to hide the fact that they have none." Their verbal inflation has no foundation. This becomes clear when they use language only for constructing *systems*.

Kierkegaard develops an incessant polemic from his observation that philosophy is based on sight and at the same time ceases speaking. He satirizes philosophy, caught up in mirror tricks of speculation. These tricks lead only to the construction of a system in which one is then enclosed. Only Socrates speaks truly, "for Socrates does not look complacently on the spectacle of Nature, Being, or his own thought. As a man of character, he achieves the ethical ideal in his life, which he risks as he incarnates his demands. And he announces the need for understanding oneself, because to understand truly is to be."

Socrates is docile in relation to the inner voice that guides him. He *listens* to the secret voice we each hear. That is why he speaks. His irony, which asks the most ungracious questions, calls itself into question. "It abolishes speculation in favor of the word." Therefore, all Socrates' teaching takes place within the framework of a dialogue, in which two speakers provide each other with the opportunity to find themselves and be born.

Kierkegaard calls this Socratic method of reciprocal (spoken!) interchange "indirect communication." In it the master and his disciple share in the quest for truth. If they wrestle, it is in order *to understand each other*. In this situation the word is action in life.

Every spoken relationship requires the mutual participation of the one speaking and the one listening, united in the same present moment. The word must be put into practice in life, or else it is interrupted. This is no theory or system or spectacle! This fundamental founding dialogue eliminates false visual knowledge (more precisely the false application of the visual to an object that is not of the visual order—or even better, the reduction of all knowledge to the visual plane!). It also eliminates the egocentric monologue of the scholar who has understood nothing, and therefore remains unable to draw from within himself any new riches!

This is where Kierkegaard's dialectic fits in, as Viallaneix shows so well. It is a qualitative dialectic (as contrasted with Hegel's dialectic, which Kierkegaard calls quantitative), and a dialectic of life rather than a system of concepts. For the word is dialectical in itself and at the same time integrated into the whole of existence. By this I mean that the word is intended to be lived.

We can stop here without considering (Kierkegaardian) repetition, which Viallaneix contrasts with speculative and fine-layered philosophy. We may stop here, since beyond this point Kierkegaard involves us in the dialectically related stages within the steps leading to Christ. These are not successive steps organized in linear progression. On the contrary, each stage adds an irreplaceable element which always takes its place in the present moment of life, like a word that has been heard. Even if the word is forgotten, it leaves its mark on life.

At this point we find ourselves in the presence of a strange and happy contradiction. The reality around us changes and flows constantly. Everything flows: *panta rhei.* The river I see is never the same. This water I am looking at races away and will never return. At every level, reality is unstable and fleeting. Consider politics or economics: every moment changes their framework. Every moment presents some loss or accident that rules out planning ahead with a view to efficient organization. History does not repeat itself; no two situations will ever be truly comparable.

Time is not alone in making reality unstable. What is the nature of reality? Bernard d'Espagnat's fine book[11] questions and upsets us. I am aware that this rock I am looking at is essentially a vacuum with atoms whirling around it. But the more physicists progress, the less able we are to grasp reality. In the last analysis, only mathematics can assure us that reality exists. We finally arrive at such refined analysis and a knowledge so subtle that reality becomes a gradually disappearing object that leaves us bedazzled.

Reality is present and yet nothing is there. What I think I grasp

---

11. Bernard d'Espagnat, *A la recherche du Réel: Le Regard d'un physicien* (Paris: Gauthier-Villars, 1981).

is not only transitory and changing, but imperceptible in its "substance" (if one can still use this word in the light of the vacuum and emptiness revealed to us by theoretical physics). We have tools for measuring, but beyond that. . . . Is everything then an illusion produced by our senses? This old question needs to be brought up again, because it leads us to an astonishing contradiction. I perceive the reality around me (such as this table I am looking at, and on which I am writing) through my sight and sense of touch. That is, I grasp it by means of my most reliable and indisputable senses. We do not need to return to this idea: I cannot doubt what I see. Yet we know for a certainty that what I see is not what I see. But what difference does this make? My sight gives me certainty concerning reality, and I need nothing more.

Here is the other side of the coin: in *Measure for Measure*, Shakespeare says "Truth is truth to th'end of reck'ning." And Shakespeare is right. Truth remains truth in relation to and in spite of everything. It is firm, stable, hard, and irrefutable. We must not relativize it just because science has changed. We must not say that yesterday's truth becomes today's error (and vice versa). We must not become so extremely liberal that we say everything is relative, so that one person can be just as right as the person who says the opposite. If truth is truth even beyond the limits of our grasp and our approximations, it *exists*. And that settles it. It remains true to itself, of necessity. In observing vanishing reality, Heraclitus says something that does not vanish, and his statement falls within the scope of truth.

Truth is the absolute or eternal. We are not able even to approach its outskirts. We do not construct truth out of bits and pieces added to one another, so as to enable us to remove them and dismantle the construction. By means of language we transmit and understand this truth that is as tightly closed and solid as a dot, reliable as a map, translucent as a crystal, but hard as a diamond. We transmit it and even discern it only through language. Truth is connected to the word and communicated by it. That is, truth is communicated by the most uncertain means, the one most prone to variations and doubt, as we have seen—by the word, that fragile thing that does not last, evaporating as soon as it has been said. Thus what we are surest of is connected with the most uncertain thing in existence; our most changeable means has to do with what is most certain.

Now here is the amazing thing: this is a godsend for us. How could we live if *our senses* advised us that the reality in which we live does not really exist in the final analysis, that it is only a tangle of whirlwinds and illusions? How could I walk if my senses showed me nothing but emptiness in front of me? How could I eat if my senses showed me the utter unreality of what I am eating? Not that everything can be reduced to the impressions of my senses. That is not what I mean. My point is that sight and touch, the senses of certainty, give me the guarantee indispensable for living, concerning a milieu that is strange and foreign to me. My certainty is false as far as exact reality is concerned, but this certainty allows me to live.

Physics or mathematics can teach me many things about reality, but they cannot contradict the unimpeachable evidence of my senses. What do I care about the fact that chemistry can give me the exact formula for the wine I am drinking? That has no effect on the great pleasure I derive from it.[12] In order for me to live, my senses must be right in spite of the scientific analysis of reality.[13]

The opposite is just as true. What would become of us if we could grasp truth with unvarying precision and express it without the slightest imperfection or without any uncertainty? What would happen if the means were perfectly adequate for expressing truth? Such a situation would be dreadful and completely unlivable. We would be pinned down once and for all in a butterfly museum. We would be there in all our splendor, unable to move any more, because everything would be said, closed up, and finished: perfect.

We have seen the horror that has resulted in the course of our history every time a person or group has claimed to express truth in its entirety, believing their word to be identical with the truth, or that truth could not be "elsewhere" or "other." This attitude has given legitimacy to all dictatorships, oppressions, falsehoods, and massacres. One person's word against another's is the only possible fragile pointer to truth, like a compass quivering in its case. And quite apart from human pretension to have a proud, exclusive corner on truth, even if we could seize truth as it is and transmit it without wasting any of it and without confusion, truth would crush us of its own weight and prevent us from living. In order to live, we need truth to be expressed by the most fragile agent, so that the listener remains free. The uneasiness which enables us to keep going involves knowing that we will never be able to grasp truth in its entirety, or be able to bring our adventure to a close by identifying our life with truth.

Some people, including Christians (I think particularly of my Protestant friends), have the profound conviction that truth is "there." They say, for instance, that "the word of God is expressed in the Bible." Even so, I must be prudent enough to say that this word is conveyed through human language: witnesses who pass it on to

---

12. Moreover, when chemists claim to be able to reproduce wine, vanilla, orange extract, etc., on the basis of their exact formulas, the result is always horrible—at least for those with a sense of taste.

13. This is part of d'Espagnat's rigorous analysis.

other witnesses. And when I hear it, I understand it with my words, my verbal images, and I speak it with my language—and I am not God, fortunately. If this were not so, human life would be closed. By these statements, I do not reduce the value of revealed truth in the slightest; on the contrary, in this way I respect it and recognize its special dimension and the depth and permanence that make it truth. If I claim to grasp and express it in its entirety, *then* it is no longer truth.

The connection between Word and Truth is of such a nature that nothing can be known of truth apart from language. This truth establishes itself over the duration of generations (Hebrew *toledoth*), in the ebb and flow of words, through our fellowship and our misunderstandings. This is where this marvelously human life is located. The most reliable thing speaks to the most uncertain world; my most flexible means expresses what is irrefutable.

## 5. WRITING

In finishing these prolegomena, we must say a few words about writing. This situation is completely ambiguous. It is a phenomenon that comes along and shuffles the cards after they have been dealt. We assume that writing is the written word. We invariably associate the two. First we must clearly understand that we associate them because of a long development. André Leroi-Gourhan has done a most praiseworthy job of showing that language was not written at the beginning, and that writing was not "canned" language![14] "Figurative art is inseparable from language; it is born from the intellectual marriage of phonation and graphic art. . . . From the beginning, phonation and graphic art have the same goal. . . . Four thousand years of linear writing have caused us to separate art and writing."

Actually we have misinterpreted picture writing and then ideograms (Leroi-Gourhan speaks of "picto-ideography") because of our familiarity with alphabetical, linear writing. In a stroke of genius, Leroi-Gourhan has discovered that present-day writing is not a normal sequence of picture writing, which would then be considered the "infancy of writing." It is true that alphabetical linearity could have originated in numerating devices, which are of necessity linear, such as notches, knotted cords, etc. Picture writing, however, is another matter, for there are two universes: "Reflective, abstract thought concerning reality, symbols which create a parallel real world, the world of language. This reflective thought is expressed concretely in spoken language, and enables people to express themselves in a way

14. André Leroi-Gourhan, *Le Geste et la Parole* (Paris: Albin Michel, 1965), I: 269–70.

that goes beyond the material present." Therefore *two* languages exist: that of hearing and that of seeing.

Compared to phonetic language, graphic symbolism benefits in a special way from a degree of independence: its content expresses in the three dimensions of space what phonetic language expresses in the single dimension of time. Images enjoy a dimensional freedom that writing lacks. An image can set in motion the verbal process which leads to the telling of a myth, but the image is not attached to the myth. Thus in the case of picture writing we are in the presence of "groups of figures coordinated within a system that is foreign to linear organization and thus foreign to the possibilities of continual speech."

In other words, there is almost complete independence between pictorial expression and vocalized expression, between the role of the hand, which uses tools, and the role of the face, which is the means of creating verbal language. "The hand creates images, which are symbols that do not depend directly on the development of verbal language. In any case, they are not at all parallel." Leroi-Gourhan calls this language "mythographic," because drawing gives rise to mental associations, series of impressions "in a category parallel to verbal myth, and foreign to the rigorous specification of spatiotemporal coordinates."

The images evoked by this language can move in several divergent directions. "The hand has *its* language in which expression refers to sight. The face has another language, which is linked to hearing. Between the two the halo prevails that gives a special quality to thought that is in the strict sense previous to writing. Gesture interprets language, and language comments on graphics." The image linked with mythological thought integrates itself into a rich and diversified system of symbolic relationships. Leroi-Gourhan thus uses the term *mythography* to designate this visual language which corresponds perfectly to mytho-logy. The latter designates the recitation of myths composed of many-dimensional and all-inclusive images that occur in succession. Here we discover the relationship between spoken and written language.

Leroi-Gourhan then shows in minute detail how the changes might have taken place: the "linearization of symbols," developing into writing, the intervention of what can be counted, the transformation of picture writing into ideograms, and the appearance of linear graphics (which took the place of multidimensional graphics). He also shows how mythological thought might have developed into rational thought: then, "at the stage of linear graphics, which characterizes writing, the relationship between the two fields evolves again: written language, which paints sounds and is linear in space, becomes completely subordinated to verbal language, which is phonetic and linear in time. Verbal-graphic dualism disappears and mankind has at its disposal a unique linguistic instrument. It is an instrument that expresses and preserves thought, which is itself more and more channeled into reasoning."

We had already arrived at this point of ambiguity and uneasiness in the written word.[15] Earlier we called it the "fixed" word: language that has passed from the order of the auditory to the visual. Henceforth it is a word placed in space, a word by which no one any longer commits himself: a word that no longer involves dialogue. The written word is inscribed in the order of reality, and therefore can be treated as part of reality, using the appropriate methods.

The written word is continually repeated and always identical; this is not possible for the true word. Ask the person speaking with you to repeat the explanation he has just given, and it will be different. But you can reread a page. In this sense, making a record or recording a tape is the same thing as writing: the same passage from temporal to spatial in involved. All these processes go from the unrepeatable to the indefinitely repeatable. They all make dialogue impossible. The word is no longer itself, but has become another world.

The written word is intermediary, which is why the world of writing or recording is so uncertain and ambiguous. However, as we have already said, language retains even in this form some of its fundamental characteristics. It is successive; although inscribed in space, it obliges the reader or listener to accept the law of time because of its successiveness. The sentence is still constructed in the same manner. I must follow it, with my eyes now, from beginning to end, and I grasp its meaning only through this flow of time. The linear aspect of language remains basic. Also, this fixed word is still related to truth, and only to truth. Being written down has not changed its

---

15. Gilles Deleuze and Felix Guattari, in *Anti-Oedipus* (New York: Viking, 1977), have made use of Leroi-Gourhan's remarkable explanation for their own ends, to further their arbitrary and burlesque design. They say that civilizations slipped into barbarism because the graphic system lost its independence and its unique dimensions, aligning itself with the voice and becoming subordinate to the voice. After this we are treated to their hallucinations, such as "deterritorialized flow" and "instrument of domination." Graphics begin to depend on the voice, but it is a silent voice from the heights or from the beyond. This voice then begins to depend on graphics. By means of subordinating itself to this voice, writing replaces it. Despotism appears at this point: "The voice no longer sings, but dictates and decrees. Graphics no longer dance or animate bodies. Instead, they are written in a fixed manner on tables, stones, and books. The eye begins to read." And all this produces both religious feeling and the despotic state. Juggling with words is always easy.

aim, meaning, or intention. It is just diluted, weaker, and no longer
backed up by a person's whole being. No longer does it have a name,
even if it does still have meaning. This word can be scoffed at in a
way that would be impossible if it had just been spoken.

At this point we can profitably recall Pier Paolo Pasolini's famous
comparison of the oral and written on the one hand and reality and
the image on the other. It brings into focus the double transformation
characteristic of our era, when technique makes everything into an
object. I cannot convey the image I see. When I place it on film, it
can be transmitted so that henceforth anyone can see it. But the other
person sees an image rather than the reality I had seen in a resplendent
moment. There is a difference: the fixed image is not real. The reality
grasped by the other person, who has not seen or known the reality I
saw, is the film itself, the screen, and the colors and forms of the
impression. He does not see the landscape and the face which were
transformed into shapes and colors before becoming a landscape and
a face. An abstraction takes place through fixation and objectification.
I can recompose these abstract spots so that they become a face, but
this is not the reality that is noticed at first.

The word is not itself either. Once it is written, it no longer has
the sting of truth it had when said by another person—even when the
simplest things were said. No one is involved any longer. The truth is
reduced to visual signs, which mean nothing in themselves; and many
of the discussions concerning signifier, signified, and sign are based
on the written word! The signs have become completely conventional;
doesn't the same thing happen to truth? Truth has become both
abstract and objective. It no longer commits anyone to anything.
Witnesses do not give their lives for written pages, but rather for
words conveyed by people.

The word when written becomes a means of abstract, solemn
discussion. A University based on writing is not the same thing as an
Academy's halls. Writing changes hearing into sight, and transforms
the understanding of a person, with his words' halo of mystery and
echoes, into the understanding of a text. This approach involves
grammatical and logical analysis, decomposition of structures, and
understanding of truth through the dull seriousness of exact methods.
Deciphering words and phrases leads us to reconstruct a message that
has lost its life and immediacy. It becomes the result of a process, of
a coming and going from the text to my knowledge and from my
knowledge to the text, with an increasingly precise method.

We must not forget that writing also affects language. Images and
our practice of reading and writing cause us to conceive of discourse
as linear, with only one meaning, and consecutive. Writing is of
necessity linear and consecutive, even when we try to sever its univo-

cal quality through a sort of written polyphony. Efforts of this nature, such as Henri Pichette's *Epiphanies*[16] or Raymond Queneau's poems, are just stylistic exercises that cannot outweigh the unrelenting mass of texts that engulf us.

Language is thus reduced by being written down. It ceases being multicentered and flowing, evocative and mythological. In this sense, and therefore quite indirectly, McLuhan is right when he speaks of a return to a world of myth through television—but not for the reasons he gives. Television, to the degree that it eliminates part of writing, causes writing to lose its rigor, or the implacable quality it gives to the development of thought. All this is lost when the written word is replaced by speech. Spoken language is then able to have multiple meanings again. These include the play on variations of a theme and the myriad directions in which the human spirit can move when listening. But this can happen only if the deluge of televised images has not done away with language altogether. In that case television will not produce any flowering; instead, the result will be the dismal disintegration of the very possibility of thought.

We all know that writing strips language of its certainty and even of its meaning, which then can be restored only after a certain thought process. We show that we sense this when we feel the need to go in the opposite direction and switch from the text to speech. This happens often, especially when we are dealing with the most creative, evocative, and truth-filled texts, such as poetry or religious writings. It is impossible simply to read them. Poetry needs to be spoken. We all know that it acquires impact and meaning only when recited. Then it becomes a living text because it is no longer a text; the speaker takes it up and *can* read it only to the precise degree that he makes it his own. He must become in turn the creator of language, with the help of the text he has been given.

The same process applies to religious writing. It is filled with life only when it serves as a support and starting point for a word that is spoken, announced, or proclaimed. In this way the word becomes current and living, having left the book's pages and flown toward the listener. What a tremendous error people commit when they consider the *verba volent* to be critical and the *scripta manent* to be something positive. Precisely because written words subsist, and persist, they are nothing but an anonymous trace. Because they fly, spoken words are living and filled with meaning. The expressions above form a useful formula for a judge who needs proof of something that is past and

---

16. Henri Pichette, *Les Epiphanies (mystère profane)* (Paris: Gallimard, 1969).

surpassed—a finished and closed matter. But they are a fatal formula for something living.

The written word is just a mummy whose wrappings must be removed someday—not to discover a few bones, but to breathe life into it again. Only the word conveys the truth of a religious message. What the written word needs is not to be considered the source of a mere code, law, or formula, or of an indefinitely repeated prayer. It must be taken at its source and given rebirth, not by repetition, but by an inspiration that reopens it. Written language has closed the mind. Like a fist grasping a diamond, it has closed its grammatical and structural trap over a vanishing whisper that it tries to translate through enclosing and containment. But instead, writing snuffs it out, and we must open the straitjacket of writing so that it becomes a freshly spoken word. That way the whisper can be perceived and received again. Then the word can start the listener off anew in his quest for truth.

# Chapter II

# IDOLS AND THE WORD

## 1. GOD SPEAKS

God speaks.[1] Jesus is the Word: "The Word was with God, and the Word was God" (Jn. 1:1). From beginning to end, the Bible deals only with the word. Non-Christians, in their usual simplistic manner, lost no time in ridiculing this concept, calling it nothing but a gross anthropomorphism. They laughingly asked what mouth God speaks with; if he has a mouth, he must be only an overgrown animal.

It goes without saying that when we read that God speaks, it does not mean at all that he pronounces words and that he has a vocabulary and follows syntactical rules. This comparison is used of course to help us understand the action and person of God. Only a very obtuse and rankly materialistic person could fail to understand

---

1. I affirm the contradiction between word and image in the Bible, contrary to the present-day tendency to meld them into one. This is done, for example, by showing that the word includes the image (Jean-Luc Blaquart), that the word contains visions as well, etc. In X. Durand's approach, "The body of Jacob became word. . . . The word of the unknown adversary is embodied. . . . The text makes the body a setting for the word," etc. Having witnessed a time when scholars spiritualized the biblical text, we now see an insistence on materializing it at all costs. There is absolutely no way to justify statements like those above. They can be made only by slipping them into the argument, using a sequence of expressions whose very accumulation makes them seem correct.

The invariable tendency throughout the Bible is to place seeing and hearing in opposition to each other, as well as the Image or Idol and the Word. What is at stake here is not a single text, but the entire meaning of the whole revelation: the opposition between YHWH and "the" figurative representations of the gods, and the very definition of the God of Israel. A pseudo-interpretation of some texts cannot overrule the overall biblical teaching.

See the excellent little article by Alphonse Maillot, "L'Oreille et la liberté," *Conscience et Liberté* (Berne), no. 3 (1979).

what the Bible says so clearly. He would have to refuse to accept this language for what it is: metaphorical, an analogy, not an anthropomorphism.

Neither will it do to reduce the expression "God speaks" to a simple "manner of speaking" which does not matter much. Let us not say that it shows a lack of analysis or the influence of Babylonian or other groups' thinking, that theologians and philosophers have understood the nature of God much better, so that we should drop the idea of a "Word" with reference to God. All these ideas are only expressions of rationalistic objections.

If "God speaks" were just an expression, it would not remain constant throughout nine or ten centuries. There would be many other expressions, images, and comparisons. But there is only one. The issue is not to know whether someday we will be able to listen and hear divine words, but why the chosen people and then the prophets, apostles, and Jesus used this particular analogy. What does it mean and what does it imply to say God speaks? What are we taught by this statement and by the continually repeated description that shows us a speaking God?[2]

Finally, let's dismiss another, more serious objection: in Hebrew, *dabar* certainly means "word," but it also means "action." Saying that God speaks does not necessarily allude to language or human speech. It may simply mean that he acts. Here we must answer in two ways:[3]

---

2. We can ignore studies like Blaquart's on the Word of God that claim to be scientific but confine themselves to imposing a classifying framework on biblical texts. This framework has no scientific value outside the circle of those who have previously approved of classification as a way of explaining. See "Parole de Dieu et prophètes," in Jean-Luc Blaquart et al., *L'Ancien Testament, approches et lectures: Des procédures de travail à la théologie*, Institut Catholique de Paris (Paris: Beauchesne, 1977). In this way the Word as revelation is excluded, and Blaquart concludes that the Word is divine because of the integrity of its message!

3. See also the remarkable study by Paul Beauchamp, who demonstrates extremely well that even when charged with power, the word is still the word: *Création et séparation: Etude exégétique du chapitre premier de la Genèse* (Paris: Desclée de Brouwer, 1970). According to Gerhard Kittel, we must distinguish two series of passages: those that refer to creation by action and those that refer to creation by the word. The latter would be subsequent to the former. Gerhard von Rad initially adopted this view, favoring two sources. The version where the word is involved was added later in this view. However, such a division becomes impossible (for example, *na'aseh* [niphal participle of *'asah*], "be done, be made, manufactured, prepared," is attributed to the "word" version, and *bara'*, "create," to the "action" version), so that after some discussion by P. Humbert, W. H. Schmidt, etc., it is concluded that the "tradition" of silent and undiscernible action was finally incorporated into and given form by the predominant word. This sort

first, we find not only the expressions "God speaks" and "Word of God" being used, but also the "words" of God are given to us. In this case, the formulation of God's language is alluded to; thus there is coherence in this set of expressions, so that we cannot dismiss the word "speak." We cannot translate it, for example, as "God acted: let there be light." We must of course have "God *said*, 'Let there be light'" (Gen. 1:3). The complexity of *dabar* shows us that God's word is the equivalent of action; it is power and it acts; his word does not fail to have effect. The word is the divine working par excellence.

Our great difficulty in this connection is that God expresses himself, acts, and is found only in his Word. We would like it if he could logically be found elsewhere—if we could make him conform to our opinions, and of course see him. We prefer concepts like spirit or energy, "God is dead so as to make room for humanity," the God who lives only in the poor person, God as image, as a kind, elderly gentleman, great judge, magnificent creator, etc. The Bible absolutely excludes all these approaches. We continually bump into the limitation which irritates us: we must understand the meaning of the Bible's great affirmation that God is manifested only in his Word. We can never grasp God elsewhere or otherwise.

The Bible vigorously opposes mystics of all descriptions, including Christians, who ascend to heaven and contemplate God by means of ascetic practices. God can never be directly grasped or contemplated face to face (Moses is the only one who is said to have done so). The only channel of revelation is the Word. And if it is a word, then it is intelligible and addressed to us; it contains meaning as well as power. This Word that created the elements and the world is the same one which, when addressed to humanity, tells us something about God and ourselves. When the Word does this it is no less creative, since it creates the heart and ear of the one it addresses, so he can hear and receive the word. Left to himself, that person would be unable to grasp the word; or rather he would find in it only a reason for condemnation and terror. This is true because of the identity between what we can understand of God's action, God himself, and his Word.

The unknowable God chooses this way to make himself known. It is not by accident that he uses the highest human faculty, entering this way, and only this way, into the circle of human intelligence. This Word spoken to us and for us thus testifies to the fact that God is no stranger; he is truly with us. This assurance was already included in the affirmation of the creative word. The God who speaks through

---

of research, in my opinion, enlightens us not at all, since the word in itself also constitutes an action.

the Word ("God says . . . ") is neither far off nor abstract. Rather, he is the creator by means of something that is primarily a means of relationship. The Word is the essential relationship. The God who creates through the Word is not outside his creation, but with it, and especially with Adam, who is made precisely in order to hear this very word and create this relationship with God. Having received the Word himself, Adam can respond to God in dialogue.

The relationship between God and Adam is not a silent, abstract, inactive contemplation, however glowing and spiritual that might be. On the contrary, it is dialogue and word. It is language, and nothing else. It is not a question of symbolic interpretation as in *Faust*. But since we are dealing with *God's* language, it is of course special, so Karl Barth could say that this word was both act and mystery. This word is not only creative power, but power to command. It is a decision of God's. It is *first of all* a decision, which is *then* inserted into history. This word is the peculiarity of the God who uses his divine freedom. Barth has demonstrated this wonderfully.

Here is the fundamental difference between the Word of God and the human word: God's Word is not just a sound which flies away and disappears, a meaning grasped one instant by the listener's mind only to fall into oblivion afterward. Rather, God's Word leaves a sure, irrefutable trace of its passage, just as at the beginning of creation, when God said "Let there be light" (Gen. 1:3). The Word resounded and light came into existence as a permanent witness of the Word spoken in the past.

God's Word is not just a part of language, it is a person. When we say God speaks, we imply that God is a person. "The Word of God is not something that can be described, but neither is it a concept one can define. It is neither an objective content nor an idea. It is not an object; it is the only object, in the sense that it is the only subject— God the subject" (Barth). The Word of God is the very person of God incarnate. There is no contradiction in the fact that the word is spoken by God and also incarnate in Jesus, since this word is what reveals God, and God has effectively revealed himself only in the Incarnation of his Son. The incarnate Word is in reality the Word fully given to humankind, so that an individual can finally be truly enlightened about God's decision concerning him, and about love and justice.

The personality of the Word of God cannot contradict its literalness and intellectuality. The word spoken in ancient times by the prophets becomes fully the Word of God because it refers to the incarnate Word. And the word newly spoken by witnesses becomes in turn this Word when and because it refers to Jesus Christ.

Since all of Christianity depends on the incarnate Word, the

Word made flesh, we must say that there is no Christian faith outside the Word; our description of the God who speaks points to what is specific and particular in Christian revelation. This leads us to give an astonishing and unique importance to the Word. If we devalue the Word even a little, we are rejecting all of Christianity and the Incarnation. Demanding that Christianity be acted rather than spoken, as the current formula has it, is thus not a way of taking Christianity more seriously. It is dilettantism.

Just as the Word is the way God reveals himself, it also reveals a person to himself. "If anyone is a hearer of the word . . . he is like a man who observes his natural face in a mirror" (Jas. 1:23). We discover our truth in this Word, which questions us on God's behalf. In the mirror we see an image of ourselves, of our natural face: we see our reality. The parallel is striking when we understand that the Word instructs each one about himself; it teaches him not just everyday reality, but his own truth—the most hidden, since it is hidden in God, and the most decisive, since one's being depends on it. One learns the truth of his being, which only God knows in its ultimate objectivity, and which only God loves in its unique particularity. In the Word God speaks about someone; the person sees himself in his abject need and his utter vanity. But because of God's Word to him, he now sees the new countenance that is given to him: the countenance of life.

This work of the Word in a person is also taught in the Bible through the importance given to the Name. The word or syllable that indicates a person is the person himself. Let not anyone speak to us in this connection of primitive ideas. A person's name is not so much a magic way of getting hold of him as it is the profound meaning of his being. To name someone or something is to show one's superiority over him or it. Adam is confirmed as the head of creation when God brings all the animals to him so that he can give each one a name (Gen. 2:19). In his sovereign power and perfect initiative Adam reveals himself to be free before God (God brings all the animals to him *to see how he will name them*).

A poet is lying when he throws off language: "I said 'Apple' to the apple, and it answered me 'Liar.' And 'Vulture' to the vulture, who did not respond." Human sovereignty is due more to our language than to our techniques and instruments of war. One can claim or believe himself to be free because of language. Naming something means asserting oneself as subject and designating the other as object. It is the greatest spiritual and personal venture.

Thus we understand why refusing the name given by God and making a name for himself was the very sign of revolt for humanity. This was the undertaking at Babel (Gen. 11): people ceased to accept God's giving them a name, ceased being face to face with God, and thus having a spiritual purpose. Instead, they decided to name themselves; that is, to assume all mastery and direction in their own lives, including their spiritual destiny. Being master of the words about oneself is in reality claiming to be one's own subject and completely autonomous.

Throughout the Bible, a person's name always tells of his spiritual reality. This accounts for Jacob's destiny as much as for the mystery of the act in which God reveals his name to Moses—YHWH: the one who is (Ex. 3:14). He causes to be, He is He. This Word's meaning is unfathomable, yet through it God reveals himself to humanity. The pattern applies to the new name to be received at the end of time by the one who has conquered, the one who will be written in the book of life. These names are only words, but it is not possible that the word be any one taken at random, or that its meaning fluctuate with the wind. We cannot create an arbitrary language for ourselves that would not matter, so that we could after all replace the Word with a drawing and someone's name with a picture or a registration number.

*   *   *   *   *   *

God creates through his Word; creation is an act of separation. The word is creator in that it names things, thus specifying them by differentiating them. The Genesis passage that establishes creation on the basis of separation contains the germ of the most modern ideas about language: it tells us that difference both establishes the word and proceeds from it. The word bestows being on each reality, attributing truth to it; it gives dynamism to reality and prescribes a fixed trajectory for it. In this way the word disentangles confusion and nonbeing.

Individual being comes from the word, because it is distinguished from the whole and given meaning by the word. Everything is given birth by the word. Things are designated because they are lacking. Only desire speaks. Satisfaction is silence.

God creates through his Word. This simple word, which has become a commonplace, first indicates to us that for God creation involves absolutely no effort at all. This is no "difficult" birth. It is not a huge struggle against chaos; it is not laborious work, arduous modeling, or a sculpture that requires supreme effort, as is the case in so many other cosmogonies. No: God speaks.[4] It is the simplest thing

---

4. Beauchamp shows the degree to which language is consistent with the very idea of creation: "The word is nearer to the notion of otherness inherent in the concept of creation: one *thinks* alone, but one *speaks* to a person. The word connotes destination, passage, or even breach and certainly decision. . . . The word chooses and sets in order. . . . Everything is given birth by the word; the word is the course of creation: things are designated only because they are lacking. Satisfaction is silent whereas desire speaks. . . . But in order to speak,

possible, and the least constrained: "God speaks and things come to be."

This leads us immediately to God's absolutely infinite greatness and power. Astronomers probe pulsars and quasars, speaking of billions of light-years, billions of degrees centigrade, billions of megawatts, and unimaginable explosions of energy. All this, encompassed in reality *within* the "God says," gives us an idea of the distance between the creator and us. These astronomic numbers represent merely the effect of a word, from God's point of view. The word creates with supreme ease, so that in this sense word and action can truly be considered identical.

The creative Word also situates God with respect to time. I was going to say "in time." Creation *through the Word* involves entering into temporality. We established above the indissoluble link between word and time.[5] This is exactly what the use of the term "word" suggests in this context: the God who speaks is a God related to time, who is located in humanity's temporality, and who does not try to be atemporal or eternal in the bad sense of the word. After all, when Genesis tells us that the first thing created was light, doesn't that indicate clearly that time is created, since light and time are inseparable?

"God spoke, and there was light" involves the same truth: time comes first, and God places himself in this time. As a result, all the later revelations that show us God intervening in History, God accom-

---

one must identify a thing as what it is, both for me and for others, in the past and the future. The *word creates a permanent status for things* in a way that the hand's gesture cannot ensure. Ascribing creation to the word is therefore *stretching beyond* the depiction of an initial moment of production which would establish a state of things, following which there would be transformations. But this 'beyond' is not a matter of thought: God . . . could have created by thought. . . . But (in Genesis) we find nothing like the concept of a double in some mental space, followed by a transposition into another space: that is, into our space."

5. The relationship between word and time from the biblical point of view has been rigorously demonstrated in Beauchamp's commentary on Genesis 1, *Création et séparation*. Creation through the Word is successive. Biblically, space is neither first nor essential. All objects are created separately in succession. Living beings, situated by God, are directed by a function which is of the order of succession: the perpetuation of life. "The plurality of species thus crisscrosses the pages of the future."

"The parallelism between the time of discourse and the time in a week illustrates this intimate relationship of word and time. God does not make everything all at once because not everything can be said all at once. But after the entire creation has been repeated for Adam, God's word ends. And the finishing point is simply the recognition and celebration of the finishing."

panying humanity and Israel in its adventure—all these are already included in the declaration "God speaks." Here we have the specificity, originality, and the unique character of this God. He is not a deity within time who is subject to the ups and downs of time (like the Greek and Roman gods): he originates time. He is not a god who intervenes in the course of history in an incoherent manner, depending on his moods (like the gods of the *Iliad* and the *Odyssey*). On the contrary, he accompanies the coherent history made by humanity. On the other hand, neither is he an abstract, philosophical, metaphysical, unfeeling, immortal, eternal God, as human reflection conceives him. He is a God who enters history through his inseparable relationship with his creation.

This relationship is created by his Word. He is a God of History, and this discovery about God is Judaism's monumental invention, which has been completely adopted by Christianity. This is the origin of all historical thinking and of History. No one else has thought in this way.[6] God, the World, Time, and History are connected through the Word.

Since he is God in relationship to Time, this excludes the possibility of his being a god of a space or locality. He is not a god of springs, of a mountain, or of a place (once he was called "God of the mountains," but this expression was used by an enemy of Israel who did not understand this God!). He is not the god of a given country. Jonah was sadly deluded when he fled far from the Holy Land, saying: "This god will not pursue me at the other end of the world." Contrary to all the gods of all peoples, this God, who speaks and is characterized by his Word, is not a local god.[7] This is because he cannot be situated in a place, since his only "place" is the Word.[8] God as creator through the Word signifies that God inaugurates history with humanity. Humanity will not be without God.

God who speaks is also God the savior. This can also be expressed another way: the God who speaks to humanity is "God with humanity," Immanuel, and then God in a human being. We must not

---

6. Contrary to what Deleuze and Guattari say in *Anti-Oedipus*. They have not understood this issue at all.

7. Contrary to a period in the historical school when scholars tried to see the God of Israel as God of Sinai (as a place), or as a god connected to Jerusalem, after which he became little by little more universal, until the birth of the idea of universalism. This is false because it considers only a spatial dimension of revelation.

8. The place of God: the expression "Heavens of Heavens" (for example, 1 Kings 8:27, King James) does not indicate a given place—certainly not the "Heaven" of the astronauts! This is a purely verbal expression, used to identify Elsewhere, the Inaccessible, the Beyond (or the Very Deep), rather than a place.

stretch this too far, and say in a metaphysical leap that God in a human being means "in every human being," implying that human beings are divine, and all that follows from that premise. In this idea the center has been displaced from God to humanity, and this goes explicitly contrary to Scripture. Only one person is called Immanuel; God became incarnate in just one. We must not leap to the generalization, even if every person is saved by this Incarnation and even if this Incarnation is in a sense a model.

A word is still what is incarnate. The Word was made flesh. Nothing else. What does this mean? As we have seen, the word is the manifestation of the most secret part of a person; it is also a proclamation. To say that the Word was incarnate means that God has manifested himself, and that a proclamation has been given. It amounts to the inalienable assurance that God is henceforth forever with us, on our side, by our side. Since judgment has taken place, it is the proclamation that Satan is excluded.

"The Word was made flesh" also means that since the Word of God was incarnate, what is visible is forever excluded. The *invisible* God came *as word*. He cannot be recognized by sight. Nothing about Jesus indicates divinity in a visual way. We will return to this matter.

During his ministry Jesus only *speaks*. He establishes and organizes nothing. He shows nothing. "The miracles?" you ask. They are signs, as the Greek word indicates: signs of the *word*. Miracles are always accomplished through the word. They are always situated in a verbal context, and come as a consequence of words. "Your sins are forgiven" (Mk. 2:5). Here the word is decisive. And then: "Which is easier, to say to the paralytic, 'Your sins are forgiven,' or to say 'Rise . . . and walk'?" (Mk. 2:5). And to show that the Son of man has the power to forgive sins, he says, "Paralytic, rise and walk" (Mk. 2:11, JE). Thus the miracle is much less than the Word.

Jesus only spoke; he wrote nothing. He wrote only once, we are told: the mysterious text he wrote on the sand in front of the accusers of the woman taken in adultery. And I think (but this is one of a hundred possibilities!) that this shows the inferiority of the written word as compared with speech. He wrote a useless, obscure, incommunicable text that was soon obliterated. But he spoke the sovereign word: "Let him who is without sin . . . " (Jn. 8:7). The word liberated the woman. It convinced the accusers and pardoned the sins. The written word remained sterile and ineffectual.

Jesus bears in himself the Word of God, so that he can say "I am the truth" (Jn. 14:6; "I am the life" means "I incarnate the creative word"; "I am the way" means that the word is a guide). "God speaks" means that the question of truth has been raised—the question of truth and therefore, as we have said, of falsehood. The "anti-God" is named the Liar. The question of truth has been raised, and therefore the question of hypocrisy for those who alter the nature of this word. In the last analysis this is the only essential accusation against those who falsify and utilize this word. I am the truth; I am myself the totality of the Word which denotes, expresses, relates, and contains the ultimate truth, of which every human word is a reflection, stammering, and repetition.

The God who speaks is at the same time the God who reveals himself, since, as we have said, the use of this term designates a relationship in which the speaker reveals who he is. The word as revelation is the Holy Spirit, who manifests himself for the first time at Pentecost in the diversity of words, in the multiplicity of languages reduced to a single understanding. Again speaking is involved. And from this starting point there is an incessant coming and going, from the revelation by means of the word to the word concerning the revelation, from the word as inspiration to the word freely spoken as expression of this inspiration.

The idea of the Word throws a decisive light on the famous *theopneustia* debate. Inspiration (not a vague spirit, a spirituality, an impulse) comes through a Word expressly spoken and understood as coming from God. But as we have seen, like all language, this word is by no means dictated or recorded on a tape recorder (the tape recorder would correspond to our brain in this analogy). This word has several dimensions: its lights and shadows, its ambiguities and connotations, its different depths. It is thus heard, understood, interpreted, and retranslated by the careful listener, who will in turn speak by making use of the freedom of the word. For the word is free.

Thus the witness will speak with his own word to testify to this word which was addressed to him. The God who reveals himself by his Word accepts entering into this game and its symbolisms, into this flexibility of human relationships, exactly as he accepts the limitations of the human condition in the Incarnation. He has given us an image, apparently visual, of the revealer, the Holy Spirit, who is represented as a dove: "He saw the heavens opened, and the Spirit descending . . . like a dove" (Mk. 1:10). He sees a void: an opening, a break, or a fault. "Like" is a comparison used to express something with no possible form. It is really a verbal image rather than a visual one. No dove appeared in the heavens. There was no vision of a dove, for the word "dove," since the story of the flood, is the consecrated and chosen *word*, simply because in Hebrew it means "messenger" as well. "Dove" means "bearer of a message." In this text there is complete identity between the dove and the proclamation of the message: "This is my beloved Son, with whom I am well pleased" (Mt. 3:17). We do not have something seen on the one hand and a word on the other. Rather, a word is borne, which implies a bearer of the word in verbal form. This bearer is traditionally a dove.

This revealer always expresses God's glory to us. All we can "see" is his Shekinah glory, which is by nature invisible. God conceals himself in it at the same time that he reveals himself by it. It is not visual, since this glory "cannot be compared with any other," and cannot be described by its shape or colors. Nothing visual can show us the glory of the Lord! Only the Holy Spirit!

*   *   *   *   *   *

The teaching involved in the statement that God speaks is not complete at this point. The word obligates us to follow it down three paths which lead to an understanding of who God is. The word is an expression of freedom. It presupposes freedom and invites the listener as well to assert his freedom by speaking. God is the liberator.[9] We must constantly remember that the God of Israel manifests himself historically for the first time in the Exodus as the one who liberates human beings from the slavery established by other human beings. God chooses his people from among slaves, in order to liberate them. The prophets continually return to this fundamental concept: this God, the only true God, frees people from all alienation.

The same spirit is at work in the New Testament. Paul's whole theology is a theology of freedom: "For freedom Christ has set us free" (Gal. 5:1). James answers (and he certainly does not have Paul's theology!): "You will be judged by the law of liberty" (2:12, JE). Freedom is the basic theme which ties everything else in the Bible together, from beginning to end. Freedom explains everything else in the Bible and gives meaning to the whole adventure of election, grace, and redemption, as the Bible describes it. It is certain that with the revelation at Horeb and the accomplishment of Jesus Christ, freedom entered the world.

Freedom has not been lived or proclaimed anywhere else. We must repeat this with conviction in our time, since it is fashionable to accuse Christianity of being a source of slavery and a means of spreading it throughout the world. Psychoanalysts, sociologists, ethnologists, and philosophers continually repeat this anti-Christian bromide, either from ignorance and in good faith or else with full knowledge and therefore in bad faith. They seize certain cases of

---

9. Among the countless works on Christian freedom, I refer the reader to Martin Luther's, and to the following modern studies: Roland de Pury, *Le Libérateur* (Geneva: Labor et Fides, 1957); Jacques Ellul, *The Ethics of Freedom*, trans. and ed. Geoffrey W. Bromiley (Grand Rapids: William B. Eerdmans, 1976).

oppression in given periods of Church history, a certain moralism and moral prohibitions dating from given periods and places, certain sermons (also localized) concerning sin or hell, and they make of these the sum total of Christianity. They do not even think about the fact that *their being scandalized* by alienation, oppression, and repression does not spring from the French revolution in 1789 and the eighteenth-century philosophers, nor from Greek thought (which is completely foreign to freedom, in spite of what has been said on the subject!), nor from Marx or Sigmund Freud. Their sense of scandal is a result of the Judeo-Christian roots of our civilization. The peoples of the Third World would never have thought of revolting against their destiny if the idea of, and the hope and the will for, freedom had not been spread by the West.

Everything comes from this first interchange: God speaks. Thus he manifests his freedom, just as a human speaker does. He invites his listener to the freedom involved in answering. God speaks; this statement contains the profound, central, supreme conviction that God is the liberator: that he never stops liberating, just as his Word never stops.

At the same time, the Word implies that this God is a God of love. We have already seen that the Word determines a relationship. God is not only creator; he is creator through the word, which means that he is never far from, never foreign to, his creation. God speaking means he is in relationship. But at the same time, this is a positive rather than a negative relationship. A relationship of love is established rather than a relationship of rejection or condemnation (in spite of what we have so often heard!) or commandment. Nevertheless, there certainly are words of condemnation. But they are much more sparse than is usually appreciated, and they are addressed much more often to the *powers* of alienation, error, hallucination, religion, falsehood, and accusation than they are to people. Money is damned rather than the rich person; more precisely, the rich person is condemned because of his money and not in himself. Political power is damned rather than the person who exercises it; more precisely, the person is also condemned because of his power over others, but not in himself.[10] People are *judged*; that is, stripped of these powers of evil, but not damned. Thus the words of condemnation when correctly understood are words of liberation for everyone. They are words of hope which certify the love of God.

We are prevented from understanding these words of condem-

---

10. For a detailed study of this important point, see Jacques Ellul, *Apocalypse: The Book of Revelation*, trans. George W. Schreiner (New York: Seabury, 1977).

nation for what they are by two different things; our thirst for vengeance and our guilt feelings. We are not pleased that God loves everyone, that his Word is for all, without limit, and that he is gracious to all. On the one hand, sectarians jealously want to be the only ones saved from the ocean of the damned; on the other, non-Christians are spontaneously scandalized by the idea that Adolf Hitler or Joseph Stalin and their cohorts and devoted followers should also be saved. But there is no real difference between these two reactions. We want people to be damned because there are people we hate and we demand vengeance. It is terribly difficult to accept grace that has no limit because God's love can know no place that is off-limits. Since God creates through his Word, it creates everyone.

Our second obstacle to understanding God's Word also has its roots within us: the feeling of guilt. Here again we are up against the trite notion that guilt feelings come from Christianity. It is true that the Church has concentrated too much on prohibitions, has declared (sexual) taboos, and has *sometimes,* in preaching on sin, internalized guilt feelings. But let no one say that humanity was free from guilt; sacrifice, found in all religions, is propitiatory or else is a sacrifice for redemption or forgiveness. In any case, the sacrifice is substitutionary and proceeds from a deep sense of guilt.[11] This very generalized guilt feeling keeps us from understanding this Word of God with simplicity, and leads us to approve condemnations *for ourselves* that go through us and above us, affecting those behind us. This situation causes us to act and prevents us from understanding these words of condemnation as words of liberation. God speaks; biblically, this means that he is Love.

We still have to deal with the word of commandment, however! Surely we cannot deny that in the Bible there are words of Law, received like a heavy burden, these complex and numerous prohibitions: the terrible Decalogue. "I am crushed under your law." First of

---

11. Unfortunately, we must constantly remind people that prohibitions and taboos do not come from Christianity, and that as far as situations that create guilt are concerned, you can find nothing better than the tangles of prohibitions among so-called primitive peoples. Just look at the analyses of kinship in Claude Lévi-Strauss's work! We must also remember constantly that the idea of sin should not lead to guilt feelings, simply because biblically, and in truly Christian thought, sin is known and recognized for what it is only *after* the recognition, proclamation, and experience of forgiveness. Because I have been pardoned, I realize how much of a sinner I was. Sin is shown to be sin through grace, and not otherwise, just as the abruptly freed slave realizes, as he sees his chains, how great his misery was. Sin is never known alone and in itself. Sin is never proclaimed. But it is true that the Church has often betrayed the Bible in this area.

all we should reflect on the fact that we *never* find the idea that the law crushes in the Bible. This is a modern idea. Biblically we always find amazement that God, the Creator, chooses to give us orientation in life (Ps. 119), and that God, the Wholly Other, wishes to let us know what justice is, when we are looking for it so eagerly. God is worshiped for this law or commandment, and Israel was able to preserve perfectly this source of amazement, joy, and radiance, as it considered the law not as a constraint but as a liberating word. This is the first way of looking at the problem.

The second is that the law is not so much in the imperative as in the future: "Thou shalt not kill" means that situated within God's love, in constant dialogue with this God, you will at last find it possible not to kill. Outside this dialogue and this word, you are, like everybody, obligated to kill. Murder and series of murders, linked to one another, are the common lot. Beginning the moment the Word of God reechoes in your life, you are able to avoid killing. The fatality of murder disappears like the other fatalities. Thus the commandment is not a hard, negative constraint, but the promise of a new life filled with freedom and joy.

The third way of looking at this problem[12] is that the law's commandments are the precise limits between life and death. Within these limits, you live fully and you are alive in all possible ways. But transgression brings with it the certainty of death—not death as a punishment willed by God and decided by him, but death as a natural destiny. If you slaughter, you will be slaughtered.

Whichever point of view one adopts, we see that the belief that the law and God's commandment are based on rank imposition by an all-powerful Master on a terrorized slave is based on a misinterpretation. This is how the situation looks from the *outside*. Unfortunately, it is sometimes the view of those who have in effect been subjected to Christianity by coercion. And the mystery of iniquity in the Church is that such things have happened. Such things could happen precisely when the Church ceased to be related to the Word; it ceased being a Church that speaks; preferring to become a Church that acts, shows, and dominates (these three things being equivalent!). The law is never coercion for the person who believes in his heart and confesses with his mouth, the one who has encountered grace, lived this experience, and is living in freedom.

Whom should we believe? The person who knows this Word of God in his life and exalts it with wonder, or the one who has not experienced this liberation, who has perhaps been crushed or coerced

---

12. I could of course never exhaust in these pages all that the law signifies!

by a family or ecclesiastical structure, and who considers this law abominable because he has known nothing but the slavery imposed by other people?

This law is in no way comparable to our codes, which are written and fixed. As commandment, it has been the object of innumerable glosses and commentaries. It is an ever living word, always new and always newly addressed to its listener. It is not the objective declaration of an anonymous legislator. The law is a renewed word for each individual, and not a fixed inscription on the facade of a monument.

Not enough thinking has been done about the breaking of the tables of the Law. The story is well known: on descending from Sinai, in the presence of the incredible pretension of the Israelites to *make themselves* a god (which they could control since they had made it) to replace the mysterious Liberator, out of anger and despair, Moses breaks and destroys the miraculous talisman he was bringing: the stone tables on which God himself had written. He acted in anger, we say. It was an act of judgment against a people who were not worthy to receive such an extraordinary gift. But in my opinion, there is a hidden meaning: here the law is *written*. It has ceased being a word. It is about to become a talisman: a magic rock, an oracle. It will of necessity be identified with the Salians' shield or any other statue. The law is dead—graven, engraved, buried in this stone.

This gift of God's Writing in material form suits the human desire to have an image of God. God knows our need to see, which is why he sends Moses down the mountain with these *visible witnesses* of his will[13] (which oppose and at the same time respond to the demand of the people, who want to see, and therefore make themselves a golden calf). For this reason the text emphasizes the fact that God himself made the stone tables to counter the vision of the bull. No direct vision of God is involved here. But his work is seen, and this vision leads one to a vision of the word. Everything is inevitably brought back to the word. This is the only concession YHWH can make to sight!

But the story goes even further: Moses breaks the stone tables. They were in themselves the image of God, the image of the Word of God. And now Moses destroys this image. Fernand Ryser says: "This nineteenth verse [Ex. 32:19] shows us then what must happen to the image of God when it enters into contact with the world: it must be broken and perish in order not to be fatal for humanity. When God comes into the world in his Son, there are only two possibilities: either the world will die, or God will die in his Son." This destruction

---

13. Fernand Ryser, *Le Veau d'or* (Geneva: Labor et Fides, 1954).

of the divine image enables Moses to destroy the false divine image. This is the basis of iconoclastic inclination for both Jew and Christian.

Finally, the destruction of this single visible, material representation of God ought to remind us continually that the Bible in its materiality is not the Word of God made visible through reading. God did not become Jeremiah's secretary and write for him (Jer. 1:9). And he has not made his Word visible. Between the written word and speech there is the same distance we have discovered on the human plane. The phenomenon is exactly the same. The Bible is not a sort of visible representation of God.

Therefore it was absolutely necessary that the tables be broken. In reality, as he brings the tables of stone down from the mountain, Moses suddenly grasps the identity of this work of sculpture with the golden calf that the people have built. God's Word must remain a fleeting spoken Word, inscribed only in the human heart. It must not be a prestigious stone, a frozen word which will be adored, replacing the ear attentive to the word. If the people adored their golden calf, which they had made, how much more would they have adored the absolute Stone which God's hands had held and on which God's finger had written!

The breaking of the tables of the Law takes place so that the commandment can remain a living word, addressed to each individual without existing objectively anywhere. The commandment remains a word, with all the unstable, direct, interpreted, and strictly personal qualities that the word involves. When people later begin to write the Law and even later the Gospels, that is their affair! But we must be clearly conscious that it is a human act. Only very rarely is it said to certain prophets: "You will write." And the proclamation "You shall write [this law] and wear it on your forehead, on your arm," etc., seems to me deliberately symbolic, and should not have produced texts actually placed in little bags, etc.

\*   \*   \*   \*   \*   \*

"God speaks. We must answer him." God creates human beings as speaking beings. Perhaps this is one of the meanings of the image of God: one who responds and is responsible; a counterpart who will dialogue, who is both at a certain distance and has the ability to communicate. The human being is the only one, out of the entire creation, who is capable of language. Like God who speaks or God who is said to speak, humanity has this capacity which comes from its creator. Speech constitutes human specificity, just as it constitutes the specificity of God as compared with all other gods. God summons a person through the word, and induces him to speak in dialogue. If God is freedom, there is someone there to live out freedom. If God is love, there is someone to respond to love through the word. The

human word exists only because it is a product of the Word of God:
I would not speak if you had not previously called me. "Even before
a word is on my tongue, O Lord, thou knowest it altogether" (Ps.
139:4).

We do not declare that God speaks because of the model of
human speech. Rather, it is because word and creation share a common nature that the speaking creator gives language to humanity, as
his counterpart. All the natural, objective characteristics we observe
in human speech (which we have noted in Chapter I) are such because
they are the characteristics of the Word as expression of God the
creator.[14] For human speech possesses eminent dignity. It is more

---

14. Here we return to Beauchamp's magnificent study, from which I must
quote an especially illuminating and powerful passage: "God did not so much
create the things I am talking about as he spoke them . . . before speaking to
me about them, so that the human word might be declared a response to his.
God made humanity the depositary of the relationship of difference instituted
by the word: men and women will establish in the world the law of their own
word, and the text [of Genesis] shows how *in this sense* they are born of God.
Why then should we insist on speaking of the human mission of 'completing'
through our work the work *finished* on the sixth day, as if God had created
nature in such a way as to leave to humanity the margin, the risk, and the honor
of this artifice? God and humanity are called to encounter each other in the
artifice of the word. By having God speak first, Genesis conceives of all human
language as a response. A human being understands through his existence that
he is in God's image. And it is through his own speech that he declares that
God has spoken. Giving the first word to God is the same as saying that the
truth of human speech, on which all existence depends, cannot have any other
depositary than God himself. Every human experience of language grasps it as
repetition: no one would speak if those who gave him birth did not speak to
him first."

The following passage also speaks of the relationship of human language
to God's: "A human being speaks of the world which he cannot clasp to
himself. Thus he transforms it into a network of relationships and movements:
into a world. . . . The word connotes destination, passage, or even breach, and
certainly decision. All language, even if it does not contain a commandment, as
is the case in this passage, is volitional. It chooses and sets in order. . . .
[Creation is the] conflict of energy and resistance, a struggle of life against
death, from which the word takes its impetus. . . . Having created things
through words, God finally speaks to a human being. . . . "

Beauchamp quotes the well-known Psalm 139 ("Even before a word is on
my tongue, O Lord, thou knowest it altogether. . . . For thou didst form my
inward parts, thou didst knit me together in my mother's womb," vv. 4 and
13), emphasizing the close relationship between the genesis of humanity in its
corporeal being *and* of its language. This certainty that human language is a
creation and a continuation of the Word of God is also found in a hymn at
Qumran. In Genesis 1 we do not see directly the creation of human language
by God, but "we see something like the circulation of an underground river,
before its appearance as a spring above ground. The words pronounced by God

decisive than action and reveals more. But most of all, human speech is invested with unlimited importance because God chose the word as his means. The fact that revelation was accomplished through the word attaches meaning and value to human language. God could have chosen any other means for his action and revelation, but he chose this particular one. Therefore human language possesses a dignity it would not otherwise have had.

Because God speaks, when a person speaks a mysterious power is attached to what he says. Every human word is called on, more or less clearly, to express the Word of God, and there is a misuse of power, an abuse of words when this is not the case. Henceforth human language has an eternal reference from which it cannot escape without destroying itself or without stripping itself of all meaning. The value of the human word depends on the Word of God, from which it receives its decisive and ultimate character. This quality is expressed in its critical value and in ethical decision. This is a result of human speech's relationship with the Word of God: of God's taking up this human word, so that there is continuity (as well as discontinuity) between them, and of human speech's finality in relationship with the Word of God. For God's Word, according to the author of the letter to the Hebrews (4:12), is "sharper than any two-edged sword, piercing to the division of soul and spirit, of joints and marrow, and discerning the thoughts and intentions of the heart." Thus the Word of God is the critical power par excellence, which of course only God can exercise; only he knows what its result will be.

The Word of God distinguishes and separates, and because it criticizes, it judges. This is because of its nature. Human language draws its function from this efficacy and power of the Word of God, except that human language does not have the same degree of efficacy and power: it can convey falsehood as well as truth.

The Word of God, since it criticizes, is also the expression of God's commandment. His Word directs; it is a commanding power and thus it determines what is ethical. Human language finds its role at this point. There is an enormous difference, however: the human word cannot determine what is ethical. But based on the commandment of the Word of God, the human word enables an individual to choose and to make his personal decision, faced with the demands placed on him. This is accomplished by means of a difficult process of differentiation and in the context of the intolerable weight of his commitment.

---

(at the moment of creation-separation) are the true genesis of human speech, the genesis of humanity. . . . The theme of the father-child relationship of humankind and God is interpreted here as transmission of the word which 'commands.' "

But when Adam speaks for the first time, he does not answer
God; he names animals. We need not linger over this frequently
explained passage. An important remark, often forgotten, needs to be
made, however: when it says that Adam names the animals, the
passage underlines the gratuitousness and ease of language. Adam
does not see names already prepared, registered in advance. There is
no natural science of words. An animal passing before Adam does
not have a name already established—given by God, for example.
Instead, Adam names; that is, he chooses the word that suits him to
designate a given animal, and then all other things.

Biblically, there is no common nature shared by language and the
name of a thing. It is after all rather important to emphasize that in a
seventh-century text, predating all reflection on language, wherever
that reflection may have occurred, we find this clear statement: the
fact of human speech comes from God; but language is made up by
the human race, which decides for itself—arbitrarily—the words, the
rules, and the syntax. Human beings choose arbitrarily with respect
to the thing designated, but not arbitrarily with respect to meanings
and structures. I need not enter into a discussion of these latter issues.

The other theme is more frequently treated: the commandment
and preeminence or domination. A name assigns a place and a spiritual value. By naming the animals Adam shows his power over them
and puts them in their place within the order of Creation. Again in
this situation, Adam takes initiative: there is no predetermined order
which Adam would limit himself to recording as he names the animals. He establishes his own order, before the Fall: a "taxonomy"
which is a free, invented expression of the supremacy God has given
him. God leaves Adam free to make this choice (*"to see what he would
call them,"* says the passage, so that *"whatever the man called every
living creature, that was its name,"* Gen. 2:19).

But in this created world, in unity and unbroken communion
with God, Adam does not give a name to his wife. It is only *after* the
Fall, in the midst of the disorder of powers, that he names his wife
*also*: "Eve, because . . ." (Gen. 3:20). This is a reflection of the
disorder of powers; for God's power is a restrained power. He does
not occupy all the space. The God who speaks also lets his creature
speak. God does not speak continually, covering over all noises and
all expression.

Each thing has its place with God in its nonassigned specificity.
Even when God's Word indicates a requirement, it leaves the other
person his complete freedom of decision, choice, and expression.
Thus no power is excessive. Every power has its limits in this Creation. This concept is also expressed in the image "God speaks." He
*only* speaks. And his listener can take him seriously or not, can listen

or not, can answer or not, as in the case of any word. Saying that God speaks is the equivalent of situating him at the level of everyday talkers. "God speaks" also foretells the coming of Jesus, who is an ordinary person and yet God. So within this order of power, human beings are also invested with a power; first of all, the power to speak.[15]

God's declaration in the first creation narrative (which is later than the second one), situating Adam as lord of creation, corresponds precisely to Adam's naming of the animals in the second narrative. The first narrative says: "Subdue the earth; have dominion over all animals" (Gen. 1:28, JE). What a lot of nonsense has been written about this passage in recent decades. Scholars have frantically tried to find here the basis for technique and all the modern technological ventures. They have tried to make this text justify what humanity does, gloriously evoking a demiurge. But these writers forget the parallelism between the two narratives, and they particularly forget that God does not give the human race an incoherent, unlimited, totalitarian power. The passage does not say that we can use the world however we like. In particular, since we are the image of God, we must direct the earth, *as* God directs Creation. We must have dominion over the animals *as* God has dominion over the worlds. "As" means "imitating," "*in the same manner,*" "with the same respect," "with the same restraint from doing all that could be done." It does not signify an unleashed, torrential, Dionysian power, a superpower, covering everything, making use of everything without order or restraint, devastating and depleting the earth.

Quite specifically, since God creates and governs through his Word, and the human being is the image of God, called by God to subdue (govern) and have dominion (command), he can only do it *by the same means*; that is, the *word.* Humanity must fulfill its royal function in the midst of the animals through the word, and not through the violence of implements. There is no allusion—absolutely

---

15. "We may be surprised that Creation should be closed and finished and that at the same time the act of creating should be crowned with the transmission of a transforming word. But the limit and the impetus do not contradict each other. Whatever the human trajectory may be, it can only have meaning in terms of its finitude. Humanity can escape from everything except from the fact of *having been,* which is necessary if it is to be able to speak and plan, on both an individual and a collective basis. It is not by accident that, in the priestly document, the Creation narrative represents the past par excellence, at the same time as it formulates and establishes the human project. Language follows the laws of before and after; it progresses and makes a path for itself toward a goal, since indefinite discourse would be discourse without meaning" (Beauchamp).

none—to technique or technology in this passage; the only power is that of the word.

The word resolves the apparently insolvable contradiction in which humanity is placed in a world created perfect and therefore complete, and yet is given the power to act and transform. The word is the transforming power in a finished world where the human word is a liberating force.[16] You find that I force the text, or limit it? I beg to differ! A simple comparison of this passage (Gen. 1:28–29) with its exact parallel in the Noachian covenant (Gen. 9:1–7) shows I am right. Between the two passages, we have the Fall (human autonomy), the establishment of the disorder of powers, and the invention of technique, expressly attributed to Cain (Gen. 4:17–22). The new world emerges from the deluge. At this point a new covenant is formulated between God and the human race. It is almost the same as the original covenant. Almost. There are two slight differences: from now on human beings may kill animals for food. This was not said at creation. And next, the matter of terror: *"The fear of you and the dread of you* shall be upon every beast of the earth . . . into your *hand* they are *delivered"* (Gen. 9:2). It is no longer a question of word but of hands; there is no more ordering and commanding through the word, but by the power of material constraint, including killing.

Technique finds its legitimacy at this point and not in the first covenant, in which the word was the only power. Why did God not simply erase this tragic period of history and begin again at the beginning? Why does he record what humanity created to its misfortune and the misfortune of the world? Precisely because this God continues to direct and command through his Word alone; because he never constrains in an absolute manner, and because he takes into account everything humankind does, including evil. He never does anything but speak.[17] But the powerful word, refused by a humanity that thought it could do so much better with its machines, has remained what distinguishes humanity and makes it human. This word is the gift of God par excellence; it is human mystery, endlessly leading to truth.

*     *     *     *     *     *

---

16. On this theme, see Jacques Ellul, *Technique and Theology,* soon to be published.

17. The evidence for these statements is found in Jacques Ellul, *The Meaning of the City,* trans. Dennis Pardee (Grand Rapids: William B. Eerdmans, 1970).

We have tried to show that biblically everything leads back to the word: God and humankind, and their relationships, their powers, the unique expression of truth, of creation, and of the order of the world. The word is everything in this revelation. Nothing is left to sight, which is nevertheless essential.

As a transition to the study of sight in the Bible, I would like to refer here to the remarkable study by Paul Ricoeur that expresses this contradiction in philosophical terms: proclamation as opposed to manifestation.[18] Proclamation, which implies interpretation, is an act of speech, with a historicity of transmission and hermeneutical activity. Manifestation is a showing of the sacred; the sacred is manifested in the Greek mysteries, but always with power. Power and efficacy are related to this visual manifestation: "the numinous element is not language to begin with. Power signifies something besides the word. . . . Power does not go through the articulation of meaning; it is *efficacious*." This antithesis is decisive: the word, relating to meaning, produces proclamation. Manifestation addresses itself to the visual sense and relates to efficacy. "The sacred opens a space for manifestation that should be called imaginal" rather than Logos. The sacred is manifested in signs to look at and also in meaningful behavior, essentially rites. The rite combines the visual with the efficacious, in order to act powerfully.

Finally, the manifestation of the sacred is expressed in a symbolism of Nature which is also related to the visual, by figures. The Greek mysteries are carried out through symbols of a *natural* sort (earth, fire, water, stars, etc.). Ricoeur shows very subtly how the (visual) rite is both associated with and contradictory to the (spoken) myth, and how the natural mystery is both associated with and contradictory to a symbolism of language. But he says this symbolism is "adherent" rather than being a true act of language (a true act of language being, for example, the metaphor, which is a free invention of speech).

The symbol of the sacred in language is *related* to the *configurations* (and therefore to the visible images) of the cosmos. This adherence to symbolism implies that symbolism in language is valid only when it is borne by the sacred values of the elements themselves. It is a silent spectacle which is imposed on language rather than an effort of language and interpretation. These are the characteristics of the Greek mysteries. It is possible to speak of their phenomenology and to describe them, but not to identify a possible hermeneutic for them, since hermeneutics is restricted to proclamation.

---

18. Paul Ricoeur, "Manifestation et proclamation," in *Le Sacré*, ed. Enrico Castelli (Paris: Aubier, 1974).

Ricoeur reminds us that the entire theology of Israel is organized around discourse, narratives, instructions (*Torah*), and prophecy—never on the basis of the numinous. Biblical myths are all *polemical* myths countering nature religions. In Israel "a theology of the Name of God opposes the mystery of idols." "Listening to the word has taken the place of looking at signs." Although rites certainly subsist in Israel, "the ritualization of life is no longer based on the correlation between myth and rite," but on a fundamentally historical vision of reality. And the result is a theology of history, as opposed to a theology of nature. Ricoeur summarizes admirably: "This difference is based entirely on the logic of meaning that I try to oppose to the logic of relationships in the sacred universe."

We have seen that paradox is the very key of language, and Ricoeur expresses this perfectly as it relates to the conflict between meaning and the sacred, between manifestation and proclamation. The symbol (in the visual world) belongs to a set of circular cosmic relationships. The "expressions at the extreme limits" show a paradoxical universe: the universe of the parables, the "proverbs," and eschatological language. It is a shattered universe, like the word itself, which brings about the breaking up of ordinary speech and refers to (or announces) what is not a visual image: the Kingdom of God. Thus speech is necessarily iconoclastic. But Ricoeur finally reminds us that it is not possible to maintain iconoclastic discourse in all its strictness, any more than sight can be eliminated, leaving us with only speech! We are in this world, not in another, and consequently we cannot avoid having images nor change the fact that images have a vital importance in our spirituality.

There are inevitably "symbolic resurgences of the sacred" throughout the history of Israel and of the Church. The sacred, the visual, and the cosmic are necessary if language is to be possible: "without the support and help of the vital and cosmic sacred, language itself becomes abstract and cerebral. Only by its incarnation in repeatedly reinterpreted ancient symbolism, by which the word is continually reduced to essentials, can the word speak to the heart as well as to the intelligence and the will—in short, to the whole person."

Ricoeur reminds us that there is a continual alternation in the Church between iconoclastic proclamation and symbolic manifestation, in the dialectic of preaching and the sacrament. In preaching, the kerygmatic element prevails; in the sacrament, visual symbolism takes over. But there is also a continual temptation to find all the truth in image and symbolism, thus excluding the word, which is less concrete, less evident, more austere and demanding. In all periods of Church history we find a renewed triumph of the image in statues, stained-glass windows, monuments, crucifixes, and relics. Although we cannot separate sight and language, only the Incarnation of Jesus shows us the correct equilibrium or synthesis, as we wait in hope for the fullness of the Kingdom.

## 2. VISIONS AND IDOLS

In spite of what we have said, the Bible often speaks of sight, in terms of theophanies, visions, idols, icons, and false gods. In reality, the biblical revelation is radically opposed to everything visual. Don't let the reader react immediately by speaking of visions, which we will consider. The only possible relationship with God is based on the word, and nothing else. This is because the biblical God speaks, and does nothing else. The word includes with it all the connotations we have mentioned above: love, freedom, and making the other person conscious of his opportunity to become a subject also. In the sphere of truth, everything is related to the word, nothing to sight.

With regard to vision, we must remember the impossibility of seeing God, maintained throughout Scripture. Yahweh says to Moses: "You cannot see my face; for man shall not see me and live" (Ex. 33:20). As Jacques Guillet emphasizes,[19] it is as if "God had a face and hands, but just when you think you could touch him, an infinite distance appears." And earlier in Exodus, "Moses hid his face, for he was afraid to look at God" (3:6). All those who witness God have the same experience: Elijah at Mount Horeb, Isaiah, and the parents of Samson.

We must choose. Shall we consider all the passages where someone is said to "see God" as equal in weight to the above passages? Must we have a "flat," nonhierarchical interpretation? I believe that in reality, concerning the impossibility of seeing God, there is a kind of constant. The other passages should be interpreted in the light of this constant. We must try to understand the meaning of each specific vision, noting what may be added in each case, and considering whether it is really said that God is seen. The passages that involve seeing God must be interpreted in the light of both the curse on images and the impossibility of seeing him.

Sight is of course not condemned in itself![20] It has its legitimate

---

19. Jacques Guillet, *La Gloire du Sinaï* (Paris: Desclée de Brouwer, 1956).

20. Sometimes, according to Antoine Vergote, in *Dette et désir* (Paris: Seuil, 1978), vision and word are united or merged by mystics. "Hearing is seeing," says John of the Cross. An essential idea is underscored indirectly by Vergote: "The mystics believe that . . . by *sight* and by *hearing*, *words* are given to them which are not simply produced by human beings." Vergote shows that John of the Cross is therefore suspicious of words which could come only from human beings: "Many people talk to themselves as if somebody were really there," he says. But because these words come "from elsewhere," "*they have the consistency of a vision.*"

place in the sphere of reality and usefulness, as a means of gaining power over objects. It is infinitely precious, but only in its domain. As soon as sight tries to enter into the spiritual realm, or claims to have access to the order of truth, it is radically condemned. It is out of the question to try to grasp God through sight (which is the equivalent of reducing truth to reality), to claim that what one sees can be God (in this case one converts reality into truth), or to make a representation of something in the spiritual realm (which is the same as consecrating a religion, since religions always belong to the visual realm). This raises the issue of the conflict between the spiritual and the religious realms. The whole visual sphere begins to be suspect, biblically, through association, so to speak, *when these things are done*—but not before.

Vision is a means or instrument—the basic element of power in action, of domination, utilization, and constraint. When the Assyrian kings wanted to eliminate their enemies' power, they blinded them. After the Assyrians, many others did the same. There is no ambiguity in the power commanded by sight, just as there is no ambiguity in reality as perceived by sight. For this reason the triple desire—to reduce God to reality, to convert reality into God, and to transform the love relationship into a religion—is explicitly condemned, and sight along with it.

But there are two completely different issues here, both placed under the heading of sight: vision and theophany on the one hand, and idols and false gods on the other. In the first tendency, one asks whether it is possible to see God, the biblical God, Yahweh, the God of revelation who also reveals himself. In the second, individuals make gods for themselves, erect idols everywhere, and adore them: idols and icons. In this second case we are actually dealing with images: objects that can be seen and that always involve a visible representation.

\*    \*    \*    \*    \*    \*

We are not, of course, going to examine in detail what is still called biblical theophany; that is, a visible, material appearance of the biblical God.[21] My general thesis is that nowhere do we have true theophany, genuinely comparable to the theophanies found in all religions (at least all those that have one or several gods). The term *theophany,* from the history of religions, has been applied to the Bible

---

21. I reserve the word theophany, as is customary, for the *visible* appearance of God, and not in the larger sense used by Beauchamp, who speaks of a visible *or* spoken theophany. This usage amounts to confusing theophany with revelation.

as a result of a superficial textual analysis, a determination to find comparable and identical elements, and simplification. A few simple explanations that are in exact conformity with the texts will suffice to dispense with this hasty patchwork.

Let us begin with an introductory remark. "Seeing the glory of God" is an expression which really indicates that God is concealed and invisible. Paul Beauchamp reminds us of two basic truths in this connection: the first is that the biblical God is usually accompanied by a dark cloud. There is a screen between him and everyone else (especially in the passages in Job: 22:14; 38:9; 36:30; 37:21). When God reveals himself, "he sweeps the heavens with his breath [*ruah*]" (Job 37:21, JE).[22] Obscurity precedes him, and his revelation of himself consists of his breath-spirit separating the cloud, but not so he can be seen!

Beauchamp's second explanation is that a remarkable piece of work is accomplished in Genesis 1: "the originality of this 'theophany' lies in concealing God instead of revealing him. This mutilated theophany, which is almost an active theokrypty [God's hiding of himself], retains only the breath-spirit (*ruah*) and the word. The other aspects disappear: shadows and light, the usual direct manifestation of God. And beyond this, the *ruah* is only present in order to suggest mystery: that God is something other than his word. Before creating there is a plan, which is not so much thought as already active and orienting itself, but we can know nothing about it. . . . Thus we have a narrative in which we do not *see* the principal agent; but this absence is given positive value." Within this framework, and in relation to this revelation, we must consider all the narratives concerning a "vision" of God.

Furthermore, working from this basis, we must proceed to establish several distinctions. In reality many things are covered by the word "theophany": dreams, signs, visions, etc. When dreams are at issue, we absolutely cannot speak of theophany. When we are dealing with a visible sign, the text is nearly always careful to speak of just a sign. Sometimes it reduces the matter even further, to a signal: God causes a flickering to appear, so that something is noticed. I find it unacceptable to consider the burning bush at Horeb to be a theophany: Moses sees nothing but the bush. The flame attracts Moses'

---

22. Just this once, I disagree with Maillot's explanation of Job's "vision" of God. Maillot believes Job's experience is narrated as a vision because it is a "pagan" text which relates to the pagan religious context. The result of the vision is not faith but the crushing of Job, who is reduced to silence. I prefer to see in Job's experience an eschatological vision. This seems to me to be confirmed by the marvelous "reestablishment" of everything in the last chapter.

attention, and the fact that the bush is not consumed intrigues him; that is all. Deuteronomy 4:15–19 clarifies this point: "Since you saw no form on the day that the Lord spoke to you at Horeb out of the midst of the fire, beware lest you act corruptly by making a graven image for yourselves. . . . And beware lest you lift up your eyes to heaven, and when you *see* the sun and the moon . . . you be drawn away and worship them and serve them, *things* which the Lord your God has allotted to all the peoples under the whole heaven." Therefore *everything* one *sees* are just *things,* created by this God who is not a thing and not visible. What matters is not the burning bush, but the word which is spoken.

The same is true of Jacob's "theophany" at the ford of Jabbok: he sees a man, nothing else, and later, tradition speaks of an angel (Gen. 32:22–32; just as in the case of Abraham's "theophany" under the oaks of Mamre [Gen. 18], or Manoah's vision [Judg. 13]). Jacob did not see God in the form of a man, nor did Abraham see him in the three men by the oaks of Mamre. As for the theophany at Sinai, we must note that everything is surrounded by clouds and smoke. The people are forbidden to lift their eyes to look (Ex. 19:21). In the Exodus story, it is never said that Moses sees God, but only that God speaks to Moses. And in the famous "face to face" passage (Ex. 33:11), what Moses sees is never mentioned—only that God *spoke* face to face, as with a friend. Finally, in the desert, what Israel sees before it is a pillar of smoke.

The essential thing is the significance of the fact that there is no real theophany in the Bible. The only possible image of God is a human being. But a human being is not God; and the visual representation of a human being cannot be taken for God—only the *living* person is this image. Therefore in this matter the visual sphere has no importance whatever. Visible things are thus signs, as, for example, the burning bush; but these signs (just as in the case of miracles) have no meaning by themselves. It is remarkable to notice that the sign must always be explained. What matters is the word that gives meaning to what is seen. When Moses turns off from the path at Horeb, the fire is only a summons; it is not the image of God. The decisive issue is not to have seen something, but to hear a word which is utterly clear, distinct, and explicit, and contains a revelation, a promise, and a mission altogether. This is a denial of all possibility of knowledge through sight, which places sight and language in contradiction with each other.

We must distinguish visions from these theophanies. The theophanies are explosive and perceptible to the senses. They are expressed in an exterior object that can be verified and that is part of the world in which we live. Visions are completely different. They

can be interior matters or "the heavens opening" (as in Mt. 3:16).
They refer to images and are *seen*, but they deal with realities utterly
different from the ones which make up the world perceived by our
senses.

When we deal with visions, we are in the presence of another
dimension of sight: one that does not refer to reality.[23] Therefore we
must consider what *vision* means in the Bible. First it seems to me
that we must remove from consideration all the passages that use the
word *vision*, but contain nothing other than a word spoken by God—
where nothing "seen" or visible to the eye is indicated. Genesis 15:1
is an example: "The word of the Lord came to Abram in a vision."
The same is true of the "vision" of young Samuel. Nothing like vision
is described for us, and we can question whether the word used in
these cases has anything at all to do with sight and image. This is all
the more true since the Hebrew word used in these passages comes
from the root meaning "to prophesy." This sort of language comes
up frequently, and means simply "revelation." Consequently we can
set these texts aside as we try to define "vision." The same is true of
the passages in which "vision" means "dream." In this case we do not
have real sight, but an illusion or an image created by the human
brain. Night visions therefore do not relate to the problem of image
and Word.

Having said this, we are left with several types of visions. First,
we have the prophets' visions: in each context we must consider that
what is seen is "*like* a human form." This relates directly to the

---

23. We must add to this the significant remark of Vergote (*Dette et désir*).
He emphasizes that contrary to what people usually think, the great mystics
absolutely do not confuse mystical experience with visions. Teresa of Avila
explicitly states that she has never had tangible visions of the outside world,
but only visions of the imagination. Furthermore, she is convinced theologically
that Christ never again manifested himself on the earth after the Ascension.
For John of the Cross, tangible visions, "even on the assumption that some of
them come from God," are in any case "obstacles to faith." "Therefore it is
best for the soul to consider them with eyes closed, without examining where
they come from." Imaginary perception is obviously another matter entirely;
but these are images that the mystic forms for himself after a long spiritual
process. On the contrary, the danger is that visions will attract the person's
entire attention, and in reality lead him away from God! As Vergote remarks
quite accurately: "The religious content of mystical visions is not different from
the content of faith; figurative representations are derived from natural perceptions." As far as revelation is concerned, visions add absolutely nothing.
"Therefore the mystic does not place his confidence in the visions in themselves. Sometimes mystics suspect that a vision is deceiving them instead of
manifesting something. Certain visible forms can conceal a diabolical content."

question of "image." But the prophet's role is not to tell about his visions; it is to convey the Word of God.

The only nonapocalyptic passage in which God is seen (since the text in Ezekiel is clearly apocalyptic) is Isaiah 6. Unquestionably in this case we are in the presence of a vision of God: "In the year that King Uzziah died *I saw the Lord* sitting upon a throne, high and lifted up; and his train filled the temple. Above him stood the seraphim; each had six wings . . . " (Isa. 6:1–2). We need to make three remarks about this passage: first, the vision takes place in the Temple. The empty Temple! The vision is related to the invisible presence in the holy of holies. Consequently we can speak of a cultic vision here. Second, it is again a vision of God in human form (seated on a throne). It is not so much God who is seen as it is the image of a man (as in the book of Revelation). Yet Isaiah recognizes this vision immediately as God. Finally, Isaiah says nothing about what he has seen; he gives no description. He practices absolute restraint; this vision *provides no knowledge about God.* It is not a revelation. Nothing "results" from what he has seen, except for a terrible feeling of unworthiness and impurity. And again, the important and decisive thing is what this Lord will say (vv. 8ff.). The vision is only a sort of shock for Isaiah, so that he will respond positively to the question: "Whom shall I send, and who will go for us?" In other words, this is certainly a vision of God, but it does not adduce anything specific. Sight is immediately absorbed and incorporated into the Word, which becomes decisive.

Furthermore, the vision itself refers immediately to the Word. Isaiah accuses himself: "I am lost; for I am a man of unclean *lips*" (Isa. 6:5, JE). That is, he is a person who does not speak the Word of God but is occupied with human words. The Word is the criterion of the possibility or impossibility of remaining in God's presence. When the seraph purifies his lips, he can become a person who speaks the Word.

We should also mention Exodus 24:10, where some scholars believe we should translate that Moses, Aaron, etc., *saw* the Elohim of Israel (replacing the usual translation: *feared* ). But the exegete also makes it immediately clear that even if the God of Israel is seen in this passage, only the pedestal of his throne is involved. The language is completely inadequate for describing the sight of divine reality. Daniel Doré quotes Peter Lengsfeld's excellent comment: "If someday a human expression were found to be directly and absolutely identical to the divine reality, such an expression would be the insurpassable and definitive manifestation of God as we expect to know him in

heaven. Then the Logos of human language would not only communicate revelation, but would be the revelation itself."[24]

Furthermore, we must note that this passage in Exodus speaks
of Elohim, whereas God was earlier declared to be Yahweh. Doesn't
this mean precisely that we can see the setting or an objectification,
but that God "in himself" remains utterly invisible? We are therefore
twice removed from being able to see God. God shows what we can
bear to see of him; and even of that, we can say or convey nothing. In
this way vision or theophany is utterly sterilized. If there is a vision,
in any case it is utterly impossible to depict it in any way whatever.
This utter uncertainty agrees with Paul's : "I know a man in Christ
who fourteen years ago was caught up to the third heaven—whether
in the body or out of the body I do not know, God knows" (2 Cor.
12:2). Here as always the relationship with God takes place "in the
body and out of the body," but we cannot tell which, because the
relationship oversteps the bounds of sight.

We must also take into account the vision of God as A. Galy
formulates it in connection with Genesis 22, in a fine study (in Jean-
Luc Blaquart et al., *L'Ancien Testament* ). Abraham's faith is expressed
in his certainty that God sees or will be able to see. And God says,
when he sees that Abraham is ready for the sacrifice: "Now I
know. . . . " Abraham *hears* the Word of God, and *affirms*: "God
sees" (therefore, he knows). The mountain is the tangible setting, not
so much of the sacrifice as of the vision. The text can be translated in
two ways: "On the mount the Lord *shows*" (instead of "is seen"), or
"sees." But in all this the only affirmation concerns God: his reality
and truth, rather than the vision a person could have of God, in spite
of the later statement: "On the mount the Lord is seen" (Gen. 22:14).
"The Lord sees and echoes Abraham, who affirms: the Lord is seen."
But these words are included in the narrative as something occurring
after God has come and acted. It is not exactly the Lord himself who
is seen, but the result of his action; and one must back up from the
action seen to the Lord to know that it was he.

Prophets are in no way authenticated by their visions. In fact,
usually when a prophet has a vision it is not an ecstatic vision of God,
but rather a completely different reality. Amos 7 and 8 are classic
examples: the vision of the basket of summer fruit, the plumb line,
etc. But Jeremiah's and Zechariah's visions are also typical: the
prophet has an utterly common experience. What he sees is commonplace, but its explanation is not. Only the word of explanation is
revelation—nothing else. What is seen belongs to the order of reality,

---

24. Daniel Doré, "Un repas d'alliance," in Jean-Luc Blaquart et al., *L'Ancien Testament, approches et lectures.*

of created things, and never goes beyond that order. It is impossible to contain the creator within the order of visible things. Most certainly the word is also something created. But there is a kind of distance established between what is said and what is observed, so that there is play between the two. And within this play something else is introduced.

The prophets even have a strange tendency to be suspicious of visions. In any case, a vision cannot contradict the word. On rare occasions it accompanies the word as a guarantee, occasionally as a framework. But there is even a tendency to criticize visions and to make the opposition between word and vision the line of demarcation between true and false prophets. On the one side we have the prophets of the word, who announce the very power of God, with no ambiguity or ambivalence, and with hard objectivity. On the other, we have the visionaries whose prophecy is unreliable, ambiguous, abstruse, and requires deciphering.

We must consider how many texts involve a vision which is primarily a false prophecy in which the false prophet argues that his vision proves he is right. A vision is both argument and falsehood. The vision is inspired by a fraudulent power which tries to pass for God and seduces people away from the revelation through the Word. The prophets often insist on the falseness of visions as opposed to the certainty of the Word of God. Thus we can say that the antithesis between sight and word is confirmed. In this connection we are told of "visions of a person's heart": what a person invents on his own, as if it were a truth from God.

Finally, the prophets also say "I saw . . . " when they refer to an understanding they have just had of reality. In this case we no longer have an abstract celestial "vision," but the sight of the real world as perceived by the senses, through which the meaning of the world becomes clear. This meaning is truth. The object of sight in the Bible is clearly the Word of God. Such an object is known only by the Word of God, as Wilhelm Vischer clearly shows. The potter's finger seen by Jeremiah becomes the finger of God. The almond branch which blooms is the haste with which the Word will be fulfilled; the cauldron whose mouth faces north is the image of God's judgment.

The prophet perceives the meaning of these material objects he sees. "Normal vision is *designation*. The prophetic vision is the *giving of a sense*. Out of the nomenclature according to human seeing . . . all of a sudden values arise."[25] The prophet's vision is an understanding

---

25. André Neher, *The Prophetic Existence,* trans. William Wolf (South Brunswick and New York: A. S. Barnes and Co.; London: Thomas Yoseloff Ltd, 1969), p. 333.

of the meaning of things and the world. Thus we might suppose that this vision has value in itself—a quality of truth similar to that of the Word. In reality, this is not so, for if vision has this power to signify, it is only to the degree that there is meaning for the prophet in what is perceived, because this meaning was *created by a Word*. It is because the vision expresses an active, living, powerful Word. It is a rich manifestation of a creative word (Claude Tresmontant); reality means nothing without this word backing it up. The prophet grasps the meaning and the sign only because he is a prophet *of the Word*, and he expresses this meaning only through words. Thus reality as seen by the prophet is surrounded from beginning to end by the word, which gives it value. The prophets' "I saw" in no way contradicts the unique truth of the Word.

In the New Testament three groups of passages evidently involve sight and vision. First, those where Jesus is concerned, in which the verb "see" is used intentionally. Next, the passages of apocalyptic character. Finally, the passages in the Acts of the Apostles.

The first group of passages is found mainly in the Gospel of John. In contrast with the initial statement, "No one has ever seen God" (Jn. 1:18), this entire Gospel emphasizes the importance of the vision that the apostles and their contemporaries had of Jesus. "You have seen me and yet do not believe" (Jn. 6:36); "every one who sees the Son and believes in him [has] eternal life" (Jn. 6:40). The word "see" in these contexts has a precise meaning: "he who sees me sees him who sent me" (Jn. 12:45); "[He] who has seen me has seen the Father" (Jn. 14:9). This implies complete unity between Father and Son. Furthermore, the Son is the image of the Father—the only image. There is no other vision of God apart from Jesus Christ; there is no other representation apart from the Son. It is impossible for a person to see God apart from the incarnation of Jesus. Again the mystics' claims are denied. There are a few related passages in the synoptic Gospels and the Epistles of John.

Considering what we have said so far, what is the meaning of this importance given to seeing Jesus Christ? It reveals something about the Incarnation. The Word entered into the world of the senses. Furthermore, as we have already outlined, the Word is related to truth, whereas images are related to reality. The Incarnation is the only moment in world history when truth joins reality, when it completely penetrates reality and therefore changes it at its root. The Incarnation is the point where reality ceases being a diversion from truth and where truth ceases being the fatal judgment on reality. At this moment the Word can be *seen*. Sight can be *believed* (because in the Incarnation, but there only, sight is related to truth). The image, which normally does not have the force of truth, becomes true when the image is Jesus Christ, who is the image of the living God. For this reason John emphasizes sight—because here reality is penetrated by truth.

But this is temporary; it is limited to the period of the Incarnation. Once the incarnate life of Jesus is over, the two orders become separate again. "A little while, and you will see me no more" (Jn. 16:16). At that point, we fall back into our frailty, back into the human condition, where reality is not truth. For this reason the Gospel of John ends with the story of Thomas, who needs to see in order to believe. When the incarnate life of Jesus is over, it is no longer possible to do so: "Blessed are those who have not seen and yet believe" (Jn. 20:29). We return to the need for believing a person's words—*only the word of those who have seen*, who have been able to certify that truth penetrated reality, that it subsists, and that the word alone is again the expression of the truth. From now on sight will relate only to reality.

After the incarnate life of Jesus, as before it, faith and sight are in contradiction. And faith is born of the Word: "You believe, not because you saw miracles, but because you ate your fill of the bread [of heaven]" (Jn. 6:26, JE). Once again the miracle is a sign without meaning in itself. Its truth resides only in the word that accompanies it and in the experience of life that it gives. Sight always pulls us away from the relationship of faith, because it draws us toward a reality we want to grasp, and because it necessarily directs us toward evidence. Seeing something implies the possibility of proof. This is exactly what Thomas asks for and what Jesus answers. Thomas had proof: things that are visible, tangible, and experienced are closely related. But wherever you have proof, or a demand for proof, the relationship is different from the relationship that faith brings. In the faith relationship, one believes without need for demonstration and without seeing anything, because faith establishes a relationship of confidence in the person who speaks. The word has significance only if I have confidence in the person speaking to me. The truth of the word depends neither on its objective content nor on its logical coherence, but on the person who speaks it.

In this case I cannot follow the same reasoning process I used for sight. In order to be understood, the Word presupposes faith, but this faith is a result of the Word that is addressed to me. "Faith comes by hearing," says Paul (Rom. 10:17, JE). It comes by hearing exclusively, and absolutely never from what one sees. Evidence and what we see appear to pull us away from a relationship of confidence and faithfulness. There is utter contradiction between this relationship with God that can only be based on faith and a relationship that would be based on sight. Sight is utterly excluded from the faith relationship. The New Testament thus confirms the Old on the issue of covetousness. The First Epistle of John speaks expressly of the "lust of the eyes" (2:16), and the most significant passage of all is the famous text in Philippians (2:5–8) that shows Jesus' anticovetousness. But we must return to the Incarnation itself: can we interpret it as the coming together of the Spirit of God and the world, the erasure of the breach, as reintegration in unity, and therefore the reconciliation of reality with truth and thus of image and word? Although the prohibition concerning making images and attaching truth to them is understandable under the old covenant, it would fall away with the Incarnation. This is true because Jesus is the image of God and he could be *seen*. He is the only possible way of seeing God, and at the same time he is the true image of humanity.

I must say that I am always dumbfounded when the *real* effect of the Incarnation is stated thus, in absolute terms. Is it possible that the modern world's atrocity and the atrocity of world history are not sufficient to convince people that the Incarnation is in reality not universal and cannot be universalized? It is now an established fact that no Christian politics, economics, society, or philosophy are possible. Can it be that this fact is not sufficient to make it clear that the argument based on the Incarnation is only a sophisticated effort to justify and legitimize our modern ventures through Christianity?

Of course the Incarnation is the coming in human flesh of the absolute God and the truth of his love. But that happened once, in a given time and place. It is as fleeting an event as the Transfiguration. The Jews are right when they say that if he had truly been the Messiah, the Son of God incarnate, things would have changed in some concrete way. They are right, in contrast to the theologians who wish to use the Incarnation to justify our current actions, and to proclaim that all of humanity has already reached some sort of divine condition.

The Incarnation is the sure promise, the pledge, the first fruits and the premise of what God will accomplish. It is the source of truth, freedom, and hope. It is all this, but it is not something already universally accomplished. It is something accomplished once and for all (in the sense that neither God nor anyone else will render it void), but as an accomplishment it is only the beginning of a wider achievement: Christ the firstborn from among the dead. But the resurrection has not yet taken place. This theology of the Incarnation as a magical mutation of human beings seems to me indefensible. It is a theology of the "already accomplished" that fails to take into account the "not yet," and the fact that we live under the Promise. So far we have only the "earnest" of this Promise.

As far as I am concerned, in spite of the criticisms of some modern theologians, we must continue to emphasize the dialectic of the "already and not yet" of the Kingdom of Heaven and the Kingdom of God. There is an "already": Christ has already come; God is on humanity's side; death has been vanquished once, and therefore once for all; evil has been vanquished once, and therefore once for all, and we can live in the certainty of love and hope. But nothing has yet been universally consummated. We have not yet been resurrected, we are not yet holy and blessed, and reconciliation is not visible, even though it is a reality as far as God is concerned. As a person outside the faith, an individual is neither assured of his salvation nor permeated by truth. He is not liberated or righteous in his undertakings.

In other words, there is no magic wand, for that is exactly what is involved in the triumphalist theology that I oppose. It says that "from now on everything is changed: God is now humanity's partner, and whatever human beings undertake (even outside the faith, even if they are utterly unconscious of God's love and will), they now do the works of God." Thus the Incarnation is taken for a magic wand. Everything has changed, whether or not a person knows, wishes, or believes it. And everything has changed concretely, in reality.

I believe this view is fundamentally antibiblical, since nothing has changed except for faith. Nothing has changed ontologically, but everything has changed at the level of *meaning*, of the sign, and of evolution. Nothing of humanity's evil and misfortune has changed, except in hope and in truth. But this truth is hidden.

This theological position also depends on a substantialist attitude (things must be changed in substance, just as the eucharistic host changes substance). But humanity is antisubstantialist and antiontological. There is no change in human nature, which in no way became divine through the Incarnation. Jesus is *one* person and not humanity. The mutation produced is the entry of truth and love into the world which had always excluded them. But this entry is as unobtrusive as the word of truth. The Kingdom of Heaven is present in our midst and is at work. It is also within us: "The kingdom is in the midst of you and within you" (Lk. 17:21, JE). But it is not in everyone.

Let us quickly recall that this is not the same as discriminating between sinners and the saved; Christians acquire no superiority through knowing and recognizing the God of truth. On the contrary, they have a responsibility and a function: the Kingdom of Heaven is a power secretly at work within the world, to change it. This is accomplished not through a metaphysical mutation but through a slow work of mysterious and invisible insertion. It is not an obvious process. Being a Christian means taking part in this work which does not change "the essence of things" but causes a new dimension of love and hope to penetrate everywhere, because of and in the true

Lord. This work takes place within visible and concrete reality, but it is not located there. And it is not yet the Kingdom of God which will come in power "at the end of time," when everything will be radically changed by the fulfillment of what is promised.

He will come "in the clouds" as the glorious Christ, and everyone will be obliged to recognize him. In the meantime, we are not yet at this stage. Christ is glorified and invisible in the heaven of heavens. And we remain on the earth, unchanged: human folly and tragedy remain what they have always been—but with the gnawing of love, the leaven concealed in the dough (but it has not yet risen), the seed hidden in the ground (but it has not sprung up), and the salt put in the soup (but it has not dissolved). So sight has not joined the Word. Sight does not have a new status, and nothing can justify the Christian imagery and the idols of all sorts that we continually erect. The Incarnation has not introduced sight into the order of truth. Only the word belongs there!

Certainly we cannot dodge the question of Jesus' being the image of God—the only possible image. But we must be most cautious in this connection. The Gospels show us clearly that Jesus' divinity was not obvious. It was in no way visible. According to the passage in Isaiah: "Nothing about him attracted attention—neither beauty nor bearing" (Isa. 53:2, JE). Continual ambiguity surrounds Jesus; although he may declare himself to be the Messiah or even the Son of God, most of the time he uses the title "Son of man." He never declares that he is God himself. He is not a visible and recognizable God in his observable reality. He is not a Tibetan-style God incarnate. It was absolutely impossible to say *when one saw* Jesus: there is God. John the Baptist discerned this by a miracle and the voice he heard, but not by seeing him as a man.

Following the Gospel writers, Origen understood perfectly this "invisibility" of the truth of Jesus: "Not all those who observed Christ's actions immediately understood their meaning. In the last days the Word came into the world born of Mary and clothed in flesh. But the eyes that saw him as a person saw one thing; their spirit understood something different. Everyone could observe his fleshly form, but very few—only the elect—received the grace to recognize his divinity" (*Commentary on Matthew*).

John's Gospel continually emphasizes the misunderstandings about Jesus. He is the image of God, because a theological reinterpretation of the Word has been effected, but he is never rendered visible and distinguishable as God in our reality. And when Jesus has ascended to the Father, when he has "found" his divinity again after the resurrection, the disciples no longer recognize him: neither the disciples on the road to Emmaus nor those on the shore of the Lake of Tiberias. They no longer see him as the man Jesus. This is why Paul places little value on knowing Jesus "according to the flesh"; the flesh adds *nothing*. Again (just as when God reveals himself to Moses), Paul can say of him *afterward*: "He *was* God present in our midst; Jesus *was* the eternal Christ," "the glory of Christ who is the image of God," or "as the firstborn of creation, all things were created in him," etc. He is "the image of the invisible God." But these things are said precisely *when he is no longer seen!*

We still have no visible image of God, and in this realm sight continues to be useless! Seeing a photograph of Jesus would not prove anything more and would add nothing to his words.[26] And I believe that in our present situation, such a picture would, on the contrary, unleash a reaction of unbelief.

For this reason the pretension of certain contemporary theological tendencies that want to eliminate God in favor of Jesus of Nazareth (since he is all we can know and believe about God) seems to me to be closely connected with this preoccupation with reintroducing the visible. They say that no one has ever seen God, but people could see Jesus, since he was a historical personality.

The desire to return to what is visible amounts to a new introduction of religion, in another guise, which takes the place of the faith called forth by the Word. In other words, the image of Jesus confirms our certainty that we are in the presence of a breach (perhaps related to the breach of holiness) between religions of sight and vision on the one hand, and a proclamation of the Word on the other. The

---

26. This also means that, since Jesus is not recognizable as God by sight, it is certainly praiseworthy to make drawings, paintings, and sculptures showing what we imagine him to have been like. But this activity can be oriented in two directions. If it involves symbolic representations, then this is perfectly acceptable and consistent with revelation. Twelfth-century sculpture does not claim to represent the real Jesus as he was; rather it tries to show in a purely symbolic manner an incarnation of the glory of the invisible God. On the contrary, as soon as someone tries to show the "humanity" of Jesus, in a kind of photography, as in the religious art called *saint-sulpicerie* and in nineteenth-century painting, then the situation becomes both ridiculous *and* idolatrous. This is precisely what is forbidden.

This impossibility of representing Jesus prevents me from believing in the supposed shroud of Jesus. In no way does it aid God's revelation. All it does is feed our curiosity. It does not allow us to understand the Word of God or to receive Truth. It contradicts directly Jesus' "You will see me no more." It tends to perpetuate an image of Jesus in our midst, whereas the only presence promised to us is that of the Holy Spirit. As for the value of the "miracle," we have seen abundant evidence for the fact that miracles have no value in themselves. Their value comes only from the Word which accompanies them. And in this case we have only the silence of the tomb.

religions of sight are related to a representable reality and they consider evidence to consist of demonstrations. The proclamation of the Word addresses itself to hearing, which leads to a different knowledge, understanding, and obedience. The two approaches are mutually exclusive.

In the same way, if humanity was created as the image of God, and if the only perfect image is Jesus Christ, this means that the living God cannot tolerate sterile material images. He requires *living images;* this is the basis of the Incarnation. "The imperceptible God desires images that are not fleeting, but neither does he want fixed, determined images" (Alphonse Maillot).

\* \* \* \* \* \*

Following these thoughts on the Incarnation, we will very quickly consider the other aspects of visualization in the New Testament. In Chapter VII we will study the Gospel of John and the vision of the book of Revelation, both of which involve us in eschatology. They both attest that access to truth in visible form is related to the New Creation, the accomplished reconciliation between God and humanity, and the reintegration of humanity in its fullness.

This being the case, we can go straight to the early Christians' visions as they are recorded for us in the book of Acts. Let's eliminate Stephen's vision, since it is apocalyptic in nature, and Saul's, since he encounters the *reality* of the living Jesus, as the disciples saw him in the Transfiguration.

Let's consider the genuine visions. They all have something in common: they are instrumental visions. The vision of Ananias, who is told to welcome Saul of Tarsus; the vision of Cornelius, who is told to send for Peter; Peter's vision, in which he is told to eat the unclean animals; Paul's vision of a Macedonian who asks him to come to Macedonia; Paul's vision when he is told to evangelize Corinth, etc. This common denominator enables us to understand that all the visions in Acts have a special meaning: it is always a matter of engaging someone in an action, giving a concrete command, or causing something to be done.

All of this is in the domain of reality and practical matters. The visions in Acts belong to the order of reality which needs to be encountered or changed. The purpose is pragmatic, and as a result these visions are adequate instruments for the end in view, but they contain nothing from the domain of truth or of spiritual revelation. Thus the visions mentioned in Scripture all coincide with what we have said about the Word's exclusiveness in relation to truth. Finally, it must be noted that such examples of vision are infrequent in the

Bible. The Bible consists entirely of the Word, whereas visions are *sporadic events.*

Having made these cursory remarks concerning theophanies and biblical visions, we can say, with certain exceptions, that truly the biblical God does not offer anything to sight. There is no showing or demonstration of God. A certain historical movement once tended to visualize the biblical revelation, in order to restore sight to its former position, and searched on the intellectual level for proofs of the existence of God.

\*    \*    \*    \*    \*    \*

Obviously visions have nothing in common with the "false gods" of which the Bible speaks—nothing in common except for sight. False gods are always gods one can see (and touch), and that very quality demonstrates their falsity and their nonexistence as gods. Isaiah's irony is well known: "You can take it and put it on a pedestal, but you can also throw it on the ground. . . . What is this god, except a piece of wood, since you can see it as it is?" From the viewpoint of our subtle ethnologists and historians of religions, Isaiah undoubtedly commits a grave error—the same error committed by Christians who ridicule statues of gods. These pagan religions are much more refined than that. The pagan "never" identified the deity with the statue. He had an abstract, superior conception of an inaccessible and indefinable divine power. I know all that. But after all, what if Isaiah (who lived in the midst of that world and belonged to it, which is not true of us) was right after all? Sacrifices and oblations were indeed offered to the statue. Prayers were indeed addressed to it. Of course, wherever representation exists, there is necessarily something that is represented.

But if the statue is so important, it must represent something utterly transient and hazy (this is the impression I get when I read the complicated explanations of certain scholars; I always wonder if ethnologists' presentations are not really poetry when they base their propositions on dubious notions grasped on the run). Belief needs to be fixed on something a bit more solid than this hazy concept.

Another possible explanation for the importance of the statue is that the representation coincides with what is represented. In this case everything Isaiah says is confirmed: such a god is nothing more than a table or a coatrack and has a certain verifiable and comfortable usefulness (isn't this really the role of deities?). Otherwise the statue will be punished: it will be turned facing the wall, etc. Surely this will impress the god!

Idols are indispensable for mankind. We need to see things represented and make the powers enter our domain of reality. It is a sort of kidnapping. False gods (they are false, but they exist!) are powers of all sorts that human beings discern in the world. The Bible clearly distinguishes these from the idol, which is the visualization of these powers and mysterious forces. People give names to these powers and forces. But that is not sufficient. They must be transferred to reality in order for us to be reassured. For we are reassured only by reality. Things that can be seen and grasped are certain and at our disposition. It is fundamentally unacceptable for us to be at the disposition of these gods ourselves, and unable to have power over them. Prayer or offering cannot satisfy, since they provide no sure domination. If, on the contrary, a person makes his own image and can certify that it is truly the deity, he is no longer afraid. Idols quiet our fears.

Images are truly filled with spiritual meaning and power; they are integrated into the sacred world, but belong to reality, to this human world. They are not in an impossible relationship over which I am not the master. Even if the idol is not itself the deity it is nevertheless the same. It has an identity and is not just a pointer. It participates in the god's existence, and is the means by which I lay hold on the deity and bring him down to my level.

Ryser shows clearly the relationship between sight and idolatry in his excellent study on the golden calf. In this narrative, Moses has disappeared. The issue is to "present to the people not just a fleeting word, related to the person speaking it, but something visible and accessible to everyone. It will be something one can be sure of and hold on to just as much as God, but more easily." Thus in this first step we have objectification and generalization: the visible object is permanent (unlike the word), and is at our disposition. The object allows anyone to see it, whereas the word is not for just anyone; it is addressed to someone in particular.

Based on this conclusion, three essential remarks from Ryser's book must be considered. First, something visible is substituted for what is heard. Ryser sees clearly the subtle truth of the matter of the golden rings: the calf will be made with the gold from the "rings that adorn the ears"; that is, which honor the organ that allows us to hear the word! "Aaron dishonors the ear; it no longer counts; now just the eye matters. Hearing the Word of God no longer matters; now seeing and looking at an image are central. Sight replaces faith. The concept that arises from a person's heart or mind is transformed into a work fashioned by human hands and takes the place of the invisible revelation that comes from above."

The second remark is that the deity represented, the visible Baal, is a god of power, possession, and domination (and fertility). What is visible is related to power. This means that humanity's desire to have a visible deity that is near and actually known leads to the making of terrible, merciless, and tyrannical gods.

The third remark comes from Aaron's proclamation as he unveils the bull: "This is your god, O Israel, which brought you up out of the land of Egypt" (Ex. 32:4, JE). This is of crucial importance: what we have here is not a switch from one god to another, but a visible image which does not remain an image! It *has now become* God himself. The image brought Israel out of Egypt.

God and the idol are the same thing, the same reality; and the idol wins. This process contradicts the explanations that say "of course, statues and depictions are not God . . . everyone knows that." No! The confusion *always* takes place. What is visible always takes in everything else. But only God takes in everything. Only he can *see* the *truth*. The passage in Exodus says: "I have seen," says God (32:9). This "I have seen" is obviously in opposition to the "sight" which the people demand. God sees both the reality and the truth. He sees the true meaning of what the people have done.

Anything may become an idol. The Bible shows us that the brazen serpent, the Temple at Jerusalem, and sacrifices can become idols when sight restricts them to a single role or a limited function. Symbols are groups of fragments of a shattered truth. Symbols become idols when the elasticity between truth and its symbols is frozen into a stereotype that humanity can finally possess.

In this connection I concur with Jean-Paul Gabus in his excellent analysis of idols: "The idol remains in a sense a symbol, since it is a concept overloaded with meaning. . . . But the idol crystallizes attention on a single element of the symbol's meaning: the serpent as healer, the Temple as a place of safety, sacrifice as a means of attracting divine favors. In practice the idol destroys the pluralism of symbolic meaning. It inhibits the circulation of meaning that normally takes place between several levels of meaning. The idol conceals the symbol."[27]

Thus there is a conflict, according to the Bible, not only with "false gods" (which do not concern us here), but also with all visible depiction of spiritual matters. The Bible attacks the security humanity draws from statues. Still we must, obviously, distinguish between the two kinds of divine statues or visualizations humanity can make for itself: the kind involving strange gods such as calves or bulls, for example, and the sort which concerns the God of Israel himself. However, the same condemnation, the same error, and the same impossibility are involved in both cases. People confuse truth with

---

27. Jean-Paul Gabus, *Critique du discours théologique* (Paris: Delachaux, 1977).

reality, and reduce what can belong only to *the order of the word* (where *of necessity they are responsible*) *to the order of sight* (*where they reign as masters*). Whether an image is called an idol or an icon changes absolutely nothing!

The paradox of idols is this: idols do not exist. In an apparently ambiguous passage, Paul speaks to us very strangely: "We know that 'an idol has no real existence.' . . . For although there may be so-called gods in heaven or on earth—as indeed there are many 'gods' and many 'lords'—yet for us there is one God, the Father . . . and one Lord, Jesus Christ" (1 Cor. 8:4–6). This passage has several levels of meaning: that of the spiritual dispute is always pointed out—there is only one God and Lord; all the rest are false gods.

But we are attracted to this passage at another level: on the one hand there are gods and lords. They really exist. They are part of the powers that claim to be all-powerful or salvific, etc., and that attract people's love and religious belief. They exist. And they pass themselves off as gods. But idols do not exist. That is to say that the visible portrayal of these powers, which is perceived by the senses, has no value, no consistency, and no existence. I could suggest a comparison: money certainly exists, but a banknote does not "exist." It is never anything but a piece of paper, and is not even a real sign anymore. And here is the paradox: since idols try to introduce a spiritual force into reality by bringing it into the sphere of the visible and the concrete, idols themselves do not exist. They exist neither as something visible and concrete (since in this sense they are really nothing) nor as something spiritual and "true-or-false" (since they cannot reach this level). They have no kind of existence precisely because they have tried to obtain indisputable existence beyond the uncertainty of the word.

The idol does not exist, but it alienates the person who makes it! Maillot shows admirably that in Deuteronomy "there is a coming together of the 'sight' one can have of other gods (their portrayal) and of religious alienation; making a god, drawing or sculpting a god means immediately bowing down to it and becoming a slave. The eye becomes not just the organ of laziness, but also of religious alienation. . . . Seeing is not only being assured of something's presence; it is also possession. . . . But the Bible shows that this immediately signifies *being possessed*."

All images are harshly condemned. The Bible speaks of "graven images," but no other sort was known at that time. Painting was almost nonexistent. "The graven images . . . you shall burn with fire" (Deut. 7:25); "Cursed be the man who makes a graven or molten image" (Deut. 27:15); "Every goldsmith is put to shame by his idols" (Jer. 10:14); "All worshipers of images are put to shame" (Ps. 97:7).

Of course, some will say that the image is not condemned in itself, but that idolatry is the problem: the image one adores, or the image made to inspire worship. Naturally. But we are still left with the strange opposition between word and image.

The God of the word cannot tolerate the gods of image. Why? The elementary, obvious answer is that these passages come from a society of images, where gods were thus portrayed, and that Israel's monotheism could not tolerate it.[28] The most spiritual religion could not accept this gross materialism. This is apparently correct (except for the fact that religions with images are not all that materialistic), but it is certainly insufficient.

A passage of Paul's clarifies the problem somewhat: people "exchanged the glory of the immortal God for images resembling mortal man or birds or animals or reptiles" (Rom. 1:23). What is the serious error? That glory has been changed into image. Glory is what shows God for what he is as God. This glory is invisible and can only be grasped approximately by the word. This glory is the reflection of God himself and can never be transformed into a thing. God's glory is a manifestation of the *truth*. It is the presence of a person.

The seriousness of making images lies not only in the fact of idolatry. The image relates not to God but to visible things (obviously it cannot exist otherwise!); it refers to *reality*. Thus there is an exchange of truth for reality, of the person for the object. It is therefore much more than a sort of competition between gods, between a true god and false ones: it is a fundamental, radical change. God really is not God any longer when he is represented. What people look at has nothing to do with truth. For this reason Paul says: "They have *exchanged*. . . . " The image is a change—in itself and not only in terms of the feelings that it produces or that produced it.

---

28. It is true that there was evolution in Israel with regard to images. Israel was probably also acquainted with images at the beginning: the brazen serpent, used under Moses' high authority, and perhaps taken by David from the Jebusites and placed in the sanctuary; the golden calf, undoubtedly an image quite acceptable to the people at a late stage, in imitation of the Canaanite bull. Perhaps there was even an image of Yahweh in the Temple. All this is possible, and as a result it gives us a rather late date for the respect given to images. The essential matter is that, given the general context of the surrounding religions, and given the general popular tendency, there was a total reversal. This reversal makes something magical of the brazen serpent and a destroyed idol of the golden calf, affirming that the eternal God is the enemy of images, at least as early as Amos and Hosea.

This reversal comes about gradually as the people deepen their knowledge of the truth of the Word, and as they learn of the radical opposition between word and image. The essential matter is the point at which the people of God arrive in their recognition of the truth, as they follow the Word of God alone.

Thus the Bible attacks not only adoration but also the image itself. This is because with the image we change not only from one religion to another but from one order to another. We leave the order of truth and move into that of reality. The prophets understand this when they show the absurdity of people who adore the creature instead of the creator. Thus the image is condemned as a denial of God himself.

This does not mean, of course, that every image, sculpture, or painting works this way! It is true only of images in the religious sphere. But just as every word draws its seriousness from the fact that God adopted speech, so every image draws its character from the place the Bible assigns to images. I repeat that of course not all images are idolatrous and demonic. But they are in effect opposed to the word, belong to another order, and are intrinsically contradictory and not complementary to the word. The contradiction situated at the level of adoration has repercussions at all levels. Images are incapable of expressing anything at all about God. In daily life as well, the word remains the expression God chooses. Images are in a completely different domain—the domain that is not God and can never become God, on any grounds.

Let us return to the warning from Sinai: "You shall not make yourself a graven image . . . you shall not bow down to them" (Ex. 20:4-5). The usual error is to refer this command only to the worship of "false gods." But this matter is already dealt with in the previous command. Here the adoration of false gods is not at issue so much as the confusion that amounts to claiming to represent by an image what one is going to worship. Not only the idol is concerned.[29] Before

29. Goux, in *Les Iconoclastes*, needs of course to find a psychoanalytical basis for the biblical prohibition against representing God and adoring images. He reasons thus: making images of gods involves making a material image (he of course avoids the problem of the *visible*, which is the explicit problem in the Bible). Given that *materia* comes from *mater* (an unfounded etymology!), this means making an image of the Mother. This can only mean adoring in a sensual way the mother figure. Therefore, "the prohibition against making images of the divinity is a radical form—the Judaistic form—of the prohibition against incest. And Moses' terrific anger against the idolaters signifies that he threatens them with castration—the punishment for loving one's mother." QED! It is obvious that anything at all can be substantiated using such "reasoning."

Furthermore, this conclusion leads Goux in an amazing way to an astonishing conclusion: the golden calf is a cow. It does not matter that all the biblical texts speak of the calf in the masculine; that the Bible tells us clearly that a bull is called a "calf" in order to ridicule it; or that we know concretely that such worship was related to the masculine fertility cult and to the bulls of Canaan or Babylon. Everything the Bible says is erased by the great discovery of the prohibition against incest. The calf *must* therefore be a cow! And all these

there is any idol, the will to portray exists. And since it is a matter of representing something as an image, visible things are necessarily involved: things that are in the sky, on the earth, and in the sea.[30] Thus what is invisible is transferred to the domain of visible things. And this is exactly what Paul means when he opposes visible (transitory) things with invisible (Rom. 1:23; 2 Cor. 4). The God of Israel denies any possible expression of himself in visual form.

True, of course, other religions in the area also had a concept of a power or "deity" beyond all visible representation (certainly in Egypt, but probably also in Mesopotamia). However, no god was excluded, and the visible portrayals were considered in effect to be gods. The visual element was basic—so basic that the nonvisualized deity was limited to an utterly hazy, uncertain, and unidentifiable existence. The visual element here is what enables people to become certain in their belief and to specify its content.

---

prohibitions must be concerned with the worship of feminine deities, who are never explicitly mentioned, with the exception of Ishtar, who comes up much later!

30. Here we must refer to the very new and profound interpretation of the commandment against graven images as related by Fernando Belo in "Universalité et contextualité," in *Parole et Société* (Paris), no. 1 (1978). He believes that this passage involves two complementary orientations: not to have images that *resemble* . . . , and the bowing down, which implies a *gathering* before (these images). The gathering is a closed one, excluding general participation, and it takes place around a scene of images "displaying the effects of resemblance in those who are thus assembled together because they have the same relationship of similarity with the images of the scene." Thus we have the image of an imaginary closed scene, with a mirror-type action so that the people cease being active in their lives (or in their relationship with God) and become passive and prostrate. The people become like *this* image and at the same time they become like each other, through identification with their object of worship. They cease being individualized and become united by images (Belo says that we are individualized by social practices; I would say rather it is by God's challenge to each person and one's insertion into this universe of the word).

This image can also become an imaginary image based on a mythological narrative with closed and mirrored language (which goes back and forth from one mirror to another). This provides an image of the god related to past events and ancestors and allows for a repetitive liturgy involving images. Thus the image produces a self-mirroring enclosure. This is what the commandment shatters, since it comes from the historical and nonmythological God, and since he starts people off on an adventure rather than enclosing them. Revelation gives no image of Yahweh; God is not enclosed anywhere, not even in the Temple. He produces in people a drive toward life and action, as they become participants in "God's story" and are sent out for an open-ended adventure rather than caught up in a repetitive liturgy. This is indeed the ultimate problem of the fixed, frozen, contemplated image.

The God of Israel, however, is exclusive. He cannot tolerate a possible confusion of himself with other gods, but in particular he cannot tolerate people's attempting any visualization of him whatever. The holy of holies is empty. It can contain a representation of things which suggest the glory of this God in a parabolic fashion, but nothing else. The glory itself is there, but it is invisible. God continually proclaims that he cannot be portrayed in any manner. And the condemnation of the golden calf, or of Jeroboam's calves, is not aimed at the adoration of foreign deities, the gods of the surrounding peoples, the idols that imitate other people's idols. The condemnation centers on the claim that the one who has revealed himself to Israel as invisible has been portrayed in a visible manner. Only secondarily could the form of a bull, which was indeed adopted in imitation of other religions, mean that they were adoring another god. The essential matter, which has not often been seen by historians, is that by claiming to represent the true God, in whom Israel believed, by pretending to visualize him, they signified by that very act that they had changed gods. Their god was no longer the Lord of Israel. This is exactly what Paul says when he recalls the sin of having changed the glory of God *into an image*.

God is fundamentally, essentially invisible. Over and over again it is proclaimed and stated that no one can *see* God and live. This is said even to Moses in Exodus 33:20 (we will return to this idea). When Moses asks God to let him see his glory, the basic answer is: "I will make all my goodness pass before you, and will *proclaim* before you my name 'the Lord'; and I will be gracious to whom I will be gracious, and will show mercy on whom I will show mercy, but . . . you cannot *see* my face; for man shall not see me and live" (Ex. 33:19-20). What follows is the famous passage in which God says to Moses that he will hide him while he passes by, and that Moses will be able to see God from behind, but no one can see his face. This means that one can see God's *trace* after he has passed: God's work and God's action after the fact. But one can never see God at work, nor God's presence.

This passage rigorously opposes seeing and hearing. We find the same idea at the birth of Samson the judge, when his father states: "We shall surely die, for we have seen God" (Judg. 13:22). I am especially interested here in the fact that sight and hearing are treated differently. This God cannot be seen, but he can be heard. If we were dealing with a "spiritualization," it would be difficult to explain why it would deal only with visible portrayal. Later Israel formulates a prohibition which seems to specify in an astonishing manner the God of the earliest period. Rather than theological progress, this signifies an acceptance of the first revelation.

The prohibition against portraying God leads to a unique situation among all the peoples of antiquity: the "empty Temple." This is precisely "the site which systematically relegates all other religions to subjective fetishism" (Goux). The empty Temple amounts to a prohibition against attributing to tangible and visible matter what belongs only to the creator of heaven and earth, and who therefore does not belong to the earthly order. This prohibition thus attests the radical otherness of God. This is the exact meaning of the well-known passages in Psalms 115 and 135; Jeremiah 10:3-4; Isaiah 40:18-19; 46:6-7; etc. Idols, made by human beings, belong to the earth's domain; they belong to "this side" (which is why people prefer them). They partake of visible reality, but this very fact demonstrates that they are not gods: there is nothing behind or beyond them; they are confined things, with no truth and no future.

The empty Temple, which is Israel's specificity, and which corresponds precisely to the temptation of the golden calf, is the critical locus of all visualization. This signifies radically that this God is truly the incomparable Wholly Other, who cannot be directly approached except through the Word that this God speaks when he chooses. The empty Temple is a critical place, just as the Word is critical and the empty Tomb is absolutely critical of all our representations of the Resurrection.

Faced with this absolute prohibition against all representation, the attitude required of the Jew, but also of the Christian, is an iconoclastic attitude. We must shatter images and destroy the statues before which people bow down. They bow down as masters who have enclosed truth within their reality, and who prevent the emergence of the Wholly Other because they have circumscribed a sacred space. Breaking the image obliges people to discover themselves faced again with the gaping void that challenges them. In the midst of fear, scandal, anger, or stupor, they are obliged to see their god fallen down, and so must raise a question and listen to a word.

But even though iconoclasm in the material sphere was the characteristic act of Christian intransigence at the beginning of the Church's history, at the time of the monks of the Egyptian desert in the fourth century, and in the Reformation, it no longer seems to concern us much. In reality, however, this is the spiritual question of our age, since it is the age of extreme visualization; but the issue no longer necessarily concerns statues! The conflict surrounding the representation of God in stone or painting no longer concerns us, because for our contemporaries, these works of art no longer represent anything. Since they are "just art," we have no reaction to them. On the contrary, iconoclasm is always essential to the degree that other gods and other representations are manifested. We no longer have to struggle against Dagon or Ishtar or Melkart, but against thrones, powers, and dominions. These are called Money, State, and Technique—the new spiritual trinity that manifests itself in quite *visible* idols, belonging exclusively to the *visible* sphere. The process (of transforming material things into deities), however, is exactly the same.

In our era, iconoclasm attacks the spiritual trinity of Money, State, and Technique. The visual sphere has won overwhelmingly, but it passes itself off for something spiritual. Only the means used (to make visible things appear to be spiritual) are different. Formerly one discerned a spiritual truth that was materialized in order to grasp it through sight. Today reality triumphs, has swept everything away, and monopolizes all our energy and projects. The image is everywhere, but now we bestow dignity, authenticity, and spiritual truth on it. We enclose within the image everything that belongs to the order of truth. The word is thus localized, and becomes space and mediocre reality. First of all, then, iconoclasm is directed at all visible signs of invisible powers. Today, much more than formerly, when we attack visible signs, all divine and demonic power is at stake, since its essence lies in these visible signs.

But there is another iconoclasm: the one that attacks portrayals of God made by Christians, even apart from statues and paintings. We also visualize in our minds, in our concepts. Only with much difficulty can we escape from spatialization (and Bishop John A. T. Robinson was right when he said that it was ridiculous to talk about the God who is "up there" somewhere above us. But Robinson seemed not to realize, oddly enough, that he also spoke of God in spatial terms when he said God was "deep down" in the depths). Only with much difficulty can we escape from our ultimate desire to bring everything back to sight, even when it is a matter of internalized sight. We need an image of God in order for our thinking to grab hold of something.

So God the Father becomes God with a white beard. The God of justice becomes the stern God on his throne. The unportrayable deity becomes the Triangle surrounded by rays of light. The God who knows all things becomes a huge eye. And we have already seen that images of Jesus, unless they are symbolic, are no more legitimate than images of God. They have no value either as representations of Jesus or as an attempt to make God show through this pious and pitiful imagery.

We must fight all these false images. They are necessarily false, because they are all situated in space and related to sight. The process is always the same. And when Gabriel Vahanian proclaims that God is dead, he refers to all these images. He attacks them by considering iconoclasm as the first act of the Christian life: the first and continuous act, the breaking down of images through the Word.

\* \* \* \* \* \*

We must constantly return, however, to the Fall. Obviously, although the word is given absolute preeminence in Creation, sight is by no means excluded. In God a close association exists between sight and word, but this poses no contradiction. A constant movement is established from truth to reality and from reality to truth. At first even Adam is given the eminent role of being the meeting point between created reality and space, where sight dominates, on the one hand, and the creator, on the other. The true creator is this one who addresses Adam through the word. This produces a situation characterized by unity of being (that is, unity of reality and truth); unity of the creator with his creation (but this is through the mediation of humanity); noncontradiction and fullness: "and when they had everything, they desired nothing."

The association in God of sight and word is emphasized by the very text of Genesis: at each stage of creation, God *speaks*; God *sees*; God *names*. He says "let there be light"; he sees "that the light was good"; he "called the light day" (Gen. 1:3-5). There is perfect continuity, and each act reflects his authenticity of being.

The explosion takes place at the moment of separation, when rupture occurs between God and humanity—and even before that. We can foresee the Fall as soon as sight is considered independently of the word; and this sight refers to the truth, appropriately enough! In Genesis 3 we read that "the woman *saw* that the tree was good for food, and that it was a delight to the *eyes*, and that the tree was to be desired to make one wise" (Gen. 3:6). This is the first time sight is a separate issue. This sight refers to the tree of the knowledge *of good and evil*;[31] that is to say, the tree of discernment of the truth. She sees; she no longer hears a word to know what is good, bad, or true. She sees—reality. She sees the *reality* of this tree. What she sees has no relationship with the word—neither with the serpent's word nor later with her own word, and finally not with Adam's word when he speaks to God.

"*Evidently*," she sees. *Evidence* becomes the sign of certainty and conviction. It is compared with fleeting words which are preserved

---

31. It is the tree of the knowledge of good and evil, and not, as some have insisted on saying, the tree simply of "knowledge"! As I have shown, this knowledge is the power to *decide* on one's own *what is good and what is evil*. [See Jacques Ellul, *To Will and To Do*, trans. C. Edward Hopkin (Philadelphia: Pilgrim Press, 1969).—TRANS.]

only by the memory: words of God, who is not visible, and words which are difficult to interpret. They contain all the laxity of freedom. These words permit no solid certainty: it is so easy to manipulate words.

"Did God *really* say?" is the only real argument. After all, am I so sure of what I heard? "Really"—that is, related to this reality. In place of all this vagueness, this open-endedness, and this memory whose uncertainty is pointed out to me, here I have the visual, indisputable evidence. It leaves no room for discussion.

I see. What I see is evident and certain. It gives evidence against the Word. This is the real "temptation," and the process by which we question truth. Rather than remaining in a fluid relationship based on listening, word, memory, choice, and response, the woman *sees* a possible way to take possession and to dominate at the level of this reality that she recognizes as the only stable one. She *hears* the true Word placed in doubt. These two facts are closely related, and based on them the opposition to images is made explicit, as the irreconcilable contradiction of image and word is ascertained (but this conclusion is a later theological construction!).

Evidence is absolute evil. We must accept nothing based on evidence, contrary to Descartes's recommendation. The evidence of reality is quite useful for action, but can in no way help us to understand the meaning of our lives. As soon as we allow ourselves to be invaded by this obsession with evidence, the discretion of the word vanishes. We become insensitive to language, which, even if it is the Word of God, loses its meaning. Thus we no longer pay any attention to it.

The utterly remarkable construction of the text of Genesis tells us that immediately after Eve's discovery of evidence for the tree's excellence, "their eyes opened" (Gen. 3:7, JE). They had been *closed* up until then! How many philosophers and theologians have fallen into a trap here. They say, "You see how unkind this God is. Adam and Eve were blind. He kept them blind. The Fall, disobedience (a fine use of freedom), transgression, and insolence toward this God, the doubting of his word and the refusal of his command—all this was necessary, so that their eyes could finally be opened. They are no longer foolish: they have become both clairvoyant and intelligent."

It is considered a blessed disobedience, a blessed "Fall," that gives birth to History and Science. Finally! "How stupid the Jewish theologians were who wrote this narrative and did not even understand what an explosive concept they included in their own representation of God. Their God is either wicked or absurd. And these theologians are certainly childish!" The historians, exegetes, hermeneutics experts, and philosophers who talk this way never realize that they themselves could be the stupid and absurd ones!

"Their eyes were opened." But it had already been said earlier that they saw light. Their eyes were opened with respect to what? Their nudity. That is the great first discovery. And that is all. All their new sight allows them to discover and learn is this nudity. And this discovery leads them to make clothing for themselves. But this has been explained as a moral matter: they are ashamed of being this way. What we have here is moral conscience and the discovery of "modesty," or the myth of the origin of clothing. But this is only a small part of the meaning of this sentence, which is much more profound.

Biblically, nudity is essentially the sign of fragility and weakness. We often find the expression "I am poor and naked" ("naked" not as an expression of this poverty, but in the sense of "weak"). And clothing is the sign of and search for protection. This is the essence of this marvelous discovery, thanks to their opened eyes: humanity is weak and without protection or defense.

Furthermore, Adam's first reaction when he hears the voice of God (in the following verse) is fear. Thus the eyes being opened in no way constitutes a point of departure for the luminous ascent of humanity. In no way does it open the possibility for humanity to understand, to assert itself, and to begin history. Instead, this even amounts to the discovery of the terrible reality that humanity without God is nothing. Without him we are without protection, without strength, and we are fragile as a breath. Sight reveals our effective reality to us.

Thus we can certainly say that this event will be the point of departure for "science and technique," since these are essentially means for escaping from this weakness and acquiring protection and power. We can certainly say that this will be the point of departure for history, since it is composed of all humanity's efforts to subsist and persist. But there is nothing grandiose and sublime in this.

On the contrary, we have here the beginning of the frightful adventure of humanity's trouble, of its misery and weakness. This is what is inaugurated by this sight which suddenly discovers reality *outside truth*—reality fending for itself, on its own, sight beyond light, which *up until this moment* had transfigured it.

This light was thought of as a light coming from God; that is, the Light of God. Human beings as limited creatures were fragile and weak, but placed in God's love; this reality was seen within the context of eternal and perfect love. It was seen by God's own sight. It was therefore a happy reality, and weakness was just one more joy, another perfection: that of the little child who buries himself in his father's shoulder. He is glad to be weak, since his father is so strong. But now their eyes are opened. They see raw reality, with realism and accuracy: reality outside God's love and therefore unpleasant, dangerous, and broken. This is the fruit of evidence. Their eyes are opened to this single and exclusive reality.

Contrary to this evidence of reality as seen, God continues to act toward human beings only through the word; that is, through proposal and discretion. God is never evident. This is another way of saying that he can never be seen. He erects and transmits signs, he calls and challenges. He speaks, and humanity must receive these signs in the adventure of listening and of the word. He speaks and his signs are never constraining; they are never as gripping as reality.

God is a God of signs, and, as we have seen, what are called theophanies on the one hand, and miracles on the other, are never anything but signs for the purpose of attracting our attention. The signs are meant to move us to lend our ear to God's voice, which is never shattering or terrifying, because it is the voice of love. "I stand at the door and knock" (Rev. 3:20). He never breaks down doors; he is never a battering ram that breaks down obstacles. The battering ram is Baal, who is visible. God sends us only signs to receive— imperceptible indications that must be disentangled from the trumpet blasts of reality; they are words mingled with all the other words broadcast around us.

Here again we have two clear and distinct universes: the universe of evidence, seen reality, humanity's universe; and that other one, of discretion and the word, of signs—God's universe. The human race of course has claimed to complete its universe through truth. Not existing truth, but manufactured truth; not the truth of love, but of power, which permits us to get a hold on dangerous and humiliating reality. So men and women monopolized language and made up signs on their own.

Human beings function on the basis of signs. "Thy foes . . . set up *their own signs for signs*" (Ps. 74:4). This passage is a very strong and up-to-date description of autonomous human effort. Thus we have no longer God's signs received by humanity, but agreed-on human signs addressed to human beings.

Of what are they signs? Here resides the great difficulty for linguistics and semiotics! The debate on this issue is continuous. Having destroyed the possibility of something signified and having retained only the notion of structures, scholars now realize that the signifier no longer has any value. We must liberate ourselves from the "dictatorship of the signifier," and therefore of structures, and counterbalance the signifier by giving all the weight to the utter uncertainty of "flow."

As a result, the status of signs set up by humankind is utterly uncertain, gratuitous, and vain. The sign no longer plays any definitive role whatever, and it refers only to itself. In this immense confusion, the signs addressed to us by God suffer, just as the Word of God is a victim of the confusion of languages. Was this confusion of languages at Babel God's vengeance? Here we have another simplistic explanation. I have discussed an initial element of the explanation of this confusion as it related to the construction of the City.[32] Here is a second element: the word related to truth; the word as communication with God—the unobtrusive word which is able to express what is deepest and most adored.

Here at Babel humanity continues along the road it began when its eyes were opened to reality and the apprehension and comprehension of this reality outside of God. The word and language play their role at Babel—to say what? "Come, let us make bricks, and burn them thoroughly. . . . Come, let us build ourselves a city" (Gen. 11:3–4). Here the word enters into reality and becomes the means of action and of reality. I do not mean, of course, to say anything so foolish as that language was not used for everyday things in the real world. It is quite legitimate to say "let's make bricks," or "please pass the bread." Language is not restricted to metaphysics or liturgy! But I mean that in a myth the elements have meaning (and are not allegorical!). Therefore, since there is such heavy emphasis *here* on this use of language, this fact is filled with meaning. It tells us that this word, which comes from the Word of God and is designed for speaking with God; this word, which is related to truth and expresses the profoundest things, becomes a means of action at Babel.

Here language is inserted into reality and is used to communicate things and information about reality—that is to say, something else entirely. And because the word has lost its basic truth, its essential root, since it no longer possesses its content, its weight and harmony, it explodes. Because human words are no longer in harmony with the Word of God, languages become separate and then diversify in accordance with their subordination to different realities. Since the word is made commonplace and instrumental, it no longer has any function except to make action possible. On the one hand it loses the unity of its origin, and on the other it acquires the diversity related to actions. Once inserted into reality, the word changed to the point where it became incomprehensible language.

Thus sight played an enormous role in the Fall and caused all of humanity and language to swing to its side. Under these circumstances, it is understandable that the Bible so often relates sight to sin.

---

32. See Jacques Ellul, *The Meaning of the City.*

Sight is seen as a source of sin, and the eye becomes the link between reality and the flesh. The eye is seen as the focusing lens of the body (but only of the body). The Bible speaks of the lust of the eye and of the eye as the source and means of coveting. Now we know that covetousness is the crux of the whole affair, since sin always depends on it. "You shall not covet" (Ex. 20:17) is the last of the command-ments because it summarizes *everything*—all the other sins. Humanity searches for other gods because it covets power; it makes idols for itself because it covets religion. Murder, adultery, and theft are always expressions of covetousness. Covetousness is equivalent to the spirit of power or domination. It is not just a simple moral question, but utterly basic.

The Bible closely and explicitly links covetousness to sight. This connection is derived, of course, from the passage in Genesis we have been examining. Eve coveted equality with God. She coveted the knowledge of good and evil. She coveted autonomy of decision. And all this resulted from her looking at the fruit. This covetousness based on evidence is the same covetousness we have seen at Babel. She looked, and the fruit seemed worth coveting to her.

We have the exact antithesis of this attitude in the famous passage in Philippians that describes the decision of the Son to strip himself of divinity, to enter into the human condition, and to make himself a poor servant, and finally to accept death—the death of the cross. The starting point of this process is: "He did not *look at* equality with God as a *thing to be grasped*" (Phil. 2:6, JE). That is, at the outset of every work of God or Jesus there is this denial of the covetousness that comes from sight. Here and only here can covet-ousness be vanquished, as a new beginning is made; and this is related to sight: he did not "*look. . .* " (even though the meaning is figurative). The Son did not look at this reality—neither at the power he held nor at the wretched condition he was assuming.

He was the Word. On earth he lived by the word. He lived in strict conformity with the Father, who does not *look on appearances*. But we always live in covetousness, which is related to evidence. Who can fail to understand this today? All human covetousness is related to the evidence of the excellence of what our society offers us: money, machines, knowledge. The evidence is clear. Therefore we must desire these things, and the current exaltation of "desire" results from this covetousness, which is unleashed by sight. Sight takes its place in the circle formed by sin, as origin and continual impetus to sin, because it is at the basis of the rupture with God as it roots itself in reality alone.

This is not to say, of course, that the word is not also an agent, means, etc., of evil! It is a fundamental aspect of evil, because it is the instrument of falsehood. But we must be careful: here the word is turned aside from its goal and (as we said in connection with Babel) is enclosed within reality; that is, it is the word subordinate to sight and an instrument of the covetousness of reality.

Let us also be clear that *we must not make a reality of this analysis of the myth.* I am not saying that the word is good and that sight is evil! Nor that the word is pure and sight impure! To say that amounts to reentering the universe of realism—the universe of this reality where sight is autonomous! I simply insist that the word belongs to the order of truth and sight to the order of reality. When the two were separated and their unity had disappeared, humanity, submitted to reality alone, entered into separation from truth. This rupture with God is called sin. Reality is thus submitted without limit to unfettered covetousness.

## 3. THE THEOLOGY OF THE ICON

Everything we have just said utterly contradicts the theology of icons as we find it in Greek Orthodox thought. We will follow Paul Evdokimov[33] in order to review this theology briefly. The icon of course is not worshiped for itself; in itself it has no value. It is not a work of art, and much emphasis is laid on the difference between the theology of the Orthodox icon and the less rigorous viewpoint of medieval Catholic theology. The object is not venerated; Beauty is, by means of the resemblance mysteriously conveyed by the icon. It irradiates "the ineffable reflections of divine Beauty." The image is clearly superior to the word: "the image shows what the word says."

Quite strangely the icon is ascribed to the Holy Spirit, who was supposed to lead us into all truth. The Holy Spirit embodies this truth. "The icon is a symbolical-hypostatic representation which invites us to transcend the symbol and to communicate with the hypostasis in order to participate in the indescribable. It is a path one must take in order to go beyond it. This is done not by eliminating it, but by discovering its transcendent dimension." The icon is an "image which leads us to something else," a prop in a mystical and transcendent quest.

---

33. Paul Evdokimov, *L'Art de l'icône: Théologie de la beauté* (Paris: Desclée de Brouwer, 1970). At the outset it is significant and basic to note that for the author, *beauty* relates only to the icon. He constructs his theology of *beauty*, in *general*, only on the basis of objects that are *seen*—painted objects. Everything related to music, poetry, the beauty of language and rhetoric, of taste and odors, is forgotten. Only one of the senses is given special status: sight, which grants a person access to the contemplation of the invisible.

The word is not sufficient. The icon is a symbol, but must be surpassed; though nothing in itself, it is indispensable in mystical contemplation. As a kind of sacrament that makes transcendent communion possible, in itself it is transcendent. The icon *alone* enables a person to *participate* in the indescribable.

The icon is thus light on the one hand (seen as the symbolic reflection of the original light), yet on the other hand it is opposed to anything that is "portrait." Icons are not portraits of the Virgin or of Jesus (thus no icon of a living person is ever possible). Icons are related only to the hypostasis: the heavenly body, the "person." The icon grasps the absolute resemblance: it takes on the very celestial figure of the hypostasis in its transfigured body—this is the icon in itself.

All this is closely linked to a theology of the Incarnation understood as "sanctification of matter and transfiguration of the flesh." The Incarnation enables us to *see* both spiritual bodies and nature as transformed by Christ. In other words, the Incarnation of Jesus has transformed the entire human species and all of nature; it is a completely finished work, and this transformed nature enables us to contemplate the divine through "indirect thought." Human beings *are* (already) deified.

This symbolic knowledge needs a material vehicle. But, starting from the symbol, by means of contemplation and true imagination with its evocative power, such knowledge grasps the figurative presence as an epiphany of the transcendent. This presence is symbolized, but *very real*. The icon guides our *gaze* toward the Highest—toward the Most High, toward the only necessity.

The icon is neither a sign nor a picture, but rather the symbol of a presence and the dazzling locus of the *mystery in the form of an image*. "The Word . . . offers itself to contemplation, as visual theology, in the form of the icon. It is [in itself!] one of the sacraments. . . . The icon shows us by its colors, and *makes present* for us what the gospel tells us through the word" (obviously, the importance of considering all this work as the expression of the Holy Spirit comes from this belief). The icon (in itself!) *participates* in the Wholly Other, by means of its *resemblance*, which becomes a process of effulgence.

The icon is also a kind of theophany. Since it has no volume, it excludes all possible materialization. It is purely spiritual: it is exclusively spiritual although visual. "It conveys an energetic presence that is neither localized nor enclosed, but radiates from around its point of condensation." The icon accomplishes what the letter to the Hebrews says about contemplating invisible things (but should this contemplation be visual and depend on our physical eyes?).

The icon of Christ, of course, is certainly not Christ. It is only an image, not the prototype. But it bears witness to a well-defined presence, and permits prayerful communion (which is not eucharistic communion, because it permits spiritual communion with the *Person* of Christ). "The presence of the icon is a circle whose center is found in the icon, but whose circumference is nowhere.[34] As a material point in the world, the icon opens a breach through which the Transcendent bursts" (no less!). Thanks to this relationship, the earthbound human being *becomes homo caelestis*. The hypostasis of Christ actually appears in icons. Coming back to the Incarnation, Evdokimov concludes: "A hypostasis in two natures signifies an image in two modes: visible and invisible. The divine is invisible, but it is reflected by the visible human object. The icon of Christ is possible, *true and real*, because his image in the human mode is identical to the invisible image in the divine mode."

Fundamentally the theology of icons involves first a switch from signs to symbols, because the icon is essentially symbolic. Then, the icon is inserted into an entire liturgy. It implies a theology of the concrete presence of the spiritual realm, and of divine light, which can be symbolically retranscribed and which is the image of glory itself.

We have said enough to show the degree to which this theology is diametrically opposed to everything that seems to me to be of key importance in biblical thinking. Furthermore we must note carefully that in the important work we have referred to, this theology is based on quotations from the Greek Church Fathers and councils—but there is almost no biblical foundation. For example, in this three-hundred-page book, the biblical foundation amounts to only two pages and seven quotations!

Because of my Orthodox friends I am sorry to say so, but this theology of the icon seems to me to correspond exactly to what we are prohibited biblically from doing: it is idolatrous. It rests on a certain conception of the Incarnation that utterly fails to take into account its unfulfilled aspect: the waiting and the hope. "Having *reestablished* the sullied image in its former dignity, the Word unites it with divine Beauty." Everything is already accomplished.

Furthermore, this theology rests on a conception of the image of God in the Creation that makes of it a concrete resemblance: "the image of God" *is* the materiality of visible humanity. This concept tries to place humanity permanently on Tabor, the mount of Transfiguration (the expression is used repeatedly: the icon transmits the light from Tabor). That corresponds exactly to the error of the disciples

---

34. We must remember that this is the definition Barth *gives of the Church* in its relationship with Jesus Christ. This shows how idolatrous the icon is!

who accompanied Jesus and who wanted to set up tents in order to remain permanently in the Transfiguration.

We must not try to find humanity's deification in God's humanization, as if God became human so that humanity might become God. Humanity goes from being a microcosm to being a micro-theos in this case. This is applied very concretely: to material, corporeal, visual humanity. The human being in himself, as we see him, is the face of God. One wonders then why the Gospels find it necessary to say of Jesus: "Behold the man." He is the *only*, the *unique* case of a human being as the image of God. But he is God's image precisely in the visible image of the condemned, scourged individual.

Here we come back, of course, to the need of visualizing in a material way what may be an imaginary, purely spiritual vision.[35] In the icon such a vision becomes an *object*, whether we like it or not, to be *seen* in the flesh. This cannot be avoided. And we should, after all, ask about the humble believers' practice. Obviously, the theological principles we have summarized above are utterly foreign to these people. So are mystical experience and the hypostatic exaltation of which the icon is supposed to be the center or the vehicle. What alternative is left open to them, then? Whereas Catholic theology remained very reserved and careful, often negative, toward images (Thomas Aquinas is an example!), a whole idolatrous tendency toward statues developed on the popular level in Catholic societies. How can we help believing, then, that the Orthodox believer considers the icon to be a god, a magic object, a reservoir of miracles, etc.? The icon becomes *in itself* the presence of God, of the Virgin Mary, or of Jesus. Everything is ascribed to the image: worship and prayer. And the well-known deviation toward superstition, which is a corruption of the faith, proceeds *exclusively* from visualizing what we are supposed to worship, pray to, and believe in without seeing *anything*.

One more matter before we leave the controversy over iconoclasm in Orthodox belief. The iconoclasts, whose beliefs were judged in the seventh council, refused to admit the symbolic character of the icon. Consequently they did not believe in "a mysterious presence of the Model *in the image*." "They could not seem to understand that besides the visible representation of a visible reality (the portrait), there is a completely different art in which the image presents what is visible of the invisible." In reality, this was not a problem of "understanding"; the iconoclasts simply did not believe this doctrine! They were accused of being docetics, of having a purely realistic view of art, since they refused to ascribe a sacred character to the icon. They

---

35. See note 23 above, on mental images.

denied that a representation of Christ or the Virgin Mary could be anything other than a representation. They denied that even symbolically the icon could have any sacramental value at all.

But the argument against the iconoclasts is utterly fallacious: it is denied that one can have an idolatrous attitude toward an icon, since an idol is the expression of something that does not exist—a fiction, a semblance, a nothing. Treating an icon as an idol, worshiping it as a natural object, amounts to destroying it. And the seventh council states: "The more the believer looks at the icon, the more he remembers the one it represents. . . . Woe to the person who would worship images." This argument is false because in many of the religions condemned in the Bible, the idol was a visible representation of an invisible religious reality, to which it referred. Idols are usually symbolical. Furthermore, this argument is also false because it melds the first two commandments into just one. The second commandment is quite rigorous: *no* representation (even symbolical!) of what is (also) in the heavens. . . ! The iconoclasts were right. But they were defeated.

As for the argument that the iconoclasts were docetics who denied the reality of the Incarnation, this rests on a cosmic conception of a realized Incarnation. This concept eliminates both the period of promise and history itself, since Jesus as crucified is considered already to be fully the glorious Christ. This "heresy" is the exact counterpart of the real docetic heresy (of which the iconoclasts were falsely accused), but it is no better!

## 4. THE WORD OF THE WITNESS

God speaks. Myth is born from this word, but rarely is it heard directly and never conveyed just as it is received, because human beings cannot speak God's words. Myth is the analogy that enables us to grasp the meaning of what God has said. As discourse constructed to paraphrase the revelation, it is a metaphor that should lead the listener beyond what he has heard. Myth is born of the revealed Word of God, but because it is figurative, it has no visible image. As the highest expression of the word, it reaches the edge and very limit of the inexpressible, the ineffable, and the unspeakable, as does the divine tetragrammaton.

Myth is the living word that soon will become a text. I only receive and know the text. And this text falls short of the myth just as the myth itself falls short of the word. Margins surround the myth as it relates to God's revelation. Our effusions, prayers, and our direct relationship are written in these margins. Margins also encompass the text as it relates to myth. In these margins are written our thoughts, quests, and questions. Correspondence is not exact, so that we will not be directly conditioned or reduced to the status of robots—saved but mechanized!

At each step I have the possibility of choice, freedom, and initiative. When I read the text, I reinsert meaning into it; I make it a word again. In a sense, the text avoids being too perfect, too absolute, too obviously identical with the very indescribable Word of God. This way I myself may speak as I make the text speak, just as God speaks (but without taking up all the available space) and then lets Adam speak.

The text that encloses the truth of the Word of God is never so exact that it only bears repeating. This text invites me to retell the myth, to recreate it. And the recreated myth calls me to listen to the ultimate, absolute Word. The Word obliges me to speak. This indivisible process implies that the text should never be fixed, reduced to structures, enclosed within itself, or understood as if it were an exact and precise mathematical formula. No valid semiotic diagram exists that can exhaust the text that is a metaphor for the Word of God. Such a text must be spoken rather than dissected.

According to the Bible, God's revelation is conveyed by the human word—by the word and nothing else. Action, miracles, and works only accompany and authenticate the word as demonstrations and accessories. Without the word they are nothing. Only the word can convey the Word of God, the sole means God used to reveal himself to us.

The importance of the human word becomes evident when we consider that a person speaking is God's witness. In and by means of this word, God speaks about himself. Just as human flesh was necessary for the Incarnation, so the Word of God is conveyed by the vehicle of the human word. The witness is the person who speaks this word in such a way that God, in sovereign judgment, declares it "True, worthy of attention, really faithful" (Barth). In this situation language is still central. But we must not forget that biblically, God's witness is the martyr (Greek *martyros*), who pays the price of this word he has spoken with his blood and life. This means that again in the Bible, word and authenticity are connected. The word commits unto death the one who has spoken it. This is an important lesson: not because of his action is the witness a martyr, but because of his word!

The nature of an action is not to signify, for it can always "signify" any number of things and suggest various interpretations. But precisely language can never be without meaning. This is not to say it cannot occasionally occur without meaning. Sometimes people even intentionally make it that way. But the true role of language is to clarify: to formulate clearly and to eliminate ambiguity. A person's honesty is measured by this standard: whether his language has two meanings. For all things have a double meaning, but the word is designed to disassociate the two meanings and to indicate them clearly. The word is oneness.

We have emphasized at length the flowing, shifting, ambiguous nature of the word. But the witness's word *must* be clear and never give an "indistinct sound" (1 Cor. 14:8). That is, the witness must commit himself entirely to what he says, recovering the unity of the person and the word. At the same time he must find the most rigorous possible form of the word—the clearest and sharpest. He must dispel misunderstandings and steadfastly repeat, emphasize, and reproduce in all possible ways the truth revealed to him.

Language, however, remains incomplete and insufficient. Therefore the Scripture entrusts us to the Holy Spirit (and this is by no means some easy solution). He is the one who takes the written text and transforms it into the Word. He transforms our murky and ambiguous words into something clear and comprehensible, with no ambiguity. But I repeat, this is not an easy solution or an encouragement to laziness: I can hope for the Holy Spirit's action only when I have done all that is possible—even impossible—to testify to the Word of God with all my means, commitment, intelligence, and effort. It is like the multiplication of the bread *beginning with* the disciples' five loaves.

Thus the one who speaks is absolutely committed as he faces others. Only his word can explain a given action or attitude and make it acceptable or despicable. Only by his use of language can such a person's authenticity be demonstrated, and his word has importance in this connection alone. Thus we are told that everyone will be judged according to his words; and again, "as I hear, I judge" (Jn. 5:30). These are surprising statements for people eager for action! Yet Jesus says: "By your words you will be justified, and by your words you will be condemned" (Mt. 12:37)! This reminds us of the ultimate seriousness of words! Here we are far removed from the modern scorn for words, far from phrases that commit no one and mean nothing. But precisely because the word is the locus of the decision *about* human beings and also *by* them, the Bible commands us to be authentic in our words. For, of course, we can misuse them: utter vain words, act on the basis of vain repetitions, pronounce blasphemous words or (more often) words of no value.

"The Kingdom of God does not consist of words," "I will know not words, but power," says Paul. "You will say Lord, Lord. . . . " All this is essential. But why are vain words condemned? Why should we be warned that people "will render account for every careless word they utter" (Mt. 12:36), if *all* words were vain, if the word was only sound and fury? The gravity of the warning lies precisely in the fact that the word is the means God chooses to express himself. In this way and only in this way can we understand the extreme importance of deforming the word, of misusing it, of falsehood! Only in this way can we understand why our "yes" must be completely and only "yes," our "no" completely and only "no." "Anything more than this comes from Satan." That covers a lot of ground: everything that tends to make the word ambiguous, that would devaluate, corrupt, or deform it.

Thus the witness to the Word of God—the one who testifies that God is the Word and speaks—is in the full sense a witness, while at the same time he restores to the human word its fullness. We have observed that all human language draws its nature and value from the fact that it both comes from the Word of God and is chosen by God to manifest himself. But this relationship is secret and incomprehensible, beyond the bounds of reason and analysis. This relationship becomes luminous and unquestionable only when the word is spoken by a witness—that is, by one who explicitly makes the connection between the divine and the human word. He must have the courage, audacity, enthusiasm, and presumption to declare, despite his deep humility: "What I say expresses the Word of God. My word projects the Word of God." This is inconceivable and must surely be paranoia. Yet only thus can all human language gather strength and find a new beginning. Such statements require the courage to look ridiculous ("Who am I . . . ?"); it is crazy to think that I could express the truth of the Most High God, knowing what I know about myself. Isn't this a potential source of pride? No, because in fact I am overwhelmed, broken, and crushed by the truth of this word I must speak. Kierkegaard lived this experience in its entirety, as did Martin Luther and Augustine. The witness cannot affirm great truths lightly.

Precisely for this reason preaching is the most frightful adventure. I have no right to make a mistake that makes God a liar. But who can guarantee that I won't make a mistake? I walk on the razor's edge. On the other hand, if my preaching is nothing but a pious, oratorical, Sunday-morning exercise, then better to keep silent. If through my words I do not proclaim the Word of God, what I say has no meaning but is the most absurd and odious of speeches. If, however, I try to proclaim God's word, I am utterly called into question by my very pretension. If I make God a liar I risk being the absolute Liar. And what if I err, substituting my ideas and opinions for God's Revelation—if I proclaim my word as the Word of God, in order to give it weight and sparkle, in order to beguile my listeners? Then my word, unratified by God and disavowed by the Holy Spirit, becomes the cause for my condemnation.

Not just any word can cause my condemnation—only the word related to the truth of God revealed in Jesus Christ. Only in this context can I be the Liar. This is the absolute risk of the Witness, the only serious risk a person can run. But only on this condition can he return to language its original authenticity.

At the same time, this person who speaks is a true witness: one who introduces something new and unexpected into a given situation,[36] thus bringing about a rupture and reversal of the situation. In a trial, the witness furnishes the key fact that *changes* the certitudes or view of the reality held before his appearance. But the witness to the Word of God produces the greatest change, innovation, and rupture that can be imagined. He testifies to the Wholly Other, the Invisible, the imperceptible dimension we call Eternity, Absolute, Ultimate, or some other name. These words mean nothing, since we cannot imagine or understand what they designate. But we use them as our only means of referring to the "different" one whose word has taught us that we are his beloved children. The witness introduces this Wholly Other into our visible, concrete, measurable, and analyzable reality. The Wholly Other takes this reality upon himself, limits it, measures it, and gives it another dimension.

No work or action can bear witness like this, but only the word, referring to the Word. Only the human word brought by one who commits himself totally to it. The Holy Spirit is necessary, but so is the witness, without whom nothing will happen. This presence of the Wholly Other is one of the most basic necessities of our society and our time, because of the many totalitarianisms, the closing up of human relations, and the terrible coldness that characterize our technological, state-controlled world.

Since totalitarian society turns everything to its own ends, the only possible challenge to it is the proclamation of a radical Wholly Other and the intervention of the Wholly Other through this proclamation. The Wholly Other—since he is incommensurable and cannot be assimilated or utilized—can produce an opening, a breaking up of the iceberg. He can allow some unfilled space and provide elasticity and play within the mechanisms.

Such a result, however, cannot arise from any internal force intrinsic to the system, because immediately it would be reintegrated into the system. Such space for freedom can only be brought about through a word, since only the word is free. But it must be a *living* word and not a leaden word. And the word can remain living only as the echo, response, and question to the other Word. This Word by

---

36. See Jacques Ellul, "Herméneutique du témoignage," in *Le Témoin*, ed. Enrico Castelli (Milan, 1975).

nature is essence and truth, independence and genesis, as well as self-producing, self-directing, and autonomous. The word continually must be begun again by the only one who creates through the Word. And the word must be continually taken up again by the Witness. Thus it must be closely connected with the person who pronounced it as his own direct and immediate expression. If such a person is absent, nothing is left.

The Word once spoken belongs to the past. But this past has no reality, so the word cannot return. Silent waves spirit it away into space. It is not language any longer. Language is heard and believed *hic et nunc*, but once spoken, it no longer exists. What remains then is what we have learned or believed through the word: our agreement (or refusal) with the other person. The word itself has disappeared, for the word is related to life, and is a part of life that can never be crystallized or preserved unaltered. Thus never can the word—neither the Word of God nor the human word—simply become an object.

Thus we return again to the word's fundamental opposition to the image. The image is an object and never anything else. Never is it living, even when it is animated; never is it the experience of a person. When God chose the Word, he adopted the means of Revelation that forbids any human familiarity or possession. God's Word can never be transformed into an object nor be at our disposition. Either God is present, in which case the Word is God's Word; or God is absent, and there is nothing. By necessity, this word is either present and direct, or else it does not exist. And when written, when in a sense it can become an object, we know well what Christ says about it: the letter is dead.

# Chapter III

# SIGHT TRIUMPHANT

Every society since the beginning of the human race has had its images; we have always seen and been filled with images. Consider our cave paintings in southern France at Lascaux, our stained glass windows at Chartres, the sculptures at Hoggar, and the high reliefs at Karnak. Haven't people always created such images? Haven't we always tried to place such interpretative filters between us and the world? Doesn't the biblical commandment forbidding graven images indicate a permanent human tendency of particular importance, since it results in such a command?

We always hear the same reassuring error: "there is nothing new under the sun—our civilization is really the same as the civilizations of earlier centuries. Why bother with this now? People are the same as they have always been." This, however, is not true. Images today are very different from those in earlier societies. For instance, earlier sculptures and paintings were negligible in number and were not the inevitable object of everyone's continual attention. Rarely did a person see an image and only under special circumstances and in exceptional places.

Who looked at the sculpture of the Greek and Egyptian temples? Probably not the peasant who lived far from the cities. We do know who saw the statues of the Chaldean and Roman palaces and the paintings and mosaics at Pompeii: kings and their advisers, rich senators and nobles—very few people (we may also mention their slaves, but they had reasons for not feeling the same joy that the images produced in their masters). Obviously these artistic creations were utterly foreign to the masses.

Turning to more recent periods, we see the same pattern more clearly: usually a rich person commissioned a work of art. The miniaturists of the Books of Hours, and later, medallion painters, enamel specialists, and still later, those receiving stipends from patrons, found work that way. Patrons at first requested their own or their wives' portraits, but later became interested in any painting by a well-known artist. Naturally, all these works remained strictly private. No reproductions of good paintings, no museums or exhibitions existed. The patrician or lord kept the masterpiece at home, for personal use. He enjoyed it alone, or with friends of the same social class. In any case, such friends would only see the painting or bust from time to time, as when they came to dinner or to a reception.

Images certainly existed. A person could even become passionately fond of one. But how different someone in the past who contemplated, repeatedly and with penetration, Grünewald's crucifixion and our biweekly herding to see the latest film. Formerly the overwhelming majority were excluded from the effect of images, and those who possessed them had only a few—which remained the same. A painting could produce joy or serve to educate someone's taste, but was not a collective force that modified the psychic structures of a group.

Images for the masses also were created, of course: stained-glass windows and sculptures in cathedrals, where individuals learned about the imaginary world and piety; and the *libri idiotarum*, to which we will return later. But these images also were very few in number and intended for the masses, who knew nothing beyond what they saw in their local church. One soon finished counting and learning by heart those few dozen scenes, always the same, unvariable and never renewed. Such images became part of one's universe, but did not in themselves form a separate, autonomous universe.

The spectator was not overwhelmed or pulled apart by these images; on the contrary, they focused his attention. And because they were familiar to him, they never carried him beyond the reality of his life. One could not then have spoken of a civilization of images, whereas this is certainly what we have now. The multiplication of images has changed the nature of the phenomenon. This is one of the instances in which the Marxist idea is correct: sufficient modification in quantity may become a qualitative change. No comparison is possible between what people have traditionally known of images and what we are now exposed to.

In an earlier time, sight was oriented toward the spectacle of nature. Nature was people's only image, their main contact with the surrounding reality. They measured this reality and established a relationship with it through sight. Sight was a means of taking nature's dimensions with a view to later action, and contemplation was always directed toward the exterior aspect of things. Only speculation, when added to sight, tried to reach beyond the superficial view.

Even one person gazing into another's eyes does not penetrate to his soul; the sentimental illusion that would have it otherwise is untenable. Such looking is truly relationship, and is a genuine under-standing of the other person, but only in his reality. This reality becomes the object of my action. It really becomes an object in relationship to me. My mere looking transforms what is into an object. This is true not only of scientific looking at matter, but also of the icy gaze of any person who considers the universe in which he moves to be absolutely his, with no reservations. The person who lives beside you is buried by this look; he is effectively transformed into an object. The proliferation of artificial images prepared the way for all this.

## 1. THE INVASION OF IMAGES

Certainly we need not go into detail about the triumphal progress of the image and the regression of the word in our society.[1] A universe of images surrounds us: photos, films, television, advertising, bill-boards, road signs, illustrations, etc. We habitually visualize every-thing. Napoleon's famous statement, "a picture is worth a thousand words," is obviously a truism for us. Let us note, however, that this must be the statement of a person of action—a realist who refers to the concrete, directly perceptible world. Obviously, for showing troop movements on a map, a simple sketch is better than detailed oral explanations. But we have converted this principle into global truth: the evidence of an image makes any other kind of expression useless. What can be shown to us, however, is necessarily of the order of reality, not truth. The world of representation, spectacle, and infor-mation is fused with the visual world.

Whenever we remain without images, information seems du-bious to us in our day. Great hypotheses of information and commu-nication did not advance until images developed. Specialists will say, of course, that this is also true of spoken information, but the historical juncture is fundamental; we now attribute visual character-istics to all information. The whole theory of communication is built on the basis of visual information, and this hypothesis is then ex-pressed by means of sketches and diagrams.

How many comments are repeatedly made about our "spectacle-

---

1. Let us simply note that tangible images are involved, and not just mental images. One of the best specialists on "mental images" writes: "It is not a true image. True images, such as photographs, are concrete objects which can be looked at, manipulated, hung on the wall, etc. Obviously that has nothing to do with what the brain's mental eye perceives" (S. Michaël Kosslyn, in *La Recherche* [Feb. 1980]). Here we have the same extension into metaphorical language as when the word "language" is applied to gestures, films, etc.

oriented society"! How much diluting and extension (like oil on water), how many elaborations and misinterpretations are attributed to this expression! I repeat: we must refer directly to Guy Debord's thought[2] (which is rigorous and explanatory) instead of attributing to him whatever we please. The spectacle-oriented society makes a spectacle of itself, transforming all into spectacle and paralyzing everything by this means. Such a society forces the involuntary and unconscious actor into the role of spectator and congeals through visualization everything that is not technique. It is a society made by, for, as a function of, and by means of visualization. Everything is subordinated to visualization, and nothing has meaning outside it.

Our ancestors' only spectacle was Nature—and Nature was not really a spectacle, since it was both the source of all possible life and a permanent threat against which one had to take precautions. Nature was not a spectacle to be enjoyed by a tourist arriving at the high point of his climb or watching an ocean storm from the shore. The peculiarity of the invasion of images in this situation is, then, that society has now substituted itself for Nature, furnishing and guaranteeing people all their means and possibilities of livelihood. This society is also our greatest danger, constantly threatening both individuals and the collectivity. *This* society has become a spectacle and can be grasped only as spectacle. Such is the extraordinary mutation that has taken place.

It is as if, two hundred years ago, someone had gathered the crew of a ship in the middle of a storm to have them attend a theatrical production of Shakespeare's *The Tempest*. We live in just such an unthinkable and grotesque situation! The spectacle of disturbances, wars, plagues and famines, airplane accidents and hijackings[3]—all this conceals everything that is not spectacle: conditions of prisoners and of the insane (or those treated as insane for ideological reasons), of assembly-line workers, etc.

Of course, we also know how to transform such suffering and alienation into spectacle and thus submerge them into our universe of images. Sight enables us to gloss over unpleasant reality by divorcing it from the order of truth. Sight permits a representation of reality that is accepted as reality and identified with it. Images become unquestionable, just as reality is. This happens because images be-

---

2. Guy Debord, *Society of the Spectacle* (Detroit: Black & Red, 1977).
3. Here we must refer to Jean Brüller's admirable drawings, from the period before he became known as Vercors, "Comme mouches en bouteille." This theme is stunningly illustrated in these drawings. "Comme mouches en bouteille," in *La Danse des vivants* (Paris: privately published by the author, 1933–36).

come more real than reality itself.[4] The representation comes to serve as our mental framework; we think we are reflecting on facts, but they are only representations. We think we are acting, when we only flounder around in a stew composed of representations of reality that come from a profusion of images, all of which are synthetic.

These images have no coherence and are continually changing. They are projected by some "magic lantern operator" who chooses, then colors, the images in variable fashion—such is our mental panorama. Such a presentation corresponds to the representation I foist upon myself. I play a role, but refuse to consider clearly who I am and who makes me what I am. Images are so much more satisfying than speech! We even praise this situation as "culture and freedom"! For example, consider this delectable passage written by a reporter for Le Monde (July 1978): "We must learn to resign ourselves to living in an audiovisual age. Most people, especially youth, read little, have poor memories, forget what they learned in school and barely remember what they see on television. Words withdraw behind images, more every day. Not just any image gets watched: only the moving, speaking image. It is not like pictures in books, but like life itself. Other images are erased by pushing a button. In an earlier time, before people could see the feature film, they were obliged to digest a crude, traditional documentary on diamond mining in Brazil or Chateaubriand's childhood in Brittany. Now all this is eliminated. Each is free to choose his own program. No one can make us 'learn' against our will."

Thus we are free—utterly free. On the condition, of course, that we enter the "audiovisual culture," that we accept the fact that we cannot do otherwise, and that in every sphere the word, discourse, and reading are on the wane. Once this is established, we are left with an admirable culture and freedom.

The text is progressively retreating everywhere. A simple examination of textbooks and magazines shows this. The turnaround took place between 1950 and 1960. Previously images were mere illustrations of a dominant text. Language was by far the most important element, and in addition there were images to make the text's content more explicit and to hold the reader's attention. This was their sole purpose. Now the situation is reversed: the image contains everything. And as we turn the pages we follow a sequence of images, making use

---

4. Who has not had the experience of being disappointed on seeing the art object he had seen in a picture? The lovely image, so beautifully presented, contrasts with the reality of the object, which is such a letdown. See the extraordinary illustrations in L'Or des Scythes (Paris: Editions des Musées Nationaux, 1975). We will return to this problem.

of a completely different mental operation. The text is there only to fill in empty spaces and gaps, and also to explain, if necessary, what might not be clear in the images. It is true that sometimes the images are clear but do not clearly communicate what the reader is supposed to learn from them. Thus the relationship has been reversed: images once were illustrations of a text. Now the text has become the explanation of the images.

## Education

Let us quickly survey our universe of images. From the beginning of his training a child finds himself surrounded with pictures and maps. Increasingly his books are cleverly and lavishly illustrated. This is now true not only of gift editions but also of textbooks, whose only goal is to address the child's senses directly, compel his attention, and awaken the kind of interest that some colorless, complicated text can no longer attract.

Even in somewhat rustic elementary classrooms photographs of scenery and reproductions of paintings are no longer hung to illustrate something taught. Their role is to insert unconsciously the beginnings of culture and to suggest a universe with dimensions that are incomparable with those of the classroom. Moreover, teaching is made easier when images are used; they not only back up a lecture but can even replace it. Everyone agrees that "an image teaches more in an instant than a long lecture." This issue is not discussed; the professors' only complaint is that they do not always have sufficient illustrative material to show all that could be shown. They would prefer to teach a subject which could be reduced in its entirety to visual symbols. This agreement, that the image teaches more than a lecture, reveals the unanimity of conviction in this area. From the very beginning of our discussion, we must cling to this agreed-on dogma, so as not to be tempted to change our minds when we have seen some of its consequences!

## Signs and Billboards

As I leave my house, I am immediately impressed by signs in the city streets. Their purpose is multiple: advertising and propaganda, proclamation and attraction. The words on a sign are nothing I would read, except in passing (would I have time to pause?). But their color, form, and design are engraved on my memory. I will remember these elements from huge billboards glimpsed at the curve in the road as they pass me at great speed above the bus; or from the immense posters with loud colors which strike me at the entrances and exits of subway stations.

Signs fill me with an imaginary world invented by people like me, and conveyed by these innumerable designs. They make me a participant in society's artistic creation, which is fleeting and colorful. This forms and deforms my reactions, manipulates my needs, and occupies my thoughts. I cannot escape this influence, however indifferent I may wish to remain to all that it praises and suggests to me. Signs are designed according to precise laws whose combination is intended to have the effect of forcing my attention and attracting my gaze. The person who boasts that he is indifferent to them is undoubtedly the most heavily influenced, albeit unconsciously.

## Exhibitions and Museums

As I continue my daily routine, it may include a visit to some exhibition or museum, be it a collection of great works or of less important ones. Of the many sorts of museums in our day, the art museum or museum of history is not the most important. We need not include a museum of seals on medieval deeds or a lace museum as major components of our image-oriented civilization. They exist, however, and for some of us they are the image that dominates our mind.

Exhibitions are much more aggressive, be they of techniques, navigation, noxious insects, or civil defense. They are composed of explanatory panels, maps, models, projections, and statistics that aim to instruct people pleasantly about fascinating things to learn. As in the case of textbooks, however, the exhibition teaches through images, through the special magic of forms. Such knowledge is intuitive and not reasoned; it causes us to grasp in a glance the totality of a reality.

A few years ago we might have thought that such cultural and educational efforts would remain rather limited. How many French people went to see the urban exhibition? But the Beaubourg Museum changed everything in France! Here we see the triumph and glorification of image, spectacle, and culture through representation. In the cultural universe of the Beaubourg, everything is dedicated to the visual domain; everything is shown (its enormous library is only a joke in comparison with the miles of images, and in any case books with pictures are the big attraction!). At the Beaubourg we witness a concentration of the methods, objectives, expectations, and realizations of the image-oriented civilization, with images of and about everything. A million visitors receive a configuration of the world they live in through this multiple exposure to images. They are taught the development of their society by images, photos, prototypes, drawings, sketches, diagrams, and slides. The result is a more frantic attachment than ever to reality—reality without truth. Beaubourg has raised the ex-position (absence of reality through presentation of this same reality) to its zenith.

## Films

Films present us with a different problem. In this case we have before us the debauchery of images—the deluge which crashes down on a person once, often twice, a week. There is no longer any doubt about their effect: psychologists and medical doctors agree that films do not leave a person intact. The emotional shock is too powerful, but not just in the story that is told: even the atmosphere in the theater, the collective darkness which leaves each person in the crowd solitary and caught up in the hypnotic light of the screen. It is common for biological as well as psychological modifications to take place during the viewing of a film: rapid pulse, changes in facial expression, which becomes ecstatic and at the same time weary and satiated.

The impact of these images continues well beyond the few hours of film viewing. Taking advantage of the relaxation in mental tension, self-control over one's feelings and emotions becomes less effective during darkness: a kind of giving up of oneself to "things as they are" takes place as the impact of images reaches its maximum. Not only the thoughts and body but the entire being of a person participates in the emotion stirred up by the film, which possesses a power previously unmatched by any other means.

The film viewer is placed in a state of emotional accessibility that opens him wide to influences, forms, and myths. Because of the images that draw him into the story, he is liberated from the restraint usually placed on some of his instincts. He projects his personal desires onto the world, because these desires wear the mask of everyday emotions. Since this situation occurs repeatedly, its effects are long-lasting. Frequent film watching creates a new personality and leads to a kind of addiction while at the same time aggravating internal lack of balance in the imagination or emotions. Obviously every frequent film-goer is not thus poisoned, but his personality is modified by the world of images whose company he keeps, as they superimpose themselves on the real world.

## Television

Film images are perhaps only encountered once a week. But they are augmented, reinforced, and accentuated by the daily images of television or the newspaper. The absolute image thus becomes familiar, brought down to the level of family and private life by television. We actually live with a continual play acted out before us; our home becomes nothing but scenery. An imaginary mutation takes place that is continually renewed and that erases and takes the shine off reality. A screen of images is placed between me and my world—a circle of images that become so much truer than my own life I cannot rid myself of them. Television is the supremely powerful drug. I end up living my existence before the very thing that eliminates me.[5]

### Newspapers, Magazines, and Comic Books

I also have my daily newspaper—illustrated, of course! Its photographs give me the feeling that I have a better grasp on reality itself.

---

5. Here, then, I find myself disagreeing with McLuhan. His theory about television is certainly extremely attractive, but must be deeply modified in order to introduce certain nuances. When he says that television does not give us images, but rather arouses sensations, that it uses the eye like an ear and destroys our reading habits, he gives us a strange mixture of correct insights and paradoxes. It is true that television destroys our reading habits, because reading has recourse to the sequence of *spoken language*, whereas television addresses itself to the universalizing and instantaneous visual sense.

But how can he say that television does not give us images? I am well acquainted with McLuhan's arguments, and possibly he could be right in the realm of the unconscious. The construction of a puzzle made up of lighted dots, which *we* make into an image, may have a profound influence on us. Here I completely agree with him. But an image is received and perceived. This image belongs precisely to the visual domain. McLuhan can say what he chooses, but when I close my eyes, I do not see what is on the screen! The eye functions as an eye. McLuhan can say that television makes the eye function as an ear because it produces something instantaneous and all-inclusive (in which sight is considered sequential and sound is seen as instantaneous) only by building on his previous hypothesis.

This previous hypothesis, however, I reject as inaccurate. With television I perceive an image that is differently made but which presents all the characteristics that images have always had (except for written language!): they are instantaneous, universal, *and* composed of dots! Look at a landscape: you have an overall view, an instantaneous impression which arises from the thousands of details which are present (as on the screen). But you do not "see" each detail! And if you stop looking, you do not find these details in your memory. Only by looking in detail would you perceive one detail, then another, and another. In the case of the image on television, you cannot perceive the details, because they disappear too fast. But how can anyone say that a pointillistic painting, made up of thousands of little spots, is not an image! In reality, television limits itself to reinforcing the world of images and challenges the logic of language! I am tempted to reverse McLuhan's statement to say that, for example, in modern music, the globalization of sounds and the artificial creation of an "acoustic bubble" make the ear function like an eye!

Is there anyone who has not had a slight feeling of frustration in reading a serious paper, such as *Le Monde*, without illustrations, or when the pictures in another paper are not clear? The readership of a million reached by the great weekly magazines shows that photographs, with their minuscule, useless, and absurd captions, are a necessity for modern people. These are admirable examples of an entire text which is little by little transformed into images, where the ideal is a story with no words.

This is the sort of story that obviously suits the contemporary individual best. He has, moreover, an extraordinary capacity for grasping even the most subtle meaning of images, whereas perfectly clear words seem foreign to him. What great shrewdness is required, on the other hand, to grasp at a glance the meaning of a surrealist poster, a baroque advertising film, or even those strange comic strips.

Comic strips are filled with allusions, asides to the reader, and details that must be noticed. The reader engages in interpreting these details without effort, grasping the meaning of the frozen pantomime. He plunges into this ridiculous, subhuman fiction—which every newspaper must now include. This is an indisputable need that testifies to the remarkable training and capacity to deal with images that modern people have acquired.

## Photographs

The image not only is offered to me—it assails me. The image I make or produce also affects me, inserting me forcefully into the incessant stream of image production. Just think for a moment about photographs—souvenirs from a trip. On my trip, I receive impressions—especially visual ones, but also overall impressions. These may include the atmosphere or phenomenology of a place, an impression that must be felt! This presupposes an enlarging of my capacity, an availability of the most flexible sort: I must perceive the largest possible number of impressions.

On the other hand, I must also "integrate" and assimilate this scene and these impressions—an unexpected, surprising, and gripping experience. Obviously then, two possible directions present themselves: one based on memory alone, involving the remembering of names and places, spectacles and meetings; the other involving assimilation; that is, making the experience of this encounter with reality an integral part of me, on both the intellectual and the human level. In the latter case I do not stop with superficial memory but appropriate (through reflection, comparison, and intellectual organization) new things into the mosaic of my existence. This requires that I offer myself to the new reality that is becoming part of me, whether a deep experience of nature or of a human milieu.

Only under such conditions can a trip become the source of a meeting between the order of truth and the order of reality. But these conditions go far beyond mere "recollection." The simple fact that I carry a camera prevents me from grasping everything in an overall perception. Even more, it keeps me from proceeding to cultural assimilation, because these two steps can be taken only in a state of availability and lack of preoccupation with other matters—a state of "being there." Both perception and assimilation must take place in continuity and in the immediate present. Assimilation cannot happen several hours afterward or later on in the evening. It must be at the moment when the impact of the new reality thrusts itself on me.

When a person is concerned with taking pictures, however, he worries about the choice of scene to be preserved (an option that separates out one piece to be remembered from the overall scene). Thus we become locked entirely into the visual problem alone. We abandon any effort at overall impression; what might have been an authentic experience is reduced to mere spectacle. Furthermore, even if you are a specialist, you become preoccupied with manipulating and fussing with the camera; the lighting and the search for the best angle lock you into a technical exercise that radically blocks out any intellectual process or reflection, the offering of yourself to the wind, the sea, or the flow of people. Even more, these concerns prevent the surging of deep exaltation in the presence of something unique; if you are a Christian, you are prevented from thanking God. No, the camera is in command. You no longer really see anything; you look at and hunt for what you are going to photograph.

When the picture is finally taken, notice that all travelers suddenly lose interest in everything else: the job to be done has been taken care of. What else could they possibly do in the midst of the ruins of the Parthenon? Suddenly they wonder what they are doing there. Once the memory has been frozen on film, they are suddenly bored. The picture diminishes enormously the experience of a trip; it externalizes it, prevents internalization, and concentrates everything on the "visual souvenir."

Looking at the picture later recalls "memories": a certain gesture or word spoken. That is all there is. It recalls no deep perception. This is obvious when one listens to the talk and conversation of people who show slides of their trips. Everything is reduced to superficialities. Just as the process of picture taking hacked off one piece of the overall reality that was to be lived, in the same way the picture, once shown, obliterates the living memory.

Memory is a part of my total life. It appears and disappears, depending on the transcription of a whole world which I have assimilated and which is part of me. It is not just a product of memorization, but a progression dependent on the basis of my relationship with the reality integrated into my culture and my total experience of life. Every memory is like a many-sided and multicolored cube in an enormous mosaic.

Pictures prohibit this movement and this return. They deal with the "picturesque," which will always be the most superficial. Here sensitivity is directed to a spectacular view and nothing else. And seeing it again causes the rebirth of false memories that are purely superficial and utterly useless. Such pictures serve no good purpose.

I can just hear the angry shouts: "You know perfectly well that you forget! Pictures serve to remind you . . . without pictures, you will forget that you went to . . . , that you saw the mural of *La Parisienne* at. . . ." What an enormous error! What *deserves* to be remembered—whatever has been lived deeply—is engraved in my being and in my memory. It changed me and made me a new person.

What about all the things I've forgotten? For it is certainly true that I have forgotten thousands of places, faces, and paintings. The things I've forgotten are simply those that meant nothing to me, those I did not live, which were just empty curiosities that remained foreign to me. They offered me nothing of value, no truth. In this case, what good is it to preserve such things on scraps of paper? I was dumbfounded by the mountains on the horizon. What picture could do anything for me? And if all I saw was a spectacle, why bother to remember it? Pictures are just an effort to prove that we really went somewhere!—that we really made the trip.

Here we have reached an essential aspect of images: in the modern identity crisis, in the midst of technical change and dispersion, images give us some certainty that we exist. Pictures assure us of our past; leafing through a picture album makes me certain that I have lived. The picture becomes the substitute for something living, just as images always do. It is the elimination of the personal and existential relationship with the world, cutting oneself off from the milieu, from other people. And it is the means of not being subject to the impact of anything new. It is also the dreamed-of substitute in terms of a false, frozen reality that takes the place of the inability to face life.

This is very symptomatic of technique: it prevents us from living but gives us the strong impression that we are living, assuring us that we are really alive! "After all," they say, "look at these faces; look at your friends. Freeze that happy, marvelous moment: the child playing, the child looking up at you. Rediscover the faces of your dear departed ones. . . ." What a lie. Either you loved them and their faces are engraved in you, woven into your thought, your worldview, and your daily experience, or you did not love them. In that case, what good are pictures? What good is it to hang on to these faces from a given moment, these expressions on shiny paper or film, if you do not have their absence burning within you?

Their absence is neither filled up nor ensured by looking at this picture. No, let's not have pictures of dear ones who are no longer with us. We should say with the poet (whose name I won't mention, since he isn't in fashion!): "Since the game is over, put down the cards; throw them away." The picture of these faces is a lie I tell myself, believing that I cared about these people, whereas no trace of them is left in me. It is another lie based on something visual: an image. What could you *say* about these people you loved? What language would be appropriate? What truth did you live because of them? What did you go through together? What of that remains with you? If you remain silent, the picture is nothing but an illusion. And if you can talk about these things, the picture should be thrown away.

"Still," you say, "photography is an art, and I can make a work of art. . . ." Certainly, certainly! I do not deny at all that people can take very beautiful pictures. But in this case we leave the subject of ordinary pictures. If I take a trip in order to take beautiful pictures, or if I photograph a face in order to produce an artistic portrait, that is a different goal and another objective. In that case I am not traveling for the trip itself, nor am I cultivating a memory. I do not take exception to the existence of photographic art but to the practice of photography by the millions who own a Kodak. In any case the ambiguity remains, and all I have said above remains valid. Even the best pictures belong to this universe of images that supplants reality itself and makes us live on a reflected and re-reflected visual plane which prevents us doubly from having access to the word.

## Liturgies: Political and Religious

It is impossible for us to go through the entire range of images. But we can hardly avoid dealing with the vivid image formed by the living picture of great liturgy. As we will see, the Church discovered the importance of things visual in order to incorporate the individual through a collective process. But we have gone well beyond those first efforts, necessarily limited, that were still restrained by the common reference to transcendent truth. The liturgical image, limited to symbolism, was only the sign of something inaccessible. We have changed all that: God is dead, and with him any notion of transcendence and truth (or more accurately, we make our own truth now). Thus we can profitably proceed to an integrating visual and bodily liturgy that knows no bounds.

Benito Mussolini inaugurated the new totalitarian liturgy, but Hitler became its great conductor. Everything visual conspired to annihilate the individual and integrate him into the whole. This included huge gatherings minutely orchestrated as to rhythm and pauses, with processions and endless parades characterized by precisely calculated movements. These great liturgical productions expressed power—at long last *visible*. And of course, since plainly visible, they had to be true. The entire nation was symbolized. Anything excluded was reduced to dust—something to sweep off the surface of the globe or scatter to the winds.

The grandiose vision obliterated objections just as it eliminated people. The image reduces truth to reality—or more precisely, this all-encompassing liturgical reality lends to any word at all the overtone of truth. The Führer's absurd, incoherent speeches could only be received as absolute Truth in the midst of the great display of huge processions and flags. Yet our world was affected decisively by those liturgies.

Of course, this triumph of images in political liturgy is only one facet of the image-oriented civilization. What Hitler created was dependent on the generalized promotion of images. The Nazi liturgies produced such a profound effect because they were perfectly integrated into this process of our civilization. At the same time, images developed and strengthened this process, giving it a new form of expression.

Exactly the same phenomenon occurs in the mass gatherings. They have the same function but are less rigorous, with everything appearing disordered and spontaneous. Strikers' parades and China's Cultural Revolution are accepted as the expression of the people themselves. How simplistic! We have only to recall the degree to which the movements of the Cultural Revolution were regulated like a ballet,[6] or to note the repression which still swoops down in China on any spontaneous movement (for example, the shooting of Tien An-Men), and to admire the amazing precision of the crowd's movements in Chinese mass celebrations. Obviously, in these events everything is spectacle, and the liturgy causes the individual to disappear in a new reality. But the Communist Party and the Communist Unions' parades are also spectacles: these tens, hundreds, and thousands of workers who move in formation with so much discipline, flanked by those who keep order. These processions are intended to demonstrate the power of the masses but in reality they expose only their passivity.

---

6. See the analysis of China's Cultural Revolution in my *De la révolution aux révoltes* (Paris: Calmann-Lévy, 1972).

Meetings, demonstrations, parades, and processions are multiplied indefinitely for all occasions. They are part of our world of images. They are as necessary to political life as is traditional liturgy to the Catholic mass. As with all liturgies, these demonstrations substitute for the poverty of word, speech, and thought.

You can say anything in a meeting. It doesn't matter. Content doesn't exist. The word becomes mere stimulus meant to reinforce unanimity. People applaud and boo when they are supposed to—at just the right moment. They are taken up with a purely visual spectacle in which the word has no meaning and no weight. The word only provides opportunity for another visual expression. Fists are raised, hands applaud. The spectacle is sufficient unto itself, as each person views himself. Liturgy, be it religious, fascist, Maoist, or popular, is a decisive manifestation of our permanent drive to reduce truth to reality by means of symbols. The technique for such integration is the image, which manifests the totality of existence in an atemporal moment and leaves us overwhelmed by an impression of power and permanence.

## Omnipresence of Images

The omnipresence of images, however, is not an accidental, sporadic, changeable fact. We are dealing instead with an almost total milieu in which all of existence unfolds more or less smoothly. Truly it is a *universe* of images in the midst of which we are set as spectators. Our eyes' function has been extraordinarily expanded. Our brain is constantly receiving the impact of imaginary sights and no longer of reality. Today we can no longer live without the reference and diversion provided by images. For a large proportion of our lives we live as mere spectators. Until the present time our perception of reality through sight incited us to action. But now the superficial spectacle imposes itself on us all day long, turning us into passive recorders of images. This multiplication of images comes together in such a tight weave that we are hopelessly hemmed in, and everyone feels a need for images. These factors make it plain that we are not dealing here with chance but with a precise progression.

Images are the chosen form of expression in our civilization—images, not words.[7] For though our era speaks, and abounds in

7. It is utterly surprising that Goux interprets abstract painting (Wassily Kandinsky, Pieter Mondrian, Kazimir Malevich, etc.) as a spiritual turning point that coincides with the prohibition of making images. Painters rediscover the spiritual authenticity of revelation and are considered prophets of the messianic world to come. Unfortunately, Goux pays no attention to the technological system and abstract painting's place *within* this system. Only by verbal acrobatics and intuitive flashes of insight can he assert the oneness of the empty temple and abstract painting (which is certainly also *empty!* ).

printed paper, so that written thought has never been as widespread as today, still there is a strange movement that deprives the word of its importance. Talk and newspapers are like word mills to which no one attaches any importance anymore. Who would still consider a book as something decisive and capable of changing his life, when there are so many of them? And a person's word, buried under the floods of millions of people's words, no longer has any meaning or outreach. The word has no importance for any listener because it is broadcast in millions of instances over thousands of miles.

A casual glance at newspaper headlines (which are, moreover, not sentences or reasonable thoughts to the person who depends on them) produces an image brutally engraved on the memory. One need not read the article in order to become acquainted with its content or to pick up a piece of information or reasoning. The headline's expression evokes a series of stereotypes that are more than sufficient to confirm and reassure a person. The news item becomes part of the collection of images that serve to feed our opinion, which is at the same time both stable and fragile.

Here we are on the verge of slogans. In slogans, words are completely stripped of their reasonable and meaningful content. All oral propaganda rests on the fact that language loses its meaning and retains only the power of inciting and triggering. The word has become mere sound: pure nervous excitation, to which people respond by reflex, or because of group pressure. If a speaker fails to make use of the magic words which automatically stir up hatreds, passions, mobs, devotion, and curses, the rest of his language dissolves, as far as his listeners are concerned, into a gush of lava, an overflow of monotony, a contemptible fog that prevents or smothers action. The word thus loses its power.

The multiplicity of images creates a strange new universe. The multiplicity of words has emptied them of their content and value. We avoid and scorn people who are always talking. In our age of technique, we know the vanity of the word. "Enough words; let's have actions." Each of us, at one time or another, has spoken these words when he was exasperated with useless repetition. Images are the language of action. But our being transformed into spectators radically changes the effect of images. The sight of reality normally moves us to action, and images are usually the language of action. But our being transformed into spectators paralyzes us for any possible action.

## 2. UTILITY

Sight triumphs because it is useful. The deluge of artificial, superabundant images creates a new world environment. Sight saves us the trouble of thinking and having to remember. It lets us live on the basis of representation and substitution. It reinforces a group's cohesiveness. The word divides, whereas images (when consciously organized) unite, as for example in liturgy.

Artificial images provide another example of that movement so often described in which, as discoveries take place, we assign to some mechanism or other a quality which was a part of our human uniqueness. The most extreme example is the computer, which is even called on to "think" in our place. Because I have my photograph album I no longer need remember. I no longer need the slow process of reflection, since I function on the basis of evidence. I no longer need to search so hard for ways of living in community, because communion is established by the image's all-encompassing identity. Techniques replace me in a growing number of activities, and the universe of images to which I belong facilitates this substitution to an incredible degree.

Images are indispensable for the construction of the technological society. If we remained at the stage of verbal dialogue, inevitably we would be led to critical reflection. But images exclude criticism. The habit of living in this image-oriented world leads me to give up dialectical thought and criticism. It is so much easier to give up and let myself be carried along by the continually renewed wave of images. They provide me from moment to moment with exactly the amount of stimulus I need. They give me the emotional level (the anger, the tender feelings, and the degree of interest) that I can tolerate and find indispensable in this gray world. Images are essential if I am to avoid seeing the day-to-day reality I live in. They glitter continuously around me, allowing me to live in a sort of image-oriented fantasy.

Images are also indispensable as a form of compensation. The word would only increase my anxiety and uncertainty. It would make me more conscious of my emptiness, my impotence, and the insignificance of my situation. With images, however, everything unpleasant is erased and my drab existence decorated by their charm and sparkle.

Above all, I must not become aware of reality, so images create a substitute reality. The word obliges me to consider reality from the point of view of truth. Artificial images, passing themselves off for truth, obliterate and erase the reality of my life and my society. They allow me to enter an image-filled reality that is much more thrilling. Even television news, when it deals with catastrophes, disasters, and crises, takes the drama out of them by making them extraordinary and thrilling—by literally converting them into something metaphysical. The more terrible the spectacle, the calmer the hypnosis of the images makes me.

The most violent film about politics, or one that denounces the worst atrocities, is in reality a means of accepting the situation. The film by itself allows me a clear conscience because I have participated in the denunciation as a spectator. As far back as 1937, with no theoretical analysis, I denounced the "pacifist" film *All Quiet on the Western Front*. It was based on Erich Maria Remarque's novel, but the images utterly reversed the meaning of what was written! I criticized the film for eliminating people's willingness to fight war, because it would actually prepare public opinion to accept war. The magic of images makes me satisfied with such a vicarious life. Even if something concrete were to indicate the opposite, I would not notice. This is the main usefulness of the continually renewed flood of images.

There is, of course, no Machiavellianism or hidden motive in this elimination through images. Only under very exceptional circumstances would an especially clever tyrant try to use all the image's possibilities. And such an effort never succeeds for very long. On the contrary, the insidious flow that gums up our thinking and our existence occurs apart from anyone's intent and without any goal in mind. It simply exists, because teachers wax enthusiastic in good faith over the efficiency of audiovisual methods, because publicity agents try in good faith to sell a product (obviously useful!), because film directors and photographers aspire in good faith to produce a work of genius, because journalists try in good faith to present their information in the best possible manner, and because television producers accept in good faith their triple mission: "amuse, inform, educate." I am not aware of any big capitalists making shady calculations in order to alienate further the poor citizenry. Nor are there plotters of collective feeblemindedness, nor perverse statesmen who use images to conceal their actions.

Some will say my analysis is deficient, I realize, since I have said nothing about some people's deep motivation through "vile capitalism" or through "the evil empire of communism." I think, however, that those who swallow those fine expressions are themselves simply victims of a fairy tale based on images and possessing only the evidence that sight gives. In this case as well, images have been substituted for the rigor of language. Images finally become like lightning, attacking us from all directions, simply because technicians involved in the use of images do the best possible job, in good faith, without asking more basic questions. The only question they ask has to do with finding something new to show—something that will be in every way useful. Let's examine the problem more closely.

\* \* \* \* \* \*

The image certainly is first of all a means of knowledge. Illustrations in textbooks probably enable children to picture better to themselves the matter at hand. Obviously, you can describe at length Michelangelo's style or the kind of life serfs led in the Middle Ages, but children will have a much more authentic impression if they see a reproduction of the Moses statue or a picture of the medallions of the cathedral at Amiens. Why describe the clothing, the work methods, and the tools, when the children are looking at them? What is true for history obviously holds equally true for physics, chemistry, biology, etc.

More strangely, illustrations also invade domains that normally would not seem to be dependent on images: literature, Latin, and philosophy, for example. In such areas an effort is made to help students understand by external means, such as pictures of people, places, and graphic materials. Thus they learn about an author's environment, which may have determined his thought or style (if you believe that these imponderables are precisely determined by the environment, that physical conditioning is decisive, and that such pictures have explanatory value for someone to whom a given environment is foreign). True or not, this presupposition shows itself correct with respect to children in our day, and this type of illustration responds to their need for something concrete. It satisfies something that a dry reading of the text would not fulfill.

But there is more! Even Latin and Greek dictionaries are illustrated. It is no longer enough to give the possible meanings of a word; we must also have it visually represented. This is superfluous. We learned Latin perfectly well without illustrations. But significantly, dictionaries followed the fashion. This shows the concern for concrete things dominating our educational practice. We must give children a precise view of things, so that words not be emptied of the objects they represent. We must not simply substitute one abstract term for another but use images to show that ancient or modern languages are alive. But such things are not done on the basis of mere theoretical concern! Scientific pedagogues did not discover the importance of images, and I am inclined to suspect that this theory of concrete pedagogy is only an intellectual explanation undergirding the sudden awareness of the need for images.

We will discuss later whether there is not really a sort of modern collective need for representation and reproduction, of which children and textbooks would be only a case in point. But we can already state with confidence that today's students could not possibly study the complicated, ugly books with small print and no illustrations like the ones used half a century ago. True, children became bored learning from such books. But let us not delude ourselves: today's children are every bit as bored, but it would be utterly impossible for them to learn from the old books. The clarity of the pages—the margins and white spaces—and the excellent appearance remove some of the boredom in themselves and give a varied and interesting appearance to a book. But only the illustrations manage to rivet modern children's flagging attention, which tires so quickly.

Today it is almost impossible for a child—but also for an adult—to fix his attention on something besides images. If a person wants to teach or to make something known in our day, he must, without reserve, represent it: express it in a picture, a diagram, or a reproduction. Oral explanations overwhelm and tire the listener; words no longer hold people's attention or their interest. Knowledge today is expressed through images.

This is also true at a completely different level: in almost all areas of thought we have introduced diagrams, curves, and graphic and statistical representation. It seems normal to use maps and cross sections in geology and geography, since these are real objects that are only simplified, diagrammed, and made more easily understood; such representation is only consistent with the subject matter. Cross sections in anatomy, static images of muscles, the blood vessels, or the nervous system, the skeleton in detachable sections, anatomical models that can be opened on several levels, and even the glass model of a human being that shows the circulation of the blood in a dynamic manner—all these are of the same order as the images we have mentioned in geology and geography.

More significant is the use of such aids in the more abstract sciences, or in those close to being abstract. In biology we can effectively move from one of the representations we mentioned to the image of a mechanism that is not directly accessible. We can, for example, grasp the very reality of the inward workings of the heart and brain and then transcribe them in an image that has no sensorial relationship with this reality. In this case an entire process that abstracts the reality of the movement takes place, and then this abstraction is retranscribed in a visible, understandable diagram that authentically expresses the reality. The electrocardiogram and the encephalogram are examples of this process. It is remarkable that just the visible image of the curve enables us not to imagine but to grasp an object that cannot be grasped in its concrete existence.

This leads us to more abstract examples. The process is the same in economics: verbal expression can certainly deal with and explain economic life. But at what a price, in terms of time, effort, and concern to find the precise word. This is so true that in economics, as in every science, the specialist is obliged to invent new words, because the traditional vocabulary does not define newly observed phenomena with sufficient precision. And after all this effort the expert realizes that what has been said is not exact and that his listeners have not carefully followed his long argument. On the contrary, how easy it is to use statistics and to draw curves based on them. Statistical curves are the images that translate economic life with its interrelationships and the evolution of a system (or a part of one) in a visual, sensory, and direct manner. Why bother to make the effort to say again in words what can be grasped through statistical curves?

We find the same pattern in sociology, where the need for images has also led to the use of curves for representing matters that could be expressed mathematically. And linguistics? Semiotic diagrams enable us to see structures. Furthermore, we should note that the process in linguistics is the same as in biology: graphic representation is the result of a process of abstracting from reality: the mathematical reasoning applied to a social body is an abstraction that then enables us to construct a graphic image. Only this image can speak to our minds. But sociology does not stop at this point. Sociograms, describing groups and interpersonal relationships within groups by means of a diagram, are just as indicative of the importance of visual means. Organizational charts, directly related to sociograms, also describe (by means of a diagram) the organization of a state, a party, a business, etc. They enable us to express not only structures but also dynamic relationships and the internal movements of the different organs. Such charts can be used in political science as well as in sociology.

Finally, the same principle enables us to reconstruct movements and relationships by the image of the psychogram in the most intimate domain of psychology. There is now no area of knowledge that escapes this tendency. This is perhaps because knowledge is becoming scientific everywhere. But it is also certainly because visual knowledge today is much more adapted to our thought patterns. Images are a true means of knowledge and the essential means of its expression. Furthermore, we must grant that in many areas of the exact sciences there is no competition between language and representation because language has become not just useless but simply impossible. Often it is impossible scientifically and technically to express discoveries made through calculation by means of words. It is generally useless to try to describe a physics experiment orally. It is utterly useless to try to explain how a radio functions by means of words. Only the diagram is expressive and comprehensible, consistent with the object.

At this stage, we are no longer dealing with rivalry between image and word; we have excluded the word. This is not the most frequent case, however; usually a verbal description is possible. But in reality we observe the image's victory over explanation in each instance. It is useless to talk at length when the diagram speaks directly and captivates.

The word *discourse* itself contains part of the explanation of this tendency. Discourse implies a long process: an indirect approach and a kind of winding movement involving successive approximations that irritate lazy modern people. Visual representation is the easy, efficient, quick path. It allows us to grasp a totality in a single glance, without any need to break up a thing and to analyze it. Explanation and precise formulation are no longer necessary when a person has been able to grasp all at once what the issue is. It is much easier to let oneself be captivated or impressed by an image than to follow an oral demonstration. It is easier not only intellectually, but we could almost say it is easier because of our temperament: a line of reasoning or a demonstration are efficacious only if they are in accord with the person who listens to them. The rigor of spoken thought must find its counterpart in a similar rigor in the listener. In order for the word to become truly demonstrative, a kind of asceticism and interior discipline are required. These cannot be acquired all at once.

The image, on the other hand, contains its rigor and its constraining force within itself. There is no need for it to find a corresponding human quality in the spectator; the rigor is transferred from the person to the object, with great ease, tranquillity, and economy! In this age of usefulness and efficiency, when we all have so much to learn and know, when progress keeps gathering speed and we are quite obligated to follow it, how could we lose time accommodating ourselves to the slow learning process involved in discourse? Just learning the indispensable skills for reading and understanding images is overwhelming enough. Why should we exhaust ourselves over an asceticism that can easily be substituted by the perfectly objective image which purely intellectual qualities (in the case of scientific images) allow us to accept?

Images have such practical usefulness: they enable us to save time and energy. No reasonable arguments can be advanced against this certitude. Images enable us to have an overall view of a fact or situation or even of reality. No verbal description enables us to understand or feel a landscape like a well-taken photograph. No spectator's testimony gives us an overall understanding of what happened in a demonstration the way a film can. Pictures furnish us the framework, the action, the actors, and the expressions, simultaneously. They give us a genuinely total *knowledge*, whose superiority over all other types of knowledge is well known. The word, however, is exceedingly poor, since it hacks reality up into isolated fragments; the phrase is so doubtful, since it depends on the person who said it; discourse is unreliable, since we must amass time and verbal constructions in order to express—always in an incomplete manner—the reality which an image gives us instantaneously.

It is perhaps significant that this synthetic knowledge has been introduced even into reading methods. In the word-recognition method of learning to read, children are taught to consider a word as a whole, like a picture. This enables them to recognize it immediately, like the picture of a house or a table. In this way it is no longer necessary to decompose words into syllables or letters. No analysis or detour through the genuine difficulty of linking letters together, which involves intellectual gymnastics. When words are reduced to the status of designs or ideograms, they surface without making any detour and without explanation in one's consciousness. They evoke what they stand for by means of direct perception. This mechanism is obviously very different from the one used in normal reading; it makes an image of the words themselves!

But visual representation permits not only synthetic knowledge; it also allows us to understand quickly. It leads us as spectators directly to a result: the image in itself furnishes a result. There is no need to follow a process or reasoned argument step by step, since it is entirely contained within the final image to which the process would lead. And the final image is the only thing that matters. Even when we look at a statistical curve, it is obvious on the one hand that we do not need to calculate the figures that made the drawing of the curve possible (unless we disagree or want to learn to draw a curve). On the other hand, it is clear that we can see in a glance the line of the curve and the result of its entire movement. We can go immediately to the last part of the curve, which indicates "the latest stage in current economics." It is obvious that an explanation does not furnish a result as simply and directly as the result of this continuous movement of the eyes. Images are the royal path to modern knowledge.

*   *   *   *   *   *

Another way images are useful shows the degree to which representation has made a decisive impact on our modern consciousness. In just about everyone's thinking today, images are considered to be proof of what they represent. You have only to see a photograph to be convinced of the reality and exactness of its subject. A photograph in itself is indisputable proof; it is a basic "given" that cannot be questioned. This common feeling is absurd. When we reflect, we know that films and photographs can be amazingly reworked and modified. Even when not doctored they can be misleading.

To mention a few well-known facts, take the problem of reproductions of paintings and statues. Everyone has been surprised by an original utterly different from its reproductions—and not only when the reproduction is not faithful to the original. It may be too detailed: one has only to change the size of a painting or isolate some detail, such as a rose from one of Velasquez's portraits. Such a rose is not even noticed when one looks at the painting as a whole. The same may be said of a crooked branch against the background of a green sky, taken from the altarpiece at Issenheim. These details truly exist, but they are not noticed, and they definitely do not have the importance that a clever reproduction gives them. In these cases the reality of the painting is not transmitted; instead, another reality has been created—a different reality, because the isolation of a detail intended to blend into the whole changes the "text" of the painting.

This effect is perhaps even more noticeable in the case of pictures of sculpture. Thanks to the consummate science of lighting, angles of vision, and framing, a photographer may choose the position and the unique moment in which a statue will take on a living form and a depth that moves the spectator. But a person observing the statue itself can never rediscover the harmony of forms which a single position made possible, nor the brilliance of the harmoniously placed blacks and whites. The spectator is disappointed by the banality of the statue, which had looked like a masterpiece in reproduction. In this case we have a genuinely artificial creation.

The same thing is true of landscapes. In front of my house we have a small, rather muddy pond. A clever photographer recently made it into both a genuine canyon and a radiant lagoon with a blue cast that was probably authentic, since it was a photograph, but which I had never seen!

If we go to the other extreme, moving to politics instead of esthetics, we find the same thing. Does anyone still remember the pictures of the massacre at Katynka, of the pits containing the bodies of Polish officers? They were presented as massacred by Hitler's troops or by the Soviets, with equal plausibility, and were used as propaganda by both sides. And consider the pictures of prisoners tortured in the Belgian Congo in 1961, which were presented as massacres carried out by the Belgians, by the partisans, or by Patrice Lumumba's adversaries, and considered obvious "proof" in each case.

Let us recall two cases in more detail. Who remembers the story of the pictures in *l'Express* magazine in 1956? Alongside Jean-Jacques Servan-Schreiber's series of reports on Algeria, quite violent in tone concerning the authorities, were pictures taken in Algeria. These showed Arabs or scenes from the war, but without captions. As was usual in *l'Express* of that period, there were allusions to the pictures in the story that led the reader to think that these pictures were "documents," and that they were sufficient in themselves as representations of the facts mentioned in the story. Then the Foreign Ministry, questioning Servan-Schreiber's story, showed that these pictures had no relation whatever with the facts related. They had been taken in other places, at other times. They were not "documents," but "illustrations," as the magazine's editors hastily explained. This scandalized public opinion to a very large degree and filled readers with suspicion. The Ministry's exposé was considerably appreciated, since the public does not tolerate photographs as illustrations. They are perceived as fact—as unimpeachable witnesses. The photograph's power of evocation should not be capable of deception.

Let us recall another typical event: in 1954, the wife of a Soviet diplomat in Australia, Mrs. Petrov, was said to have refused to return to the Soviet Union. Then she was supposed to have been arrested in Australia by two Kremlin agents, and when about to be taken away by force, she was said to have been delivered by the Australian authorities. This is how the Australian press told the story, and it was repeated in the English, American, and French presses. In Russia, the facts were different: Mrs. Petrov wanted to return to Russia, but she was arrested and held prisoner by the Australian police. The same photograph illustrated these two contradictory stories, in each case in order to make the story unquestionable and authentic. This picture published by the *Manchester Guardian* was evidence that the Australian police had delivered Mrs. Petrov from the seizure of the Soviets. Exactly the same picture was published by the Polish newspaper *Swiat* as just as much evidence that the Australian police were arresting Mrs. Petrov when she was going to get on the plane.

All these little examples are well known. It is common knowledge that film can be altered and that edited films can have a very different meaning, depending on how they are edited. We also know that the same picture can spontaneously serve as evidence for utterly different things to spectators who have differing prejudices. No caption is needed for the English reader and the Polish reader to give Mrs. Petrov's picture the necessary interpretation. *Life* magazine occasionally gives us the picture of a glowing young woman, bursting with health, laughing, athletic, and hale. She suggests real American life, which is wholesome and produces a balanced youth that is joyful, confident in the future, and a symbol of the excellence of democracy, fair play, and liberalism. But exactly the same kind of young woman— same teeth and hair, engaging smile expressing the same joy—was occasionally pictured for us in the Nazi magazines from 1936 to 1938. There she was a no less obvious symbol of the excellence of National Socialism, the beauty of the Race, and economic statism.

We find these same young women again, always with the same bust and smile, exuberance for life and enjoyment in their work, in the *RDA Review* of East Germany, or in the earliest Soviet magazines. They are symbols just as obviously of the excellence of communism, of the liberated proletariat, and of economic planning. The pictures and their meaning are identical, although the realities are a bit different.

Everyone knows this, and yet everyone continues to believe loyally in his country's photograph, attributing to it value, meaning, and significance. A word always remains the same: its meanings are so "obvious" one need not discuss them or inquire about them; the picture is so symbolic that we understand with certainty the evidence it presents.

We are not skeptical. Photographs always convince us, even though our reason tells us that they may mean nothing. Still . . . still . . . photographs place us in the presence of a fact. We make contact with the fact through sight. The image reconstructs the fact for us, and in its presence we are in the presence of the fact itself. We cannot surmount the old reflex that is inscribed on our nerves, in our deepest subconscious, and which is an expression of the oldest experience of humanity: whatever we see is real. Clear awareness of fake photographs is too recent and too unusual to be able to annihilate this experience that is as old as humanity: our eye has never deceived us about facts. We know through millions of experiences accumulated by our ancestors that the image must correspond to the facts.

We continue to identify pictures with reality, obeying an irresistible automatic reaction. When something forces us to deny this identification, we feel scandalized or ill at ease, and the most we can say is "Who knows?" But this does not happen often. And our theoretical knowledge of this possibility does not alter our spontaneous conviction. In other words, here we are face to face with a fact. Let's not forget that for today's individual a fact is the ultimate reason, the supreme value, and an unimpeachable proof. Everything bows before a fact. We must obey it. We are irrational, idealistic dreamers if we do not trust facts. It is not enough to take facts into account; we also attribute decisive value to them. No justice, truth, or humanity can stand up in the face of a fact. It decides everything.

"History will judge" comes to mean that the facts of our material victory will prove our cause was just. "Moving with history" is the same thing as moving toward the good. And when an opponent can say "It's a fact," that ends the discussion, since there is no possible answer. Our whole society cries out: "Let justice and truth perish, before we will go against the facts."

This collective submission to facts that have been transformed into values and this frenzy of wanting to know nothing but the reality of facts—these attitudes contain within them what we are seeing in our society: the triumph of things material. In this situation how can we be astonished at the decisive power that the images of facts (photographs, films, etc.) have over us? These images are charged with the same authority we attribute to facts: they are genuine proofs and unimpeachable witnesses. For this reason we are obliged to accept everything that underlies them and explains them.

Images not only confront us with facts but also impress us with their currentness. We are always bothered when newspapers print old pictures from their files, on the occasion of the anniversary of some event. These pictures undoubtedly call to mind the reality of the fact, but there is also an imperceptible withdrawal on our part. The same thing happens when we see an old film whose actors we know to be dead. Seeing Louis Jouvet, Jean Renoir, and Raimu again, living and talking, makes us uneasy. This is because we are their contemporaries. We are conditioned by all of human experience. We see neither the past nor the future; we see what is contemporary. And images always give us this feeling of currentness, presence, and immediacy. This impression is further reinforced by films, whose reality it is so difficult to resist, and even more so by television.

With television, we are present when the fact occurs, directly, as if we participated at the same moment in the parade, reception, or game. We are in the room or at the stadium, and we see what makes up events at the moment they take place. This is true even if we are actually seeing a televised film of something that happened a few days before. We may not be aware of this (we would have to be up on everything, and we are not). And even if we know it, how can we avoid being impressed by the direct authenticity of the scene before us? We are not indifferent and disciplined enough to resist being carried away by this presence. I especially distrust those who say they do not get carried away by this influence. Such people are just embarrassed by their fragility.

While images are giving us a feeling of something happening as we look on, they also give us a strong feeling of objectivity. At this point we react as modern people who have learned to distinguish clearly between the subjectivity of a person (which we must guard against) and the objectivity of the camera (in which we must have confidence). The camera does not interpret; there is no strange alchemy inside it as there is within the human brain, transforming facts into living matter, and risking the conversion of reality into truth or error. On the contrary, the camera gives us the fact it has absorbed. We have a brute fact when the camera gives us a fact it has recorded. This fact will always be the same; it is immutable. If we look at the film a hundred times, it will always give us the same scene and the same gesture. We are tempted to say that they are raised to the level of eternity by repetition. But for the spectator they are reduced to the level of the continual present.

The camera is unimpeachable in its undistortable objectivity. For our modern temperament, however, all description and reasoning are tainted with subjectivity, hence doubtful and suspect. Wherever people might be involved, error and falsehood slip in. But the camera is "honest," and gives us a fact through its image. This same problem of human error leads to the use of images in social and political science. No human reflection and observation, even the most accurate, can convince people today. Anything human is considered negligible. But statistical documents, curves, and graphics are convincing—especially if it has been possible to produce them by machine.

We easily forget that the machine is operated by a person, that it records only those facts someone considers important. This fact cannot destroy our blind faith in the machine's objectivity. When made aware of the human role in the machine's operation, we immediately deplore the fact that such a mediocre troublemaker comes along to disturb such majestic mechanical serenity.

In any case, our spontaneous impulse is to trust images produced by something "objective." We are strongly inclined to doubt what a person says, even when he has given it all his weight, all his experience and all his rigor. "No," we say, "that is not so." In history classes, when we recall the use of swearing in earlier societies, and the fact that in a trial a sworn statement could be decisive, we immediately provoke broad smiles, which show how much value students place on a person's word. It is so easy to swear and not to keep one's word. For *modern* people. But these same students have no objection to considering images as proof that binds the person photographed. Witnesses are suspect, but "objective proof" never. Thus in our society, images are genuine proof in just about every area of life. They speak to our heart and senses with an undeniable force, with a weight that comes to them from the remotest past.

### 3. TELEVISION

It is nearly impossible to deny that television has the power of adapting itself to institutions (and this is not true only of television organized for this purpose and used for propaganda; television itself is this way because of the influx of images).[8] It serves as an agent of

---

8. These initial remarks are drawn from a thesis written under my direction: D. Brethonoux, "La Télévision et le monde ouvrier." The bibliography on television is enormous. See in particular the works of Jean Cazeneuve

socialization, in the sense (for we must clarify this essentially ambiguous term!) of integration into the social body, into a collectivity, through renunciation of the individual's "being himself."[9] Television is an agent of standardization and conformity to the world. This is so in part because it moves us to dreams and psychological mechanisms of compensation; but also because of the continual dichotomy between an obviously visible object and its possible meanings, which are hidden by the multiplicity and the variety of images. Meaning is excluded, but the object is there. Television acts of necessity like an antisurrealism, like something that removes meaning. Television satisfies us, so why should we look any further? I have seen the object itself, the thing in itself.

This mutation takes place through the radical transformation of seeing into vision. We view a film. We do not perceive an object or reality through our own sight, but rather an image of this reality, seen and encoded by someone else. This image is offered to me as a simple image with no consistency, and my sight causes me to take it for reality itself. This image bears an obvious resemblance to the "signified," which is reality. But this evidence is false. That is, the evidence, judged on the basis of truth, is false. Truth in this case means only the equivalence of the image and reality, of the signifier and the signified—nothing more.

This image bears a false relationship to reality, first because abstraction takes place inevitably in the reading and visual perception of a sequence of images; second, because reality is cut up and recomposed in the image. "Audiovisual material is the reconstruction of detemporalized, dismantled reality that has been retemporalized." "Through photographs, but even more through films and television, we are witnessing a fragmentation of society into series of images. They are cut out of the social fabric and presented more or less independently from each other. . . . This universe is fragmented and without structure. Society thus comes to be seen as a place where images encounter each other, where things take place in a logical

---

and P. Schaeffer, especially Schaeffer's *Machines à communiquer*, vol. 1, *Pouvoir et communication* (Paris: Seuil, 1972), and Cazeneuve's *Sociologie de la radiotélévision* (Paris: Presses Universitaires de France, 1963; 5th ed. 1980); *Les Grandes Chances de la télévision*, with J. Oulif (Paris: Calmann-Lévy, 1963); *Les Pouvoirs de la télévision* (Paris: Gallimard, 1970); *L'Homme téléspectateur* (Paris: Gonthier, 1974); and *Les Communications de masse* (Paris: Gonthier, 1976).

9. Even if this "being oneself" is the absurd pretension to authentic individuality which does not exist, still it exists as a pretension, and I must take it into account!

manner. The cohesion of these images thus comes only from a reinterpretation of society. We move from fragmentation to recomposition (and this recomposition will be presented and taken for reality
itself). From a society of individuals and individual actions, we go to
a society of roles."

Not only the structure and the composition of reality are modified, however, but also its rhythm. An audiovisual sequence imposes
a certain rhythm of reading, so it is neither your vision nor your
rhythm.[10] The person who puts the images in sequence chooses for
you; he condenses or stretches what becomes reality itself for us. We
are utterly obliged to follow this rhythm. At no point can we say:
"Stop, image; you are so lovely." The image has gone and we will
never see it again.[11] The basic rhythm of life escapes us.

"Social reality (for example) and its televised image profoundly
contradict each other. Social contradictions are eliminated so as to
allow only a sequence of selected images to appear." I believe it
essential to realize that it is not so much a political choice that is
involved here (as the evidence might tend to make us think). Rather,
we are dealing with our need for a substitute reality in which images
are substituted for lived and seen reality. Under whatever regime or
socioeconomic organization, these effects are identical. Even if social
contradictions are made especially evident, they will *still* be erased,
deprived of their force, and eliminated by the simple fact that inevitably they will be selected images.

"Television functions on the principle that explanation equals
construction *of* reality, and description means 'constructed *by* reality.'" Images are not only fragments of reality on a screen before me.
They are not just a sequence I am compelled to follow. They are truly
a construction of reality—one which produces an explanation that
satisfies me. In the jumble of images that come from everywhere and
mix and blend without meaning, suddenly an order appears. There is
sequence and a choice made by the producer of images, and thus I
see the light. Everything is explained by the very clarity of this real
construction. It is inevitable, and pure description always leaves me
in suspense (that is, description constructed by reality; for example,
a live telecast). I need someone to explain it to me. The mere account
of what is happening does not quench my thirst to understand. I need
a clearer reality: one that is constructed and reconstructed, for me.

---

10. This is a major difference between images and the reading of something written. I read at my own rhythm, and I may go back and reread
repeatedly.

11. Unless I have a video recorder and remember to record something
that interests me!

But this visionary reality of connected images cannot tolerate critical discourse, explanation, duplication, or reflection. These presuppose a certain distance and withdrawal from the action, whereas images require that I continually be involved in the action and in on what is happening. They make me a passive spectator, but I am not removed from what is happening; instead, I am integrated into the image process that unfolds outside of me and according to a rhythm that is different from the rhythm of my thinking process and from the rhythm I would have chosen. Nothing is worse for the image's influence than to be taken apart and analyzed by language. The word produces disenchantment with the image; the word strips it of its hypnotic and magical power.

Artificial images usually avoid this danger by their short-lived nature, especially on television. The televised signal disappears, does not last, and is not seen again. It is immediately followed by another, and this concatenation of a program is precisely what prohibits any hold that the word might get on a given fragment or sequence. Each image is immediately covered by the succeeding wave, so that, in spite of the spectator's theoretical freedom, he does not interrupt his pleasure by turning off the set in order to discuss and reflect on what he has just seen. In any case, such a discussion would be useless, since one would be talking into thin air. Once speaking begins, the effect of the image already would have disappeared. This situation highlights the vanity of the television critic's task, because he necessarily prepares his column after a telecast that no one will be seeing again.

Television (but also the multiplicity of images in general) participates heavily in social control in all these ways. The person who emits and controls images produces conformity. Again, I accept that this is utterly fortuitous and unintentional—that this does not involve any intention to propagandize or any police activity. But the fact is there. Furthermore, this tendency toward conformity is not connected with a particular type of regime or alienation (such as capitalist). It takes place in any kind of society. The debate is by no means between capitalism and communism, but exclusively between individual freedom and the overall functioning of society. Even if the person producing the images is ideologically opposed to the particular society in which he lives (a capitalist society, for example), he unconsciously acts as an agent of social control. This is true simply because he participates in an enormous structure that in itself is a social machine.

A spectacle produces simultaneously two notions: (1) that since it is only a spectacle, it is easy to change (and society too!); and (2) that since it is only a spectacle, it does not produce conformity to the dominant social reality so different from the spectacle. These attitudes, however, are precisely what leads to inertia, nonintervention, and acceptance. Let us note carefully that what we have here is not an acceptance of this or that accident, incident, or shortcoming; rather, we have an overall acceptance, turning one's life over to society—a renunciation of truth. The representation that proceeds from society's structure, and reciprocally the permanent vision of a spectacle, reinforce social pressures and at the same time absorb any changes one would like to bring about. Everything situated outside the norms and paradigms of this society is reduced and incorporated. You can show the most scandalous, impressive, and provocative images imaginable through photographs, film, and television. But this never goes beyond the level of spectacle, so all such images are incorporated within the overall flood of images.

We are talking about images *of reality*. This innovative reality is incorporated within traditional images and through this process reduced to the status of conservative images. If there existed in reality some aspect of one of these images that could not be thus incorporated, a bit of doctoring would make it fit. And this altered image is all we will ever know of a given movement, group, or person, which may be unique and nonconformist. But if it is presented to me as unique, it will be marginalized by the very conformity of images.

In this way the "reality-unreality" circle of the action of images is closed. Within this process, the entire visual plane defines everything living. The result is a full and continuous society. Never is there any empty place where someone could insert some authentic action. The artificial image is always complete and we are permanently surrounded by "full" images. Our process of social conformity is effected by this permanent fullness.

The visual world leaves empty places (which usually bore the city dweller when he goes to the country! On the contrary, the sight of mountains or of the ocean is full and fills the eyes). But the universe manufactured by artificial images must keep itself filled up, so as to avoid producing boredom! Never is any empty space permitted, and this is one of the main differences between images and the word. We cannot listen to unceasing talk. The word *discourse* necessarily implies not only an alternation between emptiness and fullness; it also opens a gap in itself and in the listener. The word opens up spaces to be discovered and by this very fact is a critical force. It awakens the critical sense and arouses criticism. The word plays this role as long as it is not transformed into image and not incorporated into a visual system; as long as it is not degraded in order to join a spectacular liturgy. Under such circumstances, it would cease being the word and become merely a mute but raucous witness to the triumph of images. Humiliatingly chained to the triumphant chariot, it certifies the victory: it is reduced to noise.

This is precisely the role of the audiovisual approach: to incorporate the word into the flood of images, making it useless and empty. The spectator's mind is completely occupied with the fullness of the visual spectacle.[12] Images do not give you any respite. You can listen to a speech or the news with half an ear, while doing something else. The image monopolizes us: either you watch television or you do not, but you cannot watch television while writing letters or doing the dishes in the next room. Images captivate our entire attention, fascinating us and filling us with hallucinations, so that we abandon everything. Through this process they divert us from lived reality, from *all* reality, making us live in a universe of the fullness of images.

The crucial role of transistor radios during the May 1968 disturbances in France is well known. Combatants listened to the news while building barricades, and the effect was like an echo or a rebound. They organized their tactics according to the breathlessly reported news received from other cities and districts. It is utterly impossible to imagine the same combatants sitting in a circle in front of a TV screen to *see* what was happening elsewhere. Television would necessarily not only have stopped and prevented action, but it would have demobilized those watching it. You cannot go back to a movement that has been stopped abruptly in order to insert it into a spectacle. *From this point of view* it may be said that television is a cold medium—just like anything that requires full and inclusive attention on the part of its subject, to the exclusion of any other occupation.

Concerning television, we must return to two matters mentioned briefly earlier. Sight, when it perceives concrete reality, makes action possible and directs it. Artificial images are the very language of action. But this universe of artificial images in which we are immersed paralyzes and blocks action. We observe an absolute contradiction between reality and images transmitted through film or television. These images do not motivate us toward any action; they do not even get a person up out of his chair. On the contrary, they sink him deeper into his apathy. We look, but remain passive, because we know that we have no way of grasping the representation offered to us. The effort to get television watchers to participate in games and conversations by inviting them to call on the telephone is very intriguing. Spectators are asked to call something with a name like "action" in

---

12. "We must not say that we have entered an audio-visual or ideo-visual civilization, but rather a civilization of noise, and especially of the visual. We should call it the noiso-visual or the abrupto-visual universe, with great emphasis on the 'visual'" (Maillot).

order to participate in the spectacle, but this changes nothing in reality, since it is only a game or something equally superficial.

An image that is shown continuously and delivered to a passive spectator moves him to action only when it is propaganda. At this point, we no longer have an action desired by the subject because of some reality he has seen, but an action that has been calculated by someone else. The spectator is an object, and sight is only the means of attracting him. Besides this special case, a profound change has occurred in the artificiality of visual means. These visual media are now so centered on unreal, artificial, and conventional images that urban people (immersed in technique) tend more and more to see in them only signals and appearances. And this is what characterizes the whole universe of images that domesticate us.

Young people frequently protest against society's tendency to preempt and integrate everything, and this should lead them to understand how images work. Rather than bourgeois society, it is the universe of images that co-opts and integrates all that is done and lived, in order to reduce it to the level of spectacle. The absolute triumph of images and visualization paralyzes and integrates.

Television, however, is not the only means! Images also triumph through comic strips, even when they are "revolutionary." Whether their content is revolutionary makes no difference. What matters is the abolishment of coherent and meaningful language that says something. This is the preempting act par excellence. Images always abolish.

The comic drawings of *Hara-Kiri*, Brétécher, or Wolinski can never be anything but by-products of this triumph. We may think that we have robbed the enemy of one of his means of action by changing its meaning. We may say "We are aware that Tintin and Astérix contribute frightfully to conformism, but we have recaptured this medium, and are thus fighting our opponent on his own ground." This is utter illusion. For apart from any content is the issue of the image itself, with its perverseness. Placing oneself on the opponent's ground and trying to change the use of something (which is a favorite tactic of those who practice situational ethics) amounts to aligning oneself with the same tendency. Because it is spectacle, the image's fullness pacifies my revolutionary conscience. "I saw, therefore I acted."

This whole process not only paralyzes our intervention but also places us in a false relationship with a false reality. I take what is shown to me for reality, and reality itself fades away. Everything depends on this continual fragmentation of the reality in which I live into discontinuous images or pieces of a mosaic. These come from every direction but are blended and situated in relation to each other in new totalities. These totalities are recomposed in such a way as to be continuous. I take this continuum to be the only reality because it is the only relationship with reality that I can have from now on.

Thus the reality I see, and to which I am urged to dedicate myself, is a false reality. And the relationship I have with it is a false relationship, because two things are lacking: (1) the strength and stability of an involvement in experienced reality, and (2) the confrontation of this experience by a series of values and choices related to what I call truth. In the world of artificial images, relationships are gratuitous, fleeting, and merely interesting. But they have no more existence than any other short-lived interesting thing that distracts my attention. This false relationship shuts me out of reality, while it encloses me in a cocoon of familiarity, indifference, and jaded search for new experiences. It involves me in something unstructured that is compensated by a state-controlled economy and social control. I no longer know which reality places demands on me, or where the reality of my life is to be found. Since I know that images no longer refer to anything, I am led to choose from among the floods of images those that are the easiest to understand, instead of those which could have rich meaning. The result is that we are faced not only with a false reconstructed reality and a false relationship with reality because of mediation by images, but also with a false language.

At different points we have advanced two contradictory propositions: first, that a series of images is not a language (which would correspond to spoken language related to truth); and second, that a series of images is a language (in that its structure and its sequences are signifiers). At this point we arrive at a third proposition: images are a false language; that is, they appear to be messages and communication, but this communication is situated in an overall context that produces nothing but a vacuum. This language tries to be taken (and is taken) for the complete complex of "truth and reality." On the one hand it refers only to a fiction, but on the other hand it integrates the spectator into a social whole. In its process of encompassing everything such language neither expresses nor reveals the social whole, but merely serves it.

Diatribes against language (called a terrorist force for integration into the dominant culture) are correct only in terms of what they do not criticize: audiovisual language. Although a false language, an artificial mosaic and puzzle, it has become so much a part of our society that it meets with universal approval. This is so true that the very people who question and torture the word give their solemn approval to images despite their explosive and destructive nature. They do not realize that images cause us to conform. But their language is pure nonsense; it is happily inserted into the nonsense of false language concerning images of nothing.

"Nothing" does not, however, describe the influence of images on life. Such influence unquestionably may be observed: we live under the influence of advertising and according to the models advertising offers us;[13] propaganda and now images are having an influence on violent behavior.[14] We must certainly beware of the fact that these images have a major influence precisely when an individual lives in an unreal world whose only reality is fictitious and simulated by images.

Ruthless behavior seen in images is not related to real life but becomes normal for the person who lives in the universe of artificial images. Such behavior seems normal because images are norms in a world without meaning. The influence of the image does not act on the person himself, who then acts; that is, images of violence alone do not provoke violence. But images of violence within a world of images (where all that exists is a shadow on a screen) can lead to violent behavior.

When a person hits someone, this "someone" has no more existence than the actor so often seen. The movement of the arm itself as it strikes is only an image, and violent scenes are just a spectacle a person acts out as he watches himself. Everything is a spectacle: ghosts made of shadows, flickering lights, and scenarios worked out ahead of time. The person who is going to be hit has no reality; he represents nothing. It makes absolutely no difference whether you help a blind person to cross the street or attack him. The person striking another has become uncertain of his victim's existence. He feels like an actor in the middle of images with neither weight nor meaning. Hitting or killing give some meaning to this moment. He looks for a crisis in order to avoid this absence of being, since he too is reduced to the level of an image. Any crisis will do: drugs, orgasm, or violence. These are the only moments when the person absent from himself (because he has taken in too many artificial images) has a vague feeling of existence and self-realization.

---

13. I like to remind people that the first basic study on advertising providing life models was done by Bernard Charbonneau, in the journal *Esprit* in 1935! ("La Publicité," *Esprit*, no. 31 [1 April 1935]).

14. I am aware that questions have been raised about this topic: do movies and advertising really influence young people toward violence? Careful but positive conclusions are found in the commission's study of the question (C. Chavanon) and in the excellent newspaper article by R. Lenoir ("TV, la violence et l'image," *Le Figaro*, 10 March 1976). Images of extreme violence produce either exact reproduction (which is short-lived) or else overall behavior of generalized brutality accompanied by impoverished language.

## 4. TECHNIQUE

I hope I will not be accused of monomania just because I bring the entire triumph of images back to the question of technique,[15] because this relationship to technique is easily verified: technique makes possible the explosion of images, their infinite multiplication, the substitution of images for the word, and the construction of a universe of images. But there is also a reciprocal demand that images and technique place on each other, and, finally, a common nature they share.

First, consider the possibility of the image explosion. Obviously, the mass media surround us with images. The multiplication of visual techniques has produced this invasion of our eyes and thoughts by images. We produce images only because we have certain equipment. Without technical tools no triumph of images would be possible. First came the printing press, then photography and the explosion that followed it: cameras, linotype machines, television; and now artificial satellites that never stop producing images. The universe of images is a result of technique alone, and not of some human intention, some philosophy or economic structure, a need for profit, the class struggle, or the Oedipus complex. These pseudointellectual "causes" are advanced in every modern interpretation.

Actually things are simpler and more chilling: technique produces the means of images. It explains both their possibility and their spread and multiplication. As we have shown elsewhere this relationship involves a certain logical development: when a technical possibility exists, it must be applied. We moderns cannot leave our discoveries inactive, or relegate potentialities to the realm of the merely possible. This attitude opens the door for the creation of needs or habits imposed on people by technique's power and weight.

We become accustomed to the multiplication of images simply because this profusion is proposed and imposed by technique. And technique imposes them simply because it is possible to do so. In the world of techniques one necessarily proceeds from what is possible to its realization. When it is possible to send an image instantaneously by satellite from one end of the world to the other, the thing must be done. When the multiplication of the means used to produce images is thrust upon us, a justification for this is found immediately. But, again, all this does not take place because people wanted images,

---

15. Concerning technique and its definition, see Jacques Ellul, *The Technological Society*, trans. John Wilkinson (New York: Knopf, 1964; London: Jonathan Cape, 1965), and *The Technological System*, trans. Joachim Neugroschel (New York: Continuum, 1980).

television, or the satellites they have created. They were created by technique's process of development and then their consumption was found to be pleasant, good, and intelligent (obviously, "pleasant to look at, good to eat, and capable of awakening intelligence"). Thus we briskly entered the universe of fictitious images produced, multiplied, and spread by techniques. Since these techniques dealt with reality alone, they produced what corresponds to reality: images. These images caused humanity to concentrate increasingly on that particular, imaged reality, which became more and more unreal.

Undoubtedly it can be argued that there are *also* techniques that make use of the word, such as the telephone and radio. But two remarks may be made on this subject: first, the allure of those techniques is completely different. When the public has to choose between a television program and a cultural radio program, we know what it prefers. Images are enticing, captivating, and, strictly speaking, hypnotic, whereas this is not at all true of the word transmitted by radio. In order to listen properly to the radio, one must decide to do it, make a choice, wish to listen, and apply oneself to what is most difficult. Unless, as is usually the case, the radio broadcasts only background music rather than words. People leave the radio on, whether it is broadcasting music or talk, while not really listening and while talking about something else. The reduction of the word to mere background is obviously more serious than silence or the absence of language. It represents the devaluation of any possible content this word might have; it means utter contempt.

My second remark is very simple: the means used to broadcast images and those which broadcast the word simply are not comparable. The technique of images has effectively transformed our universe. On this point McLuhan is certainly right. When a detailed inventory of techniques of image and of the word is made, the extreme difference is astounding. Only the techniques of image are closely related and constitute a network. Techniques of the word are always casual and related to sporadic activities. Loudspeakers, recordings, cassettes, the telephone—all these are individual matters directly related to a clearly human activity. The radio would be the only technical means with the same power as visual means.

In addition, however, the relationship of the visual plane with technique is deeper than these issues; the multiplication of technical means is not the only cause of generalized visualization. Another factor is that technique has a basic need for visually oriented people in order to develop. Technique excludes discourse. In its domain, diagrams and sketches are decisive. A technical process can never be explained in words as it can be done by a drawing or a picture. Technical progression is absolutely dependent on visual representation. In order to become a technical person, one must be polarized by the visual domain. The perception of reality, the reduction of reality to usable elements, and action with respect to reality are possible only when the imprecision of language has been replaced by the precision of images. A certain mental mutation must take place in order for Homo sapiens to become a technical individual; and this mutation is effected through the visual plane's exclusion of language. This process is accompanied by the creation of another language; a statistical language which can be expressed through graphic means, for example. The language must correspond exactly to the object.

Thus we see that all techniques depend on the possibility of reducing to a drawing what had belonged to the order of the word. All of a sudden, political economics sheds its psychological and moral considerations and its problem with ends, because now everything can be reduced to Constantine Leontiev's input-output tables. At long last, things can be visualized, and therefore political economics can become technicalized. Obviously this involves eliminating what cannot be reduced to such an image. Thus a whole area of language and an entire approach to knowledge are excluded because they cannot be visualized. We must learn through sketches and obey signals in order to be apt for technical development and for the manipulation of techniques.

"But," you say, "we have audio signals." Of course! The trained ear can recognize a motor's condition by the noise it makes. We also have sirens and whistling buoys. But compare the uncertainty of sounds with the clear evidence given by a visual signal. A policeman's whistle can mean dozens of things; moreover, somebody who is not a policeman can whistle—anybody can do it. I have to see the policeman to know who whistled. On the contrary, a red light is unquestionable. This is why visual signals and signs with bright borders multiply. In order to be suited for technique, a person must become more visual than anything else. All day long he must concentrate on visual matters: during his work hours and even when he is off work. This is the first aspect of the reciprocal demands that the visual domain and technique place on each other.

The second aspect is this: we noted above the obvious usefulness of images in our day, due to their ease and speed. Now we must emphasize the other side: people molded by the technical milieu have a need to live through images. The amount of knowledge we must absorb, ever on the increase, requires that we have recourse to images. A person can discuss Israeli politics better having glanced at a map and seen a film on the Sinai campaign than if he had read a whole series of books on Israel. The reason is that he will have a better feel for reality if he has seen the images. But, of course, we are still talking only about recording images. In reality, this is one of the most useful skills in our society. Thus the matter is perfectly clear; technique requires visually oriented people. And people living in a technical milieu require that everything be visualized.

\*   \*   \*   \*   \*   \*

Going deeper, we discover a common nature in technique and visualization, images and artificial images. All involve evidence, efficiency, and something tangible and real. Technique belongs to the realm of evidence. Its results are clear. In general, either a thing works or it does not. Either we go to the moon or we do not. The rocket has left its orbit or it has not. No discussion is possible. Sight furnishes us with hard evidence, whereas talking can only produce conviction; but the transition from talking to conviction is murky and uncertain.

The same language can produce certainty in one person and doubt in another. The same phrase is true at a given moment, but then no longer. The path followed by discourse, however logical and rigorous, is not able to give a watertight demonstration. We all know contradictory arguments that are equally probable and convincing; this uncertain quality has caused people to lose patience with language.

But let's be careful: people lost patience with language only when visualization began to triumph. The time came when technique was identified with the visual realm, and technically produced visual images gave people undeniable evidence. At the same time, images gave a feeling of unlimited power. This is when language began to be thought of as just "talk," because it did not give the same kind of clear certainty and indisputable results that visualization and technique did (considered separately as well as in tandem and identified with each other).

Until this triumph of technical images, language was both the most serious act and the subtlest game. But how could the combination of seriousness and play have stood up against efficiency, which is the second similarity between technique and the visual realm? I need not repeat here what I have written about efficiency as the supreme imperative and the prime characteristic of technique. But technique is identical with images in this respect. Images always have a positive or even a programming character. An image which contains a totality furnishes us with the framework and the motivation for action. The visual realm is related to the need for intervening in reality and gives us the means for such intervention.

On the contrary, everyone knows how ineffective language is. What we call the "word" no longer has anything to do with the

Hebrew *dabar* of Genesis 1. Our "word" has no noticeable effect on a situation, is never an immediate program for action. When the word programs, becoming such an agent, it is because a kind of constraint is placed on it, or because it truly changes its "nature." With good reason Georges Sorel speaks of the image as a prime mover, when he is concerned with efficiency in connection with the action of myth. That is to say, what is spoken or told must be in effect a transformation of word into image.

The same concern is involved in the visual realm and in technique. Images are communication par excellence, and technique is efficiency itself at all levels. But without its visual aspect no technique can exist. In order to apply a means, one must see and have an image of reality. The efficacy of an image guarantees the efficacy of a given technique, just as the latter makes the former possible. In all realms, it pays. Not by accident Michel Foucault rediscovers Jeremy Bentham's panoptic system,[16] which is an astounding overall surveillance system that permits guards to keep a constant eye on everything at a glance. Foucault tries to show that this prison surveillance system actually has been extended to our entire society, which can be interpreted by means of universal visualization. But Foucault fails to mention two matters: this panoptic system is possible only through highly developed technical means; and it is necessary because the technological society requires order and efficiency.

Lack of interest in literature and the condemnation of philosophy reflect the inability of these disciplines to convert themselves into diagrams. Here we see the same concern about efficiency because the same reference to reality is involved. Sight belongs to the order of reality, as we have shown, and technique acts only in this domain of the tangible, the quantitative, and the countable. Through technique we act on things. We are doubly present in this process, through our physical bodies and as those who constitute reality. In order to become an object of technique, everything must be reified and reduced to its corporeality. Even people must be reduced to being only machines (that they submit "eagerly" changes nothing!).

Not much progress took place between Julien Offroy de La Mettrie (1709–1751) and Deleuze or B. F. Skinner; the process is always the same, both visual and technical at the same time. From the visual point of view, one says: "I have seen neither the soul nor the

---

16. See Jeremy Bentham, *Surveiller et punir* (Paris: Gallimard, 1979). The panoptic system involved a circular prison composed of cells arranged like those of a bee hive. The cells' front and back walls were made of glass so that guards posted in a tower at the center of the ring could always see all the prisoners.

spirit." Technique says: "People must become machines in order to be treated technically by the hundreds of techniques which converge on them." Reification is no longer a philosophical matter, an abstract economic issue, or a way of exploiting people that would explain their alienation. It is the result of technical development and the exclusive dominance of the visual realm. The entire person is reduced to seeing and being seen, and technique confirms this.

\* \* \* \* \* \*

Finally, the common nature shared by techniques and the visual domain produces strange consequences that really are reversals. We have said that as a person is present in the world, he perceives through sight the reality of his environment, and enters through the word into a dialectical relationship with human beings and the openness of truth. But the triumph of the visual sphere and of technique has changed all that. The multitude of images imposes finite vision on us, within a given time limit, and it is practically impossible to escape from this. We are seeing the transfer of some media from the spatial mode (newspapers) to the temporal mode (filmed and televised reporting and video cassettes). Sight makes an opening in time for us, as in the case of writing, in which the word is inscribed in space.

This is a basic reversal, and it coincides with another great movement: the effort to reduce language to sketches, drawings, and diagrams. All these efforts—reducing language to countable units, making lists of bits of information, making sketches with arrows going off in all directions, organizing A. J. Greimas-type semiotic diagrams, determining Jean Ricardou's reading grids in order to formalize fiction, the graphs of "contiguity on the horizontal axis and opposition on the vertical," or narration and fiction, etc.—all this shows nothing but the domination of technique.

Visualization is not a scientific effort but a typically technical one. It is a matter of visualizing words through the intermediary of a diagram related to language and discourse. But this amounts to making the word an object of technique. Of course, we are free to choose what we want. We should just be aware of the following two facts: first, by making the word an object of technique, we elevate excessive scientism to its highest point. By "scientism" I mean the process that has eliminated (as if nonexistent) everything that was not reducible to scientific understanding and visual diagrams. The word should have been the thing best able to resist this pressure. Now we have arrived at the point of formalizing visually everything related to the word, but at the price of excluding meaning. This is extremely significant!

Our second observation is that in making the word an object of technique, we are in no way expressing our free spirit, liberated from previous prejudices in favor of the word and language. All we express in this way is our utter sociological conformity, the universalization of images, and a thoroughgoing obedience to the generalized process of technicalization.

The lightning-fast progress of the structuralist method can be explained only by the support of the media: by the technicalization of the average person's thinking. This method does not improve or add to knowledge; it only changes doubtful understanding into something visual, which is believed to eliminate ambiguity. The relationship of the word to truth has been excluded, in order to limit us to the relationship between language and reality.

Today we must understand that while this exclusion is possible, it is the necessary condition if the word is to have some effectiveness. But it never attains as much force as visual representation. When we think of speech that has been efficacious, we always forget that it was related to a certain visual framework and certain visual impressions. In propaganda, for example, language ceases to be language and word; it is reduced to a stimulus. Propagandistic language is powerful only to the degree that its framework (the masses, marches, flags, surrounding monuments, etc.) gives it weight. The visual elements correspond to the intervention of action in the visual domain, and therefore in reality, which is the realm of technique.

# Chapter IV

# THE WORD HUMILIATED

The invasion of the verbal realm by images results in role reversal and domination, leading us to another characteristic of our modern reality: the humiliation of the word.

## 1. DE FACTO DEVALUATION

No one consciously tried to bring it about, yet the situation of the word in our society is deplorable. For this situation the people who speak are particularly responsible—not in the moral sense of guilt, but in the sense of lack and failure. The habit of speaking without saying anything has eaten away at the word like a cancer. Such people have spoken other than in poetry, myth, and the minimum necessary for legendary history. Instead of limiting ourselves to what is useful (no more and no less) for exchanging information, news, and teaching, we keep on speaking. In addition to the ritual and mystery that codify the word we insist on speaking. These days we speak without saying anything; we just chitchat.

Scholasticism, at its very origins, was not just chatter; it *became* chatter. Oddly enough, this chatter invaded the scholarly world and came to provide its security. Molière and François Rabelais bear witness to this chatter, these meaningless words. Then too, there is Shakespeare: "Words, words, words." Suddenly the tragic discovery was made that words were only words, without power to act. People became acutely aware of the uselessness of mere talk. People were not aware of this during the Middle Ages, when the word was venerated, not only in liturgy but in all its forms. After the sixteenth century, we have an avalanche of talk that is increasingly useless.

This development is easily associated with the bourgeoisie: they reduced the word to the schematic needs of business, or to conceal what people wanted to avoid saying. In this view, the word became

155

insignificant amid the elegance of the court, through Marivaux's subtle use of it in his plays, and because of everyday triteness that lacks any reference to real life. Mundane and intellectual chatter mixed together (as Aldous Huxley's *Point Counter Point* shows so admirably) finally collapse into wordlessness. Eugène Ionesco's reputation as a playwright is based on this situation.

The speaker's error comes from the absence of something "to say," so that he doesn't say anything, but (as poet Jacques Prévert puts it) just goes on talking and talking and talking. We have an excess of talk devoid of meaning and veracity. We are satiated with electoral and political speeches (which we are sure say absolutely nothing), with false conversations, and with books paid by the word (some find it necessary to write, and so become writers by trade!). In spite of the lack of anything to say, the speaker continues as if he were a word-mill moved by the wind, and he becomes responsible for the fact that no one can any longer take *any* word seriously. *No* word can be taken seriously, because the rush of these words prevents us from discovering the one which, in the midst of the torrent, has meaning and deserves to be listened to.

This devaluation of words can also be the fault of intellectuals, who give us many examples of such usage these days. We will mention only the impenitent chatter of the Henry Millers and the Deleuzes and Guattaris,[1] whose logorrhea conceals the poverty of a few simple ideas under a flood of deceptive verbiage. Their words are mere illusion, completely devaluated because they have said nothing and because of the superabundance of discourse. But this suffices for those who seize upon one glittering word and thereafter explain everything by referring solemnly to "flux" or "desire." They do this without realizing that they only repeat medieval theories concerning the *Impetus*, the Impulse, etc., from which Jean Buridan's successors were to build such beautiful effects based on vain words!

While we have a wasteland of empty verbiage, at the same time we suffer from an excess of information broadcast everywhere about everything, so that its quality is utterly destroyed. We are overwhelmed by a jumble of information: on the latest model of ballpoint pens, the pope's election, the wedding in Monaco, the Iranian revolution, increased taxes, new possibilities for credit, the conversion of the biggest polluter to the cause of nonpollution—ten thousand words of information in an instant. We would go crazy if we really had to listen to all this seriously, so the flood of words continues, and we let it flow by. After all, whether any words are involved, the result

---

1. To mention only the "greats"!

is the same: I listen with half an ear and I catch here and there a snatch of a phrase, or a moving tone of voice, but in any case the word no longer matters to me. I have been exposed to too many words and too much information. I must defend myself against these invasions; my mind closes up spontaneously, to keep me from being torn to pieces. I am like Orpheus turned over to the media Maenads; I am blown by every wind of doctrine and words; I am lured into every trap. I have stopped listening. I refuse to hear (without even realizing it).

As noise, however, the anonymous word continues to flow. No longer is any kind of relationship established. Henceforth the word is definitively detached from the one who speaks. Nobody is behind it. When language theorists take their analysis to its logical conclusion, they declare that no person is speaking, nor is there any content to communicate. They say we must recognize that in the strict sense, *it* speaks, or *one* speaks. They are mistaken, however, when they turn this into a general rule and claim to give us either an objective analysis of language or a new psychoanalysis of the "nonsubject." They are wrong to present this as something permanent. For our society and our epoch, for our intellectual or bourgeois groups, they are correct, but this is a sociological observation rather than something linguistic or psychoanalytic.

In our day, in this place, a sort of social discourse flows endlessly and is repeated twenty hours out of every twenty-four, expressed by individual mouths. The discourse is completely anonymous, even though it may sometimes be affirmed with force and conviction by a particular individual.[2] This corresponds to the speaker's anonymity. The word has become anonymous and therefore has no importance, since its only reality involved the meaning of two living persons who needed to know and recognize each other and to exchange something. Words are just wind. They pass by and have no importance: as long as no one puts the weight of his entire life behind the word he speaks, how can we take one statement more seriously than any other?

The rupture between the speaker and his words is the decisive break. If a person is not behind his word, it is mere noise. This matter of looking for the weight of truth in philosophical or political phrases (independently of the person who said them) goes back a long way. What do I care if a person lived like a coward, a liar, or a hypocrite, since the words he left are so beautiful! This is the first great vacuum.

---

2. *On the intellectual level,* of course, I consider the books of Jacques Lacan, Foucault, Jacques Derrida, etc., utterly typical of this anonymous social discourse. These writers constitute in themselves a demonstration of what they say about all individuals who speak.

In the Bible the word is an integral part of the person. It is true if the person is true. Jesus' words have no value or importance whatever if they are separated from the person of Jesus. In him there is perfect unity of life, action, word, relationship, and knowledge. The current rupture between the speaker and the word strips the word, but soon it takes on value again. But from where? Necessarily from something nonhuman, so that this value will be related to reason, science, some opinion, a social tendency, or a concept of beauty or truth. A *concept* rather than the beauty of an experience lived in harmony with itself, or the truth of a person's unity. Once related only to a concept, the word is at the mercy of all sorts of winds and changes; it loses all weight and meaning. It becomes an instrument, to be manipulated. It does not commit anyone to anything.

When the word is utterly emptied of itself, it becomes mere slogan, at the service of any structure whatever.[3] It becomes propaganda and serves falsehood:[4] fundamental falsehood, which has to do with the unity of being and the word. The word thus becomes the servant of whatever doctrine, since any political doctrine, considered in itself, is as good as another. The word may be prostituted in any venture. The anonymous word has no name and thus is not really a word. No one has spoken it. It spreads out like liquid across a world with no reference points. All the talk about signs (signifiers and signifieds, the referent and connotations) is utterly empty talk when there is no more word. This is the fault of those who speak.

\*     \*     \*     \*     \*     \*

The word is also devalued by the very conditions in which it is spoken in our day. The triumph of thought based on images implies a reduction of the word. We are all aware of the remarkable phenomenon that has left its mark on our era, the disintegration of language in various ways. We also see the word used in propaganda and advertising, in which a simple onomatopoeia or the elimination of a word's meaning is sufficient, since the word is reduced to functioning as a stimulus. This is also clear and significant in contemporary poetry, in the effort to separate meaning from the word (Abraham Moles's experiment); also in the reduction of the word to a mere conveyer of information and the tendency to analyze everything in terms of communication and information. From all this one con-

---

3. See Olivier Reboul's basic study, most enlightening, on modern devaluation of the word: *Le Slogan* (Brussels: Complexe, 1975).

4. I am not saying that propaganda is based on falsehoods concerning reality; I have shown elsewhere that propaganda is efficacious only if it refers to accurate facts.

cludes that algebra is superior to spoken language, or that images are superior to the word.

This situation is simply induced by the invasion of images. Reciprocally, based on this invasion, anything may be called language. We have the language of fashion in clothing, cinematic language, body language, etc. But it is clear that in every case a shift toward visualization and images is involved. As if without intending to, as if it were obvious, people fuse all "languages"—spoken and heard language become only a particular instance of communication. But in reality, we are dealing here with the disappearance of one sort of thinking for the sake of another.

This process confirms our tendency to live only in the present. Again, in this situation it is not by accident that we draw back and refuse to study history, and that historical continuity and significance derived from the past are rejected. This refusal obviously is not consistent with the temporal dimension of the word. On the contrary, it coincides with the fact that visual images belong to the present. An image-oriented person is a person with no past. He lives only on the basis of what images can supply. Each image contains all he needs to know; he has no need to remember or retain what he learns today. Images and the transmission of knowledge through association of images convey all one needs immediately. The uselessness of history as the study of the past coincides with this. Neither is it by accident that education loses its content. Finally, structuralism, with its crushing dominance by the synchronic element, is the method and the philosophical mode that is consistent with visual images. It is not by chance that structuralism reduces language to a relationship of structures.

The word also undergoes the repercussions of the technicalization of everything. We must become basically aware of the fact that the word is strictly contradictory to technique in every way.[5] Technique's unconditional triumph empties the word, which becomes a wandering and dispossessed servant. The word is then further reduced within the technical framework to the level of a mere instrument. The word becomes vain because of babblers, and it becomes an instrument because of techniques. The context determines evolution in this case. The word no longer needs to bear meaning; it has been divorced from what it signifies. Once again, the scientific analysts (who refer everything to language structures, since they observe that meaning is

---

5. I know, of course, that language is also a technique and the object of techniques. Rhetoric is a case in point. But there is no comparison between this technique, which belongs to the most traditional group, and what technique has become today.

useless) give a correct account not of what the word is, but of what it has become here and now.

The word is still used and is not yet entirely emptied, because it retains some of its former prestige. It is indispensable that we go on talking, though meaning and real value no longer exist, and even though we no longer make any reference to truth. After all, we have those ancestral memories according to which the triumphant word dictated God's laws to the world.

Similarly, everyone holds political language in contempt. We shrug our shoulders at its promises and lyrical excesses, but it is necessary. The politician who did not give himself over to this game would have no chance of being taken seriously. This is true even though we know that this language does not commit him to anything.

Technique makes us live in a world of action, figures, demonstrations, and efficiency. But in this context there is a double effect: the emptiness of words spoken by an anonymous speaker who is not committed to his word, and the triumphant evidence for the efficacy of action—action that is now always technicalized. The word can find a modest place for itself only if it is utterly subordinated to the efficiency and the imperative of technique. The word has become image: the word made for computers, dominated by writing, inscription, and printing, and changed into a thing, into space and something visible. Now it must be seen to be believed, and we think we have finally fathomed all of language when we can apply a semiotic diagram to it.

The word deprived of meaning by the use made of it is thus transformed into something other than itself. This temptation had been great ever since writing began, since unity was the equivalent of an image. The distortion is clearly seen when within a single society one moves from a representative sign to a syllable or a letter with the same meaning. For example, a sign that represented the ocean ends up replaced by a letter or a syllable which has nothing in common with the word *ocean*. The same sign can thus be read twice: once in pronouncing the word *ocean*, and again by pronouncing the letter *a*.

At this point the word becomes uncertain and unstable. But obviously as yet we have no real change in that common use of the word, which remained overwhelmingly dominant. With printing this changed, because so much writing came to be distributed that reading became more important than the ability to speak. The term *illiterate* is the equivalent of *uncivilized*. Civilizations based on spoken language are usually not considered to be truly developed, although from the human point of view (of relationships and the unity of the person) language dominates and writing is quite secondary. Writing has placed the word in an ambiguous and defensive position. Beginning with writing, the word began to be devalued.

The latest example of this devaluation clearly comes to us from computers. Computers went from using specialized language to direct language. Soon we will be able to talk with computers in normal language and receive an answer written in normal language. Fine. But what sort of language? Obviously computers cannot understand ambiguities, connotations, allegories, metaphors, metonymies, ellipses, and paraphrases. Computers must have unambiguous language, with no double meanings, subtlety, or complexity. We will also have to remain within a certain limited vocabulary. There can be no choice of uncommon words, no alliteration or neologism that is not yet in the dictionary but which can conjure up myriads of reactions and images in the listener. Computers cannot deal with a poem by Henri Michaux. They have neither reactions nor images.

Computers require clear language that is never ambiguous. They must be taught a syntactical approach that spells out grammatical rules precisely; then the speaker must follow these rules if the machine is to understand. Examples like this one are given: How many inhabitants do Rennes and Châlons have? Answer: zero, because the computer understands: How many people live in both Rennes and Châlons? The computer cannot understand that two questions are involved. The syntactical approach must be further refined by a semantic one in which the most important words are indicated, because they establish the meaning of a sentence. But this great effort involves converting language into something that is not the word: all the richness and openness to truth lie precisely in what must be eliminated in order for the computer to understand.

Naturally, people say: "That doesn't matter; language spoken between people will remain complex. Nothing is going to change just because we must discipline ourselves in order to speak to computers." Not so! Beginning in 1930, experts noticed that language was becoming impoverished because of the development of telegraphic style and basic English. Both of these reduce the construction of a sentence to its utilitarian elements, eliminating inflection and embellishment. Computer language completes this process. You think you still remain free to speak with someone using complex or flowery language? Of course you do! But it will be taken for an esthete's or poet's language, without importance.

This is where language's real devaluation lies: on the one hand we have "serious" language that is strong, useful, precise, and situated within society's general tendencies. It has this status because it corresponds precisely to technique and technique's development. Such language is taken seriously because it suits serious matters. On the other hand, we have a floating language, good enough for intellectuals and artists, a language for distraction and fantasy. It has no status or position, and its meaning and changes are not important in the last analysis.

Who can fail to see how much the word has been devalued by this rupture and explosion? Who could be ignorant of the fact that the same person who wrote incendiary slogans during the disturbances of May 1968 has adopted ten years later either the sober and precise language of the highly placed administrator, or else the wooden language of the militant who has become successful in the establishment?

## 2. CONTEMPT FOR LANGUAGE

Our discussion now brings us to one of the aspects of the contempt for language. We may see this contempt in two different practices related to the explosion of language. These involve the scorn of both technicians and intellectuals. From the technician's point of view, the nearly irreparable defect of language is that it is ambivalent and has many facets of meaning, so one never ends up with absolute certainty. We need to make what we say monovalent instead of ambivalent; we must eliminate uncertainty and transform language into a useful supplement to demonstration. Language usage must be purified of any reference to any unknown. Technicians who love diagrams cannot do anything with language except to make it an annex (if it must be included) to explain a given point. Language can never hold the key to meaning or to a demonstration.

For this reason we said above that the devaluation of language through subordination to computer needs is extremely important. The conversation with a computer is not limited to that situation; it becomes the model for all conversation. This was already the model, to a lesser degree, in all relationships that involved technicians. This covers an enormous proportion of language use, since it involves all sorts of technicians: administrators, jurists, economists, physicists, chemists, marketing experts, doctors, engineers, psychologists, publicity experts, film makers, programmers, etc. They represent nearly the totality of language use.

Let's have no misunderstanding: I am not talking about the specialist's language, which is impenetrable to the noninitiated. The structure and the purpose of language are at stake. "Let's get down to facts. . . . " There lies the problem. Language becomes purely instrumental and therefore in its specificity is scorned.

Technicians deny that there is any value in the scholastic type of reasoning, which is based solely on the relationship between propositions. Such reasoning seems to them to be empty and ineffectual. Certainly it lacks technical efficacy. Therefore the technician says we must eliminate this sort of communication in order to arrive at pure communication.

Language is made to transmit information—but only useful information. This can be accomplished satisfactorily only if there is no redundancy, double meaning or "interference" in the communication. "You're coming through loud and clear": that is the ideal. All uncertainty must be eliminated. We cannot waste time figuring out some meaning that comes from the beyond. We are here, on this side, and that is all that matters. Everything else is just philosophy; that is, a pastime, an odd craze some people have, without any practical significance.

Who among us has not talked with developers and builders and been struck by their irritation when we speak about a term like "the quality of life," not in vague terms, but saying exactly what the expression means. "You're a humanist," they respond. Such a response communicates clearly how much language is despised. When an expression such as "quality of life" or "environmental protection" catches on, they say "of course!" They take over the expression and apply it to any effort to "develop" land, to destroy genuinely human life and landscape, or to change the environment. "Why not? These are just words, and therefore nothing. They are just popular expressions. Let us put serious ideas into practice, such as growth and development." And when you show that these "expressions" have vast content and value, and that they involve basic choices, these people reject what you say. They refuse to be directed by words or references to values. "Practical matters are completely different from your talk," they say. And under the thin, icy politeness of the chief engineer of the Highway Commission, his scorn for the philosopher and the humanist immediately shows: "Go ahead and play with words: we'll choose a few to use for decoration; but leave practical matters to us."

But unfortunately these days I also find this scorn of language among those who should have defended it without respite: intellectuals and artists. Actually their contempt is a result of the devaluation we have been speaking about: abuse by the speaker himself. Artists who accept being confined to their role as crazies and jesters play with words. When the surrealists and members of the Dada movement attacked language as they did, people experienced a strong sensation of freedom. The dismal traditional rules were exploded; people discovered that language had a meaning other than the direct one of our everyday lives. Words carried daily life toward some "beyond." But this destructuring of words and sentences was fatal. The surrealists brought off a Pyrrhic victory: their discovery led in the end to the downfall of surreality, since it demonstrated the emptiness and the vanity of language. They dramatically strengthened the position of scientists and technicians, according to whom words are only a game. The easily achieved rupture between meaning and sound was a disaster. The surrealists meant to combat facile speech and habit. They did not realize that at the same time they were destroying one of the most eagerly pursued and difficult of humanity's conquests—an achievement that had been slowly arrived at. Connecting meaning with words was not commonplace; it was the very condition of human development and intellectual possibility. They tried to "give a purer meaning to the tribal words," as Stéphane Mallarmé put it, and the result was the discovery that there is no meaning at all.

This soon led to the language games we are now well acquainted with. The surrealists' desire to break with meaning involved the frantic search for a way out, but they destroyed the thing that made a way out possible! They produced crazy, unreasoned language. Many have shrugged their shoulders, saying: "That doesn't matter. It is just a few intellectuals, only poets' fantasies." This evaluation was far from the mark. To counterbalance technical, instrumental language that is transformed into images, we still had common everyday language, or else the possibility of restoring to language its entire sovereign dimension as the word. This was assaulted and destroyed by surrealism.[6] Anything means anything. Plays on words take the place of thought. All that was needed to play this game was to reverse the order of the factors, and this process became an epidemic. The pursuit of meaning turns into the meaning of pursuit, etc. A person can seem profound by playing this way with any commonplace.

Next came Prévert's and Queneau's playful destructuring. Then, the destructuring or dismembering of sentences, with "truth" springing from these dismemberings, according to Jacques Lacan. We also saw the mixing by multiple-track tape recorders of phrases and language sounds. These manipulations have had repercussions on all nontechnical language and can only be the expression of desperate abandon and a last effort at justifying language. They seemed to be saying: "We continue to speak this language, you know, but it is not a serious matter; just look at how we play with words and phrases. At least we are accepted as jesters; come on, let's find a little folding stool somewhere in this serious society for the juggler of words." All of us agree and answer: "You aren't saying a thing with these words (only we technicians do that); and when we feel like distraction, your tricks are amusing for a little while. It is even funnier when you use technical mixing methods to lacerate and pulverize human language."

---

6. These comments in no way detract from my admiration for many surrealist poets. The evaluation of their effect and sociological significance is something entirely different from the esthetic pleasure I can receive from a given creation or from a given poet's playing with language.

This is a frightening step to take, and its effects have spread to the entire language: you can do anything, and make words say anything. You can construct any discourse with them: they do not defend themselves. But our very human life—and not only our reason or our intelligence—is profoundly altered by this process.

Let's mention one more effort. Since the rediscovery of linguistics and Ferdinand de Saussure, the mentality of scientism has pounced upon language and has involved us in reducing the word to the state of an object: a scientific object. Now we have semantics, semiology, semiotics, and semasiology. Apparently semiotics is the broadest; it is defined as "the theory of signs and sounds and of their circulation in society" (Paul Robert's dictionary). The Lexis dictionary gives "general science of signs and modes of signifying." So language is only one of the modes of signifying. Linguistics is only one branch of semiotics.

Semiology is "the study of systems of signs in social life" (Robert); that is, systems of signs have a social function. Note well: signs almost always refer to visual things. To the degree that linguistics is one of the possibilities of semiotics, this means (implicitly; this is never admitted!) that language is reduced to relationships between signs, whose model and description are visual!

Even semantics (the study of language from the point of view of meaning) does not have the word as its reference point, but is rather the "means of representing the meaning of what is said" or the "signified of lexical units in relation to their signifier." Since all this is supposed to be done in a scientific fashion, irreducible units exist at the base of semantics: "sememes," which are minimal units that differentiate meaning.

I find it astonishing that on the one hand linguists can reduce plays on words, nonsense expressions, and paradoxes to differentiating units, and on the other hand they include the word in a science of signs that are definitely visual. I purposely "misunderstand" at this point, because all studies in semiology claim that this discipline excludes the word, but this is not so! Thus the spoken and heard sign is included, but the model is "shown and seen."

As professionals, linguists and structuralists take language extremely seriously, yet they treat it as physicists and chemists have treated matter: with utter scorn. They treat it as a mere thing on which scientific discipline is supposed to exercise its rigor. Treating the language as a submissive object is like treating the word of God scientifically. Can anything escape from the triumphant imperialism of the scientific method? A speaker's claim to evoke something which cannot be submitted to scientific analysis is held in contempt in this situation. "You believe in the mystery of the word? Come along; we are going to perform its autopsy, and you will see that there is no soul under my scalpel."

This attitude involves contempt for the word, which had given people the impression and sense that there was a fissure giving access to the beyond. Now we are told that no beyond is involved in the word—only precise structures in discourse. Everything that is not strictly speaking *dis-cursus* is rigorously reduced to structural relationships. And the *dis-cursus*, which exists only in the imagination and belief of the speaker, must be implacably destroyed.

There is no meaning. Everything in a text is reduced to structural relationships. This amounts to negating the word that escapes the scientific method. Since this method is law, according to the procedure followed in every science, let's exclude as unreal and unimportant anything that cannot be subordinate or an object. For despite Edgar Morin's question, scientists still are the subject (even when they pretend not to be) and nature the object. We have not yet reached the stage of humility in our relationship with the word!

Two tendencies become clear in this context: on the one hand, language is seen as arbitrary; on the other, the signifier becomes overvalued. Both tendencies coincide in their implicit contempt for language. First, language clearly has come to seem arbitrary. No natural relationship exists between a word and the thing it designates. No onomatopoeia reproducing the ocean's sound designates the ocean in language. We have no howling sound that means "wolf" in language. Therefore language is an artificial creation: the word and the thing are not the same. No aspect of a given thing is included in the word for it. The word is pure convention. Children are taught the word not as a necessary means of survival but as the arbitrary imposition of social convention.

Such statements belong to the "order of evidence" and are ruinous for language and the word. If we accept such statements we are not bound by anything. No syntactical, etymological, or common-sense rule has any reason for being. And since everything is arbitrary, why not change, overturn, and upset these words and rules? After all, we would just be replacing one arbitrary element for another. This process amounts to the negation of history (which is quite normal, considering the connection we have observed between the word and history). Also negated is the serious nature of language acquisition. The next step is to plunge into phonetic spelling, the creation of basic English, and the playful destructuring of language. Nothing matters anymore.

All these efforts invariably remind me of the ridiculous adventure of the members of France's 1791 Constituent Assembly. Since they considered the French provinces to be purely conventional and artificial, they wanted to divide the country into equal, square pieces. At least that was rational. Of course, the human factor is denied; but this calling into question of language has all the logical reasons and evidence on its side!

We encounter the same contempt for discourse and for the word when people hit us on the head with: "the important thing is not at all to know what is being said, but to determine where the person is speaking from." This notion is always stated triumphantly, and as if it were a very serious matter. This is too much! The word's content and what it expresses? Utterly unimportant! On the other hand, it is essential to know if the speaker is bourgeois, an intellectual, a worker, a student or a professor, a judge or the accused, etc. In reality, as with all these linguistic "discoveries," all that is involved is taking elementary ideas and making them look impressive by covering them over with pseudoscientific vocabulary. Simple ideas are turned into something absolute by the scientific establishment, so as to crush that remainder of language that is not scientific. By this very process and by their very scientific quality, such ideas become *false,* in the same now well-known way that pieces of reality do when science makes a fragment of reality its object and thus alters reality and loses its object!

"Where a person is speaking from."[7] If this means that the same

---

7. I would like to cite another example of such obvious matters, transformed by science into manifest error through the artificial cutting up of reality. What follows is the beginning of an excellent article by J.-L. Lavallard from *Le Monde* of 26 Jan. 1977. It takes its title from Paul Claudel's expression:

THE EYE LISTENS: BABA + GAGA = DADA
We look with our eyes and we hear with our ears. At least that is what we think. But two British research scientists, Harry McGurk and John Mac-Donald, of the Psychology Department of the University of Surrey-Guildford, have just proved the opposite: our senses do not have such separate functions. These researchers have shown conclusively that we also "hear" with our eyes. What they have discovered is true generally and applies to children as well as to adults. It is true for each of us and is not limited to deaf people who learn to read other people's lips by observing their lip movements.

The discovery began with the disconcerting result of an experiment. The subject watches a sound film showing the face of a woman speaking. This woman repeats the same syllable twice every second. She pronounces GA-GA. But the sound track accompanying the film is not the original one. It has been recorded with BA-BA instead of GA-GA. So the subject's ear perceives BA-BA, whereas his eyes see a person who says GA-GA. The person conducting the experiment asks the subject what he perceives. The answer is disconcerting. The subject does not hear BA-BA as we might expect (only 2% of the adult responses correspond to the sound track). He does not hear GA-GA either (0% of the responses). Everyone (or almost: 98% of the responses) claims to hear DA-DA!

The phenomenon is very deep-seated. The authors of the study claim that even they cannot rid themselves of the illusion, although they know phrase spoken by a judge and by the accused does not have exactly the same implication and meaning, so that we must interpret what is said on the basis of who said it, then we are dealing only with an utterly obvious fact that has always been known. In this case, we are

---

perfectly well what is said and what is seen. When they close their eyes, they hear BA-BA correctly, but as soon as they begin looking at the image, they perceive DA-DA again.

These results are astonishing. They show clearly that the perception of sounds is not just an auditory phenomemon, but that it is the result of complex operations in the brain, where the information from our various senses arrives before the brain makes a conscious analysis. Furthermore, even in the case of this sort of auditory information, visual information often wins out. Among the subjects who claim to hear one of the two actual sounds (auditory or visual), those who perceive the "visual" sound are almost always the majority. . . . The eye wins out over the ear.

What can we say about this experiment? Based on this study, can we really arrive at the conclusion that "the eye wins out over the ear"? It may show that we partially lip-read, which is obvious; every deaf person knows this. In this case nothing has been discovered. Or else the experiment shows that we hear a *totality*; that is, a *person* speaking, with his face and hands. The word is an expression of the entire person and cannot be separated from the speaker; this is just what we said above. In this case, again, nothing new has been discovered!

There is nothing else to be learned from this experiment. The rest is absurd and demonstrates nothing. It is absurd because the researchers make a person say sounds that mean nothing! And the person watching the film is asked to tell what sound he perceives, whereas he is expecting a word. The discrepancy between sight and hearing when a *sound* is involved has no significance at all as far as language is concerned. It is no more significant than *seeing* a worker five hundred yards away wielding a sledgehammer and hearing a horn honk from the same distance. Obviously, when I see the sledgehammer hit, I expect to hear the sound of its impact. And that's all we can say!

The significant thing about this experiment is not what it might teach us but the unmasking of those who designed the experiment. For them, language amounts to noises and sounds, so that choosing any sound at all allows them to draw conclusions about language. Sounds are deformed through mixing what is heard and what is seen, because they are just sounds, with no referent. Had they used words with meaning, no confusion would have taken place. We often have this experience when seeing a poorly dubbed foreign film. I hear the French phrase and I see the German pronounced on the screen, but I in no way confuse the German with the French!

In this case again, pseudoscience makes no discovery, because it eliminates the basis of the problem! All that is involved is contempt for language! Some-time later, writing about Joseph Losey's film, *Don Giovanni*, Christian Zimmer wrote "The ear sees" (*Le Monde*, 1 Feb. 1980), in a fine criticism of Losey's stagecraft, which overshadows the opera itself. Losey is much more interested in space than time, and the result is that the music suffers the effects of his temptation to be realistic.

being warned of the importance of fine-tuning what is said—*but this has always been done*. But when it is transformed "scientifically," the expression "where a person is speaking from" means that there is *nothing else* in language other than the expression of "where the person speaks from"; that is, one expresses *only* his (class!) interests. This is foolishness. But it is a foolishness which coincides with the widespread scorn for language! Today meaning is excluded—any meaning—and political, social, and other conflicts take its place. Language is considered to be an instrument of domination. We will return to this idea.

This tendency to view language as arbitrary is related to the second tendency mentioned above: the overvaluation of the signifier. The signifier becomes the interesting reality. What it signifies and the relationship of the sign to values or thought is no longer thought important. How often is it said: "Meaning does not matter to us; we do not perform structural analyses of the text in order to understand it better. In the same vein, the intention of the speaker, or what the author wanted to convey, is unimportant. The only things that concern us are the process of transmission, the mechanism of circulation, the organization of the signifier, and its structure. All our attention centers on this signifier" (probably as a reaction against the idealism of previous generations, which were interested only in the thing or idea to be expressed). The result is that such scholars deny not only meaning, but they also deny that there is anything "to say"; they deny there is any thought preceding the emission of the signifier. Thought comes from what one writes or says. What is to be said results from what has been said or from some mechanical stimulus.[8] When we have examined the structure of the signifier, we have learned from it all there is to know. The signified is established through speaking and writing, and thus has no preeminence. Meaning comes from the

---

8. We must again refer the reader to Ricardou's scholarly and enlightening analyses of the New Novel (*Problèmes du nouveau roman* [Paris: Seuil, 1967]; *Pour une théorie du nouveau roman* [Paris: Seuil, 1971]; and *Le Nouveau Roman* [Paris: Seuil, 1973]) for an understanding of just how far this process of eliminating meaning can go (see Jacques Ellul, *L'Empire du non-sens; L'Art et la société technicienne* [Paris: Presses Universitaires de France, 1980]). Let us especially recall the disagreement Ricardou raises with respect to Jean-Paul Sartre's thought on the thing "to be said." For Ricardou, Sartre's main weakness is believing that there exists a thought which is going to be expressed. Actually, in conformity with the hatred of meaning, Ricardou shows that all we ever have is something "said," and that language produces itself through the working of its structures.

meaninglessness of writing in itself. Moreover, this has little importance, since, as we have said, meaning does not matter.

At this point we do well to ask ourselves the reason for this overvaluation of the signifier. I can see two reasons for it. First, it can be observed! I cannot observe the signified, nor the relationship of the signifier with the signified. These are "philosophical" problems. On the contrary, I can observe the emission of a phrase, its circulation, deformation, and audition. I can even make nice diagrams of this process. This shows in the first place that this attitude follows the traditional "scientific" tendency: only what can be observed and analyzed by the classical scientific method is important (or even exists, in the extreme view). Since only the communication process involving the signifier can be thus analyzed, it is the only thing that matters to us. Everything else is a metaphysical argument that serves only to confuse the scientific relationship between subject and object.

In addition to these considerations, we now arrive at the "diagram," which is of fundamental importance. At last we can transpose this elusive language into images. We can make a sketch of how communication and even information work. Now we have our feet on the ground, having risked involvement with the signified in imagination, myth, and poetry.

The second reason I can see for the overvaluation of the signifier brings me back to technique: it squares with the technical mentality. We want to see how the thing works: the process of circulation and deformation. As we indicated above, the process is what matters. It just so happens that this is what interests the technician. Finalities do not concern him, nor does meaning! Without knowing it, structuralists are possessed by the spirit of technique. The ideal is to be able to transform everything that exists into a machine: language, communication, and relationships all become machines. Deleuze and even Morin are typical in their choice of terms: a century ago, only a few eccentrics wanted to reduce living beings to machines. Now it is the dominant term.

Machines do not ask questions about the why of things, or about ends or meaning. The only consideration is how a thing works. And this is in reality the preoccupation concerning language and communication. "Machinitis" explains perfectly the reason for the overvaluation of the signifier, which amounts to the invasion of language and the word by the technical mentality. Since we are invaded from all sides by the multiple functions of things, we are obliged to follow this path and reduce everything to this procedure. Here again we find the mania for reducing everything to the same thing, to a single model. Since the dominant model is technical, everything *must* become technical. The least technical of realities (I insist that this is so!), the word, must be cut up until it has been reduced to something that can be dismantled. In our mechanistic obsession, we confuse what can be dismantled [démontable] with what can be demonstrated [démontrable]. Since we have been able to dismantle the "communication-information" complex and the signifier, we assume we have "demonstrated" all there is to the word.

We have examined the two root causes of this raving overvaluation of the signifier. But as soon as one has eliminated the signified, this question is inevitably asked: "After all, is the signifier really so important?" Never does it occur to anyone to go back and give priority to the signified again. No! People assume that the elimination of the signified is over and done with—and well done. Everyone agrees that nothing has meaning. The word does not say anything. People just continue on their way in the descent into the hell of contempt for the word. The signifier is still part of the word. And despite all scientific efforts, it is impossible to keep the word in a sealed jar. It always slips out again; all its edges and shreds of meaning or flashes of truth cannot be kept under cover. People are not comfortable with a completely mechanistic and mechanical word, even when it has been reduced to the level of a signifier. There is always an element of chance remaining, an unforeseen fissure. This is clear when one goes back to the studies of Henri Lefèbvre or Robert Escarpit.

Well, then, why not also get rid of the signifier? The merry venture of Deleuze and Guattari in demolishing the signifier is well known. Their operation is possible only if one has previously excluded the signified. Once this is done, you are left with an imperfect and inconsistent machine. It can be accused of exercising an unacceptable, inadmissible dictatorship over the "desiring machine," the person. The signifier that was magnified at the previous stage becomes a tyrant at the same time as it becomes ridiculous and illegitimate. Simply by demonstrating the illegitimacy of the signifier (which is easy to do as soon as it no longer refers to a signified!), you can make it obvious to everyone that we need to be liberated.

Now the process is complete. There is no more word by which language is reduced to a vague phenomenon without importance. Such vagueness was strictly subordinated to desire and ordinary fluctuations. We have followed step by step the process of the incredible contempt for the word that has progressively dominated Western intellectuals. This contempt has expressed itself in stammering, stuttering, silence, the hiccups, periods indicating ellipsis, strings of nonsense, alliterations, onomatopoeia, inflated typographical arrangements—all meant to replace a language no longer spoken. We no longer know how to speak it because it is not a technical and mechanistic language.

At this stage of contempt, language became literally anything except the vehicle of a message, the originator of meaning, or the place of dialogue. Speaking is anything at all except saying *something* to *someone*. I tremble as I write the last sentence! What a small-minded bourgeois I am; how reactionary, how backward and conservative; and what a refusal of progress! What a right-wing, antirevolutionary mentality! But those who judge this way have not understood that their attitude is neither leftist nor revolutionary, however much they may think so. On the contrary: it is just a simple, trite reflection of the most insipid, conformist, and benumbing technicalism.

I say "benumbing" because when a technician really does his job, he is working on the level of reality, and that is fine. But when an intellectual transposes the technical mentality into his domain and wants to treat everything like a machine, he is simply being conformist; he attains no reality, and behaves "like a child without a mother"! My mother the machine: that is the great lesson we learn from Deleuze and Guattari. Language has become anything at all: a social adapter, an instrument of control and conformity, a signal, ideological reproduction, a framework, alienation of the speaker, etc. It has become anything at all, but never the creative source of meaning; it is never a word borne by a human being and therefore a human word.

## 3. HATRED OF THE WORD

Despising discourse and language was not enough. After scorn the next stage was hatred. To get a feel for this one must read the writings of Maurice Roche—or many others—that reek of hatred for the word. They no longer stop simply at ridiculing the word and demonstrating its futility as inadequate human expression. They find it necessary to destroy it, to dismember language, not stopping as before on the level of a theoretical analysis but going on to a practical level that brings disgrace on language.

What we have here is not just the poverty of expression of one who does not know how to speak, who has a reduced vocabulary and lacks coherence in his thinking. Nor is it the quest of the philosopher or formalist who considers language as an object. We are dealing rather with the deliberate act of someone who possesses a perfect mastery of language and wishes to kill it. He does this by means of a ridiculous exercise designed to demonstrate that the word conveys nothing, says nothing, and that the speaker is nothing but a machine gone haywire—or that was never working right in the first place.

The dividing line comes at this point. At the stage of contempt for language, everything was reduced to machines. Then at this stage of hatred for the word, it is a matter of machines that are out of order, gone haywire. Language is nothing but a grotesque series of syllables, sounds that refer to nothing and signify nothing except mental breakdown.

Robert Pingent and Claude Simon perform exercises in style that are anything but innocent. What they really express is an unquenchable hatred both for our intellectual heritage and for our devotion to efforts at interpersonal communication. A kind of furor against anything that could be verbalized (Ricardou) comes over the intellectual—a hatred of meaning. He feels it necessary to detach himself at all costs from what the other person meant, since it might have import.

This furor and hatred look suspicious! They really amount to avoiding the hard questioning that comes from language itself. Language poses the possibility that there might be a crack or fault in the wall we have frantically and deliberately built to isolate ourselves within meaninglessness and subhuman delirium.

Moreover, hatred of the word becomes more bitter through identification with hatred for humankind. But oddly enough, such hatred expresses itself as a desire for human freedom. The problem is quite simple; the first theme is: language is constructed. It has a limited vocabulary, a syntax, expressions, and a fixed spelling. Therefore it is both normative and at the same time follows norms which the speaker himself has not established.

We learn to speak. One or several adults teach us the language. Thus we are made to conform; we are molded, enclosed. As soon as I learn a language I am deprived of my freedom. What freedom? Why, to create *ex nihilo* my own language. And this is an unacceptable deprivation—a violation of my most sacred right: the right to construct myself as a person.

I am forced to enter a prefabricated scheme; I am taught to speak according to a certain model. Scandalous! I hate this language simply because as an adult I look back on my childhood and realize that it is no longer possible for me to return to the stage of complete innocence and freedom, where nothing was determined in advance and absolutely all possibilities were open. Now all these possibilities have been taken from me. I was forced by language to behave in a certain way and thus left frustrated. I continue to be frustrated because I cannot create my own language. Someone overpowered me when I was innocent and defenseless. The instrument of that power was language.

This eloquent protestation overlooks one major factor: language does not consist of inarticulate howlings into the sea wind. Rather it is—and is *only*—the means of making a connection between one person and another. And if such a connection is to exist, a code is essential—an agreement regarding the meaning of the sounds and signs employed. Without such a code, no relation, no communication, no connection is possible. Language absolutely cannot exist without it. The frenzied effort to place ourselves at square one is utterly naive.

Language, since it is language, is necessarily something given. Just as Jean-Jacques Rousseau's *Social Contract* is never the initial agreement; it is *always* a given. And if we refuse this given, the language simply does not exist.[9] Nothing new or free has been created through such a refusal; it represents no innovation or liberation of humanity.

Such furor against language is nothing but another illustration of Blaise Pascal's "he who would act the angel acts the brute." By trying to be liberated from a language that is learned, along with its accompanying conditioning, one simply gives up all possibility of relationship with others, and forgoes the one thing that makes humankind truly unique: the word. Such an effort leads not to a new level of freedom, but to foolishness. I do not say "to an animal-like existence," because it is impossible to "return" to an animal stage, after having had the use of language and then trying to kill it. Language has made me what I am. Taking such a passionate position against language is not simply the scornful analysis of a phenomenon, as in the previous section. Rather we are confronted with the kind of rage experienced by someone who feels himself trapped with a tongue which he cannot loosen, and who begins to hate his torturer.

This stage of immediate reaction by someone who awakens to his lack of freedom is soon superseded when he comes to the ideological phase. Language is not just the abstract conditioning I was made to undergo when I was still impressionable as wax. It is rather a conditioning that made me agree with the dominant ideology. Now the cat is out of the bag! Language is an instrument of oppression and alienation used by the ruling class to keep the oppressed classes in bondage.

Look at this picture: even before a single word was spoken, evil leaders, cruel tyrants, had the dark design of enslaving others. To entrap poor innocent people who were without any malice, the despots invented a subtle instrument of enslavement out of whole cloth: language. They imposed their language on these poor innocents so that, when they began to speak like their masters, they quite naturally adopted their masters' ideas. Thus they became an obedient and bleating flock.

You find what I have just described ridiculous? But it is only a

---

9. In this connection it would be good to reread G. K. Chesterton's wonderful story, "Professor Chadd's Madness," in *The Club of Queer Trades* (Chester Springs, PA: Dufour, 1962).

slightly exaggerated expression of the formula that is accepted as true with no questions asked: "the ruling class makes the oppressed class learn its language in order to turn the oppressed into prisoners of the ruling class's ideology and to prevent them from thinking." Language is not a neutral instrument that conveys anything whatever or that can be made to serve any and all purposes (certainly this much is obvious!) Rather it orients discourse, and therefore thought, in a certain direction in advance. It is an instrument of social control, much more to be feared than the police or censorship, since it is internalized. It is an element of control anchored in the unconscious, lodged there at an age when we cannot react.

Thus a person will think according to the mold which was forged by the ruling class. He will receive in his person its patterns of thought, its prejudices, its points of view. More than any other means, language constitutes a tyranny over thought, thanks to which everything works by "reproduction" (the famous reproduction theory!). No one can escape from it—we are prisoners of the authoritative meanings.

The next element in the analysis is a fury against this language that imprisons me every time I speak, and that forces me to side with the ruling class. Such an angry cultural revolution is indispensable if I am to free myself from bourgeois culture. But who can help us escape from all that language itself conveys (since even the counterculture is encapsulated in this conformist, sterilized language)? Most solemnly then, the reign of Anti-Word begins, and everything is gladly embraced that produces clear-minded, deliberate "destruction" of the exchange value of the word.

Beginning with such obvious facts, we can easily see what drifting has taken place—all resulting from the combination of para-Marxist ideology and a simplistic analysis of the relationship between language and culture. The emptiness of this intellectual attitude (so widespread in our day) is easy to demonstrate.

The first criticism, obviously, concerns the concept of language connected with this attitude: how can anyone fail to see that this violent diatribe is valid only if one subscribes to a mechanistic and rigid concept of language and the word? This absorption of the contribution of language into bourgeois ideology—language as an instrument of domination—would be a fact only if language were rigorous and precise, if the phrase corresponded exactly to the speaker's intention. It would be true only if the word reproduced ideology precisely, including no halo or haze, no empty spaces or margins. The listener would then have to receive the word with the same precision, understanding exactly what the speaker means.

But we know that this is not at all the situation. On the contrary, discourse is full of empty spaces; there are fractures in the word and gaps in language. In other words, the listener must interpret: he inevitably learns, understands, and receives something quite different from what was said. To be sure, I do not deny that today's culture is the achievement of the bourgeois class, or that its ideas haunt everyone's mind. But perfect reproduction of the bourgeois mind-set does not take place. Alien creations and images are born elsewhere, in the gaps of language!

Note that this famous accusation applies *only to visual "language." Images, films, and television convey the dominant culture, express the bourgeois mentality, absorb alien tendencies, and neutralize potential threats from other cultures.* How remarkable that in these raving imprecations against "reproduction," spoken language and the word are attacked rather than film! This indicates the prestige attached to visual images! Meanwhile we hypocritically accept the preconceived notion of the visual as popular culture. Enough of that!

A second criticism is then immediately apparent: how can language be accused of conveying nothing but the ideology of the ruling class, images of capitalism, and the bourgeoisie's "truths"? How can it function as an ideological appendage of the State, ensnaring us and making us conform? How can anyone substantiate these claims when historically the word has continually constituted a revolutionary ferment and been the instrument of the great rebels? What means did Robespierre and Saint-Just use? And Marx and Lenin? Language was their strength.

The dominant antibourgeoisie mentality expresses itself neither by images *nor by action,* but first of all by a new word. This word is coherent and reasonable, and expresses an analysis, an idea, knowledge, criticism, aspiration, and a utopia radically different from all the words and teaching of the ruling class. Where would these instincts come from if all ideology reflected the ideology of the ruling class? How could language express the revolution if it were only the devoted agent of bourgeois efforts to produce conformity?

In reality the word is revolutionary in itself. Just as it was the agent of humanity's formation in the midst of the animals, so the word in our day is the agent of the great refusal. *Only* the word is revolutionary, and only language can lead to the realization of human hope. This is because of language's relation to truth. The ruling class has to fight an enormous battle to prevent this mole's undermining of the status quo. They need to have a sense of purpose, in order to castrate the word, to domesticate and to circumscribe it—sap its strength—to make language a simple neutral instrument!

How can anyone fail to see that this war against organized language, this hatred for the word, means accomplishing the bourgeoisie's goals? This struggle can only neutralize the one force that challenges the ruling class! The switch from Marx's language to Antonin Artaud's or that of the Dada movement enables the bourgeoisie to breathe a huge sigh of relief. Since language is destroyed and no longer expresses anything, there is nothing left to fear! And what insane foolishness to believe that by destroying language, by destructuring it and denuding it of meaning, something revolutionary is accomplished! Propaganda, in fact, can work only when language lacks clear concrete referents.[10] The sort of "revolutionary" we have been discussing accomplishes the one thing required to make him as susceptible as possible to the influences of the dominant propaganda!

Can utterly incoherent, meaningless discourse, stammering, or intestinal rumbling do revolutionary deeds? Unfortunately the notion that language is the enemy only conveys the absolute poverty and helplessness of its zealous advocates. They can accomplish nothing against this society (which they fail utterly to understand), so they wreak their vengeance where they can, attacking something defenseless (words!). They misdirect their revolutionary energy against an imagined foe, achieving great victories against a weak construction. They pride themselves on their profundity, while the oppressor rejoices to see his adversary destroy what is potentially his own most faithful ally! Hatred of language and the word only manifests the impotence and vanity of conformist pseudorevolutionaries, the likes of which abound among the intelligentsia.

At this point we must virtually exegete from Goux's book (*Les Iconoclastes*, p. 67), since it presents itself as philosophically and scientifically neutral. Goux tries to show that while abstract painters spiritualize painting, the invention of perspective betrays an individualistic, egocentric, and bourgeois point of view. Perspective involves the representation of reality and the reification of the sign.

Then Goux tells us that "if the theory of the sign conceived of meaning as intrinsic, as attached to the material signifier, that would be a fetishist and reifying illusion." "There is no signifier that signifies in itself. The reification of the sign [that is, the sign considered in itself and having meaning on its own] could appear to be metaphysically naive unless one understood its foundations, which are a result of the bourgeois capitalist manner of signifying."

The first point is quite remarkable, since Goux has just described how idols work. One might suppose, therefore, that the Canaanites in the tenth century B.C. conformed to this "bourgeois capitalist"

10. Cf. Jacques Ellul, *Propaganda: The Formation of Men's Attitudes*, trans. Konrad Kellen and Jean Lerner (New York: Knopf, 1965; Random House, 1973).

manner of signifying. By no means. For Goux, the forms of consciousness related to primitive modes of production and exchange cause every people, every act to be charged and overcharged with meaning (therefore the visual and the auditory are identical).

But later on, "there is a movement that results in tendentiously eliminating meaning from reality as consciously perceived, except for a **limited sector**,[11] that of the signs of language and writing. These, on the contrary, are overcharged with meaning. It is as if the linguistic type of signifiers and their **abstract semantic** articulation *absorbed* all the loose meaning (the abundant and unattached meaning), granting themselves the exclusive right, the *monopoly*, of meaning. As a result, nonlinguistic reality was deprived of immediately perceived meaning. . . . Now this monopolizing action by the signifiers must necessarily be accompanied by a putting of the world into perspective, from the point of view of an egocentric subject. . . . One might expect the object of perception to be overloaded with meaning by the constant projection of a subject who does not situate himself reflexively and for whom **everything** in perceived reality is profoundly symbolical (i.e., signifies in an immediate sense). But in reality there is a tendency toward deprojection in the course of which the linguistic signs alone are charged with the totality of available meaning. . . . "

Thus the problem is that language and the word are overcharged with meaning and are true bearers of meaning. This is presented as an impoverishment, a loss of the meaning that should be superabundantly present in everything. It is seen as a monopolistic (a loaded word!) process. Language is called a "limited [symbolic] sector"! But this attitude results from hatred of the subject, of everything personal or living, and preference for the diffuse, the inextricable forest of symbols, the impersonal, and the collective. And in one sense Goux is right. Language and person or subject are indeed related, and conflict exists between language and the forest of symbols with unattached meaning. That much is true, and corresponds exactly to what the Word of God describes for us when it condemns idols. And in the opposite sense, this conflict, reflected by Goux, is what we experience because of the loss of the speaking individual.

Last of all, this hatred for the word is expressed in another tendency. Not only must we demolish organized, meaningful language, but furthermore, reasoning individuals cannot accomplish the task. On the contrary, the true reference point must be sought in the individual who speaks this language spontaneously: without reasoning, without content, without logical order or clarity. When the

---

11. Words in italics are Goux's emphasis, those in boldface are my emphasis.

"lunatic" speaks, the underlying meaning is completely different from what his words signify. The language of the schizo or the neurotic (rather than the paranoid individual, who smells badly of fascism!) becomes the model and the ideal. What we have here is a determination to set aside reason, to cut the connecting thread between word and reason, by destroying coherence.

And in this connection we observe strange magic at work: the lunatic destroys communication, meaning, and continuity—and he is admired for it. People swoon over such great originality! But what does this have to do with language? Pompously calling it "the language of breakdown"[12] does not help any, since this name serves to indicate that language has ceased to exist! Without either meaning or communication, everything is reduced to an emission of sounds, which could be replaced by other sounds or by anything at all!

Lunatics, of course, have a language. But can it be a model? Can it signify liberation in a more authentic sense, going beyond dreadful rationalisms and rationality? We are dealing with the magic and fascination associated with a radically different world. The lunatic has always held this fascination for those who were looking for truth beyond simple human truth. They gave us a god "astride" the lunatic, the lunatic "possessed" by a demon, in communication with the beyond, or the lunatic as bearer of illumination, of direct knowledge not filtered through the human brain. Now we have the search for a language beyond language, sought in the lunatic's destructuring of it.

These senseless phrases are praised, and it is declared that they constitute an attack on organized language, on language as a norm. This language supposedly reveals to us the reverse side of the language

---

12. Michel Thévoz has increased his efforts since his *Le Langage de la rupture* (Paris: Presses Universitaires de France, 1978). In *Ecrits bruts* (Paris: Presses Universitaires de France, 1979), he publishes sample texts by lunatics. These people have distinguished themselves by breaking with society, its established values, and, of course, its conventional language. All have been hospitalized (hardly a criterion, of course!), and one of them (Laure) claimed to have been St. Peter's wife. I am by no means judging here. But these poor texts are only stammerings, distortions of words, combinations of sounds, utterly without content or reference—mere alliterations. And when intellectuals seize such texts and declare that they constitute "revolt," a break with the established order, an argument against the repression of language, acts of resistance to academic culture, I say that these intellectuals are gutless, impotent voyeurs. Trying to proclaim the "freshness" of these aimless texts, or their "primary" character, is pointless. Instead they are texts that betray an inexpressible poverty, impotence, and misfortune. For that reason the people who wrote them should be loved and understood. But to exalt these texts and consider them powerful is nothing but an indication of the death of the word among intellectuals.

of oppression and a refusal of social conventions. The break with ordinary language and "its basic axioms: linear progression, the primacy of meaning, concern for communication," is admired, along with the devaluation of the meaning of words.

In the face of all this, we should perhaps wonder *for whom* this madness has meaning. And *how* is the meaning of such a profound destructuring expressed? The answer is that it has meaning only for someone with a well-developed hermeneutical skill; that is, a very able interpreter. As for *how*, the meaning of the destructuring is expressed only by means of the most rigorous and expressive language! Michel Thévoz involuntarily demonstrates this. His work consists of restoring meaning to something devoid of meaning—establishing communication between people who utter these senseless words and the listener or reader! Thus by means of the very best language—language filled with meaning and communication—these inaudible verbal explosions take on some sort of value! Such utterances contain no more "attack on the very foundation of language," no more destruction of the word, than when someone from China speaks Chinese to me, and I understand not a bit of it!

In the case of the lunatic, however, we have an interpreter. But the situation is somewhat different. When it is claimed that the lunatic expresses his refusal of social conventions when he speaks, I accept this as the understanding that the interpreter offers me. But naturally I ask: if there is no meaning in the lunatic's words, why try to find one? If the words and structures of language have absolutely no value, how can we try to find a message in them?

I fully agree that these lunatic discourses should be studied in order to diagnose the patient who pronounces them. At the same time, I agree that such texts can have in their lack of meaning a great power of poetic suggestion, that some are genuine poems (at least within the post-surrealist concept of poetry). But again, the only person who understands, feels, and interprets is the one who speaks the coherent language of "reason"!

As for being charmed by the fact that these writings ridicule "established discourse," and by the way they "remove us from the realm of language,"[13] such joy depends on the simplistic notion that there exists *an* established discourse and that "being removed from the realm of language" constitutes progress. But if this is so, one wonders why these authors continue to write perfectly understandable sentences, taking care to communicate! Ridiculing the word, which they revel in so much, really amounts to contributing to the

---

13. C. Delacampagne, "Des fous de génie," *Le Monde* (26 May 1978).

victory of the mobs' power, and that of shadows and murders. And social agitation is never innocent!

\* \* \* \* \* \*

But we are left with a nagging question: however did these things manage to come into being—this collection of clichés (hollow but thought to be profound!), this hatred of language, and this simplistic equation: "established discourse = ruling-class = language"? In particular, how were such ideas able to spread to the degree that they are now commonplace? There exists of course a whole trend in favor of the irrational, which places value on antireason, and I have criticized it elsewhere.[14] I'll not repeat myself here. But I believe two themes can help explain this situation. The antilanguage attitude expresses sociological conformity to the development of visual images and the concentration on the visual. The lunatic's language suddenly seems fascinating because it fails to transmit any idea or continuity. It evokes images and ushers us into a world of unusual, baroque *visions*. In other words, such language constitutes the victory of visual images over the reasonable or proclaiming word. This victory is expressed through hatred of discourse and language.

Such an attitude constitutes simple obedience to the dominant "social-technical" trend—simple conformity to what is going on at all levels of our society. In this case we have a refined expression, produced by consciousness raising, of something utterly trite: the reaction of the most ordinary comic strip reader or television watcher.

As we have often noted, the more insipid the reality expressed, the more violently revolutionary and explosive it sounds. The more commonplace the conformity to society's underlying tendency, if that tendency is active but has not yet been exposed, the more nonconformist it appears.[15] In all such cases, people are adopting a pseudo-revolutionary stance, in exact conformity to the normal, logical consequences of the invasion of visual images. This is true whether one proclaims the decisive importance of corporal expression, the devaluation of the word as compared with mime, the renewal of institutional instruction, or liberation through "rough" art or nudism (I have purposely chosen an apparently incongruous mixture!).

But we must recognize that after all something more is going on than just simple conformity or automatic reaction, which is just the reflex conditioned by the triumphant visual image. The hatred, fury,

---

14. *The Betrayal of the West*, trans. Matthew J. O'Connell (New York: Seabury, 1978).

15. See Jacques Ellul, *A Critique of the New Commonplaces*, trans. Helen Weaver (New York: Knopf, 1968).

and accusation which are expressed against the word are not merely the product of sociological conformity. Something else is at work here. I believe that this rage takes its root in the conflict between truth and reality. Between a potential openness on the one hand—to truth which could come from inaccessible depths or the beyond—and on the other hand the right to retreat within oneself. Between "we are not alone in the world" and "me, only me."

Hatred of the word expresses the refusal of a given truth to be read between the lines or heard in the silent moments of discourse. This truth vanishes when we concentrate exclusively on reality and the concrete, on what humanity has accomplished. All modern thought tries to imprison us within this reality and nothing else. Modern thought tries to make us consider reality as truth—the only truth, truth itself. Truth verifiable by science. Truth constructed within reality. The truth of Marxism founded on reality alone. Reality as the criterion of the true, the good, the just. Language continually casts doubt on this claim. This idea must be endlessly reaffirmed, and therefore meaning, openness, and the uncertainty of oral and written language must be destroyed. Only this can explain the hatred and the triumphal chord struck by those who claim to have disintegrated discourse and meaning. But in the final analysis the conflict is religious.

# Chapter V

# THE RELIGIOUS CONFLICT BETWEEN IMAGE AND WORD

## 1. THE CHURCH INVADED BY IMAGES

The Church allowed itself to be invaded by images.[1] It wanted to become visible, establishing itself on the foundation of evidence. This developed alongside the theology of the Church's power and the lust for power, which became incarnate in the institution.

I am terribly sorry to have to say such unpleasant things about the admirable works produced by Christian art. I marvel at this artistic flowering. I am moved to adoration before Fra Angelico, the Chartres statuary, the fair God of Amiens, the tympanum at Moissac, and the worship-inspiring judge of Strasbourg. Yes, this is all undeniably very beautiful. And it is all perfectly Christian in its symbolism, but not when it tries to show the mystery as unveiled by images. This is true even of the stained-glass windows and the *libri idiotarum*. Sculpture is Christian when it limits itself to what can be shown: devils and demons. The tempter of Strasbourg—now there is something visible! All else is an error.

---

1. In one sense Goux (*Les Iconoclastes*) is right to call into question the images that have proliferated in Christianity. But he errs when he considers that this is inherent in Christian revelation and when he speaks of "the Christian heart that clings to holy images and places its faith in their immanent truth." What he describes here is a complete distortion of the gospel. Although at certain times the Catholic and Orthodox Churches and very uncivilized milieux could be described by these words, they become the expression of fundamental ignorance when presented as an absolute. Unfortunately this ignorance is confirmed throughout Goux's book whenever he has the misfortune to speak about Christianity. How astonishing to state that the "Christian trinity has a human face"! And that only the eternal Jewish God has a "radical otherness." Goux seems to be utterly ignorant of Christian thought and theology.

Naturally, I do not at all condemn those who worked with such great perfection as painters, sculptors, and architects. They worked to the best of their ability, with all their faith, consecration, and service, in order to praise and glorify God. These workers were all simple artisans, and the error did not take place on their level. On the one hand, they were marvelous artists; on the other, they were authentic, dedicated Christians. They wanted to serve God with their art, and in effect, they did serve him. That is to say that God surely accepted their work, which is part of the glory of the nations that will be fully integrated into the heavenly Jerusalem.

They accomplished the prophetic act of reconciling sight and the word. But as we shall see, it is only a prophetic act; that is, it relates to the end of time. Furthermore, the error lies at this point: in believing that it was not an act related to the end of time, but a contemporary act that authorized the Church to consolidate its power. Visualizing God's message brought in its wake all sorts of consequences in terms of magic, superstition, idolatry, paganism, and polytheism. Whether we like it or not, the abundance of images, ceremonial beauty, the visual triumph of liturgy, and purely visual symbolism—all these things were the main source of all the medieval and later errors in the Roman and Orthodox Churches.

I said above that it was quite necessary to distinguish between these admirable artists and the Church leaders and theologians who chose to incline everything toward the visual plane. They did this for the sake of efficiency (this is clearly stated and repeated: we must have images because they are more efficacious; in order to see, as Paulinus of Nola says, "if the sight of these shadows when enameled and set off by colors doesn't make some sort of an impression on these crude and stupid peasant minds"). The purpose of images is to strike the imagination, to arouse interest in religious subjects, to "frequently refresh our memories concerning Jesus Christ crucified for us, or to persuade us to follow the faith and the piety of holy persons" (The Colloquy at Poissy, 1561).

But images also teach: they give a résumé of the Bible and Christian doctrine in altarpieces, stained-glass windows, and bas-reliefs: "These are like stories written for the simple and ignorant." However, even so these images produce a feeling of adoration that goes far beyond mere teaching. "Naturally, people love images; even small children love dolls, especially if they are well dressed; they put them in some prominent place and show them a certain respect. This childlike attitude crosses over into religion. Just as dolls are children's idols, images and statues are grown people's dolls, which are more honored if they are well dressed. For, since all our knowledge comes through our senses, we need an object to worship that appeals to our senses; we need to see something that compels our attention. We are also drawn to this by visual pleasure and by the ease of images. For it is easier to look at paintings than to understand doctrine, and easier to make a person from stones than to remake a person in God's image" (Charles Dumoulin).

The sixteenth-century debate over images, which is echoed in the above quotation, also shows a final aspect of these creations: for people in the Middle Ages, as for all those who came before them, images are always endowed with a certain spiritual meaning. They are never solely representation, design, or esthetic. Mainly they are bearers of a message or power. They are an integral part of the sacred world and therefore indicatory, significant, and inviting. You cannot fail to feel their charm. Even if you do not wish it, they take you off to a supernatural domain of worship or magic that is not of this world. They are always means and intermediaries, idol or myth; they are never mere distraction. If they are an evasion, it is an evasion toward the supernatural rather than the imaginary.

These images thus played a role radically different from today's secularized, rationalized, popularized images. Because they were scarce, permanent, and sacred before the eighteenth century, images held a very special position in human life, not at all comparable to the place they occupy today.

But in the Church images very quickly became the glorification of humanity and of individuals (baroque sculpture concentrates everything on visualizing the apostles' and saints' power and their dynamism; finally, the Church's power is visualized and fills simple believers with terror and admiration). The cathedrals were erected to the glory of God, certainly; but they attested the indisputable power of the Church. These images are associated with the determination of the princes of the Church to dominate society. Their aim no longer is to serve and bear witness to the crucified Savior, the Savior of the poor, but to model society according to principles and ideas based on a philosophy drawn from a synthesis of the gospel. They have a desire to dominate and conquer. They are concerned with efficacy—not to draw people to the compassionate Savior, but to cause them to obey God's and the Church's commandments. This efficacy neatly parallels the ecclesiastical institution's triumph. We will return to this relationship. For now, let us just note a series of true and indisputable relations: between the will to power, the will to act in concrete reality with efficacy, the visualization of a message that had existed only on the level of the word, the creation of images as a result of this visualization, the elimination of love in favor of Truth as formalized in dogma, and institutionalization at all levels. This sheaf of factors cannot be disassociated. And sight and image are the key to it all.

Here again I repeat that I do not mean that sight is evil, sinful, etc., or that images are bad. The falsehood lies in reducing what belongs to the order of truth in order to make it enter through visualization into the order of reality. Of course Christian statuary was not idolatrous in itself! And Suger's theology, to which we will return, was perfect. But through necessity, fatality, and the force of events, it produced idolatry.

The explosion takes place in the fourteenth century, just at the time of the worst spiritual, moral, and human disintegration of the Church. There were certainly many statues and representations before this, but they had an entirely different meaning and content, so that they could scarcely be said to involve the temptation to make a visual representation of mystery. During this period we see the profusion of images—of all images—and the cataclysmic appearance of visualization's effect on the people. Precisely when the Church is involved in its worst crisis, it falls back with all its weight on its institutionality, which it magnifies, and on the utterly idolatrous image utilized for every end.

Both the institution of the Church and the image have the same goal: efficacy. Images are efficacious in the transmission of the gospel. The popular preachers of this period are unanimous in saying that only images are persuasive. They are efficacious in holding people's attention, they have a mystical efficacy, and they are efficacious in fighting pagan beliefs—but in such a way that these beliefs came to dominate.

Art and theology experienced a complete mutation in this century of spiritual and human disasters. Georges Duby proposes a bold and fascinating thesis: he says that until the thirteenth century the people were utter strangers to Christianity, except for its completely formal aspects. In the fourteenth century the people enter fully into participation in spiritual life; there is a quantitative expansion of what had until then been limited to clerics. The Church opens up, so that there is now a *possibility* of participation. Verbal expression is too complicated and difficult, so there is direct recourse to images as the simpler way. The people begin to look while participating. They do not get lost in abstract adoration or knowledge of negative theology: they require something concrete.

This movement is accompanied by a sudden change in theology that takes place at the same time: "sight presided over the birth of love and gave it its nourishment . . . everyone at that time was convinced of it . . . to love, one had to *see*." So mystical theology takes the place of discursive theology. The ideal is to contemplate God himself. In order to do so, one must begin by contemplating pious images. "Make yourself present at Calvary by *looking* with your soul . . . see with the eyes of your soul how they drive the cross into the ground." Seeing gives greater certainty and a more accessible object.

Images begin to occupy a central position in piety and theology. And, of course, all these images (statues, paintings, and stained-glass windows) represent scenes from the Bible or the life of the saints. But at the same time relics are images that are presented more and more lavishly: "reliquaries are converted into monstrances, which are transparent cases that enable one to see the holy bodies." Liturgical images also appear; at this period the liturgy and its ornaments and gestures become more spectacular and visual.

As a result, the word is repressed. It doesn't much matter whether anyone understands what is said. What matters is to see what is done, and thus to participate physically. "This is why the display of relics has such an important place in fourteenth-century rites. This is why the Mass is interrupted for such a long time at the moment of elevation, when the consecrated host is offered to the *sight* of the people." Images in Bibles become more and more embellished; there were "Bibles for the poor in which the story was cut up into sections by a series of simple, expressive images. But there were also corporeal images: the body's participation in the sacred mysteries. Collective acts were created in which the entire population of a village mimed the Passion narratives. In these mimes both body and soul tear themselves away from everything that restrains them." These are the *sacre rappresentazioni*.

It is much less important to live one's faith than to mime it, participating with one's body. Knowing revealed truth matters less than being involved in a corporeal imitation of it. For some, gesture is the main thing; for others, seeing replaces everything. The body occupies a position of considerable importance through a sort of contagion. Was there mystical content in these activities? For some, this was indisputably the case: "H. Suso, *miming* Jesus' Passion, proceeded toward the contemplation of an image of Christ crucified."

In any case, these brief notes show that our modern thinkers, so proud of their inventions, were in large measure preceded by others. When I hear serious scholarly presentations of the pedagogical role of images, I remember that all this was *precisely* stated by clerics and friars in the fourteenth century. I often think about the utterly convinced, impassioned look of those who talk about the new theater and its unheard-of discovery of direct participation, in which the spectator enters into the act; and the pride of the specialists and young people who rediscover the body (struggling against this abominable Christianity that has covered over, restrained, and eliminated the body) and tell us pompously about corporal expression, which will replace useless spoken language. It is through the body, mime, and the contagion based on visual stimulation that one transmits . . . what? No, we no longer transmit anything. We only participate. Just listen to all these innovative, revolutionary statements, these discoveries of things never before known in the West (since, of course, the peoples of the Third World have retained the authenticity of corporeal expression, spontaneous theater and ceremony, carnivals and bodily participation in the Mass). When I hear all this, I suddenly find myself right back in the fourteenth century, when all this talk—exactly the same thing—was already being heard, and from Christians! This great contemporary vanity (like discovering the moon, because we are ignorant of everything) rests also on other foundations. To these we will return.

For the Church and the fourteenth century, this rush toward images, toward the "realization" of spiritual and revealed truth, ends up of course in magic and the coarsest of beliefs. This is a far cry from theological rigor and the precision of the word. Instead, we have effusion of feeling, flaggelation, "mystical crises," and worship of images in themselves. It is at this period, for example, that people begin to believe that it is enough to "*look at* the image of Saint Christopher to ensure one will not die in mortal sin on a given day." Images take on supernatural efficacy—images in themselves.

Here we are at the opposite pole from faith, in the most incredible superstition. In the name of efficacy, preachers spread the worship of images, ignoring the distance that the sign implies, and without any reference to a signified. The directness of sight and evidence attributed everything that was taught—Jesus' miracles, for example—to the image itself. When we speak of "medieval superstition," we must refer it primarily to the fourteenth century and to this explosion of things visual, corporeal, represented, and of reality.

From this point on the easy way is open. People must be made to see. So they will go from statue to statue, immersing themselves in seeing increasingly fascinating things, ending up with the baroque and the "glories" of the seventeenth and eighteenth centuries. Until then, God had remained beyond representation, but with the advent of the glories, God could be seen. Artistic representation will become more and more realistic in its detail, culminating in the vulgar religious art called in France *sulpicien*. If people need to see, and if a statue has power and holiness in itself, it *must* cease to be a sign, and reproduce reality faithfully and photographically.

All this coincides with the fundamental identity crisis of Christianity in the fourteenth and fifteenth centuries, and to the crisis in the relationship of Church and society. The identity crisis is double: the loss of the certainties of the faith, and the loss of systematic theology. This is the period of great social and popular crises, such as the Black Death; one-fourth of Europe's population disappears within a two-year period. Death triumphs. The certainty of the words of the gospel is doubted. God is not all-powerful, since we are experiencing such tragedy. People felt they could not have confidence in the Church's traditional preaching, since the Church was unable to protect them. They needed other protections and means, other sources of help and certainties. They lost faith in the promises; one must clutch at visible reality, which at least gives us something unquestionable.

Systematic, integrative theology is lost in the midst of the most terrible disputes, which are political as well as religious. Nominalism, secularization, and negative theology triumph. All speech can do is fall silent. Since a person can no longer understand or develop what is left of theological discourse, he falls back on visual things and contemplation through a mystical gaze.

But during the same period we have the Church's internal crisis (the moral crisis, the Avignon papacy, and the Great Schism) and its external crisis (the Church repressed by the political powers and confined to religious matters). The Church responds to this double crisis by increasing its reliance on the visual and institutional planes. The Church does not accept its privation and its reduction to wandering and poverty; it does not choose to return to its status of "wanderers and travelers of the earth" and to pure evangelical preaching in a state of destitution (as St. Francis of Assisi and *many others* had prescribed a century earlier; but they were immediately betrayed by their successors). Instead, the Church persists in its desire to consolidate its power. And since truth no longer has any weight, the Church will triumph in reality—visible and institutional reality.

This is the great century for the institution, as well as for visualization; the two always go together (in our day as well). This is true because institutions are a construction of reality—an effort to grasp reality, a superstructure of reality grasped by sight. Thus institutions are a normal consequence of visualization. If reality is all that counts (economic, political, social, familial, and professional reality), if all of human life is reduced to our social and productive being, and if everything takes place in this world, the *corollary* of this discovery of the primacy of the senses is *the will to organize institutionally*. The Church tried to resolve its multiple crisis by developing and strengthening itself institutionally.

Institutionalization and visualization—the two reinforce each other. The institution arises from visualization and from the invasion of images, and also reproduces this invasion. The power of images is established on the very foundation of the institution. We must have something to show. Only institutions fill this need. We must have something spectacular and flamboyant, and the institution allows us to have popular celebrations and fireworks. Liturgy becomes sumptuous, and the Church becomes the showing Church because the institution organizes things and manifests itself.

Even the strictly spiritual mystical tendency (seeing God) can exist only on the basis of the institution. Because the institution is solid, forms a good framework around people and things, and makes society function, the mystic can dedicate himself to his passion, his detachment, and his contempt of everything. Administration must be perfect if the political or military genius is to function. Without administration, nothing works. And while it is true that too transcendental a theology leads to a complete liberation from the powers of the world, to a rupture that authorizes absolute powers, the reverse is also true: a strict, precise institutional system authorizes and produces a purely spiritual mysticism. Sight is the common denominator of the two.

The relationship between the visual order and institutions, which was quite clear at its beginning in the Church, is found again in its entirety in our day. Thus the boldness of modern theater, of gesturing, of corporeal expression, and the revolutionary explosion of the abolition of spoken language in the theater are possible only thanks to subsidies granted by the State; that is, thanks to the generosity of the institution. There is actually a deeper agreement: reality alone matters to both the theater and the State.

In the conclusion of the conflict between the word and idols, where we observe the complete triumph of images in the Church, we must become aware of the fact that it is primarily a religious conflict. First of all the conflict is situated in the religious world: in the Church. There the triumph of reality and the elimination of truth take place. This world closes in on itself, denying the possibility of another opening that is specifically maintained by the word. The word migrates continually, from one world to the other, from the transcendent to the immanent. The image belongs to this side and is sufficient unto itself.

Nowhere but in the Church is the primacy of vision created and the word progressively excluded. The Word is sung and becomes liturgical; the Word in an incomprehensible language[2] subsists only as an element of the spectacle. No longer is it a word that bears meaning. The Word is excluded and replaced by liturgical gestures, colors, changes of clothing, incantations, and litanies.

---

2. We must not forget that Latin was, at least beginning in the twelfth century, utterly incomprehensible to simple believers, just as it is today!

Nowhere but in the Church was created the primacy of the institution over social action and ethical questioning. These latter both belong to the domain of the word. The primacy of the institution involves rigidity and the creation of law as the complete solution to people's and society's problems.

It is in the Church, and nowhere else, that new scientific thought was formulated. This kind of thinking is attached to the reality of things, unlike previous thinking, which was attached to interpretation or discourse. This new thinking came from the laity and was secularized; it dealt with this world—the real, visible world—and only with this world. It was not thinkers, philosophers, and scholars outside the Church who developed this thinking against the Church: only clerics, and often churchmen, formulated this transformation. Secularization was born of and in the Church, as was the concept of modern institutions.

All this was directed by the affirmation (within the Church) of *human glory* and the desire to *possess the world*. This is the enormous mutation. And all the laity, materialists and realists, who will follow only carry on what begins at this point. Human glory and possessing the world are attitudes in life that are expressed by the primacy of sight over everything else.

The spread of images that the modern world has experienced began in the Church. Its source was in the "enthusiasm" for images in the Church that is the precise counterpart of the abandonment of revealed truth, of the meaning of the word, of the humility of the Incarnation, of the discretion of revelation, and of the uncertain openness to the beyond and to the echo. The Church opted for what is visible, and with it, for power, authority, efficacy, and the agglomeration of crowds around a reality[3] that was at last seen and grasped. This was a radical choice of what would be *shown*; it involved showing and demonstration. But the Word was no longer present. This was because the conflict between sight and language and between idols and the word is essentially a *religious* conflict, when a rupture occurs between reality and truth.

Revealed truth does not try to annex reality, to assimilate it, or

---

3. Of course, I know that this choice was made before the fourteenth century. But many ambiguities and uncertainties in this orientation remained, and they are erased beginning in the fourteenth century. I also know that the Church multiplied images before the fourteenth century, but they were utterly different and had another meaning. On this subject see the admirable book by Georges Duby, *The Age of the Cathedrals: Art and Society, 980–1420*, trans. Eleanor Levieux and Barbara Thompson (Chicago: University of Chicago Press, 1981).

to cause it to mutate. On the contrary, reality tends to assert itself as truth—as the only, exclusive truth. And when the Church, charged with the responsibility of revelation (which is not religion; if revelation remains authentic, it cannot be part of a religion), opts for reality, it involves the real world in becoming a religious world. The Church thus causes the world to construct the religious meaning of images— all images—and the religious superstructure of reality—all reality. The anti-Christian movements of the eighteenth to the twentieth centuries will follow precisely the same path, simply reversing the signs; that is, they will make the new secular religions[4] into a weapon of war against the Church, which will get what it deserves.

Finally, today, according to Maillot, "liturgical renewal is in reality a transformation of Christian worship into Canaanite religion; it involves staged worship in which the visual aspect tries to drown out the word . . . but we must be especially concerned about the teaching of children and what was called until recently 'catechism.' Everything else is now done in catechism classes: scribbling, drawing, dissecting pictures, film showings . . . they have utterly forgotten to come back to the written word."

## 2. ULTIMATE VALUE AND THE CAPTIVE WORD

In this section we will consider a preliminary approach to this religious conflict in the context of the non-Christian religious universe of our modern world, rather than in the context of Judeo-Christianity. The visual image's triumph ushers us into a religious universe that is different from the universe of the word. The conflict seems to take place in two different domains: that of "ultimate value" and that of excluding what is hidden.

In the first case, the central question is "in what do people place their confidence today?" They rely not on the sight of a reality that surrounds them, but rather on the multiplication of artificial visual images that constantly attract their attention. The situation in which we find ourselves is contradictory: the visual order places supreme value on the reality in which I live. I am subject to this confrontation, and sight actually allows me to position myself in reality and to act on it.

But the multiplication of artificial images changes this relationship. These thousands of changing images scatter my attention, provoking hallucination and hypnosis as I am submerged in them. The resulting dizziness and the enormous mass of visual stimuli tend to

---

4. See Jacques Ellul, *The New Demons*, trans. C. Edward Hopkin (New York: Seabury; London: Mowbrays, 1975), concerning this whole movement.

ascribe ultimate value to reality. Everything, and the truth about everything, must henceforth be situated with respect to this reality of images. Not only situated, but judged, appraised, and evaluated. A thing's value depends on its relationship with this reality and on its ability to find a place in and modify it. Anything that fails to act on visible reality has no importance.

Obviously I am not speaking here of conscious, clear, and philosophical thought; we are dealing rather with the spontaneous feeling of the average person whose brief thoughts are led by the images that are part of him. But this preconception of the average person is the religious attitude of an age. It is not a matter of an explicit ritualized religious value given to this reality, but simply a belief in its ultimate value. This coincides strikingly with Marx's philosophical thought, for example, when he wanted to gauge the truth of a thought by the *Diesseits*, the reality on which the thought could have a grip. In Marx this idea expressed a conscious and systematic materialism. That the tone has now changed is evidence of the effect of visual images.

Everything must be referred to this visible reality. It serves to decide between true and false in one's thinking. Actually, true and false are not at stake; rather, it is a matter of correct and incorrect. This is because an exact science can produce a technique that acts on this reality or explains reality; but this has nothing to do with truth.

Furthermore, this confusion in contemporary language is typical. "Correct" and "true" have become synonyms; so have "false," "lying," and "incorrect." But there is a world of difference between these terms that is not perceived. Visualized reality tries to supply the means of controlling everything in the domain of thought, philosophy, and theology (visualization is at the root of most contemporary theological conflicts!). But the situation is much more complex than this remark would lead us to believe. For everyone knows that visualized reality is visual only through the technical transmission of images. It is not an experienced reality, but a reality that comes to us indirectly through the mass media. As we have seen, this is what assures the visual domain's triumph. It situates the individual in a universe he believes to be real, since he sees it; but it is a purely fictitious world. It is fictitious because it consists of nothing but an environment made up of images that are absolutely nothing but images.

The only effective reality the individual encounters is that of his TV screen. Everything that takes place on the screen and that the individual takes for reality is simply a pointillistic system of electronic signals. But he takes it for genuine reality, and I have shown elsewhere that this reality is infinitely overvalued in comparison with the reality one can actually live. What is shown on television becomes the important reality, whereas what is lived no longer matters. The stupe-fying multiplication of images constitutes a whole *universe* of images in which we are situated.

In other words, there exists, on the one hand, the concrete reality in which we live, but it ceases to matter because it lacks the sparkle and exciting impression given by images. We progressively detach ourselves from reality, whether it is "everyday life" (work and family) or "political life" (in the practical and concrete sense).

On the other hand, we have the imagined reality, made up simply of images, which makes an illusory universe for us. But this universe is so fascinating and gripping that we prefer to situate ourselves within it and live by proxy. It is not exactly an imaginary universe (although it is this, but in a special sense; for our imagination has not established it; rather, it is established by the imagination of those who construct these spectacles), but it does constitute a universe. This spectacle is artificial.[5]

Of course, you could say that the other universe (of everyday life) is artificial, since homes, marriage, and now also conception and education are the products of artistry. But there is a world of differ-ence, since I can act on this second universe. I can intervene, and my decision is woven into the constitution of the world in which I live. But the other universe is artificial in the sense that I can in no way affect it; it is made outside of me. Thus through this multiplication of images I end up living in a universe from which I am excluded as subject. I am without responsibilities, without action, dialogue, or power.

We place our religion in this reality. That is, we believe only what takes place through this means (the image, which becomes the uni-verse of images). We receive our values (cultural and moral) from this spectacle. We establish our modes of mediation with respect to this spectacle, which becomes the locus of our strongest gratifications and frustrations. A person pays closer attention to the means of communication than to a worship service!

Thus there is a double process: supreme value is ascribed to images, to the visual which triumphs over the word; then the universe of images in which we are situated is established. This is a purely visual universe (the word plays only an auxiliary role in it), but it is an illusory vision. The second process is an ancient religious one: visible reality is a source of greater religious certainty: I see, and I

---

5. For me there is no pejorative connotation in this word. I do not give special preference to the natural by placing Nature in a position of eminent value. But in this context we are considering the consequences of an exclusively artificial universe, in which everything related to Nature is excluded because it is merely represented.

attach my confidence, my experience, etc., to what I see. Then I
establish a religious world (the divine world) that is entirely visualized.
It is primarily imaginary and secondarily illusory. I can tell about it in
endless detail, with increasing accuracy (the idols as images of the
gods, and then the infinite multiplication of deities according to their
functions).

*Visible reality transferred to the illusion of images becomes our
ultimate reference point for living* (not for thought!). But the value we
attribute to it is strictly fictitious, since it proceeds from mechanisms
and is situated in a fictitious universe. A modern individual's beliefs
are all situated within that reality. He never expects anything other
than a *visible change*; any other kind seems fallacious. He places his
hope in processes that transform the visible; the expansion of revolutionary beliefs is always exclusively situated in this milieu. No one
believes any more in the creative or the founding word. This conflict
between sight and word has to do with the ultimate value a society
adopts for itself.

The present humiliation of the word is only the current version
of a permanent reality: people detest the fundamental word, which
nevertheless establishes them as *human* beings. As can easily be
imagined, this is the central drama of every individual; it is another
aspect of the death instinct. It is the key to the suicide wish and the
real truth concerning the radical separation in a person's heart. It
explains his explosion when he denies what he has believed.

With brilliant insight, Kierkegaard has seen this better than
anyone.[6] Viallaneix has gathered his thoughts on the subject under
the title "Captive Words," because all human words are overpowered
by dissonance. And among these captive words can be discerned the
forgotten word, which is the word of creation, the frozen word of
philosophy, and the poetic word that is sung. We are made to live
these words, but they have become incomprehensible to us when
spoken; they lead to misunderstanding. The entire creation speaks,
but instead of listening to this word, we want to see the secret of this
creation. We want to see, and this leads to scientific demands. The
words of creation, the world's song, and the echo of Nature become
confused words. According to Kierkegaard, God speaks this way, and
creation tells of its creator. But we grasp only an echo that is actually
a parody or a counterfeit of the creative word, which as human beings
we can no longer hear because of our rupture with God. Nature
"promises harmony and speaks to us of a divine message; but it gives

---

6. For this analysis I return to the first part of the previously cited book
by Viallaneix, *Kierkegaard et la Parole de Dieu*. In this section, Viallaneix has
thrown light on the degradation of the word especially well. But one should
read her entire book.

us only incomprehensible signs which have to be interpreted." This is
made essentially impossible by parasites on the wavelength and by
interference, which prevent us from understanding this first indication
of a possible word. These "noises of life" usher in all sorts of
dissonance and drown out the intelligible word.

Kierkegaard then shows with prophetic vigor the kind of noise
we experience today, whose importance he had discerned: the racket
of the city, of speed, of politics and revolution, the racket of the press
and of advertising, "urban chattering and gossip, like a snowy whirl-
wind"—all this (and what would he say in our day!) utterly suffocates
the word. "The problem with the daily newspaper is that it is expressly designed to glorify the present moment"; "nonsense, gossip,
foolishness . . . these things are caricatures of the word; they transform it into impious chattering, yack-yack, so that the content of the
message is scattered by senseless noises." "The retransmission of
objective information is a parody of the communication of knowledge." Faced with this mockery of language, Kierkegaard's only possible response is "the catharsis of silence." Silence these noises and
fall silent oneself. Nothing but silence can allow a person to hear a
word of truth again as it traces its path through the echoes of nature.

Instead, people attach themselves to these noises. Thus they
enter into another domain of the captive or betrayed word: the frozen
word of philosophy, which claims to be listening for the ideal. Here
again Kierkegaard appears to be amazingly ahead of his time, as he
poses the basic question of the relationship between word and language. But he situates the question in its relationship to the rupture
between human beings and God, between the word of human beings
and God's. "For the divine code, Nature's code, and the human code
are different. It follows that a person who tries to understand God's
message by himself is condemned to replace it with another message,
from another language, which is human language." "The person puz-
zled by the jumble of words that creation whispers around him refers
them to a linguistic system which he hopes will be able to tell him
these words' meaning. . . . The word is developed into a language;
that is, it finds itself dialectically united to a language."

Kierkegaard proposes an observation (that for his time is astonishing) in which "the basic error in modern times is just this: being
continually concerned with what one needs to communicate, rather
than with the nature of communication." But after profoundly studying language as an ideal object, he discovers what we thought we had
just recently discovered (Viallaneix deserves the credit for showing
the extent to which Kierkegaard was ahead of us here!): that "each
element of society has an element of discourse that corresponds to it.
Both perform a function—one in life and the other in language. The

workings between these elements take on the same form. In short, there is an isomorphism in the human universe and the universe of discourse. Based on this fact, a human typology can be conceived based on an analogy with the study of language."

Language expresses what is deepest in a person, so that it should be clear and coherent. But its reality is quite different: confusion and gibberish. Human discourse has submerged us in misunderstanding and noncommunication, because language has triumphed completely over the word (Kierkegaard gives an extraordinary demonstration of this). So "language and thought are swallowed up by the same chaos." Once again, Kierkegaard connects this contemporary perversion with our inability to hear the Word of God. We substitute our own approach: logic, for example, or philosophical speculation, etc. It is pointless to fill in these outlines, which are found in Viallaneix's book.

The third movement, concerning the word as sung, is similar: the poet could speak a true word, but poetic communication has been degraded, so we need a rediscovery: another kind of discourse, which would give poetry back its authenticity. "*Nature's sounds* resound with vain echoes, because the first word gets lost, with the first impulse. *Those who construct systems* (philosophers) try without success to catch meaning in the rigid mesh of their abstract concepts. They get bogged down in the chatter of their own reflections and refuse to budge, with all their knowledge. *Poets* improvise imaginary interpretations of the message that their ear perceives; but they get lost in the field of the possible. None of these is able to restore communication with God or to understand his language, by their own efforts."

Thus the humiliated word of our society, with its particularities, its excessive destruction, its squandering of discourse, its inflated style, and its nonsense, is the continuation or the final result of a long, slow process that took it from the beginning to us. It amounts to the permanent destruction of the word, understood and shown by Kierkegaard, who sees it as beginning with the rupture between God's Word and the human word, between humanity and God. But the universality of this process does not at all diminish the value that the word and language have had in all societies, nor the strangeness of what is happening today. Looking at the present situation we cannot merely say: "This is just what always happens." Or, "This condition is permanent, since it all began with the Fall." With this point of view, we have no reason to be concerned! To the contrary, we must make this our current concern, since it is an existential question posed to each generation. We must pose it in today's terms, and not in eternal, abstract terms.

Finally, we must realize that not by accident Kierkegaard raises the issue and perceives this rupture of the word and devaluation of language. He shows both tendencies to be universal, right at the beginning of the modern era; that is, just at the moment when this humiliation was about to begin.

## 3. THE EXCLUSION OF WHAT IS HIDDEN

The second aspect of this controversy is that visualization excludes what is discreet and hidden. The first debate over the triumph of sight excluded spiritual and religious matters and questions concerning truth. This facet of the debate involves us more specifically in the elimination of the Christian revelation. The triumph of things visual involves a radical negation of Christianity (this is probably the central issue in the present crisis). For the triumph of images makes acknowledgment of the Incarnation impossible; the hidden God is not God, precisely because he is hidden.

It is not by accident that the enormous popularity of the "death of God" was born in our world of images: the impossibility of representing God visually leads inevitably in our day to the impossibility of his existence. God is dead—but beyond all the explicit reasons generally offered, he is dead because he is not visible. We can have confidence only in a visible God who is clearly manifested, exclusively in the visual dimension. When we contrast the successes of science and technique with the failure of religions, we always place ourselves in the visual domain. There even exists a denial of sacred history, the secret history of God with people, which is a mysterious and uncontrollable process that can only be told. All we accept now is common, collective history, which is unique and has no duality. Since it is visible it can be written up in newspapers. It is made by people, so if we continue to believe in God, we include his action with that of people who make history: government officials or revolutionaries, depending on our political tendency.

In the same way the Kingdom of Heaven hidden in the world is excluded. All Jesus' parables concerning the hidden quality of the leaven or of a seed (things that work secretly and are not seen) to which one can only bear witness by the word—all this has become absolutely unimportant in our day. For we require, as our only acceptable truth, what can be photographed, with results we can measure statistically, and which we can represent graphically. This hidden Kingdom is as uninteresting to everybody these days as the promised "Paradise."

The Word which testifies that "My kingdom is not of this world" means, as far as we are concerned, that it does not exist, since it can neither be represented nor visually verified. At this point we are suddenly flung into another dimension: politics. It can be said that politics essentially belongs to the visual domain (it uses the word as a means subordinated to ends that can be visualized), whereas the spiritual and religious conflict is of the order of the word. Thus the word-sight conflict is also played out in this area.

Politics involves the disclosure of everything latent, bringing these elements to the light of day so their efforts can be evaluated. Politics means power and capturing the means of power. And power is necessarily located in the visual sphere. Even biblically, when the Word is revealed as power, it produces visible results (the Creation!). But according to Paul's reasoning, the things that can be seen were made by the invisible ones. Politics, on the contrary, tries to go only from visible things to visible, and to circumscribe everything within the efficacity of power. This is the opposite of the process of witnessing, which never coerces and never gets involved in competition for power. It always leaves the listener with his independence, because the witness always proceeds from the visual to the word.

The current controversy over the Resurrection is a special case. The Resurrection as it has been related to us is impossible, because we can no longer believe in the creative power of a word. Conversely, we cannot conceive of this Resurrection in our visual universe. Here the word goes back to something hidden and is an unobtrusive, discriminating word: separation by this word is the first decisive revelation. The visual, on the other hand, is the universe of nondiscrimination, related to the totality and to unity with violent contrasts. Everything essential about the Christian revelation is called into question (with different degrees of seriousness) by the basic reference to images and by mistrust of the word.

\* \* \* \* \* \*

Most modern theological controversies reflect this conflict. They include the elimination of theology for the benefit of politics, as well as the denial that God is the Word; the denial of the validity of prayer, as well as the impossibility of transcendence and revelation. In another area, that of ethics, the calling into question of behavior judged previously to be Christian (listening, patience, obedience, waiting, vigilance, along with many other modern tendencies) only signifies the primacy of the visual over the oral, and the judgment of ineffectiveness made on a visual basis.

But, were it not for the role of the mass media and the universe of spectacle, we would be involved in a very old, merely renewed, controversy. I am inclined now to say that the above positions are taken not only because of the visual domain but because of the visual domain's mutation by means of the technical establishment. If this is true, these ethical and theological judgments are nothing but the result of a sociological process and involve the acritical acceptance of the universe of images.

Furthermore, many theologians conformed to their common unfortunate tendency and committed themselves to the direction society was moving, going down the easiest incline; that is, they adopted images with enthusiasm and began to be ashamed of the word. How many proclamations on the modernization of the Church and evangelism have we read and heard, always with the same content: modern individuals are disgusted with discourse; they no longer listen or read; on the other hand, they watch television. If you want to be effective, you must work with images and give up talking. You must change liturgy into corporeal expression, into living tableaux, into captivating spectacle, and transform spoken discourse into popular songs and rock music. These do not say anything, but through their rhythm they involve people in a sort of communion that comes not from the Holy Spirit but rather from people's identical reactions to extreme stimuli.

When the Catholic Church oriented itself toward visualization, it committed the greatest possible error, all in the name of efficiency. This error contributed to a double process that expressed the great temptation of the Church: on the one hand, the transformation of revelation and faith into religion (thus imitating the world's religions); on the other hand, the attempt to produce a Christian society, a Christian civilization, a Christian world order. This could be accomplished only by visualization and by surrounding all life's realities with images.

However, the tremendous perversion which was accomplished in the West between the eighth and eleventh centuries (earlier in Byzantium, where the even greater importance of the icon begins in the fifth century) seems to me quite different from what is happening today—different from two points of view. First, everything worked due to a symbolism that was both created by the Church and clearly understood by the faithful. In this symbolic process everyone progressed in an authentic spiritual instruction. But today the churches provide poor spectacles in which nothing commits people through new symbols; they are just nourished by fleeting, ready-made images that lack depth.

The second difference is that the medieval Church created this tendency. It had discovered the importance of sight on its own; it was innovative in statuary and liturgy. The Church was producing what no one else did! It was creative. All this involved a theological error, but at least it was inventive. In our day, in contrast, we have only the most insipid imitation of what is being done everywhere else; the

Church follows the sociological tendency. Everybody produces television programs; well, then, why shouldn't we do like everybody else? This is the beginning and the end of modern Christian wisdom.

But the motivation is the same: efficacy. Images are more efficacious, especially when broadcast by the media; therefore . . . ! And we must have images that respond to the good public's expectations! The corollary is that the word is destroyed. What a frenzy Christian theologians have displayed for accepting structuralism or the theory of incommunicability. What sadistic joy they find in endlessly repeating that the person listening understands nothing of what the speaker says. If the word does not connect, if nothing is communicated by the word, well then, let's give up and stop talking. And what eager agreement with the idea that language is tyranny, that discourse is nothing but the expression of an undue, illegitimate superiority of the speaker over the person listening. At least, agreement concerning the word's uselessness is reached with a special kind of frenzy among Protestants, even though the Reformation centered everything on the word. But this contempt for the word tries to justify itself with the most obvious observations; it is shown to have the most commendable intentions, and is clothed in the clearest *evidence* and the best good sense.

We must improve our evangelism techniques. People no longer understand Christian vocabulary, so we must change it. This is both true and false. It is much more serious than a simple matter of vocabulary; a different choice of words cannot really change the situation. What people do not understand is not certain words but the word itself, whatever its content (unless it becomes mere nervous stimulus in a propaganda context). You can rejuvenate your vocabulary all you like, but you will not be any better understood, because the manner of thinking, the value of the word, the fact that one can no longer trust a person's word—all this is called into question!

The essential fact is that people today are utterly indifferent to the question of truth. This is because not only their individual existence but all of society attracts their attention rigorously and systematically to the domain of reality. This is accomplished through the power of techniques, which get a hold on their minds through images. People are indifferent to their destiny and the meaning of life: all this has become mere "literature," and this expression tells the whole story! People are committed to the great technical venture; they devote themselves to it, and images express this involvement perfectly.

Thus, someone will say, we must adapt to this: since people no longer understand the word, let's replace it with action. This is the temptation of Christian activism: good works, worker priests with a commitment to a union or politics. As we have said, action falls within the province of images. Action genuinely reaches people and lures them, because they find themselves in reality; and action, on most people's scale of values, rates infinitely higher than the word.

Since people no longer understand the word, we should use propaganda: "audiovisuals," expositions, and large gatherings where the word will be only background noise or a pretext. Such a gathering is an image in itself. You have the crowd, orchestration, projectors, and, in this context, someone who speaks and is nothing but an image himself: Billy Graham is the perfect example. Certainly all this will touch people in the crowd.

Telling the story of the Bible in comic strip form is undoubtedly efficacious. The only problem is in knowing if such a comic strip is still the Word of God. In the final analysis, the basic question is why we want to reach people. Let's remember Jesus' word to the Pharisees: "You travel over sea and land to make a proselyte, but when you have him you make him twice as bad as yourselves" (Mt. 23:15, JE). This is not exactly the problem we are dealing with, but it is vital that we ask ourselves whether the means we use are able to convey the truth of Jesus Christ. These means can move people, gather them, convince them, and even bring them to church. But such means really convey nothing of the truth of Jesus Christ to people. They merely recruit people by leading them into all sorts of misunderstandings about Christianity.

Action can be a means of entering into contact with people, as can gatherings or film clubs. But such contacts do not lead anywhere. Neither action nor films convey any truth, since, like images, they are unable to convey anything besides reality.

An exposition that is supposed to be evangelistic is dangerous for the gospel. What can a Church of the Word possibly *show?* Images? Of what? For Protestants the matter is obvious: images of the past can be used: old Bibles, old engravings. But can these convey the truth of Jesus Christ? On the contrary, won't such images involve the spectator in all sorts of misunderstandings and confusion? He will be led to identify the Church's life with its history, to confuse humble Christians with heroes, to think of Christianity as a religion, and to identify rites and numbers with truth. That is to say that such efforts lead people into utter falsehood. All images include within themselves the same danger. Thus theologians, priests, and pastors are contaminated by the relentless triumph of images. Once again they enter the order of necessity, abandoning the order of freedom. Instead of straining toward truth their concern is for reality.

In this connection the most unthinkable reversal takes place: when all of Christianity is based only on the word, and the word is accepted as the Word of God that can be expressed only by the human word corresponding to it, then the contempt and abandonment of this human word inevitably signifies abandonment and contempt for the Word of God. By allying itself with images, Christianity gains (perhaps!) efficacy, but destroys itself, its foundation, and its content. In reality nothing is left to say—not because the word is false, but because images have emptied it of meaning. And pious Christians have been gripped by the "evidence" that these visual media and this rash of images are good, lovely, and pleasant to taste, and able to make them wise.

# Chapter VI

# THE IMAGE-ORIENTED PERSON

At this point we come to the greatest mutation known to humankind since the Stone Age. The delicate balance between seeing and hearing, word and gesture, was broken in favor of signals and sight. Western people no longer hear; everything is grasped by sight. They no longer speak; they show. Nevertheless, we are inclined to consider contempt of discourse—the hatred of the word and language that has gripped us so—as a problem only for intellectuals.

Isn't this just a clerical controversy? A matter for those who abused the word, exhausted language, vainly tried to find a new phrase, and who, out of spite, despise and hate that which has served them so well? They are intellectuals, poets, politicians, churchmen, professors, and lawyers, but also scientists and philosophers—all a bit like the doctors satirized by Molière. They are people for whom the word has become a doormat on which they could always wipe their feet; it is made of something soft, always pliable, which could be abused in all sorts of ways.

Everything had been said and then some, so that each time it seemed possible to advance, a hand was raised at the back of the lecture hall to remind us that Lu Xun or Hippodamus had already said that. The result is an infuriated rejection. We needed to get out of this cage and these repetitions; we needed to enter the real world where at last everything was not identical to everything else. We had learned such fine lessons from science.

Is this an issue for intellectuals that bypasses the common person? Not at all. First, we must not forget the incredible influence of intellectuals on society and today's public opinion, at least in France. We live in an era that is completely different from those that preceded it, when it might have seemed that intellectuals carried no weight and that their ideas had no repercussion on society. Although this was never really accurate, the repercussions of the intellectual revolution made themselves slowly and progressively felt. At present intellectuals have had a direct hold over the public since they began to have access to the mass media. Intellectuals are no longer scholars in a little heated room, like Descartes, writing for a few specialists and showing only their absentminded professor's look in public. Now they speak on the radio and are seen on television. They are part of the ordinary person's view of things. Even the intellectual who is not "committed" promotes more formulas and opinions than systems or complete doctrines, and this is exactly what is called for. We find him speaking "live" for the public on whatever the subject may be, just slightly beyond what the public can comprehend, but in any case giving the public what it expects.

These words spread because they belong to an image: the death of God; the death of humanity. These things are spoken: the class struggle, imperialism, structures, systems, desire, sexual freedom, machismo, phallocracy. . . . We do not much know what they mean, but these terms involve in themselves a kind of magic that makes us feel good when we use them. By means of these terms the ordinary person becomes part of a trend or fashion. But such image-formulas, which are at first used at random, settle in our subconscious in successive layers, repeatedly feeding our minds, so that in the end they determine our convictions and the positions we take on issues.

Today's intellectuals are extraordinary shapers of public opinion, provided they have access to television and can at the same time express themselves just a bit beyond what the average person feels and expects. Thus when people see and hear intellectuals massacre the language, hold the word up to ridicule, and endlessly state their hatred of reasoned expression, the public soaks it up. How could people fail to welcome eagerly what coincides so perfectly with their own convictions (for example, that intellectuals are useless quacks, that only efficacious action matters, etc.) After all, even intellectuals are saying it! The word is more suspect and ridiculous than ever! This great intellectual controversy has in effect moved to the popular level; thus the hatred of the word has won over even the humblest people.

## 1. THE CONSUMER OF IMAGES

"The hatred of the word has won over even the humblest people"; but at the same time the common person has experienced a mutation that gives him access to the world of images. This mutation took place not because people reflected and chose it (consciously preferring sight and this imaged universe) but as a result of the change in environment and circumstances. No deliberation or conscious choice was made. Artificial images became profuse, and thus the environment we live in changed. We have involuntarily chosen these artificial images.

We prefer looking at our pictures to looking at the landscape, and when we do happen to look at a landscape, we look at it as if it were a photograph: "Pretty as a picture!" We are better at grasping the beauty of a work of art in reproduction than in the original. We have changed without noticing that anything was happening to us! As usual, when the technical world changes, it seems to all of us that these are just neutral tools that are placed at our disposal, while we remain sovereign and unchanged. I am still myself. The things that are multiplying are at my service, but I remain intact. This is the naive claim of the ordinary person[1] who does not even ask himself this question; the scholar considers the question and remains sure of his ground. Yet, generally, we are completely changed by our means, and in particular by our image-laden environment.

This change was all the more complete because we were in complete accord with it. That hatred of language proclaimed by intellectuals coincided perfectly with the inadequacy of everyone's language. And the rash of images harmonized quite well with all modern human tendencies, since we were already influenced and changed by the general working of techniques. We had already become different, and in order to be comfortable with our new selves we needed images, both for distraction and because of their usefulness. Thus there existed on the one hand the technical possibility of an indefinite production of images, and on the other the ordinary person's desire to receive them.

I have an unquenchable thirst for more and more of the images that are so dear to me. Why should this be? First, because of my laziness and the ease afforded by images. Everything becomes so simple when transformed into images. When a Beirut building caves in, I see it. I am more involved than if I had read an account of the fighting. The rapid flow of images gives me a direct grasp of the event, and of many others like it. I do not have time to linger over them. I want to see so many things. . . . And furthermore, I have to keep learning more and more. Not only *is* there in an objective sense a lot to learn, but *I must* learn it. For this reason images are essential.

Thanks to images I will learn directly the new techniques of my trade and the information I need to know. I have total and direct

---

1. I use this expression, "the ordinary person," a good deal. It comes from the Italian: *uomo qualunque*, on which I wrote a rather careful study to show that it could be a scientific sociological category, and an indispensable one at that: "La Notion d'homme quelconque en tant qu'hypothèse de travail sociologique," *Revista de Sciencias Sociales*, 1964.

contact with things that would be terribly complicated if I had to go the slow route of discursive analysis, then synthesis, progressing from stage to stage by intellectual assimilation.

But there is something even deeper: we live increasingly separated from the natural environment (we frantically try to rediscover it when we go on vacation). When we lose contact with this reality, which used to be the essential reality of our lives, we develop an extremely deep need for another reality. Modern people are the only living beings in a nonliving environment. Because they live in a new abstract, theoretical milieu, unrelated to their tradition, they cannot yet conceive of this technical milieu[2] as reality. The modern person thus considers nature his refuge, but it is a fiction that we still live in nature. And we have extreme difficulty conceiving of ourselves as excluded from nature (or that Nature has been excluded!) and involved in another universe. The fiction is that we are still, as always, in a world of water, wind, trees, and animals. Yet the real universe in which we find ourselves seems unreal to us. Concrete, automobiles, steel, and asphalt seem like "accidents."

At the very moment we sink into this double fiction and refuse reality, we become obsessed by reality and the concrete. All we care about is action on reality; ideas and thoughts are swept aside, leaving only what is concrete: money, machines, my trade. Nothing but concrete issues matters in our beliefs and our choice of life. This is an astonishing contradiction. But then the merciful image comes along to resolve it for us. Images coincide with reality.

We feel relaxed and joyful at continually rediscovering nature through images. We feel right at home again when we see these majestic pictures of the ocean, these clever animal films made possible by the telephoto lens. We never knew nature so well, never saw it so well. Thanks to these images we can drink in the sea breeze and the mountain air. At the same time the image gives us the technical universe in its hypostatic reality.

The mechanical world that so often troubles us becomes magically present and familiar through images. But this familiarity is *shown*; that is, made majestic, noble, and superior—it seems to deserve being shown and admired. *Mirari*: mirage. The image as mirage reconciles contradictions, makes absent nature present and real again, makes the technical milieu familiar and admirable, and quenches our thirst for something concrete and real. Images counterbalance all the abstractions. And they restore to us at last a reality in which we can live: the reality of the world of images.

---

2. See Jacques Ellul, *The Technological System*, on technique as a milieu.

We are in the process of seeing the fulfillment of Edgar Allen Poe's prophecy in which the painter, impassioned by his mistress-model and also by his art, "did not *want* to see that the colors he spread on his canvas were *taken* from the cheeks of the woman seated beside him. And when several weeks had passed, and very little remained to be done, nothing but a stroke on the mouth and a glaze over the eye, the mistress's spirit still flickered like the flame at the base of a lamp. Then he put on the final touch, put the glaze in place, and for a moment the painter stood in ecstasy before the work he had finished. But a moment later, he was struck with panic, and shouting with a piercing voice: 'It is truly *Life* itself,' he suddenly turned around to look at his mistress. She was dead." Nothing ever constrains us to face what is dying when we see it so alive in our images.

Because of all this people themselves have changed a great deal. They are first of all consumers of images.[3] The technical individual belonging to the Western world has been described in many ways: the man of the masses (José Ortega y Gasset), the organization man (William H. Whyte, Jr.), the extrovert, the quantitative man (Bernard Ronze), the technical man, the other-directed man (W. Miles), and many others. Each of these is certainly correct. And each of these analyses enables us to gauge the deep psychological, moral, psychic, spiritual, and intellectual change that has taken place. It is a veritable mutation.

We are not sure we can understand thoroughly what really has happened to each of us, but I believe one of the decisive factors in this mutation is that we live continually in a world of images, that is, in the continual unshadowed presence of all of reality. We live in the present, without fail. The present image erases the past and prohibits expectation by bringing the future into the present. Seeing the present implies the present realization of our desires, without delay. A government that says it needs two years to resolve a crisis is a doomed government. An ethic that teaches us to wait and move patiently toward a goal is automatically rejected. Any promise made for tomorrow converts the one who makes it into a liar. "Everything, right now" is the notion that comes from the presence of images, which in effect get us used to seeing all in a single glance. Thus reality is completely present. *Mustn't* reality therefore be completely present? For imaged reality is. But images are reality.

Thus when our experience of reality disappoints us because it does not square with our image of it, this cruel disappointment

---

3. See all of Jean Baudrillard's books on the consumption of symbols.

immediately convinces us of the injustice of the situation. We see marvelous automatic gadgets. They exist! We see incredible surgical heart or brain operations. They are done! Then why aren't all sick people taken care of in this way? Why isn't everything automated? Since it is possible, why don't we reduce the workday to one hour? Why not have everybody on vacation all the time and cared for with the most recently developed machines? Since things are not this way, there must be some dark scheming, Machiavellian calculations, and sordid selfishness involved. Someone is determined to keep the worker alienated and to keep the poor person ignorant and ill. "They" alone—employers and fascists—prevent the coming of the marvelous society presented to us by images. The continually reborn belief in the coming of an ultimate era is scandalized that the time has not already come. The entire strength of Marxism is based on this belief (an amazing reversal is involved when Marx, a model person of the word and discourse, inspires a movement that develops and sustains itself only through images and as a consequence of the psychology based on images!).

But the present reality as seen through images, which is only the reality of the technical miracle, is also the menacing and dangerous present. We see birds slimed with oil; and the slow, majestic rising of the fatal mushroom cloud has become the continual vision of our destiny. Here we are faced with a catastrophic present constantly represented before our eyes; a continual menace confronts us through the images we see. This does not involve some hoax we can expose through language; nor can we use words to soften the effect of the threats that surround us: we see them as if we were in their very presence.

And when the threats are not real, images still surround us with the fictional threats of horror films and stress-filled movies. As if reality were not enough! The word never had either this function or this power; certainly it never possessed this continual presence. Real or fictional images make us feel we are witnessing the end of the world. This is a logical consequence of the imaged ends of the world and of civilizations we are continually shown.

Thus we have these two trends: the demand for everything immediately, and the dread of the end of the world, both of which stem from the infinite multiplication of images. These trends work together to produce on all sides apocalyptic and messianic tendencies, or at least the coming of an ultimate era. This is the first of the great changes we undergo. The second is the mutation of our intelligence and intellectual process.

## 2. THE INTELLECTUAL PROCESS

Images produce an intellectual process different from the ancient one or the one developed by classical education. It goes without saying that this process is not completely new; of course, since sight existed, and since people themselves chose their images, they *also* thought by means of images and entered into this kind of thinking. But this was limited and not frequent, because images were not dominant. The new factor in our day comes from the effect of visual reproduction's triumph over all else, which involves us in the domination of one form of thought. This supremacy is new, even though we are not dealing with a completely new form of thought.

What are its characteristics? First, thought by association and suggestion. But in this case the association is of images rather than ideas. Films and newspapers have filled us with visions. We are inhabited by photographs, so that our subconscious supplies us with them whenever it is stimulated.

But the stimulus is itself an image. When we glimpse a picture, a process whereby images recall one another is immediately set off. These images cause us to go from one idea that is represented in this manner to others that have no necessary relationship between them. Forms, colors, movements, landscapes, and faces associate themselves with each other, then carry us along with them. Furthermore, we feel no need to resist this process, since it is pleasant to let ourselves be led and dominated, up to a certain point. Naturally, sound associations exist as well, and we could speak of similar phenomena in this realm. But we live in a universe of images rather than sounds.

The word, although prevalent in our day, has lost its *reasoning value*, and has value only as an accessory to images. In turn, the word actually evokes images. But it does not evoke the direct images related to my personal experience. Rather, it calls up images from the newspaper or television. The key words in our modern vocabulary, thanks to propaganda and advertising, are words that relate to visual reproduction. They are stripped of all rational content, so they evoke only visions that whisk us away to some enchanted universe. Saying "fascism," "progress," "science," or "justice" does not suggest any idea or produce any reflection. It only causes a fanfare of images to explode within us: a sort of fireworks of visual commonplaces, which link up very precisely with each other. These related images provide me with practical content: a common truth that is especially easy to swallow because the ready-made images that showed it to me had been digested in advance.

Make no mistake here: this is how modern people usually think. We are arriving at a purely emotional stage of thinking. In order to begin reacting intellectually, we need the stimulus of an image. Bare information or an article or book no longer have any effect on us. We do not begin reflecting on such a basis, but only with an illustration. We need violent visual impact if thought is to be set in motion. When we jump from image to image, we are really going from emotion to emotion: our thought moves from anger to indignation, from fear to resentment, from passion to curiosity. In this manner our thought is enriched by diversity and multiple meaning but is singularly paralyzed with respect to its specific efficacy as thought.

Furthermore, the emotional quality of what we moderns call our thought produces an extreme violence of conviction combined with extreme incoherence in our arguments. I refer here to ordinary people and not to an intellectual elite. We do not involve ourselves in studying the meaning and consequences of a fact calmly and objectively. The fact asserts itself through its image and associates itself in unchallengeable fashion with other images which, in this mode of thinking, are its true context. Emotions justify as well as provoke or command opinions, which still seem intellectual and reasoned.

Prejudice and stereotypes did not originate in our time. Passionate thinking was well known earlier, and Romanticism has furnished us some of its finer types. But it may be that ordinary people had less pretensions to thinking and reasoning in earlier periods. Certainly they were given less systematic visual incitements to set off their emotions. This is precisely what seems to be new: this pretension to information, to a sensible opinion, and to widespread thought among the people is related to a particular form of image association and to passionate reasoning, which is a direct consequence of such images.

We must add to this first characteristic the result of what we have already observed: images cause us to grasp facts in an overall manner. It is thus a matter of intuition. And this is exactly what we observe. Visual means of communication set in motion an overall mechanism of apprehension. We grasp the entirety of a situation or a reality by means of an instantaneous intuition. We can observe in practice the development of this intuitive kind of knowledge in young people. They understand all at once; their perception places them at the very heart of reality.

Such intuition is remarkably efficient. It is a very strange kind of knowledge: it involves a kind of direct communication of knowledge, as if it did not pass through the brain, as if reason were absent and intelligence had nothing to do with it. A mysterious link seems to be established between the person showing the images and the spectator. Images are chosen to produce this sort of secret understanding of reality, and in fact they reach their goal. Sometimes even without being clearly conscious of the fact, we know what a given image meant. A sort of sympathetic vibration of knowledge is established between those who are indwelt by the same images. Sometimes they would have enormous difficulty expressing in words what this means. They could not transpose this certain knowledge into words. They take refuge in adjectives and allusions; gestures compensate for the absence of vocabulary.

Yet this knowledge exists. It can be communicated, but only by means of other overall images. Intuition must again play its role, as communication is established from the entirety of one being to the entirety of another, through the intermediary of something visual. This image carries more meaning than other images received but is devoid of reason.

The words *understanding* and *communication* in themselves involve a kind of mobilization of being. And this is what is produced in this kind of reasoning or transmission of knowledge by images. We said above that images transmit reality itself to the spectator, with formidable energy, insistence, and strength of impact. But we also said that images possess emotional force. These elements, when combined, explain why it is that when modern visual means are used, spectators do not remain passive. They participate very quickly in the unfolding of a spectacle and feel personally involved. But an intellectual attitude is *also* involved; that is, in visual communication the spectator is "in on" what he sees; he clings to what is transmitted (which is why such means are so efficacious in teaching—because of the spectator's interest and participation).

But this means that there is no longer any distance between subject and object. This is normal if we reflect on the fact that sight, when used in the context of nature, creates direct communication with reality. It implies that one is involved in *this* particular reality and quickly leads a person to action. But when the image has become artificial and is purely a means of knowledge, the reaction persists. I feel directly involved in what I see, just as prehistoric people did. And if I am seeing objects or ideas, I am not truly independent; I cannot really take my distance from these objects. From the intellectual point of view, this means I cannot really exercise my critical faculties. The use of images to transmit knowledge leads to the progressive elimination of distance between a person and his knowledge, because of the way we are made to participate when this means is used (this is, of course, in perfect accord with technical civilization, and to be desired by its standards). The critical faculties and autonomy of the thinking person are also eliminated.

Thus we could say without any exaggeration that knowledge transmitted by images leads to a kind of thinking that presents two characteristics (besides those noted above: intuition and association).

First, this thinking is based on evidence: the image that creates this thinking gives rise to a feeling of evidence and a conviction that it is not based on reason. This kind of thinking explains the reaction we so often note among our contemporaries: when someone asks them to give the reason for their opinions, they answer: "It's evident." This thinking, which creates prejudices and stereotypes, is the domain of the unquestionable. Obviously you cannot dispute with an image, and you cannot challenge the hero of a film. But this extends to the mental images produced by the film: there is no criticism or debate possible, because these involve differing methods of thought. What produces immediate assent cannot bear the discussion process. The conviction acquired in this way can only be attacked on its own ground: by other images and other "evidences."

But we must admit that in this case we usually have a confrontation of two systems of images that do not coincide and cannot be communicated. Psychologists (especially Americans) have been very aware of a problem that had a great deal of impact about twenty years ago: the growth of prejudices and mental stereotypes (which are the basis of racism, among other things). It is agreed that these are irrational, ready-made images: a person does not consruct this image himself from scattered traits he gathers together. But it seems that more attention should be given to examining the following factors: such images are not a transposition of discourse and words, from articles and conversations. They are truly the mental reception of images in the material sense: posters, photographs, etc. Stereotypes are ready-made images received as is, from outside. Such thought based on evidence is always effectively translated into images. Say "progress" to an ordinary person, and he will answer "machine."

The other characteristic of this kind of thought is that it is always "committed." It is, for instance, thought related to action, especially political and social action. Imaged thought, based on and fed by and stirred up by images, is of necessity committed in the social context which creates these images. Such thought refers to the reality that is transmitted to it through visual systems; there is no possible escape from this. For we must not forget that all the images that deluge us refer to the context of our society.

True, there must be agreement between the spectator and the image shown to him. A historical film, for example, can succeed only if the spectator sees himself mirrored in it, or if he can relate his time to the historical period of the film. Excellent documentaries on Auguste Rodin, Honoré de Balzac, and Vincent van Gogh were commercial failures, because they struck no chords in the spectator.

In order to succeed images must genuinely reflect our society. Then they involve the spectator's thought in judgments and decisions that are related only to technical, economic, and political life. It is certainly not by accident that precisely at the time we were invaded by images, scholars came up with the theory of the need for commitment in thought. This commitment cannot remain independent of what is shown to it; and what is shown is nothing but the political-social context.

Thought based on images can be neither abstract nor critical. Of necessity it is thought related to the milieu. I am not saying whether this is good or bad. I simply note that again in this case intellectuals have worked out theories to justify the inevitable. For unconsciously, they could not avoid being subjected to the enormous weight of billions of images (just like other people). Yet consciously, they were well aware that maintaining the demands of critical and independent thought involves a complete break with the rest of humankind. This would make it impossible for them to play their role as genuine intellectuals. They must think like everyone else if they expect to be at all believed by the masses. Thus their conscious and unconscious minds agree in taking them down the path of thought that involves images, evidence, and emotivity.

\*     \*     \*     \*     \*     \*

At this point, however, we find ourselves coming to a dangerous turn. Teachers who work out illustrations and make use of films to make knowledge more accessible scarcely concern themselves with such effects. This is because they are convinced that the mode of thinking that involves images and intuition can fit in perfectly with the traditional mode of thinking by reasoning and discourse. An unreasoned and unproved conviction exists that the two kinds of thinking complement each other. Yet it seems clear that the enormous difference between the two keeps them from being complementary. They are *opposing* mental attitudes, which presuppose essentially divergent capacities and training. This can already be seen rather clearly as early as Descartes.

The word also originates a specific mode of thinking. Experience tends to show that a person who thinks by images becomes less and less capable of thinking by reasoning, and vice versa. The intellectual process based on images is contradictory to the intellectual process of reasoning that is related to the word. There are two different ways of dealing with an object. They involve not only different approaches, but even more important, opposing mental attitudes. This is not a matter of complementary processes, such as analysis and synthesis or logic and dialectic. These processes lack any qualitative common denominator.

The very object of these two thought forms may not be the same.

The word necessarily gives rise to a mode of thought by demonstration, following a logical or dialectical process. Here we will omit the word as incantation, since language calls for a logical internal law of construction that presupposes a rigorous relationship among its terms. In the classical order the word trains the mind for demonstration. A correctly constructed, reasoned argument is convincing because it corresponds to the internal law of language and to the rigorous requirements in the very structure of a sentence.

A person must believe in language if he is to be open to the meaning of a reasoned argument. But for a person used to the value of the word, reasoning leads to correct and satisfactory knowledge. Moreover, the word has no meaning if not integrated into this kind of a context. No matter how elementary or utilitarian a demonstration may be, no matter how rudimentary the language, the word nevertheless moves in this domain of reasoning. Always in some way it addresses human reason. The word is the instrument of this reason and can be used only because a common reason attributes a certain construction to the word.

Communication on the basis of the word is primarily the communication of experiences or feelings that can be grasped by the intellect and conveyed by intellectual values. These experiences and feelings undergo an intellectual process and are then addressed to another person's intellect. The word must pass through this sender and this receiver. An impact value or emotive power of the word may also be added, though these really are not necessary but simply superfluous. The word at first does not involve the whole being, nor involve it directly, but reaches a person only through a more or less lengthy process. It leaves a certain distance between people when they speak to each other.

The word does not belong to the order of evidence. As we all know, a simple rough statement, lacking reasons and context, is always disappointing to the listener. Except in the case of propaganda, a listener expects a demonstration, and is not satisfied with a statement lacking rational proof. The word is inevitably linked to this need for reasons and to this roundabout method, even if we are not conscious of the fact. Evidence and direct comprehension are not language's strong suit. All spoken communication is a laborious construction by a person who elaborates his demonstration as rigorously as possible, leaving as few lapses as he can. It is also a construction in the case of dialogue, in which a progression is shaped by active exchange.

Images leave everyone in an icy silence that can only be transcended by total, intuitive communication. No interchange is involved. The word, however, is the means of human relationship and dialogue, which is the dialectical exercise of experience. The word requires reasoning and the use of analysis and synthesis, even when these are involuntary. Language is this way because of its very structure. Don't we use the term *analysis* precisely to designate the process by which we understand a sentence? Such analysis is not carried out on the basis of some naturally given set of facts, but rather is based on a previously formulated result of synthesis. And synthesis takes place continually on the basis of the results of analysis.

A person who has been trained in rhetoric, in the strict sense of the word, can no longer learn in any other way. His thinking necessarily takes place in the world of reasoning, dialectic, analysis, and synthesis. This is not without its dangers, of course: we are aware that words can be abused. We know how an illusion allows us to take these symbols for reality, and how empty talk sometimes fails to be attached to anything concrete. Sometimes confusion between rhetorical reasons and reason exists. But these abuses in no way affect the authenticity of the intellectual mechanism that is formed by and for the word.

A person who is trained in this way always distrusts intuition and images. Intuition appears to him to be without foundation or certainty. A scientist always distrusts "feminine" intuition. We cannot take seriously the knowledge that the first human beings could have had of plants and animals, knowledge based on their pure "intuition." Psychic and "spiritual" phenomena that do not belong to the domain of reason seem like illusions to us, like stories of ghosts and mediums. On the basis of reason we cannot really accept healers, who are intuitive individuals, even if we consult them.

Nor can an intellectual trained by the word consider images to be accurate and adequate. They are always suspect as far as he is concerned; at best they are accessories that have no meaning apart from the explanations that accompany them. We find exactly the same disposition of mind in the person accustomed to thinking by images and intuition. Since he yields to evidence and needs this evidence, he resists demonstrations. Reasoning irritates and exasperates him without convincing him: what good are such roundabout methods? Why such a slow pace? Why stop at every step to secure one's position, when he can have the result in one move? Intuition can enable him to grasp the totality in a flash. The most precise demonstration possible will not convince such a person, because he is desensitized to reason. The sequence of the parts of a reasoned argument does not strike him as at all necessary.

I recall a group of young people who were fervent in their political concerns and whose education had been based on images. They listened to a magnificent lecture on Algeria in 1959—a lecture astonishing in its documentation, intellectual rigor, fine analysis, and solid synthesis. The practical conclusions of this presentation flowed in a precise manner from its premises. Afterward these young people said to me: "That's very good. No doubt he's right. But we 'feel' differently." They knew nothing of Algeria, of course, except for images. This anecdote seems typical to me of the misunderstanding between word-oriented and image-oriented people.

The word really cannot reach those who are oriented toward images. To such people it seems utterly empty, like vain talk. A person cannot take seriously what proceeds from the word when he is accustomed to the palpable, concrete, and living aspects of images. The word seems like wind, or like something without life. Thus the problem is not just a genuine inability to think in the two modes, a necessary exclusion of each by the other. It is also a genuine refusal to use both forms of thought. The person who is accustomed to one of the two has only scorn and distrust for the other. This is not surprising, because images are the opposite of demonstration; intuition is the opposite of reasoning; and the association of ideas excludes any possibility of the rigor of logical thought. We must not think that a person is absolutely free to play both games at once, to use two instruments equally, because they condition the whole person so profoundly. We are modified by our own means of expression, and the dominant use of one means prevents our valid use of the other.

\*    \*    \*    \*    \*    \*

If these hypotheses are correct, we now come to the specific area of the lie. First, audiovisual lies. Audiovisual means mask a series of graduated lies (not deliberate, explicit, conscious lies, of course!). The first is simply the presentation of this method, this pedagogy, this technique, as a great human creation. It is passed off as good, like a sort of new ideal that brings with it all sorts of progress. But no "creation" is involved: it is simply an inevitable de facto situation. Quite simply, we could not have done otherwise. The audiovisual process is imposed on us and is part of the technical world's necessity.

The lie also has a second stage: the audiovisual method is said to be a successful means of reconciling sight and hearing, image and word. It represents the latest advance in a pedagogy that already had been greatly improved by illustrations. Television is the most highly evolved teaching instrument. Other associations of images and words, such as slides and video techniques, will be grafted onto it. Images enable us to make things comprehensible when no form of discourse could explain them. When a person has seen a flower open on a large screen, or the back of a chrysalis split, or sperm penetrate an ovule, he will never forget what he has seen; it will stay with him permanently. Without words, of course! And this is the first step in the lie: no words are used, whereas we are continually told that this method involves the equal association of images and words, with precise correlation. In practice this is easy to corroborate: ask a pupil to explain what he has seen! "Well, . . . " And here his words end!

We must not make a secret of the fact that students' increasingly poor examinations stem precisely from this conflict: pupils take in images, and we require that they respond with discourse. Switching from one to the other is impossible. Generations of students that were taught rhetoric and Latin found a way to escape the seriousness of the word by superfluous verbiage and by imposing a purely formal technique on the word. Today we have the same evasion, but now it is aided by the triumphant image and the destroyed word.

In the audiovisual realm, the image is king. The word, practically useless, is in any case a serf, not an equal. At best, the word is used to provide the name of what is seen on the screen but is eliminated for all other purposes. Furthermore, anyone who needs convincing has only to listen to the vain talk and the comments that accompany a series of images: pompous discourse falsely poetic; dead time filled up with pseudo-poetry! This is natural—what could you possibly add through words that could compare with images?

Of course, audiovisual methods can be useful in learning: for example, foreign languages. It helps to see an image and hear the sound that goes with it. But the word in this case is reduced to exactly that: a sound. What is learned is not the depth and profundity of a language, including its formation and its verbal and syntactical structure; only good pronunciation is involved. Far be it from me to say this is useless. On the contrary, what is learned in this case *is* something useful, but only that! And useful only at the level of the objects or actions to be shown. For audiovisual methods limit themselves to what can be shown. What is useful at the level of pronunciation has to do with everyday language. What use is the teaching of Goethe's German or Shakespeare's English? The answer is obvious. What is the use of teaching a dead language? This agrees exactly with what we said above about visual images. They are related to efficacy, utility, and reality.

The audiovisual lie, however, wants us to believe that one really learns a language this way. But a language is tied to the entire psychology of a people, and to its history and literature. Yet one can know nothing and still be able to carry on a conversation in a given language. Ionesco has shown well the distance between this conversational level and true language. The serious thing is not the use of the audiovisual method but that what is learned in this way eliminates all the rest, which is considered not "useful."

Audiovisual methods extend our entire society's discrimination against what is not useful and efficacious. Even when the goal is to learn a utilitarian language, the word is excluded. Images render no service to the word, nor to thought. The audiovisual method faces us with the exclusive spreading knowledge of technical reality. Nothing else is involved. And when this method triumphantly extends to everything, we witness, as in the case of computers, the process of excluding everything that cannot adapt to it. We can never emphasize this elimination enough: anything that cannot be dealt with through computers ceases to exist. Whatever is not transmitted audiovisually does not matter.

This exclusion is clearly manifested in certain scientific statements; for instance, that only "reality" can be the object of knowledge. And reality in this case is defined as we described it briefly in Chapter I: what is measurable, quantifiable, defined, noncontradictory, and identical to itself. Only this reality can be known and can thus be the object of scientific research and *true* knowledge. At this point reality is consciously identified with truth. This is the basis of most epistemological research undertaken since the triumph of images.

To the degree that audiovisual methods are improved, philosophy declines. Philosophy is not of the same order, either in terms of the way its thought develops or with respect to the level of language involved. It is claimed that the audiovisual method is the servant of thought, whereas in reality thought is excluded by the continual invasion of images. Audiovisual methods immerse us in reality alone. And reality takes up all the available space and becomes all-important.

Then in a reversal of the sort in which our age abounds, thought is excluded. This takes place hidden by the insistence on the contrary: the pretension of autonomy and of the individualization of the person who is learning. Such education is said to produce a critical mind and a capacity for judgment, whereas these are precisely what images eliminate. In this way it is claimed that we are enabling people to arrive at the full use of their intellectual powers, whereas this is excluded; we are supposed to be freeing the human mind, but we are merely bogging it down more than ever in the exclusive visual world and the preoccupation with things technical.

The audiovisual method cleverly excludes the word, all the while claiming to integrate it. In this method every word refers to images. We are told that "the word that cannot be visualized is nothing but empty dreaming, soap bubbles, and vain talk, since it lacks reference to reality and therefore to the truth." This process of elimination is powerfully reinforced by the enthusiastic and naive assistance teachers provide. They have no idea what they are doing or of the degree to which they are manipulated—not by some evil genie but by the working of the technical system.

We are faced here with one of these twisted mechanisms that abound in this system (we are tempted to take them for something conscious, since they seem so clever, but they are unconscious). Audiovisual teaching, which is so efficient, is false not only in claiming to associate word and image equally. It is false also in the sense that it is the smokescreen covering over the mutation in our mode of thinking, as we have just analyzed it. We must not be allowed to realize what we are in the process of losing. The most extreme case can permit no possible choice between what we use as the instrument of thought and our instrument for recognizing reality. We must not feel the depth of the break between these two processes of human intelligence; still less must we feel our break with what has been until now the grandeur of Western thought.

Audiovisual methods utterly obliterate this conflict and this break. They enable us to believe in good faith that we are in the midst of a great reconciliation, and that we can be both Socrates and an engineer working on the computer analysis of fluid mechanics. Audiovisual methods lead us to think that we can successfully associate technique with culture, and even that a more evolved stage of technique will enable us to dedicate ourselves to the blissful joys of purely intellectual, spiritual, and esthetic creation: "The famous idea of a humanistic technical culture is a real possibility—just look at audiovisuals!" People are scandalized by the sort of analysis I make, showing the increasing divergence of two irreconcilable types of thought that will never come together. They cannot come together, since the evidence of the one excludes the changeability of the other.

That the audiovisual method thus plays an eminently ideological role here should not surprise us. This ideological mask leads us into an awareness of a broader dimension of the problem, in which the audiovisual question is merely one startling aspect rather than the only factor. Things visual give us access to reality. The multiplication of images roots us firmly within reality. When the word is excluded, we lose the sense of truth. *But reality belongs to the world of necessity.* Everything about it is both necessary and evident. *The word is both the locus and the expression of freedom* (or, if one prefers, the pretension of freedom, or its intention or illusion, as well as the falsification of freedom). Wherever the word is excluded or subordinated, freedom is eliminated. When a person is subdued by images, he is situated in a necessary world filled with necessities. He sees what he must know, learn, do, and decide. He accepts necessity at the very time he accepts images. But to the degree that evidence is always involved, he never *becomes conscious* of this necessity.

Thus we find ourselves faced with this double mutation: one is shut up within necessity alone, and it is impossible to become aware of this. But we know, at least since Marx, that the first (and sometimes the only) act of freedom is becoming conscious of necessity. As soon as a person recognizes that he has been conditioned, this means that he has taken a position with respect to this necessity. He situates himself outside it in order to see it. Furthermore, he can define himself as conditioned only if he is free. Unless he were conscious of freedom or willed to be free, he would not even know that he was subject to necessity.

This distance taking, however, can only occur by means of the word. The invasion of images causes us to be not only in a universe of things, but also in an imaged reflection of this world of things and realities. We are locked up in this world because of the many-sided, polyvalent, incessant quality of images, and because of the way images symbolize things. All this affects a person so that not only is he subject to the necessity of reality, but he also becomes incapable of considering this reality as a combination of necessities. He is trapped at the level of his experience and at the same time by the images reflecting this experience. Through the abundance of images this reflection gives him the impression that Everything is possible, that Everything is always new, and that circumstances are so fluid that he can influence or master them. But since all this takes place in a sort of magic-lantern universe, it never goes deeper than an impression. This is all that is required if an individual is to be demobilized and more completely integrated into fictitious battles.

The word, however, through its very imprecision, involves the freedom of both partners. We have seen that it respects the freedom of the listener, but it expresses and even produces the freedom of the speaker when he chooses to say what he finally says, and chooses to eliminate other things he could have said. The word creates a free space between two people, through the possibility of understanding and misunderstanding. When the word becomes imperative, it places the listener in a situation of free choice. In the last analysis, the image-oriented person has lost his deep freedom by penetrating into this milieu of images produced by technique.

## 3. SPACE AND VISUALIZATION IN MODERN ART

Today all authors (with one exception, whom we will consider) agree in noting the extraordinary victory of the visual and spatial over the temporal and auditory in the art world. For painters, space has changed its character. Robert L. Delevoy[4] provides us with an admirable analysis of this fact: in the classical conception, space was considered the locus of relationships between objects. This idea gives way to the notion of space as a phenomenon: "an unreal milieu, where tectonic values, tensions, articulations, and the sequence of forms" move freely and are self-sufficient. "The spatial virtualities of color are associated with constructive mechanisms, distribution, and the montage of signs" (the terms of this analysis are significant, since they spontaneously evoke technical processes).

Space has become the basic dimension in art—all art, including music. A nonspatial esthetic representation of the world no longer exists. Yves Bonnefoy feels tragically ambivalent about this certainty: "nothing will take place but the place." Words propose an "abode." Bonnefoy is totally committed to localization; but after this exaltation of space, he says: "I cannot keep myself, *however*, from reaffirming that impersonal poetry without time is *wrong*." But after all, we are guilty of this wrong!

At the same time that space wins out over time, the visual replaces the auditory. Schaeffer explains the degree to which the meaning of visual images depends on the word or discourse. The text attests. The image shows the fact and thereby lends itself to a multitude of interpretations. "The universe in constant motion, the phenomenological universe of the course of events, substitutes itself for a whole system of fixed reference points which are in static equilibrium: the world that can properly be called the world of dis-course. This indicates the naïveté of professors who count on the image to visualize the abstract. . . . In an image-message, misunderstanding . . . is the rule."

Yet everyone agrees in proclaiming that we have here a new language and a new art. It wins out over what was only language: the filmed novel replaces the novel. A whole trend develops the idea of writing a novel fragmented like a film.

Such interpenetration is no longer limited to the domain of the comic strip but becomes characteristic of the "best" writers: Marguerite Duras, who dedicates herself to the filmed novel in *Nathalie Granger* and *India Song*; Alain Robbe-Grillet, with *Glissements progressifs du plaisir*. In some cases a film director and a novelist work together to produce the novel for a film, the counterpart of the cinematic transcription of the novel (for example Patrick Modiano and Louis Malle in *Lacombe Lucien*, Tonino Guerra and Federico Fellini in *Amarcord* ). We have utterly left behind the old technique: a

---

4. Robert L. Delevoy, *Dimensions du* XX<sup>e</sup> *siècle*, Art, Idées, Histoire (Geneva: Skira, 1965).

film based on the novel by . . . , or the film as simply an illustration of a story. The reason is that translation from one medium to another presupposes difference and opposition, with the result that it is always unsuccessful.

The intertwining of the two is now complete, but to the benefit of image and to story's detriment; to the benefit of the spatial at the temporal's expense. Language in visual form unfolding in space replaces verbal language unfolding in time.

Music also has developed spatially since the end of the nineteenth century, with what has been called the victory of pictorial genius over musical genius. It is obvious that painting traditionally has been spatial, but it also has undergone a modification, rejecting all optical illusion, so as to become only "something that is there." The painting is nothing more than itself—the real space it occupies. The discovery of space by painters and sculptors has been endlessly stressed for a good reason: the objects produced or reproduced matter less than the *space* between them, the meaning, the concentration of forces, the distribution of the space. The play of light and color serves only to heighten the value of the space.

This development harmonizes to an amazing degree with the impact of Technique. Technique is a conqueror of space and both requires and takes for granted a maximum of space for its development. In this connection Jean Merkado's sculpture (exhibited at the Bourdelle Museum in 1975), for example, is significant. On the one hand it is purely technical: it consists of geometrical forms held together by mechanical connections, which suggest groups of machines. On the other hand it denotes space. Everything about it constitutes experimenting with space: empty space, volumes, masses, and materials. "The important thing is what happens in the empty space, between the masses. . . . " The most technical modern sculpture has no meaning or value in itself. Representation counts for nothing; the situation in space and the cutting up of space are meaningful, exactly as in the case of Technique!

Although music involved continuation and becoming, sound is not limited: it leaps beyond its limits. With Claude Debussy "the spatial conception of sound surfaces" begins. And after him follows a veritable atomization of melodic models. Disparate elements are superimposed on one another. Igor Stravinski quite consciously institutes combined space-time (overall, of course, this was a very necessary tendency: a given length of time is the amount of time necessary to cover a given space). Many talk of the impressionists' influence in this area. Subjective time—the time experienced in music—declines progressively as music becomes a collection of objects.

Such music expresses life (duration!) less and less as it becomes, for example, the expression of computation. This would seem to objectify life. Thus music becomes a sort of parasite on painting. Music rejects its temporal depth and precisely circumscribes each bundle of sounds in its specificity. In turn, music itself becomes at each instant "something that is there," without a future.

Moreover, this generalization of space in all the arts, this victory of visualization, is expressed in many guises. For example, consider the influence of the discovery of the universe of the infinitely small and of the strange world of molecules and atoms with their structures that are at the same time spatial and yet never really correctly representable in space. This influence shows up frequently in contemporary painting.

We have the same problem with the influence of speed, which involves a different appraisal of the relationships between things and space itself. Far and near are no longer considered in the same way. Everything is equally present. The modern individual thinks on the basis of isolated facts placed in a relationship governed by speed. Mobility, in all the arts, assumes a "functional role" (Delevoy). This mobility, a determining factor in film as well as in painting or music, is spatial: it integrates the temporal in space in a precise manner.

Architecture accentuates this preeminence of space to an astonishing degree. Ricardo Bofill, with his group, "Taller de Arquitectura," declares that "Life is in space, Time is in space; *nothing exists* but space." "An esthetic which incorporates the contradictory values of duration, change, the simultaneous and the successive, is being elaborated. At the same time the spectator can now participate in the process of the work—by devouring the optical substance of a spectacle that is destined to have a continuing birth" (Delevoy).

This is possible, of course, only to the degree that everything temporal has *become* space. And the same influence is at work when we note with Paul Klee that the spectator is himself watched by the painting. No longer is it sufficient to learn to see what the artist offers to sight. The spectator must feel himself integrated into the space of a painting, which is no longer decoration or an invitation to meditation but a place where one is called to live. One is involved in such a place because here, as with television, one is bombarded by strong motivating influences. The spectator becomes himself a part of this space. Thus in art, space becomes everything, just at the exact moment when we are deprived of space by the very development of techniques that absorb and annihilate it.

Last of all, the question of instantaneousness comes up in this context: mechanization in art demands an esthetic experience based on an instantaneous response. (And here we obviously come back to McLuhan: instantaneousness as opposed, for example, to the discovery of a text written sentence by sentence; global understanding; instantaneous introjection. To be sure, a machine can be instantaneous, but aren't we reducing human beings to machines when we attempt to obtain the same reaction?) Does instantaneousness have an esthetic quality? In his remarkable essay on art ("Technology and the Future of Art," *Massachusetts Review*, 1966), A. Efron gives a long demonstration of the contrary. In particular, he emphasizes that the instantaneous is not at all an "experience."

It is true nonetheless that instantaneousness is the goal not only in film and modern music but also in painting and sculpture. Painting (armed with psychological and photographical data and chemicals) is supposed to act on our nervous system itself, without going through our consciousness. But is this not, again, the negation of the human being? The spectator must have no past, no future; his whole being must be tied to the instantaneous sensation. This is a strange turn for art to take. It is reduced to a huge ear that can take in torrents of sound but can only vibrate in unison. This music becomes cosmic (John Cage), and such painting is the expression of fields of force, but the price of this expansion is that humankind is eliminated.

Instantaneousness is really an illusion. Instantaneousness in art is impossible. Efron recalls that Norbert Wiener has demonstrated at length that people and machines operate at two levels differentiated by time—on two distinct time scales. This opposition sets a decisive limit on the possibility of synchronization (except for the coercion of people into such synchronization, as in the case of industrial "rhythm"; but this can only be done externally). This limit exists because of the *qualitative* difference between these different time scales.

In the domain of art, this difference implies a radical opposition between art and electronic technology: as long as some relation exists between art and human beings, there cannot be any sort of instantaneous art. With the ideology of instantaneousness and immediacy in art, with the ideology of spontaneous creativity (the happening, etc.), we are in the presence of a clear-cut integration into the technological process and a total denial of everything that has ever been considered art.

In addition to the succession of televised images with no temporal relation between them, Arnold Schönberg and jazz give us an example of the dissolution of time. Their musical elements tend to be frozen; everything becomes an immediate and omnipresent construction. The twelve-tone scale is a static technique which brings the listener continually back to identical material. Time is frozen in all contemporary art. Only space is filled, and it is the area of our genuine activity.

Note that the visual and space are the typical locus of Technique.

What we grasp through techniques are dimensions and spatial structures. "Only people living during the era of the airplane could have ensured the development from Edgar Degas's expression to Maurice Estève's. I doubt that either Estève or Alfred Manessier was an aviation enthusiast, but, more revealingly, they were tempted to imagine the optical reactions of their contemporaries who did fly airplanes. . . . Why not grant that artists do their utmost to translate not the reality of the mechanical vision of a world crisscrossed by flashing machines, but rather the concept that gave rise to the creation of these machines and that results from their use? This dominance of spatial interest derives from the fact that Technique refers only to reality," and this reality is nothing but space.

For Technique, time is unreal; it is only lived. Of course, there are techniques *of* time, and we all know the decisive importance attached to the advent of the clock by historians of techniques. But this only adds to our argument, since techniques of time always consist of a *cutting up* of time, a cutting into sections. This process really amounts to a negation of time, which does not exist on its own but only in its spatial reduction. Time goes by: the hands of the watch move *in space*.

Technique never grasps anything but space. That is why the famous time-travel machine is a dream of science fiction: the machine is localized. It acts on a given space and has absolutely nothing to do with time. It is even the negation of time in the sense that it always reproduces the same motion. The thousandth time, the product that comes out of a machine or the motion of a piston are identical—no time has passed. The machine follows a pattern of rigorous similarity, because it deals entirely with immediacy and space.

Technique permits a taking over of space, but as far as time is concerned, Technique can only reject and deny it. By the same token, visualization is apprehension of reality *as* Technique—or a machine—apprehends it. Techniques can teach us to see a thousand times better, a thousand times more. They enable us to see new universes, or an unexpected detail in a familiar face. But space is always involved. Techniques do not teach us to listen or to hear. They never enable us to penetrate meaning. And in the great conflict that we have noted with respect to the denial of meaning, we see an echo of this triumph of visualization.

An object seen can have innumerable meanings. Only language, something auditory, can unravel them. No longer is any meaning left to look for. The object is there, and nothing else. So language disappears. No more additional knowledge exists. The very objects of sight and hearing are possessed, since they are inscribed in a certain space.

Just as they are. The artist will have to take possession of these instantaneous realities.

And if he refuses? He will simply no longer be on "the same wavelength." No one will listen to him or see him. As far as the public is concerned, he will not exist.

Experience is no longer interpreted through the flow of time (memory, language, etc.; technical influence also plays a role in the widespread suspicious attitude toward memory!). Instead, experience exists "as is." "Paintings, faces, events are henceforth cracks in reality that are much more effective than the fictions of language!" (Schaeffer). But fiction was the explanation of a given space in a temporalized version. For a century we have been following the directly opposite path. The fact is there, but reason has now vanished.[5]

---

5. For a more detailed analysis of art in the technological society, see J. Ellul, *L'Empire du non-sens.*

# Chapter VII

# RECONCILIATION

This, then, is our situation today: through the eruption of unlimited artificial images, we have reduced truth to the order of reality and banished the shy and fleeting expression of truth. Strangest of all, we are not dealing with the identification of truth with reality already found in science. Instead, this "reality" is really fiction—literally simulated, depicted. This reality is falsified, but it constitutes the new visible human universe. It is a visible universe of proliferating images produced by all sorts of techniques. No longer are we surrounded by fields, woods, and rivers, but by signs, signals, billboards, screens, labels, and trademarks: this is our universe. And when the screen shows us a living reality, such as people's faces or other countries, this is still a fiction: it is a constructed and recombined reality.

Modern people thus are deprived of reference to truth at the same time they lose their situation in lived reality. This situation is intolerable. It produces acute suffering and panic: a person cannot live deprived of truth and situated in fiction. He does not know exactly what makes him suffer, but despairing to be when he has no real being, he lives with a latent panic and an unconscious vanity. He must find a way out at all costs; he must restore truth. But truth cannot be separated from this reality, because of the devaluation, impotence, and captivity of the word. Since the only path remaining is sight, the truth recovered is constructed around images and visible things. This is one of the basic facts of our time: "We will make gods we can see, and they will go before us" (see Ex. 32:1).

In this rational, positivistic, scientific world so devoted to economic growth, we observe the resurgence of the most ancient human impulses. But since our reality is no longer nature, the gods chosen for us to see are those of the technical and political world. They are the gods of consumerism, power, and machines, and they range from dictators to atomic piles. Now everything is invested with an extra dimension: it is not lived reality, but since this reality is visualized, it is magnified, idealized, and made sacred, through the symbolization accomplished by the mass media.

In this way a new idolatry or worship of icons is born in our midst. The process is identical to that of idolatry in the earliest times, but its object is no longer the same, since the earlier objects no longer exist. It is pointless to make ourselves an image of the powerful Bull to symbolize fertility: we need instead to magnify machines and electricity, through their images. Just as the king had magical powers, now movie stars and dictators have it. Propaganda gives us symbolic persons, such as Youth and Palestinians. Woman is given back her inverted role as absolute idol through images.

How could it possibly be otherwise? The irreparable rupture of sight and hearing is the irreparable sign of our "lost Paradise." Men and women will never again see either God or the tree of knowledge of good and evil. From now on they will search in the dark. Since they are excluded from Eden, all that is left is an echo of inaccessible truth. All the other signs of this rupture, which theologians have called the "Fall," are exterior or historical; only this one is inscribed in human "nature"; only this one stays with us from the first day to the last.

To see truth is impossible. "Neither the sun nor death can be looked at directly" is the modern, lay version of "No one can see God." This rupture leads to an infinite number of consequences in all of life, especially this: seen reality cannot be true. It exists, providing the framework and the milieu; it is useful and indispensable. But it gives human life no meaning. It provides no light concerning our own meaning or that of our actions. It gives us no direction to follow. It leaves us, as fragments of this reality, to flounder as best we can without a compass or a sextant, in the midst of the continually shifting waves of this world. Humanity encompasses the world in its view, but this world is utterly lacking in signs, unable to open itself, giving no clear direction.

The wonder is that humanity has not gone even farther astray. What it knows best remains empty and meaningless. Truth could at last give humanity the key to life, could calm its worries, provide the reason and the answer to the question "Where do we come from and where do we going?" Even better than an answer, truth could give us the direct vision of what our joyful rest will finally be. But this truth can be only vaguely heard, as a word transmitted in the midst of so much jamming, so many noises, uncertainties, and misunderstandings. This is mainly because the word is fleeting and never preserved, becoming at best a memory after it has passed. But who does not remember how untrustworthy and obsolescent memories are?

Thus the truth is known through echoes and fragile transmissions and never realized any more than the word. How often have we heard about the famous discord between the inspiration of one's plans and their realization? The revolutionary, reflecting over the results of a superb, enormous movement, or the political leader, contemplating the field after the battle, will say "This is not what we intended." Is this simply the difference between a project that did not turn out as intended—for lack of calculation or forethought—and its result? Does this mean that projects and inspiration are not to be taken seriously, and that only the concrete, actual result counts? No, this difference goes deeper: it stems from the rupture between truth and reality. Projects, utopias, intentions, and doctrines—all these belong to the order of truth, and are known and created by the word. Translating them into something realized, moving from them to action, has to do with the order of reality. In that explosive moment when truth enters into reality yet is never incarnated, everyone can see the results.

Thus I have not, at any point in these pages, intended to claim that hearing and the word are *superior* to sight and image. Let me explain: I would be more inclined to say the contrary. Only sight enables us to have full knowledge. Only sight gives certainty, enables us to be guided and get our bearings. In our present condition, in which we can no longer "see" truth, the word is the only locus of truth for us, and we cannot dispense with truth. The word is fragile and uncertain, but extremely precious. We are left with only the word. It is our last resort, but is irreplaceable for establishing communion between us, and also between us and something as indispensable to us as our daily bread. We will never live by bread alone, but by every word that comes from the Father.

Thus, in our present condition, this word in its very insufficiency is the only gift we have to keep us from sinking into hell. Without the word, human life is hell. Sartre was right when he spoke of the *look* of others set on us. And his hell, his "no exit," is just that—the look that cannot discover any truth, while words are vain and empty, conveying nothing and not permitting anything to be changed. The explosion is without remedy.

Repeatedly, as we have felt the gravity of this rupture, we have tried to find a remedy for it. Repeatedly we have tried to restore truth through sight, or to unite sight and the word in a bundle of corresponding factors, as if to restore the unity of our being. Such were the ceaseless efforts of mystics and Gnostics of previous eras; they centered everything on sight. Certainly what they saw is conveyed in words, but truth at last is seen; the orders of angels, "Paradise," and the procession of light all belong to the visual order. Theirs were efforts to reestablish at last the full relationship and the indisputable knowledge that are indispensable to us, and which we grasp only in shadows and figures. Such efforts are invariably failures. The mystic, even if his experience is true, can never enable another person to share it; he can only talk about it. Exactly! And all have experienced the tragedy of discovering that words are inadequate to express the fullness of what they have seen.

In our day, through technique, this reconciliation or possibility of access to truth through sight is no longer the province of mystics but of ingenious gadgets. And here we find the heart of the lie exposed above concerning audiovisual methods. They claim to mend what was ruptured and to restore unity of being through the precise relationship they foster between sight and hearing, thanks to increasingly sophisticated gadgets. But in reality they signify the final exclusion of truth, or else its reduction to some secondary, accessory use. Such methods empty the word of its value and reduce truth to efficacious, usable reality.

No gadget, however ingenious, will enable humanity to discover the meaning of life (and notwithstanding certain brilliant philosophers, we cannot live if our life has no meaning). Nor can a gadget enable us to recover a relationship of communion with other men and women (and we cannot live if we are hopelessly misunderstood).

The audiovisual venture is identical to that of the mystics, though in another epoch and different cultural context, with a different concept of reality and truth. In the period of the mystics, truth seemed transcendent and they needed for it to become real; it needed to be encountered fully, and only sight could bring this about. In our day, only reality matters; the important things are those that can be defined and measured. So we try to make this reality into truth, bring truth to it, include meaning within reality. And the word, as the only witness to truth, must thus be incorporated into images. This was the path religions took toward idols; it was the forbidden path. "You will not make for yourself any representation of things. You will not worship them" (Ex. 20:4-5, JE). The worship of reality amounted to the proclamation that reality was the only truth.

## 1. LIGHT

At this point how can we neglect the divine presence of light? "God is light" (1 Jn. 1:5). It is a frequently used metaphor! Light enables us to see. How could we fail to understand the entire Gospel of John, which speaks of nothing but this light? How can we fail to take into account the wonderful theology (believed to be the work of Dionysius the Areopagite)[1] of light springing forth in a series of leaps? Duby writes of this theology:

> God is Light. Every creature participates in this initial, creative light. Every creature receives and transmits light. Every creature receives and transmits divine illumination according to its capacity; that is, according to the position it occupies in the scale of being, according to the level at which the thought of God has placed it hierarchically. The Universe, which is the product of an irradiation, is a luminous bursting forth that descends by cascades. Light emanating from a first Being establishes each created being in its immutable position. But the light unites all of them. As the bond of love, it floods the whole world, establishing order and cohesion. Since every object reflects the light to a greater or lesser degree, this irradiation, by means of a continuous chain of reflections, causes a reverse movement, from the shadowy depths. This reverse movement reflects back toward the source of its radiance. In this way the luminous act of Creation itself establishes a progressive upward motion step by step toward the invisible and ineffable Being from whom everything proceeds. Everything returns to him by means of visible things which, at ascending levels of the hierarchy, increasingly reflect his light. In this way what is created leads to the uncreated by a scale of analogies and harmonies. By elucidating these relationships one after the other, we advance in our knowledge of God. As absolute Light, God is more or less veiled in each creature, according to whether it is more or less resistant to his illumination. But each creature reveals him to its own degree, since it liberates that part of light it receives in the eyes of anyone who will look at it with love.

This admirable composition harbors all the traps of sight as the aim of truth. For it moves continually from purely spiritual light (and the author speaks of light here only by comparison and analogy, because he is unable to find a better expression) to the sun's light, which illuminates creatures, revealing their form, color, movement, and reality. The spiritual light becomes temporal, natural light, and Pseudo-Dionysius's ambiguous theology will later inspire Suger's very concrete structures. In the latter, the light of the Invisible becomes the light of the Sun. This theology needs sight and reality in order to express the inexpressible and to coordinate truth and reality in one overall entity (the Creator and his Creation).

How can we fail to see a reflection of all this in the Christian

---

1. See the wonderful study of this theology and its consequences by Duby, *Le Temps des cathédrales*.

thought of the theology of the *sol invictus?* The sun is the source of light and life (this traditional religious expression becomes in our day a rigorous, precise scientific formula; it is no longer ecstatic poetic delirium, but the expression of the best of our world's knowledge. All life is born of and proceeds from the sun).

What a tempting way to reconcile a broken universe. But we must constantly come back to this limit, the same one marked by the flaming cherubim at the entrance to Eden. The *sol invictus* is not the God who created the beginning, he whose word inaugurated the worlds. It is not Love, Meaning, or Truth. Its implacable flame can lead us only to "the divine Nothingness." This light is a matter of analogies and parables, nothing more. Nothing becomes visible because of this light.

We must return to the prologue of the Gospel of John, where the balance is correct. "In the beginning was the Word. The *Word was* the *light* of the world." Here unity is basic. Word and Light are united.

In Creation the relationship between word and light is established in a complete fashion: light is an *effect* of the word. God says:

> Be—light
> Was—light
> Saw—light
> Separated the light from the darkness
> Called the light—day

The word and light, its effect, appear as penetrating each other completely and as utterly transparent. Form and content concur. But this takes place at the moment of creation, as in the prologue of the Gospel of John where the New Creation is considered, and it happens again in the book of Revelation. Undoubtedly light is the special being that gives access to both truth and reality. As a product of Truth, it literally gives rise to reality, since in Genesis the creation of light marks the appearance of time.

The creative Word causes light to spring forth the first time it is spoken. But this is a secondary light. It merely expresses the fact that there is no shadow, hidden place, duality, secret, mystery, or ambiguity in the one who speaks this word. At its origin this word is perfectly clear and involves no reservation. Light penetrates everything to manifest and make clear all that could be hidden. Up to this point, while we have no rupture, there is subordination of the light. It is the *first* creature, but it is a *creature*. Nowhere is it said that God *is* the light, and even less that the light is God. The light proceeds from him. The Spirit of God is a spirit of light and not of darkness; even less is he a blinding Spirit.

Life and light are clearly identified with each other. Life is the light of the world in the sense that what is alive must become the criterion of all judgment and evaluation. By the light we can understand and evaluate everything that happens. Life is light in that by it we discern; we have a touchstone which enables us to recognize, among other things, good and evil, because they are identical with life and death. But if someone tells us that God lives in inaccessible light, or if God is surrounded by unbearable light, or if "light lives with him," or the day of the Eternal God will be light and not darkness, and that this light penetrates everything and will make clear everything that was hidden, then we see that light accompanies God. It is associated with him and is truly his first creature. But the light is not God.

We can say to God: "God, you are my light." By this we mean that through God, through his revelation, we know what he chooses to reveal to us. Then we also see the world and ourselves from God's perspective, differently than we see them naturally. Jesus says of himself, "I am the light of the world," but he also says "*You* are the light of the world," so there is no identification of light with the inaccessible God who is beyond all definition. As a person who bears the *word of truth* Jesus and all those who receive the truth become light. This *word enlightens* both the person and the world, both the mystery of life and the mystery of our relationship with Love. This light does not give us a view of anything; it gives us a revelation of our relationship to Creation.

Light is the first creature. Thus the Father is called the "Father of lights," and those who receive the revealed word are designated "children of light." The light goes from the Father to the children, and they become bearers of this new creation. But in no passage is this a matter of sight.

This light could have signified reconciliation and the reintegration of sight into truth. But this did not take place. "The light shined in the darkness and the darkness did not receive it. . . . This was the true light which enlightens every man as it comes into the world. It was in the world and the world was made by it, and the world did not know it. It came to its own and its own did not receive it" (Jn. 1:5, 9–11, JE).

Therefore the wonderful coming and going of light as seen by the Areopagite does not exist and did not exist at an earlier time. This movement was the norm in Creation, strictly its only *norm. But it is no longer the norm of the world we live in.* Night and darkness have become the normal situation; our sight is limited by this darkness that lets us see only as far as our hand can reach or we can see.

Light came, but as a *streak* or a *ray,* a beam that makes a hole in the darkness, piercing a thick darkness that remains dominant. Beyond our atmosphere, in interstellar space, darkness reigns: galactic night. And the earth moves through this night. A single beam of this light occasionally crosses the darkness, is reflected, and enables us to see something, but how long does it last? The same is true of truth and life.

The darkness did not receive the light. It did not show in a clear, evident, blinding manner that Jesus was the Messiah, the Christ, the Redeemer, both the Son of God and the Son of Man. Only his human reality, in all its human weakness, was seen and seemed certain, in the spiritual night. When we try to reduce Christ to his historical dimension as the exemplary person, Jesus, we confirm this primacy of sight. This process shows us only a poor, unfortunate, innocent Jew who was put to death. When we reduce Jesus to this historical figure, we obey not so much a concern for the truth as the dominance of images in our thinking, as they substitute themselves for truth. The image of the Incarnation is the violation of the truth by a visible reality. What is visible veils and hides the truth. We concentrate our sight on this carpenter's son, on this wandering preacher, and thus we cannot understand the fullness of his message. We fail to perceive what is behind and beyond, but also what is in, his appearance.

We read enigmatic narratives in which the glory of God's truth sometimes becomes visible. In the Transfiguration, for example, the human appearance, what is visible in Jesus, is maintained, but at the same time the truth of his participation in the divine bursts forth. The spiritual light becomes a physical resplendence. Indisputably, the disciples see this. God's truth, which explodes in this negation of time, brings about the fusion of opposites. But, just so, it is unbearable that sight should make these people, who have been dead for a thousand years, appear as living and present. It is unbearable that the disciples' everyday friend should be clothed with the glory of God's truth. Terror stricken, the disciples say foolish things. This moment cannot last. Immediately, Jesus becomes the ordinary person they knew so well. Nothing of this retrieved unity could remain.

The Emmaus pilgrims have the same experience: in this case they do not see a blinding light that encircles Jesus' body. First he is surrounded by mystery: "Who is this person who talks like this?" And when the mystery is unveiled in the breaking of bread, when they recognize with their eyes that it is Jesus whom they had known so well but who had died—then everything disappears. Everything disappears and they no longer see anything. This takes place precisely at the moment in which they arrive at the unity of reality and truth: when the Jesus they see and recognize, and who is quite real, becomes at the same time the one who bears this extraordinary news: "The dead person has been raised." At that moment truth is surrounded by death as a halo. This man who had accompanied them was dead. His resurrection is the encounter, the rediscovered unity of reality and truth. Jesus' real life, which he had lived on earth as corporeal and visible, is reunited with his true life, created at the same time as light and truth.

For this reason I reject modern interpretations of the Resurrection, all of which try to avoid this scandal. They speak of the Resurrection as a myth designed to help us understand the truth of God. Or a Resurrection in the heart of the disciples who testify to the fact that Jesus is truly alive because they continue what he was. Or the Resurrection as simply the appearance of the Church. They offer us a Resurrection (which could not possibly be such a ridiculous event as a dead man coming back to life!) that is an image testifying to the eternal triumph of Life. Or the Resurrection as a political insurrection, or a manner of speaking whereby the disciples certify that their master was truly the bearer of life and truth for everyone.

All these interpretations evade and deny precisely what the Bible tries above all to make us understand: the reconciliation, reunion, and encounter of reality and truth, word and image. We said above that trying to reduce Jesus to his historicity amounts to following the separation by denying the truth. If this is true, this other desire to reduce the Resurrection to these mythical or political modes amounts to following the separation by denying reality and truth.

Such interpretations of the Resurrection amount to denying that anyone could *see* the crucified Jesus' body alive again. They are thus a denial that the truth of life had rejoined the reality of the body that was dead. It is fundamental and crucial that Jesus came out of the tomb *bodily*. Although we cannot exhaust the meaning of the Resurrection, we must understand that *first and foremost* it was this actual return to life of the one who had entered the place of the dead, in the depth of the abyss.

Thus the Resurrection was a fleeting intervention of light in our darkness. It vanished as soon as it was recognized. We have the same announcement in the encounter between Mary Magdalene and the Gardener, which includes this enigmatic injunction: "Do not touch me, for I have not yet reascended to the Father" (Jn. 20:17, JE). What is the point of this "Do not touch me"? Why does he give this reason: "for I have not . . . "? I think this is related to the heart of what I am trying to say: in this risen Jesus who can be seen, truth has completely rejoined reality. This is utterly new, because reality is penetrated by truth. And at the same time, truth becomes certain because it is visible.

But there is an insurmountable distance involved for those who remain in our situation; we cannot yet grasp in a lasting manner and hold on to this new thing in Creation (as on the mount of Transfiguration and at Emmaus). It disappears as soon as it is glimpsed, because the end of time has not yet arrived. "Because I have not yet reascended to the Father: you cannot lastingly see and grasp this until after the return; that is, when the end of time has come and everyone will see the accomplishment of this reconciliation." These words lead us to the last biblical discovery: the reconciliation of word and image, of reality and eschatological truth.

## 2. RECONCILIATION

We will not go back to our brief consideration of visions and theophanies. We must try to go on from there. Visions of signs or visions as dreams are just things that precede a personal encounter with God. Furthermore, such visions are sometimes the same as words ("God spoke in a vision," of which nothing is known; nothing is said of the vision, but the *word* is reported: Gen. 15:1; 46:2; Num. 12:6; etc.). The encounter, in itself never visual, is always considered a moment of ultimate significance for a person.

A personal vision of God is considered each time to be like a death sentence: thus Isaiah receives the vision (Isa. 6) and must go through the purifying fire if this vision is to be a beginning and not the end. But the rupture is total. And the prophecy which results from it is a prophecy of condemnation and judgment, with a final promise (Isa. 6:13). Ezekiel does not say he actually saw God, but rather describes the fabulous accompaniments of his glory. The result of God's presence seen in time is a prophecy of condemnation and final judgment. In both cases, the prophet announces that the people cannot hear the Word of God. Only the prophet listens to this word related to the end of time.

One cannot see God and live. A mutation in life stems from this encounter, because the prophet has entered a moment of ultimate significance. He has entered death and a new birth, which involves an absolutely new beginning. Something absolutely new is established with no continuity between what the person was before and after his encounter with God. The vision that preceded the encounter is an *ultimate* vision.

As for visions in which someone discerns a nonexistent object (Zechariah's ephah) that leads to an explanation, or visions that unfold like a story (Daniel's and Zechariah's visions), these have to do with apocalyptic vision. We will speak later of these, but must note at this point that such visions always have a twofold dimension: historical (by which they are related to the concrete, existing situation, with a message for the people of Israel) and eternal and final: the vision is not just the announcement of God's intervention in history but also the proclamation of ultimate truth. For example, the vision of dry bones in Ezekiel is clearly "historical," but how can we fail to see in it a prophecy of the Resurrection—that is, an eschatological dimension? Zechariah's visions all have this twofold dimension.

Indeed, how could we believe that God's judgment (always contemporary in these visions) would be limited to a temporal judgment and nothing more? The God of Israel is the God who entered the history of his people, a God present in this history who accompanies his people; yet at the same time this All-Powerful God is also the Eternal God of hosts. His word and the visions he gives are not limited to a given time and place. All Zechariah's visions (the horses, the measuring line, the lampstand and the olive trees, the ephah, etc.) are visions of judgment. The vision of the New Jerusalem in Ezekiel, or in Daniel the vision of the animals, the shining man, of Michael, etc.—everything that is seen is always related to a final combat, final judgment, a new creation, or a resurrection.

I believe this rigorous and constant relationship between what is *seen* and eschatology to be extremely significant. Sometimes it is explicitly expressed: Joel proclaims that in *"the last days . . . the young men will have visions and the old men will dream dreams"* (Joel 2:28, JE). And Job declares: *"when my flesh is decomposed, my eyes will see him"* (Job 19:26, JE). Thus visions are bound up with the end of time, and the possibility of seeing God in the fullness of his truth and reality can appear only when present reality—ours and that of the world in which we live—has disappeared in order to be replaced by another reality.

We find sight treated the same way in the New Testament, as when Jesus says, "Blessed are the pure in heart, for they shall see God" (Mt. 5:8). Seeing God does not take place in time, in our present reality, but rather is an ultimate vision, dependent on purity of heart. This expression indicates something absolutely new and radical in human life: not a renewal in a temporal and accidental, uncertain and transient sense, but a heart that has become utterly pure, like Isaiah's lips—these are the marks of the New Creation.

Likewise, of course, the Transfiguration is the sight of the resurrected Jesus already in his glory, as we will see him at the final judgment—Jesus seen in eschatological perspective. The same thing applies to Stephen's vision, when he sees the heavens opened as he is about to die. This is not a dream but the sight of what can only be seen as a new and ultimate reality.

Now we come to the book of Revelation. One of the characteristics of John's Apocalypse is clearly the multiplication of visions.

Sight plays a decisive role in this book. Everything depends on visions: of God's throne, of the glorified Christ, of the very glory of God, etc. But, of course, these visions are suspect: they are considered to be either imagination with no foundation or else a sort of literary construction. In other words, apocalyptic writers, and John in particular, are thought to have had no vision; their writings amount to just a manner of speaking: a literary genre. That is, to express truth at that time and in that milieu, it was necessary to make it depend on vision.

Sometimes it is believed that the prophets really had visions: that Isaiah really saw the glory of God as he says. This could have been the basis of an extremely violent dispute among the prophets: those who really had visions, and those who did not and only claimed to have seen them. Thus visions have a reduced importance within the whole of prophecy, the essential matter being "God says," or "the Word of God."

Then, progressively, visions become more important. But they also lose their rigor. In the case of Zechariah, for example, visions appear to be so identical with what they are supposed to mean that they almost give the impression of being simply an ad hoc illustration. We might say that something like this happens: a prophet has something to say. In order to make it gripping, expressive, and troubling, he can do something (Ezekiel's prophetic acts: the vine, public fasting, etc.), thus *acting out* the word in front of the public in order to make it directly understood. Take Jeremiah's yoke as an example: he shows the people what the word means.

From this practice of a living tableau the prophets move on to the description of their vision. In this case a vision is presented as a sort of riddle or as a means of shocking people. It is not certain whether the prophet actually saw something, but he uses a tableau or a sign to illustrate his message. He appeals to sight to make the revelation complete. However, when a man of God says he saw something, surely it is a difficult thing to affirm that he saw nothing!

Interpreting this matter as a question of historical evolution is too easy. Scholars say that the prophetic concept of revelation was replaced by an apocalyptic concept. They often say this with a shade of contempt, as when one of them writes: "writers of apocalyptic are no longer prophets. Whereas the latter proceeded by means of free oral expression of the word, the former are writers, for whom vision and divine revelation are nothing but a literary form" (Joseph Scharbert, *Morale et Ancien Testament*). It is hard to see on what grounds we would decide that apocalyptic writers had no real visions and that visions are a "literary genre"! (Is it believed that they are *also* a genre?)

The above quotation is significant, however, in that it makes clear that in apocalypses we no longer have any spoken message. Instead, a completely different process is used; one moves from visions to another form of expression: writing. Almost certainly the prophets became writers: they go from visions (which I believe they really had) to writing. So books or pamphlets are circulated. We no longer have a person dealing directly with a crowd to which he speaks.

True, visions are more appropriately described in a book than expressed orally in public. Probably Isaiah wrote down his vision immediately rather than speaking of it concretely in public. That is, a vision produces a text that is seen, since reading is a visual operation. Reading combines vision and word in that ambiguous form, the frozen text made to be spoken, as it waits to live again by being reconverted into speech.

A second facet to this, however, is much more important: if prophets had no visions, why did they use such a means to express revelation? Why reintroduce sight, since everything was centered on the word, and since everything continues to exist only through the word? Why all these detailed concrete descriptions? For we must consider the fact that the proportion of visual elements increases as we go along. The book of Revelation is entirely constructed on the basis of visions. It is probably the highest point of apocalyptic literature, not only by virtue of its content, the strength of its thought, its continuity, and the progression of its message (whether historical-critical exegetes who are clever at slicing a text up into thin layers agree), but also because of the interpenetration and rigor of its images. Everything is presented in such strongly visual images that the reader cannot help "seeing" them, and the word formulates the images. The word does not just declare truth but relates to the image and its background. The word relates not to the direct meaning of the image but to its symbolical and permanent meaning. The message does not itself become an image—seeing is not enough for understanding; but the message comes from an intertwining of what is seen and the word, which alone is able to reveal the surreality of the image. By this I mean that we are not dealing with just literary talent or a novelist's trick.

Sight must be stimulated, and even an imaginary vision must be represented as image. But apocalypses usually are a proclamation of the "last days": the Judgment, and the New Creation—at least those apocalypses preserved in our biblical canon are.

Gnostic-type visions refer to a static divine system (an organization of celestial hierarchies or "Heaven") and enter into "Eternity"— and we might say that Ezekiel's vision, for example, of cherubim, animals, etc., is of this type, very rarely found in the Bible. Then we have the truly apocalyptic visions, which are inserted into a movement, a progressive series destined to move toward a final moment.

This final moment can be an encounter with God in the absolute (which calls an individual into question existentially); or the discovery of the God who acts in history but places his people in a situation of ultimate significance; or the apprehension of the last days, with a view toward the "end of the world" and a completely new creation.

In all three cases, the apocalypse or apocalyptic visions express an irreversible radicalism. And I think that the process of the vision expresses this: up until that time, a Word of God entered history with the unpredictability of the word. It penetrated a reality that was foreign to it, and at the same time placed humanity in a contradictory situation. An apocalypse, on the contrary, uses vision, precisely because it announces the last days and the end of this contradiction. It amounts to toppling over everything into the new creation, where reality returns to the status it had "before the Fall." At this point (but only here) it becomes possible to *see* what could not be seen during the course of history.

Thus apocalyptic vision is not a more or less dubious literary device, nor a fashion of its time; rather it is perfectly consistent with its object. When it bears witness to the final reconciliation, the recapitulation, this reconciliation clearly encompasses all of reality. Therefore sight's apprehension of this reality, along with vision, becomes with and like the word the adequate mode of expression of *this* revelation of the work of God.

## 3. THE REDISCOVERY OF ICONS

We ended up earlier with a very harsh judgment on icons, but here we see that reconciliation affects them as well! It is actually quite remarkable that everything in the theology of icons is perfectly acceptable from an eschatological perspective, as long as it is a present affirmation of what will ultimately take place. Icons become part of an eschatological liturgy: they relate to the encounter of future life (Evdokimov, p. 23). They take us into the Lord's advent. They show us "the anticipation of the transfiguration of the whole human being." They enable us to penetrate the mystery of the "eighth day": "Icons from the perspective of religious experience give us a foretaste of the vision of God in the light of the eighth day" (but this theology forgets just one thing: that we have not yet arrived at the eighth day!). Evdokimov himself says precisely this: icons are an "eschatological task," an "art allied with the apocalyptic vision of the last things."

At this point we can agree again: this use of sight, this reconciliation of Vision and the Word is uniquely eschatological. It is promised and it is the promise of the end of the Fall; but it has not yet been fulfilled. As part of the theology of the last things (belonging

only in that theology!), it certainly is not in a direct line with speculative thought, but neither can it produce a present "demonstration."

One can try to defend icons by saying "they explain the ultimate
consequences of the Incarnation: the sanctification of matter and the
transfiguration of the flesh." It is good to *explain* this, but certainly
never good to show it as an accomplished reality, since the flesh is not
yet transfigured. Paul explicitly states that we can know nothing of
what this transfigured flesh will be, or what the immortal, incorrupt-
ible, glorious, spiritual body means. We know nothing of what all
this means, and we are even less able to show it.

I fully agree that we can say "the face-to-face vision of the future
time will be the vision of the incarnate Word," but the reference here
is future. Even symbolically, we cannot visually represent this incarnate Word in his glory. In other words, icons remain false in their
pretension to be symbolically shown reality. But they are acceptable
as the recall of a promise and as a reference to the reconciliation of
sight and word not yet accomplished, but simply announced. They
are acceptable on the condition that they remain at the level of recall
and reference, that is, with no reality, no liturgical role, without
attracting piety or prayer (but this is precisely what they have not
done!). They must be simply a signpost we consult to know in what
direction God is leading us. But no one meditates on a signpost: we
continue on our way!

Throughout his theology of icons, Evdokimov declares at each
step that icons show something eschatological, that they are the
actualized presence of the end times. This is highly significant. In
other words, as an eschatological *theology* announcing the reconciliation of truth and reality within that of word and image, this theology
of icons is perfectly correct and true. But this absolutely does not
authorize us to make real, concrete icons, showing what is concretely
invisible to our carnal eyes. No analogy or mirror, no allegory or
symbolism can give contemporary people on earth an image of the
invisible God before the new creation. He was incarnate once in Jesus,
who *will come back* in a glory that we can in no way depict for
ourselves.

## 4. THE GOSPEL OF JOHN

As we consider the announcement of the Reconciliation, we
must deal separately with John's Gospel, since it is the biblical book
which most continually deals with the matter of sight and vision (but
not images!). The verb "see" recurs continually (more than one
hundred times) and is undoubtedly one of the essential themes of this
book. This may be because "John" belonged to the second genera-

tion, which had not *seen* the Lord in the flesh. This generation questions whether sight is important. Paul dismisses the matter in short order by asserting that whether one saw Jesus alive makes no difference (2 Cor. 5:16).

John grapples with the issue in order to demarcate and establish the status of sight. This relates, of course, to his theology of light. To what would light correspond and whom would it show, if sight did not necessarily exist to receive it? What light and what sight are involved here? Four themes seem to intersect: (1) the discrepancy between what is seen and what is said about what is seen, together with the whole problem of seeing invisible things; (2) sight as a limit and degree of certainty on the part of the witness in his testimony; (3) the ambiguous and contradictory relationship between sight and faith; (4) sight as promise and eschatological dimension.

However, all these expositions, which insist so much on sight in this world (through the carnal experience of encountering God in Jesus and in the course of history) are nevertheless framed by two great statements: one at the beginning of this Gospel, the other at the end. The first is: "No one has ever seen God" (Jn. 1:18). The last one is: "Blessed are those who have not seen and yet believe" (Jn. 20:29). In other words, the whole long development of this idea should be read between those two poles. This whole thought process concerns sight, the importance of vision, its relationship with revelation, and the question of the status of things visual. All this is situated and relativized by the theological statement and the exhortation at the beginning and end of John's Gospel.

"No one has ever seen God." We must realize, then, that nothing in this Gospel can refer to a direct vision of God. This confirms all that was already stated in the "old" covenant. God is not knowable to the same degree that reality is. He is not observable through this sense that gives us a guarantee of certainty. This can produce a negative theology, and in fact there exists here an insurmountable barrier to our pretension to knowledge and recognition.

John adds: "the only Son . . . has made him *known* to us (Jn. 1:18, JE). Thus knowledge apart from sight is involved. Just as he can never be seen, God cannot be recognized. He is always unexpected, does not fit into our human panorama, perspective, or totality. He cannot be situated in any reality or be the object of any of our treatises based on evidence. Sight necessarily refers to something other than God.

As far as Jesus is concerned, we need something other than sight in order to call him "God." John's Gospel will lead us to identify him in this way. Its preliminary statement prohibits us from speculating about our intrinsic possibilities, and from proceeding to construct a

God who would necessarily be analogical with what we can see. This is so true that this Gospel—sometimes called Gnostic and said to be influenced by Gnosticism—is undoubtedly from its very beginning the most anti-Gnostic, because the path of Gnostic light for knowing God is closed off. The entire Gospel must be read in this perspective.

At the other end of the Gospel, the point of arrival, sight is blocked in the name of faith. Sight is devalued in comparison with faith, and it becomes impossible to legitimize sight in a universe governed by faith. Only those who do not see are "blessed"; that is, only those who have not seen, and who therefore have the only possible true relationship with God (because it is not based on sight, and seeing God is impossible).

Jesus declares us happy if we did not know him according to the flesh, during his lifetime, in his reality, because he requires of us the absolute leap: the risk of faith that is the only guarantee that we love him. We are blessed if we did not see him resurrected, if we did not place our hands in the scars of his wounds, if the Resurrection remains outside that reality for us. This is so because he asks us to enter the folly of this Resurrection that can be received only by faith; it ceases to be folly if it can be verified. And we are always trying to rationalize it (by saying that the Resurrection is the Church, or the poor, etc.) in order to stop the scandal—that is, we always try to come back to sight.

Thus John's entire teaching on sight is located between these two basic statements; we must continually go from one to the other. Clearly it is no accident that this Gospel begins with this statement and comes to a close with this benediction. It is obviously intentional, and John enables us to move ahead on the basis of what he gives us as starting point and testimony.

(1) Throughout this Gospel we find a clear discrepancy between what is seen and what is said about what is seen. This is because the reality that is seen is invisible. First of all, we have Jesus seen by John the Baptist. He sees Jesus and says: "Behold, the Lamb of God, who takes away the sin of the world!" (Jn. 1:29). John the Baptist sees simply Jesus the person. He describes him in such a way as to clothe him with a truth which does not come from sight. "Behold"—not Jesus, the person I see, but the Lamb of God. The reality he sees is encompassed and transcended by what he cannot see. "I saw the Spirit descend as a dove" (Jn. 1:32). No one saw this: God is invisible, and the heaven from which the Spirit comes is not the atmosphere, but the invisible heaven. The word *as* means that it was not a real dove. Seeing is not seeing. *In effect* John saw nothing.

The same thing occurs when Jesus "sees" the profound truth

about a person; he discloses what is not visible in the person: "Jesus *looked* at him, and said, 'So you are Simon the son of John? You shall be called Cephas (which means Peter)'" (Jn. 1:42). "Jesus *saw* Nathanael . . . and said of him, 'Behold, an Israelite indeed, in whom is no guile!'" (Jn. 1:47). Jesus declares the hidden truth about the person who comes to him. He has seen only what anyone can see, yet what he says goes beyond and reveals "the essence of being," which sight could not possibly reach.

We find the same relationship in Jesus' final conversation with his disciples, when he announces that he will send the Spirit: "the Spirit of truth, whom the world cannot receive, *because it neither sees him* nor knows him" (Jn. 14:17). The World—carnal individuals—can know only what it sees. One must see in order to accept. And this Spirit is one of the invisible things; that is, he is not part of accessible reality. Thus the world cannot receive this Spirit, because it confuses what is visible with truth. The Spirit of *truth* cannot be grasped by sight.

This text is central to the opposition we have outlined between the order of reality (grasped by sight) and the order of truth. In the same way, two verses later, "Yet a little while, and the world will see me no more, but you will see me; because I live, you will live also" (Jn. 14:19). When he is dead and gone, Jesus can no longer be seen by the world; he no longer belongs to the domain of visible reality. But since he will be alive, he will be seen by those whose "sight" extends to what is invisible; that is, they will move to another kind of sight—not of reality, but of what is hidden.

This kind of sight is not without its dangers. Jesus' enigmatic comment to the Pharisees shows this: "If you were blind, you would have no guilt; but now that you say, 'We see,' your guilt remains" (Jn. 9:41). If a person remains in the sphere of reality, of what is accessible to sight, and makes no claims beyond that, Jesus says he is blind (blind to God's truth) and without sin, because he does not claim to lay hold on God, to pierce and to know him through sight. Such a person does not claim to identify seen reality with truth, which is infinite, absolute, and mysterious. Since this person does not claim to define God or to make gods for himself, that is, to possess the fruit of the knowledge of good and evil ("then their eyes were opened," Gen. 3:7, JE), he is without sin.

The religious person, however, claims to see. He claims to encompass truth within the reality he sees. He claims to see by his own means—with his fleshly eyes he sees the invisible God (sees him, discerns him, makes him clear, etc.). Because he makes sight intrude into what is not its domain, such a person is a sinner. Beginning with himself and depending on his sight, he tries to accomplish through his own approach and strength something that can only be an extraordinary gift: to see the invisible.

The above passages from John harmonize with two others (showing once again the essential agreement of the Scriptures): one in Paul, and the other in Hebrews. Both passages focus on this same going beyond sight toward invisible things. "We look not to the things that are seen but to the things that are unseen; for the things that are seen are transient, but the things that are unseen are eternal" (2 Cor. 4:18). This passage shows how completely visible things are identified with concrete reality, which is by nature transitory. In Hebrews we read: "faith is a demonstration [something shown!] of unseen things. . . . By faith we recognize that the world was formed by the word of God, so that what is seen was not made by visible things" (Heb. 11:1, 3, JE). This passage shows how completely the Word is related to what is not seen!

Although the above two passages reveal the opposition between visible things and reality on the one hand and invisible things and truth on the other, their central theme is the "sight" of "invisible" things. This appears to be an obvious contradiction—a radical impossibility. Thus faith involves a kind of mutation which directs sight to a different domain than the one it deals with naturally.

Why speak of sight then? Obviously, we cannot use these passages to say that God becomes visible! They do not say that the invisible becomes visible! Or that our sense of sight acquires a "third eye." Why do these authors insist on sight? The letter to the Hebrews gives us a clue when it says that "faith is a firm assurance" (Heb. 11:1, JE). Certainly this sight of invisible things is not concrete, material sight of invisible things. And certainly it is not a matter of a "vision," like those sometimes found in Acts, for example, in which certain elements of the invisible are made apparent. What we have here, I think, is a metaphor in the strictest sense of the word; that is, as we have already said, sight when related to reality gives us complete certainty concerning that reality.[2] Reality when seen is as obviously certain as the word when heard is uncertain. In this sense, these passages tell us that by faith we have access to a full and complete certainty, comparable to the certainty sight gives us in the domain of reality. Seeing invisible things means having an apprehension as of reality, a possibility of certainty, and a guarantee of such things'

---

2. I remember, of course, that we know today that this certainty is false, that our sight is conditioned by cultural factors, and that an object is not seen "in itself" and as it is in itself. But it is still true that in common usage sight identifies an object and we cannot spontaneously doubt this reality.

existence; just as when I look at visible things I am sure (through my sight) of their existence, form, color, and distance.

(2) Thus I can associate with this interpretation a series of passages that associate witness with sight: "John bore *witness*, '*I saw* the Spirit descend as a dove from heaven, and it remained on him'" (Jn. 1:32); "And *I have seen* and have borne *witness* that this is the Son of God" (Jn. 1:34); Jesus answered "Truly, truly, I say to you, we speak of what we know, and bear *witness* to what we have *seen*" (Jn. 3:11); "He who *saw* it [the crucifixion] has borne *witness*—his testimony is true, and he knows that he tells the truth—that you also may believe" (Jn. 19:35).

Obviously, this relationship between sight and witness is not fortuitous. In each case the witness is related to sight (and I could refer to other, less significant texts that also link the two). Sight neither authorizes the witness nor provokes it; but John's insistence is clearly based on certainty. A person can give testimony only when he is absolutely sure, beyond a doubt; I would say he must be positively certain. Sight gives us this kind of certainty, this indisputableness, concerning reality. For this reason, John refers to sight. On the one hand, "we *know* that what we *say* is true." But in testimony, this knowledge based on the word does not count; what matters is metaphorically visual certainty: we are as sure as if we had seen with our own eyes. Based on this, we can bear witness.

(3) The Gospel of John places us within the central problem of sight and faith, which is not a simple matter. Alongside passages that apparently say that faith is based on sight, others say exactly the opposite (one sees because he believes). Still other passages, and these are the most numerous, emphasize the misunderstandings and misinterpretations that sight produces in the domain of faith.

We will begin with the third type: "A multitude followed him, because they saw the signs . . . " (Jn. 6:2). What follows is the feeding of the five thousand; after this, Jesus observes: "you seek me, *not because you saw* signs, but because you *ate your fill* of the loaves" (Jn. 6:26). They have gone beyond the sight of signs and miracles, in order to enter an existential and living relationship, the choice of "eternal life."

In another connection, the dialogue between Jesus and Philip typifies the misunderstandings concerning sight: "'If you had known me, you would have known my Father also; henceforth you know him and *have seen him*.' Philip said to him, 'Lord, *show* us the Father, and we shall be satisfied.' Jesus said to him: 'Have I been with you so long, and yet you do not know me, Philip? He who has seen me has seen the Father'" (Jn. 14:7–9). We will not get involved at this point in the endless debate over the identity of the Father with the Son!

Let's just notice that sight—the fact of seeing Jesus in his flesh and bones—brings with it no knowledge or understanding of who Jesus is. This is corroborated, of course, by Peter's confession and Jesus' response: "flesh and blood has not revealed this to you . . . " (Mt. 16:17). Sight does not eliminate misunderstandings.

On the contrary—all sorts of *misinterpretations* are made possible by sight. Here we should note that John's Gospel, which, as we have said, emphasizes sight so much, is also the Gospel of misunderstandings and misinterpretations! It can be considered the Gospel of misunderstandings because *people have too much confidence in what they see!* The spectator's eye fools him, especially when he thinks he has grasped something through sight! This is the theme of John 9, and, as Maillot emphasizes, it is also Nicodemus's problem: "Nicodemus, when he has seen Jesus' works, thinks he *knows* who he is. . . . And Jesus reminds him that seeing is not enough if one is to know; he must be born again."

The rupture between sight and faith is plain in John 6:36: "you have seen me and yet do not believe." And this is corroborated by John 6:40: "every one who sees the Son and believes in him. . . . " But this means "everyone who sees him *as* Son of God" (and not as Jesus the human being). And the terms "see" and "believe" are not correlated but separated by the word "and": it is not "sees and believes" (because he sees), but "sees and also believes." Thus this passage, which might appear to place special value on sight, is on the contrary an affirmation that sight must be spiritual, and that faith does not depend on it. When Jesus is asked to do a miracle so it can be seen and thus lead to faith (Jn. 6:30), he answers by speaking of bread from heaven which makes no concession to sight. Finally, sight can provoke hatred of Jesus: "now they have seen the works I have done, and they have hated both me and my Father (Jn. 15:24, JE).

In other words, Jesus' works drive us to a decision and oblige us to take sides. But when we base ourselves on sight, that is, on the sight of his works, without going beyond their appearance, this sight inevitably leads us to consider them frenzied, preposterous, morally unacceptable, etc. Thus we are led not just to indifference but to hatred of the one who has such pretensions.

At this point we come to a controversy that is not yet ended. For in the last analysis, the attempt to apply "scientific methods" to revelation and to Jesus amounts to trying to make them part of the visual domain. Since we are situated strictly in the sphere of reality we try to reduce Jesus to a visible, concrete reality. This may involve sifting his actions so as to leave only what is possible scientifically, or applying historical or structuralist methods in order to arrive at the point where everything about Jesus is explained. This process can only lead to rejection of Jesus as Lord and Savior. Our eyes see reality but not truth.

If sight were complete and enabled us to see the invisible, then such a process would lead to different results. But for this to work, sight would have to be something more than sight. This is the meaning of the famous passage: "He has blinded their eyes and hardened their hearts, lest they should see with their eyes and perceive with their hearts, and turn for me to heal them" (Isa. 6:10, quoted in Jn. 12:40). Conversion and faith become in some sense impossible when their eyes see what they see. The eyes given us for the purpose of seeing the glory of God in its reality have been closed by the Fall. There is indeed no need for a new intervention by God in order for people to be blinded concerning the truth. People refer continually to sight as the ultimate criterion, but it is blind to ultimate things.

The "seeing of invisible things" of which we spoke above is a new dimension in sight. This shows us another relationship between sight and faith: sight becomes true when it proceeds from or is transformed by faith. Faith discerns real things that are not present to ordinary sight. The entire narrative of the discovery of the empty tomb is striking in this connection (Jn. 20). Simon Peter enters the sepulchre and *sees* the linen cloths on the ground, and the cloth that had been on Jesus' head "rolled up in a place by itself."

The other disciple also sees, and he believes. He sees the emptiness, the empty tomb, ascertains that the body is no longer there, that the wrappings have been undone, and that the cloth from the head is on the ground. This is all he sees; that is to say that actually, in the domain of reality, he sees nothing. And he believes because he has discerned something invisible in this visible spectacle. He apprehends the Resurrection because the body is no longer bound by the wrappings, and because Jesus' face is no longer covered by the cloth (according to a traditional allegorical exegesis, this means that the body is freed from its earthly weight and that the glory of the divine face is no longer hidden behind a veil of flesh). Based on this empty reality that he sees, he believes.

But faith preceded sight in this case. The disciple believed in this Jesus; he believed that he was the Son of God, so that he sees reality, and *in* (and at the same time *beyond*) this reality he sees the Resurrection. Thus the prophetic promise made by Jesus to Martha is fulfilled: "Didn't I tell you that *if* you *believe* you will *see* the glory of God?" (Jn. 11:40, JE). The possibility of seeing this glory is based on faith. First there is recognition of the truth, belief in the revealing Word, and then, as a consequence of this, the sight of invisible things, the sight of the glory of God, becomes possible. That is, reality and truth are joined here, yet sight is restored to its fullness.

The passage from one to the other is especially emphasized by the last passage we will quote: "A little while, and you will see me no more; again a little while, and you will see me . . . because I go to the Father" (Jn. 16:16–17). The disciples fail utterly to understand this statement. From our vantage point, the thought is clear: "you will see me no more in the flesh, with your sight based on reality. But I am going to the Father, and because of this, you will receive the Holy Spirit. He will transform your sight, making you capable of seeing invisible things." Thus they would see him again, but in a different way, with a plural dimension: they would see Jesus himself glorified, but they would also see him in the body of Christ which is the Church, and in the Eucharist. They would also see him present in the poor and the suffering. We see because we believe. We see because even the most carnal eyes have now been opened to a surreality—to something beyond reality that is nevertheless not to be neglected.

(4) Jesus expressly and explicitly calls his disciples to see him by means of the word. He invites them not to seek beyond sight, trying to grasp some further or more secret mystery of God. Jesus calls them to see his reality as the totally revealed truth of God, and the word remains weak. The roles are reversed: previously, images illustrated the word; now, the word is a mere explanation of the fullness of the image given in Jesus. This importance of sight is radically confirmed in John's passages on the Resurrection: the first disciple entered the sepulchre "and he saw." This is repeated throughout the encounters with the empty tomb or with the resurrected Jesus. Mary Magdalene sees two angels. She sees Jesus standing. And when she returns to the disciples, she bears this message: "I have seen the Lord" (Jn. 20:18).

John's Gospel insists on sight as long as Jesus is present. His presence on earth is an exceptional time, a unique moment in which it is possible to encounter the fullness of truth by means of sight. The final fulfillment is already taking place. The end of time is present and being *accomplished*. But with Jesus' death and his going to the Father, this period is closed. The Incarnation *has* occurred but is no longer visible. People saw the Father in Jesus, but Jesus is dead: "a little while and you will see me no more; again a little while, and you will see me again" (Jn. 16:16, JE).

Thus sight is truly essential. Fundamentally, John presents Jesus' presence on earth, the Incarnation, as a sort of continual transfiguration (whose narrative he omits). But Jesus' death brings us back to the previous situation. We no longer have any way of seeing Jesus and thus of seeing God. We only hear things said about him. We come back to the word alone, and the relationship of faith ("Blessed are those who have not seen and yet believe," Jn. 20:29). Thus Jesus' visible presence on earth also relates to the end of time. It concerns the situation in which the reconciliation has taken place, in which word and sight are united, and sight gives a more direct, assured, indisputable view than anything previously experienced.

Thus as far as I am concerned, everything in Scripture that refers to sight sends us back to this promise concerning sight in the last days, or else to the fact that sight's reconciliation with truth is an eschatological matter. At present this reconciliation signals the presence of the end times. We can distinguish two emphases in the Gospel of John: one involves the assertion that Jesus' presence *is* in itself the end of time. The time is fulfilled because he is present. The other emphasis contrasts knowing and seeing, thus underscoring that a temporary situation prevails.

Jesus is present with the first disciples, and he says to them: "you *will see* heaven opened, and the angels of God ascending and descending upon the Son of man" (Jn. 1:51). "You will see"! Thus ultimate reality will be seen: heaven opened, indicating direct access to the Father, the moment of the final restitution, the triumphal entry into a recreated Eden, and the angels: the genuine coming together of "earth" and "heaven," of reality and truth. Thus sight is restored in its fullness, but this is possible only at the end of time.

All this takes place because Jesus is present. Precisely the same condensation of History into a single dot of ultimate significance, the condensation of time into reality, enables us to understand "your father Abraham rejoiced that he was to see my day; he saw it and was glad" (Jn. 8:56). Here again sight is involved, but in the way it will be at the end of time, when everything is present in the same manner. Sight no longer will involve a succession based on the succession of reality.

Everything related to "seeing" the Resurrection belongs to this same order. The Resurrection is in itself our entry into eschatology and the entry of the *eschaton* into our reality. After this, nothing can happen to change what has been accomplished. This applies to the apostles when they see "nothing," as we have indicated (Jn. 20); it also applies to the statement "They shall look on him whom they have pierced" (Jn. 19:37; they will see him in his glorious reality; that is, at the end of time), which is situated in this proclamation of the end. Lazarus's resurrection, with the statement "if you believe you will see the glory of God" (Jn. 11:40, JE), is also a prophecy of the ultimate resurrection. In that resurrection, the *vision* of God's glory is bound up with the presence of the *eschaton*; that is, the time when ultimate truth will be clothed with the evidence of visible things from "here below," from here and now. We must most assuredly connect the certainty of the Witness, of which we have spoken, with this future certainty.

In the meantime, Jesus enables us to know. His presence leads us to the knowledge of God: "No one has ever seen God; the only Son, who is in the bosom of the Father, he has made him *known*" (Jn. 1:18). But this ambiguity remains: Jesus did not enable us to see God, but he has transmitted knowledge of God because in the flesh he was God and visible. He is the knowledge that is described in the previous verse as "grace" and "truth." This knowledge is alluded to in many statements about glory (the Son of man has been glorified, and God has been glorified in him).

This knowledge, however, is not something based on sight but rather on his very presence. In Jesus, truth rejoins reality, and reality becomes true and the bearer of truth. Visible reality no longer belongs exclusively to the domain of the practical or of human separation. Instead, there is fullness. Because of the Incarnation, "Heaven" and "Earth" are joined, but this new situation is only temporary—while Jesus is visible and concretely present on earth. He is the premise, the "pledge," the point of departure, and the firstborn from among the dead. But we must live this as a promise while we await the reconciliation with him of our divided being. Then truth will become visible and evident and will no longer be the truth of the hidden God. With respect to images and the word, this is what we await. But this relates to the New Creation, to which we will return.

The Gospel of John thus locates sight's position perfectly with respect to revelation, and does not clash in any way with the rest of Scripture. John situates the final point at which reality and truth rejoin. In the Kingdom of God, there is no more separation. The rupture brought about by the Fall of Adam is obliterated. This rupture involves the opposition (not only this, but this in addition to other things) between truth and reality, so that there is no more truth in the real world where Adam lives. This is because God is no longer *in* this world. And there is no more reality in truth, because the Creation is separated from its Creator, and has refused him. And in his love, this Creator did not annihilate it or replace it with another creation.

The end of time is the point at which reality and truth reunite. In this sense we can say precisely that the Incarnation was already the end of time. But its presence was temporary! In the New Creation there will be no more opposition between the two orders. This is expressed by the phrase "God will be all and in all" (1 Cor. 15:28, JE). Truth will rejoin reality perfectly, will penetrate reality perfectly, will inhabit it totally. But this also means that sight will rejoin the word, that we will *see* face to face what we have heard about (in the earthly kingdom, we could only hear about it, since God chose the word as his instrument).

We will see: this is exactly what is promised to us by the Resurrection. When our "corruptible flesh is clothed with incorruption, and our mortal body is clothed with immortality" (1 Cor. 15:53, JE); in this text also we find that sort of glorious transmutation of reality clothed with truth. Then sight will attain to truth, because it will no longer be separated from reality.

Then "we will know as we have been known" (1 Cor. 13:12, JE), for it is true that God sees us perfectly. But we are continually reminded of this important difference: God sees us, though we do not see him. He knows us not only according to our truth but also according to our reality. And we are promised that "then" we will know in the same way. But since this is in effect one of the important characteristics of this new world to come, then it is clear why sight is especially chosen as the mode of revelation concerning the end of time; this will be the meaning of the New Creation.

Thus it is possible to see, but we can see nothing that concerns the truth of today, nothing for the present time. The unity of the word and sight relates only to the end of time. And this unity characterizes these new heavens *and* this new earth. Already this unity is manifested in the mode of revelation used in the apocalypses.

However, this confirms what we observe concerning the present Time: the radical and decisive opposition between the word and sight. If it is true that the two forms and objects of knowledge meet only at the final moment of history—if nothing less than the end of this Eon and the creation of a New World are required for sight and the word to be reconciled—then this implies that there is in the order of truth a deep, total, and essential rupture between word and sight in the present age. It is artificial to pretend to reconcile them, vain to believe that they complement each other, and wrong to hide one's face in horror at their hostility.

Thus the certainty of the great reconciliation (between sight and hearing, vision and word, what is shown and what is said) at the time of the New Creation—but only then—prohibits us from mingling them. But also this confidence situates us in a perspective different from the one of traditional theological research. Two theological concepts contradict each other: that of the synthesis of *hic et nunc* and that of the final reconciliation lived now in hope. This contradiction is probably best made explicit at this point in our argument. I might say that the concept of synthesis is characteristic of all the philosophical theologies, usually Catholic or Orthodox. The concept of contradiction is specifically a biblical concept.

In the first concept one always seeks to reconcile contradictory factors (or even poles) by means of a directly accessible synthesis. But the contradiction is resolved sub specie aeternitatis, in the present moment and permanently. In other words, when achieved, a *stable* synthesis results that necessarily takes on a metaphysical appearance. Scholars thus try on this basis to resolve the contradiction between image and word, and seek to escape the prohibition against making images (by saying that only worshiping them is forbidden). This is the road to visualizing Mysteries, to icons, to the Golden Legend, etc.

The Bible, on the contrary, shows us the reconciliation between image and word, between reality and truth, as the end point and the metahistorical moment reached after the historical process of contradiction. In the course of History we have no exclusion, divorce, or radical strangeness; but encounter and synthesis are impossible. In the course of History there is only evolution through reciprocal influence: the contradictory relationship (but it is a *relationship*!) that is necessary if there is always to be something *new*. This new thing, however, can never be included within a structure or expressed in an institution, for these congeal all possibilities of evolution and change. This relationship can be lived only in the integrity of contradiction and in the hope of reconciliation. But it must always be a present hope: a hope that changes the situation now, or that prevents a situation from occurring, since the basis of this hope is something already accomplished.

## 5. CHANGE

"Thus we must beware of congealing salvation history in a pattern that kills more than it expresses. We must remember the priority of history. The only way of preserving what God had to say to us is respecting as much as possible the events (words) by which he said it to us. The *word* became flesh, and it is accessible to us only through the 'flesh' of history as it is preserved for us" (Maillot). What consequences does Maillot's statement involve for today? The word is a vital center in our world, the main locus of the general crisis, the living sign of our alienation—our era's palpable SOS.

The word is greatly mutilated, cadaverous, and almost dead, but we must become conscious of what this means: our whole civilization is loathed along with the word. The word signals our civilization's possible death and provides the channel through which the poison can get in. Anyone wishing to save humanity today must first of all save the word.

The word is the place to begin. It is humiliated, crushed, and meaningless. We must restore its royal domain and its demands. The enormous mutation made possible by biblical revelation assures us that this effort does not amount to a pointless venture or an attempt to try out a risky path. The final reconciliation between image and word, between reality and truth, essentially won in the person and work of Christ, is given and promised in its fulfillment. Based on this assured, absolutely certain reconciliation, which, however, is not yet visible or accomplished, we must devise our works and paths. We are not alone, for we have the company of him who consummates this reconciliation. We are not rash, since we know the clear direction of this reconciliation.

Thus the rediscovery of the sovereign word cannot work against images by excluding them or by trying to humiliate them in turn or cast them into outer darkness. Could we do this, even if we had a passionate desire to do so? Each thing should be honored in its function, in its respective truth or reality.

At the same time, however, we must continually remind ourselves that although the reconciliation comes *at the end* and only at the end, it is both *already given* (in the knowledge and conviction of what will take place at the end) and not yet realizable. We must maintain this distance and specificity without fusing things. We must not pretend that the end has already come and that we can therefore fuse and synthesize. We must not convert eschatology into a reality by producing the reconciliation here and now, arbitrarily, through our own determination and means.

We come back repeatedly to the same struggle between ourselves and God. On the one hand we must do what God has decided must be done. But we must not begin ahead of time, before the fulfillment of the time willed by God: the *kairos*. This is extremely difficult. Jesus provides us with an example of the most profound obedience in that he not only does what God expects, but he does it at exactly *the proper moment*. We must not act like Abraham who, in his impatience to have the son promised to him, decides to have him with Hagar, since his wife is too old. But the time was not right. Nor should we do as the disciples did: they wanted the Judgment to take place right away, *hic et nunc*. Jesus' response is that if they pull out the tares now, they will also kill the divine seed.

Thus the long-awaited reconciliation of image and word and of truth and reality is certain, but we must not try to manufacture it with our techniques and metaphysics here and now. What we must do in this time and place, based on the certainty of reconciliation, is to hear the command to iconoclasm, which resounds continually. We must insist on the necessity for an understandable language for communication and work for the continually renewed opening up of everyday language.

(1) The command to iconoclasm:[3] we must commit ourselves continually to this difficult eviction of images from the domain of truth. They must remain what they are: useful, unexcelled means for reality and action, good in this realm. But they must not claim to go beyond this, not claim to evict the word, not lead people into worshiping images. Thus we are committed to combating this worship: in television, the skimming of newspapers that consist mainly of pictures, the reducing of thought to comic strips (even if they are wonderfully clever—especially so if they are), the framing of thought, research dependent on the results and possibilities of images, and the allurement of sketches and diagrams, but also the hypnotic effect of the automatic functioning of computer terminals.

All these attitudes are genuinely religious, though by no means is this apparent! A visible miracle takes place before our eyes. Since it has become an everyday, repeated miracle, it is all the more gripping. The command to iconoclasm must first of all firmly attack audiovisuals, whose lie we have exposed. We must warn of their great danger. When the word is integrated into a rigid series of images, it mobilizes at the same time both our view of the movement and our hearing of the explanation. This involves our *entire* field of perception in passive participation. Discord is abolished—the very discord that had pro-

---

3. Goux has given a perfect demonstration of the importance of iconoclasm. But amazingly, he considers our era iconoclastic, thanks to Marx, Freud, and abstract painting. These destroy philosophical images, he says! But the *real* invasion of everyone by images is what matters, so we must proceed to a real iconoclasm and not a fictitious one such as what Goux accepts. Vahanian, on the contrary, has understood the problem perfectly. He shows how real iconoclasm is an inevitable result of faith (Gabriel Vahanian, *La Condition de Dieu* [Paris: Seuil, 1970]).

However, in a remarkable insight, Goux (in *Les Iconoclastes*) sees that the messianic world is the world of nonrepresentation. But his whole thought is doubly flawed: (1) he considers in isolated fashion the commandment against making graven images, and therefore considers that the abstract paintings of Pieter Mondrian and Wassily Kandinski obey this commandment. He arrives at this conclusion without realizing that the central issue of the commandment is not the fact in itself, but the contemplation and bowing down to worship. Abstract, nonrepresentative painting doesn't change a thing!

(2) Goux's second error involves believing that the messianic world is presently realizable (for example, by way of abstract painting). He has not grasped the messianic world's eschatological character, involving a promise for the end times, which brings with it not the absence of all representation but the reconciliation of image and word. Goux quotes S. Zohar: "the messianic world will be [and I agree that it is future!] a world without images in which no more comparison will be possible between an image and what it represents." But this has nothing to do with painting; Zohar refers to the world of reconciliation, in which "God will be All and in All" (1 Cor. 15:28, JE).

duced (by means of contradiction) reflection concerning the individualized situation of the "thinking" subject. The word no longer evokes anything. On the contrary, it becomes a force for reduction, since it is reduced to the field of displayed, fictitious, and simulated reality.

The individual's margin of interpretation is reduced or even annihilated through audiovisuals, since symbol and content are fused in a realism which tends toward perfection. At the same time, the real situation thus recreated leaves the spectator without any possibility for active intervention. The audiovisual image no longer furnishes any stimulus to action. The word furnishes no stimulus to reflection. The result is absolute paralysis. Audiovisual techniques are "thus a new stage in human evolution; a stage that bears directly on the most human of characteristics: reflective thought" (Leroi-Gourhan).

The lie that ought to provoke our iconoclastic decision goes on: we are continually told that audiovisuals will bring about human perfection by economizing "imaginative" effort (in the etymological sense of taking the word and forming images from it). For the audiovisual image is ready-made: it is there, and the word fits it perfectly. We forget all too easily that imagination is the basic characteristic of intelligence,[4] so that a society in which people lose their capacity to conjure up symbols also loses its inventiveness and its ability to act. Each person loses his ability to produce symbols imaginatively; gone are the vital operation links in relation to the body's expression and to the beyond. Iconoclasm is indispensable with respect to this appalling antihuman war machine, which is what audiovisual techniques have become. In every way they are comparable to ancient idols, which required human sacrifice before they would show their truth. We must denounce this and show our scorn for the way they destroy. We must continually begin again, calling for individual reinterpretation.

But audiovisuals are not the only area in which iconoclasm proves necessary. We must also explode the illusion of the image as truth by obstinately refusing to believe "evidence," refusing to be deluded by statistics, graphics, or the products of computers. Only a word that is not the word can declare that "the computer says. . . . " A computer must never, ever be accepted as an ultimate reason.

---

4. Without going too far back, I refer the reader to the works of François Laplantine, *Les Trois Voix de l'imaginaire: Le Messianisme, la possession et l'utopie: Etude ethnopsychiatrique* (Paris: Editions Universitaires, 1975); Cornélius Castoriadis, *L'Institution imaginaire de la société* (Paris: Seuil, 1975); *The Crossroads of the Labyrinth* (New York: Urizen, n.d.); and Lewis Mumford, *The Myth of the Machine* (New York: Harcourt, Brace & World, 1967).

Computers are sometimes useful in their narrow domain (*very* narrow, despite their many possible applications). We must be iconoclastic with respect to computers, which are pretentious devices that arrogantly substitute themselves for the word and for reason. Our iconoclasm must attack all abusive scientism, everything that tries to pass itself off as truth, except for the word, which is characterized by chiaroscuro and hesitation. It is filled with meaning and is evocative and provocative.

We must oppose triumphant methods, the elimination of ambiguities, and the resultant foreclosure of possibilities for the truth (which slips in through the gaps of coherent discourse). No gaps, of course, are left in computer language, algebra, and scientific certainty. The frozen surface of our intellectual world is like a smooth glacier. Rich and superabundant images have invaded everything; but then left only a desert. They have become the very key to science. We must radically deny that science can account for everything human, because truth always may be expressed through human beings.

Scientism (be it psychological, sociological, or psycholanalytical), biological intervention in the embryo, test-tube babies, modification of chromosomes, personality changes through chemotherapy—all these are the result of identifying reality with truth. All depend on the triumph of things visual over the word. Our firm refusal must interpose in each case, in order to reestablish the possibility of risk associated with the word and meaning. Naturally, we are not called to object to science as such, but only to its idolatrous pretension to be exclusive, substitutive, and reductionist.

We oppose science only when it becomes merely an image, basing itself entirely on images and translating everything into images, yet claiming to integrate everything in the world, and myth in particular. Psychoanalysis's claim to be a science and at the same time to integrate myth (Oedipus, etc.) is extremely significant and disturbing. At this point we must say no. Myth, like anything else, can be considered an object of science, of course, but we must realize that in this way the essence of myth is lost since it is robbed of meaning (Lévi-Strauss). But when myth becomes an instrument of science, the result is that such a science can never be established. Deleuze is right: if analysis is to be scientific, it must exclude the Oedipus myth!

We must challenge science as a spatial entity: when it claims to include time while reducing it to something spatial. We must challenge science as related to reality: when it pretends to be the whole truth by limiting and excluding everything that goes beyond it. Science tries to exclude anything it cannot reduce. Hence we must also challenge this reductionist process itself: "everything" is defined as what can be categorized or reduced by the scientific method.

Finally, we must interpose in the religious realm. In view of the eruption of modern religious feelings and multiple religiosities, we must challenge visual mysticism. This includes the inward look, gurus, physical-spiritual exercise, transcendental meditation, neo-Buddhism, and apocalyptists. People must become clearly conscious of these movements, since all belong to the order of visual mysticism. All cultivate the famous interior silence, so that vision can develop! At the same time, the corporeal emphasis invades: frenzied shaking in religious meetings, trances and hysterical singing (ostensibly to express joy), organized pseudocelebrations, cults in which snakes are ecstatically shown and manipulated—all this claims to give strong expression to religious truth but only signifies the invasion of hypnotic images. It amounts to the exclusion of the word and the annihilation of revelation. God's path toward us is hermetically sealed off, replaced by people possessed of some visually expressed power. Our no to all this must be radical.

Certainly our iconoclasm should not work against images in themselves, since they are perfectly legitimate, good, useful, and necessary for life. We oppose their imperialism and pride, the covetousness and spirit of conquest they inspire, and their pretension to be without limits.

(2) We must not forget, however, that the promised reconciliation has value today. We should now be living not its beginning but *its reality as a promise.* This means that iconoclasm can attack only the transformation of images and visual things into idols: objects of belief, worship, and mysticism. We should not attack images when they are reduced to their proper level, function, and role. People unquestionably need esthetic expression, for example. This need, expressed through the creation of a beautiful image, receives its validation through the promise.

The problem comes when this beautiful image becomes the bearer of all truth for its creator—when it expresses the whole person. André Malraux's hypostasis of art can serve as an example. Sight, images, and representation are indispensable and covered by the promise. The first Christians' or the sixteenth-century Reformed Christians' iconoclastic fury took aim at worship of images rather than the object itself; they opposed confusion rather than reality. They were trying to return reality to its proper limits.

Images constitute our indispensable environment, on the condition that we *see* them as they are. Ecologists carry out the work of the promise simply by considering our human environment in its genuine reality. They judge reality on the basis of truth.

Reality is also an inevitable vehicle for truth, however. We must relive the conviction that truth amounts to nothing without this incarnation. We must live out again what Marx correctly affirms: the decisive importance of *Diesseits*, which prevents us from losing contact with reality. This expresses exactly Jesus' saying about praxis. Unless put into practice, truth is nothing; and praxis alone amounts to penetrating visible reality, as in the case of visualization. Thus again, sight, image, and reality should be restored to their authenticity, beyond iconoclasm. But this can be accomplished *in this world* only if we understand that God's promise also covers sight, image, and reality, since the same promise that authenticates them also *limits* them precisely.

(3) The third major ethical direction concerns the necessity of comprehensible language. Language is made to be heard and understood. Language brings the word to us. Only vanity and idealism believe that a pure, absolute word exists that is not clothed in language. The word exists only with and through language, and language is designed as a means of communication, as understandable, reasonable, and coherent. The lack of comprehension of something said signifies the absence of language.

Since truth can be conveyed by the word, we must defend coherent language energetically. At this point I would like to call to mind what Paul says in 1 Corinthians, precisely on the subject of these impassioned, frenzied words that were believed to conceal a deeper revelation than rational and comprehensible language. If languages that express demon possession exist, there must also be a language that expresses possession by the Holy Spirit: the famous "speaking in tongues." Paul does not reject it; rather, he critiques it:

> Make love your aim, and earnestly desire the spiritual gifts, especially that you may prophesy. For one who speaks in a tongue speaks not to men but to God; for no one understands him, but he utters mysteries in the Spirit. On the other hand, he who prophesies speaks to men for their upbuilding and encouragement and consolation. He who speaks in a tongue edifies himself, but he who prophesies edifies the church. Now I want you all to speak in tongues, but even more to prophesy. He who prophesies is greater than he who speaks in tongues, unless some one interprets, so that the church may be edified.
>
> Now, brethren, if I come to you speaking in tongues, how shall I benefit you unless I bring you some revelation or knowledge or prophecy or teaching? If even lifeless instruments, such as the flute or the harp, do not give distinct notes, how will any one know what is played? And if the bugle gives an indistinct sound, who will get ready for battle? So with yourselves; if you in a tongue utter speech that is not intelligible, how will any one know what is said? For you will be speaking into the air. There are doubtless many different

languages in the world, and none is without meaning; but if I do not know the meaning of the language, I shall be a foreigner to the speaker and the speaker a foreigner to me. So with yourselves; since you are eager for manifestations of the Spirit, strive to excel in building up the church.

Therefore, he who speaks in a tongue should pray for the power to interpret. For if I pray in a tongue, my spirit prays but my mind is unfruitful. What am I to do? I will pray with the spirit and I will pray with the mind also; I will sing with the spirit and I will sing with the mind also. Otherwise, if you bless with the spirit, how can any one in the position of an outsider say the "Amen" to your thanksgiving when he does not know what you are saying? For you may give thanks well enough, but the other man is not edified. I thank God that I speak in tongues more than you all; nevertheless, in church I would rather speak five words with my mind, in order to instruct others, than ten thousand words in a tongue. (1 Cor. 14:1–19)

Clearly Paul in his critique of glossolalia does not express himself like a mediocre, commonplace rationalist! Furthermore, the present fashion among Christians and theologians of rejecting Paul, of being suspicious of him, is utterly characteristic of all eras of intellectual carelessness and incoherent faith. Paul disturbs by his rigor and precision. It may be possible to rave deliriously and to say anything at all about the Gospels, but with Paul this is much more difficult!

As I said, Paul does not express himself like a mediocre rationalist: his judgment against speaking in tongues is based on love of neighbor. Language (not in all circumstances, but in the Christian understanding) must serve to construct, exhort, and console. It must enable the other person to edify himself in his relationship with his brother. You can console only if the word you speak is clearly understood. You can strengthen the other person only if he receives some meaning from what you say. You can help edify the other in his faith and in the truth only if he can use what you say for himself. Apart from this there are only confused and incoherent noises that serve no purpose. It would be more accurate to say that, yes they do serve a purpose: they startle people, lead them to believe the moon is made of green cheese, keep them at a childish level, and spread either terror or worship, both of which are absurd. All this is unchristian.

For Paul language is thus not just a common instrument of communication but the vehicle of a revealed truth that is common to everyone. Therefore it should be used for the benefit of all. It should always bring us back to concern and love for the other person, so that we take into consideration what can serve him. Paul alludes precisely to the common people: the humble people who do not have great spiritual gifts and whom we must help to advance.

Paul does not deny that speaking in tongues is an expression of the Holy Spirit ("I speak in tongues more than you all"). But he does indicate that this incomprehensible, incoherent, mystical language involves a direct relationship with an incomprehensible God. If it is true, therefore, that Christianity is a life of love, how could it be lived in solitude, face to face with God? Thus, out of love for others, speaking in tongues must be made understandable to everyone.

Speaking clearly and reasonably expresses love of neighbor, whereas today's passionate efforts to destroy language express nothing so much as the basic solitude of modern people. Undoubtedly I would greatly surprise our modern intellectual philosophers and poets (though they will never read these lines!) by explaining to them that their hatred of understandable language merely confirms the basic catastrophe of our society: human solitude and the technicalization of relationships. Thus (in a very routine fashion, incidentally) these members of the intellectual elite content themselves with carrying to extremes the worst social tendency. They make things worse by allying their intelligence with such trends and justifying things as they are. Intelligence has surrendered its strongholds and abandoned the fight.

No truth, depth, wisdom, or opening (into unknown worlds!) can be found in these pseudolanguages of lunatics and little children. Such languages fail to open into any world that might be behind this one and truer than this one. The most we can accomplish is to listen to the stammering of the unconscious, an echo of primitive times (which are *in no way* better because they were primitive!) through these languages. We experience a kind of emotion, explosive force, or truth in listening to these languages, not because it is really present in them, but because this brutal rupture causes something we used to have to spring up in us.

Personally, I have a great appreciation for surrealist poetry. But I know perfectly well that if an expression strikes me, if a word sequence calls up visions within me, it is not because these things are present in the poetry. Rather, the thing was in me, and the sound of the poetry was the trigger that set it off. The vocation of language is different.

Hatred of language, fanned into flame by miserable talk that rationalizes it, amounts to nothing more than hatred of human beings—of everyone but ourselves, of course—and the refusal to communicate. I enclose myself within a magical universe of symbolism without symbols, which opens for me alone onto vague and vain terrains. Hatred of language and worship of the language of people who are mentally ill are of precisely the same nature as a heroin addict's attitude. He is enclosed within his basic solitude and confirms this definitively through drugs.

Furthermore, everything Paul says is completely confirmed by what we see in the Old Testament: we know that prophets spoke in tongues and entered into trances. But nothing of this has been handed down to us. Only understandable prophecies using language were preserved for us as God's word for his people. Similar is the case of Jesus: never do the Gospel writers[5] allude to convulsions, oral ejaculations, or "prophetical" or Pythian trances! Never! Jesus speaks everyone's language: the clearest, most everyday language. His everyday, commonplace language encounters his stories—the extravagance of his parables—and thus an extraordinary element springs forth and explodes with new meaning (Ricoeur). Thus in Jesus we observe the same determination to use reasonable language, as the perfect vehicle for the absolute Word. He avoids hermetic language, double meanings, and elliptical expressions. Parables are rather a means of conveying meaning.

In conclusion, as Christians, we must support firmly the value of understandable language, which alone can communicate the Word. We must challenge energetically all the snares and temptations of mysterious, mystical, delirious, and fiery language. In the world as it is today, the recourse to such languages amounts to surrender and betrayal of humanity.

(4) Within this requirement of an understandable language, however, another possible orientation exists (I do not claim to exhaust all the possibilities; the reader must make the effort to find out for himself in what areas this requirement can be applied in our day! The analysis of lying advertising language is an example!). We must struggle (in a Christian way!) for an *open* language.

If language is to be a vehicle for the word and a possible translator of truth, it can only do so as an open language. That is, a language that permits a continual adventure. This is the only positive facet of the actions of the people I have just attacked, who invoke the language of insanity in order to destructure social language. They want an open language that is not stereotyped, and they are right to oppose wooden or leaden language. But their remedy produces a disease that is just as bad. For while this passion for the language of mental illness destroys reasonable language, it produces utterly closed discourse.

The admirable thing about language (and undoubtedly for this

---

5. We know, of course, that these Gospel writers are "suspect," just like Paul. Like him, they represented the dominant ideology, so that they translated Jesus' revolutionary message into bourgeois phraseology. See Jacques Ellul, *L'Idéologie marxiste chrétienne* (Paris: Centurion, 1979).

reason the parable of God's self-revelation refers to God as the word) is precisely the contradiction, conflict, and tension between the fixed structures of language, the fixed meaning of words, and the grammatical relationships, on the one hand; but on the other, the ability of these exact means to accomplish something that is not at all fixed. They can transmit the most fluid, the newest, the most secret, and the most heartrending things that exist in us and in the world. Each time it is used, stereotyped language can become the living, innovative word. But in order for this to work, language must remain open; that is, it must remain susceptible of being newly filled with unexpected content.

We could say (being especially careful not to force the comparison) that we have here the perfect tool, with which the sculptor can produce and bring to light something that did not exist. This tool does not condition the will, intention, or skill of the sculptor. The problem with this language (which is both marble and chisel) is simply the necessary resistance of the material and of the tool. The demands of expression must be stronger than the resistance, so that the resistance will manifest the seriousness of these demands. Language both structures and verifies the truth of the word, which remains unspoken if it does not bear a strong, expressive charge. But in order for this structuring and verification to remain possible, language must not be closed. By this I mean that the means must not prevent innovation; nor may it determine the work in an exact fashion. The magic chisel must not sculpt by itself, independent of the sculptor's hand.[6]

A tendency to close language exists, as does a tendency to reinforce this closure ideologically. That is, the tendency exists to realize the fears of the zealots of insane language. This closing comes from the social context itself: from ritual, repetition, and redundancy. As a result various forms of discourse are closed: political discourse; but also (as T. Kuhn has shown) scientific discourse (within what are called scientific methods, which exclude all innovation, or else within thought paradigms); ideological discourse (which limits itself to indefinite repetition); and catechetical discourse, whether it be Christian, Stalinist, or Maoist. Everyone convinced of the decisive character of the word—and still more everyone who considers biblical revelation his authority and has understood that everything depends definitively on the Word of God—must enter into combat against these closures. They exclude not only human language but also the possibility of the intervention of the Word of God.

---

6. This is simply a comparison. I do not mean to say at all that language is simply a tool or a machine for us to use.

We must insist, then, on two particular aspects of this closure, which are too rarely emphasized: a religious aspect and an administrative aspect.[7] Although there is much chatter about ideological and cultural language, certain matters are insufficiently dealt with.

Ritualization as a tendency and temptation of every religious universe is, of course, well known. We know of the relationship between myth and rite. Clearly there is value in such practices as repetition in prayer, of redundancy within worship and ceremonies, and of liturgy in the collective consciousness. Also evident is the necessity of fixed limits to give a sense of community; a strict framework in order to establish the relationship between the people and the celebrants (whether religious, military, inaugural, political or other types of ceremony are involved); and finally of stereotypes in order to avoid delirium just where it could so easily appear, in the expression of religious feeling! Ritual and liturgy are useful in producing a language that ceases to be evocative and thus avoids the risks of new elements. This language instead is confined to a soporific, incantatory, and reproductive role. Any open-endedness in religion, no matter what it is, is so dangerous that we feel a need to ritualize. But the ritualization of discourse amounts to the closing of any possibility for the word. Such ritualization always implies the transferral of the word to the visual universe (for this reason ritualization involves a considerable proportion of visible ceremony).

Here we are faced with a permanent characteristic of religions. And faith founded on Revelation through the Word alone (which refers to a God who only speaks) cannot tolerate this ritualization. Rites are fundamentally religious, whereas the biblical revelation is antireligious. Rite, like religion, involves fetters, closure, and framing, but the word is explosive and liberating. This is true of the word at work in language, and an understandable language at that; but it is true nowhere else and in no other way. Thus we discover a new contradicting factor between religion and biblical faith; this contradiction is beginning to be recognized and accepted.

We must not err in this: even when religion appears to be unfettered, it still remains utterly polarized and is never truly liberating. Thus, although we deplore the disappearance of festivals, we must not forget that festivals in traditional societies are never spontaneous: they are precisely governed by the ritual calendar. People broke loose in Saturnalia, Lupercalia, and Bacchanalia on a given day, at a precisely determined time; and at a certain hour, everything returned to normal. People freed their instincts on command, at the moment deter-

---

7. I omit the closing of language through advertising and propaganda, which I have studied at length in *Propaganda*.

mined by the stars, the calendar, etc. This plunging return to a group's origins, to chaos, was not invented; it was commanded. It has never been otherwise. This explosion of delirium and desire has only one goal: to make the social order better accepted and to make community constraints more bearable through a regulated liberating of the instincts.

Thus festivals also are ritualized: they are religious and amount to the establishment of new fetters, the renewing of old ones, and the possibiity of integrating and tolerating repression. They are never liberating. Only the word, the proclamation of truth by the word, the invention of the word, the reference to God who is the Word and to the Word that is with God—only these are liberating. They alone constitute the opening of an adventure, the position of an absolute beginning each time.

It is not by accident that freedom is a creation of the Judeo-Christian world. This very thing has involved us in the scientific and technical adventure, just as both democracy and socialism are products of this liberation through the word. But these always include the opposite threat of utter incoherence, either in politics or in thought, *and* the threat of absolute closure, in politics (dictatorship) and in thought (orthodoxies or scientism). Incoherence and closure are the two equal and complementary faces of falsehood. But every time the word surfaces again. Only today, vanquished by technique, has the word grown dim, become diluted.

Alongside this closure by ritual, we can find another example in administrative secrecy (which is the prolongation of secrecy in business and military or scientific secrecy; administrative secrecy is more serious, however, because it concerns everyone in the modern State and is the expression of a caste in power). Administration has created its own language and keeps secret its plans and projects, its decisions regarding action, and its procedures. Those who are subject to such administration cannot have any sort of open relationship with it. "Open house" or receptionists are just tricks whose function is to make the secrecy more acceptable without revealing any of the reality involved.

We are faced with a fight for freedom, for an opening of the word that is decisive for individuals and society. No rationalization can legitimize this secrecy. Everything must be explainable, discussable, and continually followed; and final decisions must result from a genuine dialogue—not a fictitious one like the current "consultations." If we want to return the dimension of truth to the word, we must break down the triple wall of administrative secrecy (triple in its hermetic language, its appearance of regularity, and the objectivity of its decisions).

All the more difficult is the requirement of the opening up of language, the struggle against all closures and enclosings, because our temptation is to accept and even justify such closures. Our repeated lie declares: "That's how things are. They can't be any other way, so they must remain that way."

In our day we observe a reinforcement of the closing up of languages through the analysis of language's nature (a closed analysis!) and through the philosophy that says "it must be this way." This reinforcement of closure comes from the reduction of everything to systems or structuralism and everything that gravitates around structuralism. Structuralism's value as a method of analysis is obvious. It even contributes a valid understanding of texts, as do other approaches. Clearly, it makes a certain light sparkle that can illuminate aspects of language not often appreciated. However, it does not go beyond these values and can only be one method, one approach, *among others*. It has no corner on truth. Structuralism says nothing about meaning and should never close our minds to meaning. It cannot claim to be exclusive. We must refuse structuralist *ideology*, which excludes meaning and reduces language to nothing but the interplay of structures.

Meaning filters down precisely in between the structures—in the gaps and incoherences. Furthermore, meaning is not something the speaker or writer fails to express, and that comes to light only in the structure, in the relationships between language units and their correlations and contradictions. Semantics and semiology, which reduce everything to the interplay of signs, are insufficient. The word goes beyond systems. But it can be imprisoned when the system is reinforced and the philosophical condemnation of the person speaking is just the other side of the coin, the reverse side being the power of technique's means when joined together against the freedom of the word.

You say that the freedom of the word doesn't matter much? You insist on freedom in *action*? That demand is all very fine, but in our day, recovering the freedom of the word and the word of freedom (that is, the truly innovative word) amounts to the *whole* of experiential liberty. In order to obtain it, we must be capable of risking our very lives. We will not recover the freedom of the word by some apparent audacity of crazy ideas or by some political adventure. Thus today, one of the aspects of our struggle is the refusal to reduce everything to a system, and the refusal of ideological structuralism.[8]

---

8. But we must be on our guard! Any serious structuralist will agree with this suggestion and say he is prepared to reject ideology, claiming to be purely scientific. The two are closely allied, however—so closely that I have never been able to find one without the other!

## 6. THE FREEDOM OF THE WORD

"Negativism! Again this time, everything you have said is negative: iconoclasm, struggling against the closing up of language, fighting the irrationality of the lunatic's language, and what else? What positive proposals do you have, and what program do you suggest?" I could answer in learned fashion with the positivistic dialectic of negativism: in the final analysis, only the No produces change and advance.

Again in this case, however, I prefer to refer to the simplest of images: a person is chained fast, by his feet and wrists, with forged chains. He has no way of freeing himself. You come with a sledgehammer and you break his chains. At the material level your act is purely and exclusively negative: you have broken some chains that were a fine product of human technique. You have destroyed the work of an artisan or of a large business concern that shows human progress. You are entirely negative—especially since you do nothing else. You have broken a lovely iron object that is now useless. And there you stopped. You have constructed nothing positive, that's certain.

But was I also supposed to take the freed prisoner by the hand, make him my pupil, and teach him what he should and could do? Doesn't this purely negative deed produce freedom? Now that he is unfettered, the person can stand up, begin to walk, and choose where he wants to go; he could do none of this before. Well, let him do it! But only *he* can do it, and if he prefers to stay hunched up in his prison wishing for his chains back, what further positive deed can I do for him?

This is precisely our situation. Whoever accuses my analyses and research of negativism and considers iconoclasm and the criticism of structuralist ideologies or of romanticizing insanity to be a purely pessimistic orientation proves just one thing: that he loves his chains. He is not ready to risk the adventure of freedom that begins with the freedom of the word, which requires a great effort and an enormous commitment!

The only positive action we can take is to open a space into which we must dash forward. In this manner we can discover the word's real nature, the unparalleled risk of truth and falsehood, and the extraordinary adventure of rationalizing or freeing from slavery. This is the open space before us. It requires a dialectical advance of our minds that are accustomed to the linear technological process; it requires the reintegration of the temporal into a spatially oriented civilization; and it forbids us to stop in our tracks.

As soon as the word becomes free again, we are involved in a whole set of contradictions. But they are necessary for life, particularly for life in the midst of division, such as the division caused by the smashing of the monolithic audiovisual world. Since the word is made to unfold and develop endlessly, we must continually refuse to stop. A spatial orientation presupposes stopping in the place which finally suits us. The visual world involves stopping; I must freeze and frame things. But the word stops no more than time does. No instant can last, nor can time be suspended. The word is the same. We must move ahead to meet what is advancing toward us: the great eschatological recapitulation of human history.[9]

Today we live in division and contradiction the life that one day will be unity, balance, and peace. We live in tension the life that promises a flowering (this is especially true of couples, who *exist* only by means of the word and not by means of sex!). We live in dialectic what will be the calm of the lotus flower. We live in conflict the life that promises reconciliation. We must not refuse this single possible mode of living: division, tension, and dialectic, as they are expressed and implied by the word. For apart from this mode all that exists is petrification, rigidity, decomposition, and death.

We can live this life only to the degree that we know that the reconciliation is already won, and that in Jesus Christ word and sight, proclamation and experience, space and time, are united. We need to know that we will see this reconciliation, that we "will understand fully, even as [we] have been fully understood," that we will see "face to face" what we have heard about (1 Cor. 13:12). Job says: "I had heard of thee by the hearing of the ear, but now my eye sees thee" (Job 42:5). Based on this certainty, without which we have nothing to live for and without which the conflict would be intolerable, we can return to the daily struggle to make the word resound, alone and unshackled. During the space of time that separates us from this final sight, may the word resound for human freedom and for God's truth.

*Dedicated to the memory of my friend*
*Yves Hébert*
*who died July 12, 1979,*
*as I was writing this last page.*

---

9. For Ellul's concept of recapitulation, see his commentary, *Apocalypse: The Book of Revelation*; and *The Meaning of the City.*—TRANS.

# WORKS BY
# THE SAME AUTHOR

*(In order of their first publication, usually in French)*

## I. HISTORY

*Etude sur l'évolution et la nature juridique du Mancipium* (thesis). Bordeaux: Delmas, 1936.

"Essai sur le recrutement de l'armée française aux XVI<sup>e</sup> et XVII<sup>e</sup> siècles." Académie des Sciences Morales et Politiques' prize, 1941. Apparently never published.

"Introduction à l'histoire de la discipline des Eglises réformées de France." Manuscript which awarded Ellul the "Agrégation" degree at the University of Paris Law Faculty, 1943. Apparently never published.

*Histoire des institutions.* Vols. I–II: *L'Antiquité;* Vol. III: *Le Moyen Age;* Vol. IV: *XVI<sup>e</sup>–XVIII<sup>e</sup> Siècle;* Vol. V: *Dix-neuvième Siècle.* Paris: Presses Universitaires de France, 1955–1980.

*Histoire de la propagande.* 2d ed. Paris: Presses Universitaires de France, 1976.

## II. SOCIOLOGY

*The Technological Society.* Trans. John Wilkinson. New York: Knopf, 1964; London: Jonathan Cape, 1965.

*Propaganda: The Formation of Men's Attitudes.* Trans. Konrad Kellen and Jean Lerner. New York: Knopf, 1965.

*The Political Illusion.* Trans. Konrad Kellen. New York: Knopf, 1967; New York: Random House, 1972.

*A Critique of the New Commonplaces.* Trans. Helen Weaver. New York: Knopf, 1968.

*Métamorphose du bourgeois.* Paris: Calmann-Lévy, 1967.

*Autopsy of Revolution.* Trans. Patricia Wolf. New York: Knopf, 1971.

*Jeunesse délinquante: Une expérience en province.* With Yves Charrier. Paris: Mercure de France, 1971.

*De la révolution aux révoltes.* Paris: Calmann-Lévy, 1972.

*The New Demons.* Trans. C. Edward Hopkin. New York: Seabury, 1975; London: Mowbrays, 1975.

*The Betrayal of the West.* Trans. Matthew J. O'Connell. New York: Seabury, 1978.

*The Technological System.* Trans. Joachim Neugroschel. New York: Continuum, 1980.

*L'Idéologie marxiste-chrétienne: Que fait-on de l'évangile?* Paris: Centurion, 1979.

*L'Empire du non-sens: L'Art et la société technicienne.* Paris: Presses Universitaires de France, 1980.

*Changer de révolution: L'Inéluctable Prolétariat.* Paris: Seuil, 1982.

*FLN Propaganda in France during the Algerian War.* Trans. Randal Marlin. Ottawa: By Books, 1982.

## III. THEOLOGY

*The Theological Foundation of Law.* Trans. Marguerite Wieser. Garden City, NY: Doubleday, 1960; London: SCM, 1960; New York: Seabury, 1969.

*The Presence of the Kingdom.* Trans. Olive Wyon. Philadelphia: Westminster, 1951; London: SCM, 1951; New York: Seabury, 1967.

*The Judgment of Jonah.* Trans. Geoffrey W. Bromiley. Grand Rapids: Eerdmans, 1971.

*Money and Power.* Trans. LaVonne Neff. Downers Grove, IL: Inter-Varsity Press, 1984.

*False Presence of the Kingdom.* Trans. C. Edward Hopkin. New York: Seabury, 1972.

*To Will and To Do: An Ethical Research for Christians.* Trans. C. Edward Hopkin. Philadelphia: Pilgrim Press, 1969.

*The Politics of God and the Politics of Man.* Trans. Geoffrey W. Bromiley. Grand Rapids: Eerdmans, 1972.

*Violence: Reflections from a Christian Perspective.* Trans. Cecelia Gaul Kings. New York: Seabury, 1969; London: SCM, 1970; London: Mowbrays, n.d.

*The Meaning of the City.* Trans. Dennis Pardee. Grand Rapids: Eerdmans, 1970.

*Prayer and Modern Man.* Trans. C. Edward Hopkin. New York: Seabury, 1970.

*Hope in Time of Abandonment.* Trans. C. Edward Hopkin. New York: Seabury, 1973.

*Apocalypse: The Book of Revelation.* Trans. George W. Schreiner. New York: Seabury, 1977.

*The Ethics of Freedom.* Trans. and ed. Geoffrey W. Bromiley. Grand Rapids: Eerdmans, 1976; London: Mowbrays, 1976. The French version, *Ethique de la liberté,* published by Labor et Fides (Geneva), contains some material not included in the English version. This is especially true of the third and final volume, entitled *Les Combats de la liberté* (1984).

*Living Faith: Belief and Doubt in a Perilous World.* Trans. Peter Heinegg. San Francisco: Harper and Row, 1983.

*La Subversion du christianisme.* Paris: Seuil, 1984 (soon to be published in English by Eerdmans).

## IV. BOOK-LENGTH JOURNAL ARTICLES

"De la signification des relations publiques dans la société technicienne: Un cas de passage de l'information à la propagande." *L'Année Sociologique* 3rd series (1963): 69–152.

"Impressions d'Israël." *Foi et Vie* 76, no. 4 (Aug. 1977): 1–72.

"Le Travail." *Foi et Vie* 79, no. 4 (July 1980): 1–50, 63–86. This is actually a group of articles, most of which are pseudonymous.

## V. AUTOBIOGRAPHY

*Perspectives on Our Age: Jacques Ellul Speaks on His Life and Work.* Ed. William
H. Vanderburg. Toronto: Canadian Broadcasting Corp., 1981; New York:
Seabury, 1981.
*In Season, Out of Season: An Introduction to the Thought of Jacques Ellul: Based on
Interviews by Madeleine Garrigou-Lagrange.* Trans. Lani K. Niles. San Fran-
cisco: Harper and Row, 1982.

# INDEX
# OF NAMES AND SUBJECTS

Aaron, 76, 87–88

Abraham, 74, 75, 77, 255

Abstraction, 26n.8; and God, 55; and images, 45, 130, 131–32, 140, 214; in language, 70; of modern environment, 207; and writing, 45

Action, 35, 85; as ambiguous, 107–8; and images, 144–45, 202; and judgment, 108; and language, 21, 29, 38–39, 64–65, 108, 127, 151–52; and propaganda, 145; and reality, 230; and sight, 6–10; social, 191; and Technique, 160; and truth, 27, 260; and the word, 49–50, 54, 100, 110, 201, 267; and the Word of God, 107

Adam: and Eve, 17, 66; and the Fall, 97–99, 252; and God, 51, 107; as mediator, 96; as namegiver, 52, 66–67

Administration, secrecy in, 266

Ambiguity: and action, 107–8; vs. computer "language," 161; and God, 233; human, 25; of images, 32; importance of, 258; and Jesus' divinity, 83–84; and language, 3, 8–9, 18–19, 22, 23, 25, 107–8, 162, 171, 175–76; in prophecy, 78; and reality, 72; and sight, 72, 243, 248; and structuralism, 154; and the word, 109; of writing, 42, 44, 160–61. See also Objectivity

Analysis and language, 133, 134

Apocalyptic and visions, 237–41. See also Eschatology

Arbitrariness of language, 166, 169, 173–74

Architecture, 224

Art, 181, 221–27; in the Church, 84n.26, 183–88; vs. icons, 102, 103; and instantaneousness, 227; modern, 16, 94, 112–15; in museums, 118; vs. reality, 116n.4; and science, 224; and Technique, 225–26; and writing, 42–44. See also Film; Music; Painting; Poetry; Sculpture

Audiovisuals, 7n.2, 116, 144, 217–20, 231, 269; in education, 129–32, 217–20; as efficient, 218–20; in evangelism, 202; as ideology, 217–20, 231, 256–57; and language, 146; and necessity, 217, 220; and passivity, 256–57; as reconciliation of word and image, 217–20, 231; rhythm of, 141, 142

Autonomy, 52–53, 99; and audiovisuals, 219; and the Fall, 68, 101; and images, 113, 212; and sight, 102; and the Word of God, 111

Barth, Karl, 51, 104n.34, 107

Baudrillard, Jean, 24, 208n.3

Beauchamp, Paul, 49n.3, 53n.4, 54n.5, 64n.14, 67n.15, 72n.21, 73

Beauty and icons, 102

Belo, Fernando, 92n.30

Bible: its human language, 41–42; and icons, 104; in images, 187; and mysticism, 50; and reality, 32; and sight, 71–102; and truth, 32, 41–42; and the word, 48–71; as the Word of God, 51, 63; as writing, 63

Blaquart, Jean-Luc, 48n.1, 49n.2, 77

Bourgeoisie: and ideology, 263n.5; and language, 155–56, 157, 172, 174–77

Certainty: and faith, 246–47; and the Fall, 96–97; and images, 36, 187,

189, 191, 194, 216; and language, 16–19, 20, 151, 160, 162, 163, 182; and noise, 13; in prophecy, 78; scientific, 258; and the senses, 39–41; and sight, 7–8, 40, 230, 246–48; and truth, 40–41; of the witness, 243, 246, 251; and the word, 230; and writing, 46

Charbonneau, Bernard, 147n.13

China, 125

Christendom, 200

Church, 183–92; and freedom, 58–59, 61; and images, 30, 70, 200; and oppression, 58–59; and sociological trends, 200–201; and the Word, 61

City: and images, 12; and noise, 196

Closure, 25, 29, 229, 254; and idolatry, 92n.30, 94; and images, 190, 191; and language, 19, 23, 32, 182, 255, 258–59, 263–69; in linguistics, 24; of relationships, 110; in religion, 265; of systems, 38; and television, 143; and truth, 41–42; and the Word of God, 107; and writing, 47

Comic strips, 37, 121, 145; and the Bible, 202; as sacred, 256

Commandment. See Law

Commitment, 65, 108, 268; and images, 200, 211, 213–14; and language, 33, 158, 160; of the witness, 108, 110; and writing, 44

Communication, 21; and images, 114; in Kierkegaard, 196

Computers, 128, 219; and language, 161, 162; as sacred, 256, 257–58

Condemnation, 109–10; in the Bible, 59–60; as liberation, 59–60

Conformity: and ethics, 35; and images, 26, 35, 145, 146,181–82; and language, 172, 174–76; and Technique, 154; and television, 140, 142–43

Conscience, 31; and images, 129

Consciousness and language, 36

Covetousness, 81, 101–2; and images, 259

Creation, 49n.3, 53–54, 78, 85, 96, 232–35; and the Fall, 252; in Kierkegaard, 195–96; and language, 50, 51, 64–68; and power, 199; and the word, 53–54, 59, 60

Criticism, 94, 221; and audiovisuals, 219; and images, 10, 34, 36, 128, 212–13, 214; and language, 34–35,

46, 176, 215; and light, 234; and pessimism, 34; and reality, 34; and television, 142; and the word, 65, 143

Dada movement, 163, 177

Debord, Guy, 114–15

Deleuze, Gilles, 44n.15, 55n.6, 152, 156, 170, 171, 172, 258

Diagrams, 107, 114, 134, 139, 152, 162, 170, 256; in education, 131–33; and Technique, 149–50, 153

Dialectic, 10n.3, 25, 40–41, 70, 153, 214–15, 269; biblical, 253–54; and dialogue, 17; and images, 8, 128, 207, 256–57; in Kierkegaard, 39; of the Kingdom, 81–83; and language, 39, 215–16, 264, 267; of language and sight, 14; and relationships, 16–17; of sight and hearing, 2–3; vs. Technique, 268; and television, 141; and the word, 268–69

Dialogue, 16–17, 18–19, 23, 25–26, 39, 172, 215–16; vs. images, 215–16; in Socrates, 38; and writing, 44

Dionysius, Pseudo-, 232–35

Doré, Daniel, 76–77

Duby, Georges, 186, 191n.3, 232

Ecology, 67, 259; and language, 163

Education: audiovisual, 217–20; and images, 11, 117, 129–32, 187, 212, 214; in reading, 134; and the senses, 14. See also Audiovisuals

Efficiency, 39; in the Church, 185–86; in evangelism, 201–2; and images, 11–12, 131–33, 151–52, 184–85, 186, 188, 200, 201, 211–12; vs. language, 151–52; and sight, 69; and Technique, 151–52; and truth, 231

Ellul, Jacques, works: *Apocalypse: The Book of Revelation*, 59n.10, 269n.9; *Betrayal of the West*, 181n.14; *Critique of the New Commonplaces*, 181n.15; *De la révolution aux révoltes*, 125n.6; *L'Empire du non-sens*, 169n.8, 227n.5; *The Ethics of Freedom*, 58n.9; "Herméneutique du témoignage," 110n.36; *Idéologie marxiste chrétienne*, 263n.5; *The Meaning of the City*, 68n.17, 100n.32, 269n.9; *The New Demons*, 300n.4; "La Notion d'homme quelconque en tant qu'hypothèse de travail sociologique," 206n.1;

*Propaganda: The Formation of Men's Attitudes,* 158n.4, 177n.10, 265n.7; *Technique and Theology,* 68n.16; *The Technological Society,* 148n.15; *The Technological System,* 148n.15, 207n.2; *To Will and To Do,* 96n.31

Emotion: and language, 215; and thought, 210–12, 214

Escarpit, Robert, 171

Eschatology, 85, 184, 237–41; in Job, 73n.22; and prophecy, 237–41; realized, 241–42, 253, 255, 256n.3; and recapitulation, 269; and sight, 243, 250–53; and vision, 238–41. *See also* Apocalyptic

Espagnat, Bernard d', 39–41

Ethics, 28, 199–200; vs. institutionalization, 191; and language, 35; situational, 145; and the word, 65

Evangelism, 201–2

Evdokimov, Paul, 102–6, 241–42

Eve, 17, 66; and the Fall, 96–99, 101

Evidence, 26, 99; and the Church, 183; and covetousness, 101; and the Fall, 96–99; and images, 36, 114, 134, 135–39, 188, 213, 214, 216, 257; and language, 16, 34, 97, 166, 215, 216; and reality, 34, 220; in religion, 85; and sight, 80; and Technique, 151; and truth, 10n.3. *See also* Images; Reality; Sight; Spectacle; Vision

Exodus, 58

Expositions, 118–19, 202

Facts, 31, 137–39, 267

Faith: vs. images, 30, 188, 189; vs. sight, 80–81, 87, 243–54; and the Word, 80

Fall, the, 229, 241, 249; and human autonomy, 68; and language, 197; and sight, 96–102; and truth, 96, 252; and weakness vs. power, 97–98

Falsehood: as closure and incoherence, 266; and language, 32–33; and truth, 28, 32; and the word, 101–2

Feminism, 35, 216, 229

Festivals and religion, 265–66

Film, 12, 26, 138, 213; and novels, 222–23; psychological impact of, 119; and reality, 31, 128–29, 202; and truth, 30, 202

Foucault, Michel, 152, 157n.2

Fourteenth century: Church and society, 188–90; images in, 186–87; mysticism, 186–89; theology, 186–89

Freedom: and the Bible, 58, 266; and commandment, 66–67; and the Fall, 97; and Greek thought, 59; and images, 116; and language, 23–24, 66, 173–74, 179; vs. necessity, 202, 220–21; and television, 142; and truth, 41; and the word, 57, 58, 110–11, 220–21, 267–69; and the Word of God, 68; and writing, 107. *See also* Liberation

Gabus, Jean-Paul, 88

Galy, A., 77

Glory: of God, 90, 93; human, 191

Glossolalia, 260–63

Gnosticism, 240, 244; and sight, 230–31

God: character of, 97; as creator, 78; as "dead," 95–96, 124, 198, 205; as exclusive, 92–93; glory of, 73, 90, 93, 252; and history, 54–55, 237–38, 241; and humanity, 54–56, 59; as indefinable, 234; as invisible, 56, 58, 71–77, 79, 83, 84, 92, 93, 99, 102n.33, 104, 105, 110, 229, 232, 237–39, 242, 243–46, 253; and language, 48–71; as liberator, 58–59, 62; as light, 231–34; as love, 59–60; name of, 53, 76–77, 106; as savior, 55; and space, 55; and time, 54–55, 238; as visualized, 95; as Wholly Other, 27, 32, 61, 94, 103, 110; will of, 255; as the Word, 264

Golden calf, 62–63, 90n.28, 91n.29, 93, 94

Gospel of John, 231, 242–54

Goux, Jean-Joseph, 5n.1, 91n.29, 94, 126n.7, 177–78, 183n.1, 256n.3

Graham, Billy, 202

Greek mysteries, 69

Guattari, Felix, 44n.15, 55n.6, 152, 171, 172

Hearing, 13–14, 37–38; and language, 14; and sight, 13, 14, 26n.8, 27–37, 42–44, 63, 69–71, 93, 167n.7, 204, 229, 231; and time, 13, 26n.8, 27. *See also* Language; Meaning; Truth; Word

Hidden things: vs. images, 198–203; and language, 16

History, 137; and the Fall, 97–98; and God, 54–55; and images, 159, 198; and the Incarnation, 106; and language, 20–21, 24, 166; and myth, 21; vs. nature in Israel, 70; and prophecy, 237–38; and the word, 254

Hitler, Adolf, 60, 125, 135

Holy Spirit, 250, 260, 262; and icons, 102, 103; and the Incarnation, 81; and light, 233; present with the Christian, 84n.26; as revealer of God, 57–58, 244; and the Word of God, 108, 109, 110

Hope, 254

Iconoclasm, 63, 94–96; as Christian duty, 94, 255–60, 268; and faith, 256n.3; and Greek Orthodoxy, 105–6

Icons, 102–6, 254; and the Bible, 104; and eschatology, 241–42; and sight, 102n.33; and worship, 242

Ideology and language, 174–77, 264

Idolatry, 86–96, 177–78, 184, 186, 229, 259; Christian, 83; condemned, 89–92, 93; and icons, 104, 105–6; and reality, 87; as security, 88; as slavery, 89; and statues in Catholic societies, 105; vs. the word, 191

Image of God, 67; in humanity, 85

Images, 31, 37, 75–76, 112–54, 259; and abstraction, 42–45; artificial, 31–32, 45, 126, 144–45, 192–94, 205–6, 212, 228–29; as autonomous, 113; biblical, 187; as certain, 36; characteristics of, 5–10, 26; and the Church, 30, 70, 183–92; as compensation, 128; condemned, 71, 85, 89, 112, 126n.7, 254; and conformity, 26, 35; and covetousness, 259; defined, 1; directness of, 36, 206–7, 212; and dread, 12, 209; and efficiency, 151–52, 184–85; and evidence, 134, 135–39, 220; vs. faith, 30, 188; and freedom, 116; function of, 255, 259; of God, 71–72; and history, 159, 185–92; and impatience, 208–9; increase of, 30–31; as instantaneous, 36; as intermediaries, 185; irreversibility of, 9; in Israel, 90n.28; and language, 34, 37, 116, 121, 126, 146, 176; and liturgy, 29–30; and lunatic language, 181; and meaning,

147; and miracles, 30; vs. mystery, 26; and necessity, 220–21; need for, 70, 121, 126, 128, 130–31, 150–51, 206–7; and passivity, 126, 212; and power, 151; and the present, 138–39, 207–9; and reality, 27–28, 30, 31, 115–16, 128, 140–41, 143, 144, 146, 188, 207–8; vs. reason, 206–7, 210–17; and religion, 29–30, 194–95; and society, 213–14; and the subconscious, 36–37, 210; as substitute for living, 119–20; as superficial, 123; as symbols, 84n.26; and Technique, 11, 148–54, 181, 207–8, 221; and theological error, 184; and time, 159; and truth, 29–30, 31–32, 146, 191, 256, 257; usefulness of, 206; and violence, 147; and the word, 48n.1, 90–91, 97, 102–3, 111, 130–33, 143–44, 158, 185, 190, 192, 210, 214–18, 220–21, 250; and worship, 184–85, 256; vs. writing, 116–17. See also Evidence; Reality; Sight; Spectacle; Vision

Incarnation, the, 51–52, 57, 62, 71, 79–85, 235, 242, 243–45, 247–48, 249–52; and icons, 103, 104–5; vs. images, 191, 198; interpretation of, 81–82, 103, 104–5, 106; and the word, 55–56; and the Word of God, 107

Individual, 140; vs. collectivity, 124, 125; and images, 141

Information: and images, 114; and language, 3–4, 16, 17, 158, 163; and sight, 6–7, 8; superabundant, 156–57; vs. the word, 196

Inspiration of Scripture, 63

Instantaneousness: and art, 224–25, 226–27; of images, 9, 10n.3, 36, 133–34, 211–12, 216; and language, 15, 21; and sight, 14, 21; and Technique, 225. See also Time

Institutionalization, 185, 186, 254; in the Church, 189–91; and visualization, 189–90

Ionesco, Eugène, 156, 218

Isaiah, 71

Jacob, 48n.1, 53, 74

Jesus Christ, 33, 56, 67, 75n.23, 81, 83, 101, 104n.34, 255; baptism of, 57, 83, 244; divinity of, 55–56, 67, 83–84, 105, 235, 243, 244–45, 247, 248, 250, 252; and freedom,

58; and glossolalia, 263; as image of God, 79–81, 83–85, 104–5; images of, 84, 95, 103, 106; as light, 233, 234; his parables, 198, 263; and science, 248–49; shroud of, 84n.26; and the Word, 48, 51, 56, 158. See also Creation; Incarnation; Resurrection; Transfiguration
John, Gospel of, 231, 242–54
John of the Cross, 71n.20, 75n.23
John the Baptist, 57–58, 83, 244
Judgment: and actions, 108; of God, 237–38; and language, 108; and prophecy, 237–38; and the word, 65

Kierkegaard, Søren, 37–39, 109, 195–98
Kingdom of God, 70, 71, 82–83, 252

Lacan, Jacques, 157, 164
Language: abstract, 70; and action, 21, 29, 38–39, 64–65, 108, 127, 151–52; and ambiguity, 3, 8–9, 18–19, 22, 23, 25, 107–8; as arbitrary, 66, 166; characteristics of, 3, 22–26, 264; vs. closure, 19, 263–69; and commitment, 33; and connotation, 17–18, 20; contempt for, 149, 162–72; and Creation, 64–68; and culture, 174–76; defined, 1; devaluation of, 33, 34–35; and dialectic, 39; dignity of, 64–65; vs. efficiency, 151–52; and ethics, 35; and evidence, 34, 97; and falsehood, 32–34, 65; fragility of, 40–41; and freedom, 23–24, 66, 68; hatred of, 146, 172–82, 262–63; and history, 20, 24; human vs. animal, 3, 19, 20; and image, 3–4, 34, 116, 121, 126, 146, 176; as imperialistic, 169, 171, 174–77, 201; importance of, 38; as incoherent, 197; and judgment, 108; and knowledge, 36; of lunatics, 178–80, 262–64, 268; vs. materialism, 34–35; and mathematics, 18, 19, 20; and meaning, 74; vs. mystery, 69; and myth, 21, 26; vs. paradox, 23, 24–25, 26, 34, 70; and the person speaking, 33, 57, 80, 111, 133, 139, 157–58, 160, 167n.7, 178, 267; vs. power, 69; and psychology, 35; and reality, 12, 22–23, 27–28, 32–33, 53, 220; and reason, 214–16; and relationships, 16–17, 18–

19, 20, 21, 23–26, 38–39, 42, 51, 53n.4, 59, 63–64, 215–16; and repetition, 64n.14, 264, 265; vs. sight, 12, 37–38, 74; vs. sounds, 167n.7; specificity of, 22–23, 28, 162; and symbolism, 69; and Technique, 149–50, 153, 159–62, 170–72; and television, 46; and time, 10n.3, 14–16, 22, 26n.8, 36, 44, 54, 224–25; and truth, 22–23, 27, 33–34, 40, 42, 160, 176, 260, 261; understandable, 255, 260–63, 265; vain, 33; vs. violence, 23; vs. vision, 75, 76; and the witness, 107–11; and the word, 196, 260. See also Hearing; Meaning; Truth; Word
Law, 59, 60–62, 65, 66; and freedom, 66; vs. human codes, 62; and institutions, 191; as liberation, 61–62; tables of, 62–63; as word, 63; as writing, 62–63
Lengsfeld, Peter, 76–77
Leroi-Gourhan, André, 42–44, 257
Lévi-Strauss, Claude, 60n.11, 258
Liberation, 58; and condemnation, 59–60, 61; vs. religion, 265–66; and the word, 266. See also Freedom
Light, 96, 98, 230–37; and Creation, 232–34; divine, and icons, 104; in John's Gospel, 243; and life, 234–35; and truth, 234–35; and the word, 233
Linguistics, 3–4, 16, 24, 99–100, 157, 158; and images, 132; and scientism, 165–70. See also Structuralism
Literature, 169n.8. See also Poetry
Liturgy, 124–26, 184; and closure, 265–66; fourteenth-century, 187; and icons, 104; and idolatry, 92n.30; and image, 29–30, 128; and institutionalization, 190; and mass gatherings, 125; and myth, 69–70; and power, 69, 125; and religion, 265; as spectacle, 200; vs. truth, 29–30, 202; vs. the word, 190, 192
Love, 28; and God, 59, 98–99; and sight, 186; and truth, 185
Luther, Martin, 109

McLuhan, Marshall, 26n.8, 37, 46, 120n.5, 149, 224–25
Magazines, illustrated, 121
Magic, 184; and images, 188

Maillot, Alphonse, 48n.1, 73n.22, 85, 89, 144n.12, 192, 248, 254

Marx, Karl, 29, 113, 176, 177, 193, 256n.3, 260; and freedom, 59, 221; and language, 209

Marxism, 175; and images, 209; and reality, 31, 182

Mass media: and images, 193; intellectuals' use of, 205; and symbolization, 229

Materialism, 29, 138; vs. language, 34-35

Meaning, 4; and images, 147; and language, 19, 74, 164-73, 175, 177-80, 182, 264, 267; in life, 97, 229, 231; and reality, 8, 9, 231; vs. the sacred, 69-70; and structuralism, 159-60, 267; and Technique, 153, 226; and television, 140; and writing, 45-46, 160. See also Hearing; Language; Truth; Word

Means, 40-42, 149, 206, 217; in evangelism, 202

Memory, 121-23, 124, 128, 229; and Technique, 227

Middle Ages and images, 200

Miracles, 74, 84n.26, 99; and images, 30, 188; and language, 56; and sight, 247, 248; as sign, 80; and the Word of God, 107

Money, 101; condemned, 59; and iconoclasm, 95

Morin, Edgar, 166, 170

Moses, 53, 58, 62-63, 73-74, 76, 87, 90n.28, 91n.29; seeing God, 50, 71, 84, 93

Music, 26n.8, 38, 167n.7; and radio, 149; and space, 222, 223-24, 225

Mystery, 25-26; and icons, 103; vs. images, 26, 183; vs. language, 69; vs. reality, 26; and sight, 186, 250; and truth, 26; and writing, 45

Mysticism, 71n.20; and the Bible, 50; and icons, 102-3; and institutionalization, 190; and language, 263; and sight, 230-31, 259; and visions, 75n.23

Myth, 152; defined, 106; and history, 21; and language, 21, 26, 43; and liturgy, 69-70; and reason, 43; and the Resurrection, 236; and revelation, 106; and science, 258; and television, 46; and writing, 46, 106

Names: in the Bible, 52-53; and language, 66

Nature: vs. history, 70; and images, 194n.5, 207; and reality, 207; and sight, 113; vs. society, 115; vs. symbolism, 69

Necessity: vs. freedom, 220-21; and images, 220

Neher, André, 78

Newspapers, 120-21, 127, 153, 196

Noise, 2, 13-14, 26n.8; vs. language, 168; vs. the word, 195-96

Objectivity, 52-53, 111, 114, 165-66, 170; and images, 11, 12, 133, 138-39, 212; and language, 15, 24, 33; and music, 224; and sight, 5-7, 9-10, 13; and truth, 45; of the Word of God, 51. See also Ambiguity

Openness. See Closure

Opinion, 24, 26

Oppression: in Church history, 58-59; through language, 174-77, 179-80

Painting, 208; abstract, 126n.7, 256n.3; and images, 9; and language, 177; modern vs. classical, 221-27; and reproductions, 134-34; and sight, 13

Paradox and language, 23, 24-25, 26, 34, 70

Paul: 58, 77, 84; modern rejection of, 261, 263

Philosophy, 24-25, 37-42, 152, 153, 195, 196-97, 256n.3; vs. audiovisuals, 219

Photography, 30, 36, 84, 121-24, 128, 134-39, 148, 206, 207; as art, 124

Poe, Edgar Allen, 12, 208

Poetry, 18, 25, 180, 195, 197; and the person speaking, 46; and space, 222; and speech, 46; surrealist, 262. See also names of individual poets

Politics: and language, 160, 264; and liturgy, 125-26; vs. poetry, 25; and power, 59, 199; and the word vs. sight, 199

Posters, 114, 117-18; in revolution, 26

Poverty, 250

Power, powers: in the Church, 183, 184, 185, 189, 191; condemned, 59; and covetousness, 101; and Creation, 199; and the Fall, 66, 68,

98; and false gods, 87; of God, 66; human, 67; and iconoclasm, 95; and idols, 89; and images, 151; and language, 68; and liturgy, 125; and politics, 199; and sight, 69, 87; and truth, 99

Praxis. See Action

Prayer, 199; and writing, 47

Preaching, 109–10

Prévert, Jacques, 156, 164

Propaganda, 177, 201, 215, 263, 265n.7; and action, 145; in evangelism, 202; and images, 117–18, 142, 210; and language, 127, 154, 158; through photographs, 135–37; and symbols, 229; and violence, 147

Prophecy, prophets, 75–76, 184; and glossolalia, 263; and idols, 90; interpretation of, 239–40; and meaning, 78–79; and sight vs. word, 239; true vs. false, 78; and visions, 77–79, 239

Protestantism: and images, 202; and language, 201

Pseudo-Dionysius, 232–35

Psychoanalysis and myth, 258

Psychology and language, 35

Queneau, Raymond, 46, 164

Rabelais, François, 15n.5, 155

Radio: and music, 149; vs. television, 144, 149

Rationalism, 49

Reality: and action, 230; in Acts, 85; vs. art, 116n.4; and criticism, 34; defined, 10n.3; dominance of, 30–31, 33; and evidence, 34; vs. faith, 189; and the Fall, 96–98; and idolatry, 87, 231; and images, 27–28, 30, 115–16, 126, 128, 140–41, 143, 144, 145–46, 188, 192–94, 207; as imperceptible, 39–40; and language, 10n.3, 12, 22–23, 27–28, 32–33, 53, 220; and Marxism, 31; vs. mystery, 26; and necessity, 220; and precision, 33–34; rejected, 207; vs. revelation, 191–92; and the senses, 40–41; and sight, 6–10, 40, 71–72; vs. signs, 99; and Technique, 30–31, 123, 193; vs. television, 120; and truth, 22–23, 27–28, 29–32, 40, 53, 72, 79–80, 85, 88–89, 90–91, 95, 96, 98, 114, 122, 125–26, 154, 182, 186, 189,

190, 191, 202, 219, 228, 229–30, 232, 233–34, 235–37, 245, 249–54, 258, 259–60; as ultimate value, 192–95; as unstable, 39–40; vs. visions, 75; and the word, 100; and writing, 44. See also Evidence; Images; Sight; Spectacle; Vision

Reason: vs. images, 210–17; and language, 36, 178–79, 214–16; and lunatic language, 180; and mythological thought, 43; opposed, 181; vs. Technique, 162–63

Reconciliation: of sight and word, 184, 241, 269; of truth and reality, 249–55, 256n.3, 259–60; of word and image, 241–42

Reformation and language, 201

Relativism, 40

Religion: vs. Christianity, 202; and closure of language, 265–66; vs. faith, 200; and festivals, 265–66; and images, 29–30, 194–95; vs. liberation, 265–66; and liturgy, 265; and power, 59; vs. revelation, 191, 200, 265; and sight, 72, 84–85; vs. the Word, 84–85

Resurrection, the, 83–84, 238, 249, 250, 253; and art, 94; and eschatology, 250–51; and faith, 244; and the Incarnation, 81–82; interpretation of, 236; as reconciliation of truth and reality, 235–37; and the word, 199

Revelation: vs. images, 199; and myth, 106; vs. reality, 191–92; vs. religion, 191; vs. theophany, 72n.1; and vision, 243; and the Word, 50, 57

Revolution: and images, 26, 145, 195; and language, 172, 176–77, 181

Ricardou, Jean, 153, 169n.8, 173

Ricoeur, Paul, 69–71, 263

Robinson, Bishop John A. T., 95

Ryser, Fernand, 62, 87–88

Sacrament: and icons, 103, 105–6; vs. the word, 70

Sacred: and images, 185; vs. meaning, 69–70; modern-day, 228–29; as necessity, 70; and sight, 69

Salvation, universal, 56, 60, 81–82

Sartre, Jean-Paul, 169n.8, 230

Schaeffer, P., 139n.8, 222, 227

Science: and art, 224; and the Church, 191; and the Fall, 97–98; as idolatry, 258; and images, 11, 132; and language, 3, 19, 33, 264; and myth, 258; vs. poetry, 25; and reality, 248–49; vs. religions, 198; and structuralism, 267n.8; and truth, 31, 40; and the word, 266

Scientism, 3, 219, 258; as closure, 266; defined, 153; and linguistics, 165–70

Sculpture and Technique, 223

Secrecy as closure, 266

Secularization, 191, 192

Sight, 5–12, 112–54; and action, 6–10; and ambiguity, 72, 248; and artifice, 11–12; and autonomy, 102; in the Bible, 71–102; in the Church, 191; and covetousness, 101; dominance of, 37; and efficiency, 69; and evidence, 80; vs. faith, 80–81, 87, 243–54; and hearing, 2–3, 13, 14, 26n.8, 27–37, 42–44, 63, 69–71, 93, 167n.7, 204, 229–31; in John's Gospel, 242–54; and language, 6, 8–9, 12, 37–38, 74; in liturgy, 265; as metaphor, 78, 246–47; in philosophy, 37–39; and power, 69, 87; and prophecy, 239; and reality, 40, 71–72; and relationships, 113–14; and religion, 72, 84–85; and the sacred, 69; and sin, 100–101; vs. truth, 27, 72, 79–80, 95, 115, 230–31, 234, 249, 253–54; and vision, 140, 239–40; and the word, 78, 83, 87, 96–97, 102, 184, 195, 199, 230, 239–40, 251, 265. See also Evidence; Images; Reality; Spectacle; Vision

Signs, 45, 177–78; as autonomy, 99; biblical, 73–74; clarity of, 150; from God, 99–100; human, 99–100; and icons, 104; and language, 3–4, 160; and miracles, 80; outdoor, 117–18; vs. reality, 99; and society, 165

Silence, 25–26; and the word, 196

Sin: in the Bible, 60n.11; and covetousness, 101; and sight, 100–101

Slogans, 127

Social action and images, 213

Society and language, 196–97

Solitude and language, 262–63

Soviet Union, 135, 136–37

Space vs. time in science, 258. See also Time

Specificity, 66; human, 3, 14, 63, 68, 128, 164, 174, 195, 225; of language, 28, 162

Spectacle, 114–15; in art, 224; vs. experience, 122–24; and liturgy, 126; and passivity, 127. See also Evidence; Images; Reality; Sight; Vision

Spengler, Oswald, 3, 11

State and iconoclasm, 95

Stereotypes and images, 213

Structuralism, 3–4, 16, 24, 25, 45, 132, 140, 159, 165–66, 169–71, 267; and ambiguity, 154; and closure of language, 267; and ideology, 267, 268; and Jesus Christ, 248–49; as scientific, 267n.8; and Technique, 153, 154, 170; and theology, 201; and the Word of God, 107. See also Linguistics; Taxonomy; Systems

Structures as fixed, 254

Subjectivity. See Objectivity

Suger, 186, 232–33

Surrealism, 121, 180, 262; and language, 163–64

Symbol, symbolism, symbolization: biblical, 70; Christian, 183; and icons, 102–3, 104, 105–6, 242; and idolatry, 88; and images, 184, 200, 221; and imagination, 257; of Jesus, 84n.26; and language, 19, 69, 178; and mass media, 229; vs. nature, 69; in picture writing, 42–44; in the sacrament, 70; in visions, 240

Syncretism, 28

Systems, 24, 25, 38; assimilation into, 110; and closure, 38, 267; in philosophy, 197. See also Structuralism

Taxonomy, 49n.2, 66. See also Structuralism

Technique, 110, 122; and action, 160; and art, 225–26; and audiovisuals, 217, 219–20; and Cain, 68; and the city, 145; and closure of language, 267; vs. culture, 220; vs. dialectic, 268; and dread, 12; and efficiency, 151–52; and evidence, 151; and the Fall, 98; and Genesis, 67–68; and iconoclasm, 95; and images, 11, 31, 128, 148–54, 181, 201, 206, 221; and language, 23, 149–50, 153, 159–67, 170–72; and mastery, 10–11, 12; and meaning, 226; as a milieu, 207; and modern painting, 126n.7; as neutral, 206; and objectivity, 212; and objects, 45; and the possible, 148–49; and reality, 27,

30–31, 123, 193; vs. reason, 162–63; and relationships, 262; vs. religions, 198; and the sacred, 228–29; and sight, 199–200, 226; and space, 223–26; and spectacle, 115; and structuralism, 153, 154, 170; and time, 226–27; vs. truth, 231; and the word, 149, 266

Television, 23, 128, 129, 138–47, 153; and the Church, 201; in education, 217; as image worship, 256; and information, 16; and language, 46; and myth, 46; and passivity, 144–45; vs. radio, 144, 149; and reality, 119–20, 193–94; and writing, 46

Temple, empty, 76, 94, 126n.7

Teresa of Avila, 75n.23

Textual analysis, 45

Theater: and liturgy, 187–88; and the state, 190

Theology: Catholic, and icons, 102, 105; conflicts in, 199–200; fourteenth-century, 186–87, 188–89; Greek Orthodox, 102–6; and images, 184; and reality, 193; and sociological trends, 199–200

Theophany, 237; biblical, 72–77, 99; and icons, 103; vs. revelation, 72n.21

Thévoz, Michel, 179n.12, 180

Time: in Creation, 233; and God, 54–55; and hearing, 13, 26n.8, 27; and images, 9, 159; and language, 10n.3, 14–16, 22, 26n.8, 36, 54; and reality, 9; vs. space in art, 221–27; vs. space in language, 268–69; vs. space in science, 258; and the will of God, 255; and the word, 111, 268–69. See also Instantaneousness

Totalitarianism, 110

Transfiguration, the, 85, 235, 237, 238, 241, 242; and icons, 104–5; in John's Gospel, 250

Truth: as abstract, 45; and action, 27, 202, 260; and the Bible, 32, 41–42; and certainty, 40–41; characteristics of, 40; and computer "language," 161; vs. correctness, 193; defined, 22, 28–29; and the Fall, 96; and falsehood, 28; vs. film, 30; and freedom, 41; and images, 29–30, 31–32, 146, 191, 228, 256, 257; as inaccessible, 228–30; and language, 22–23, 27, 33–34, 40,

42, 160, 176, 260, 261; vs. liturgy, 29–30; and love, 185; manufactured, 99; and mystery, 26; need for, 228–31; and power, 99; and reality, 10n.3, 22–23, 27–28, 29–32, 40, 53, 72, 79–80, 85, 88–89, 90–91, 95, 96, 98, 114, 122, 125–26, 154, 182, 186, 189, 190, 191, 201, 202, 219, 228, 229–30, 232, 233–34, 235–37, 245, 249–54, 258, 259–60; as risk, 268; and science, 40; vs. sight, 27, 72, 79–80, 95, 115, 230–31, 232, 234, 249, 253–54; as stable, 40; vs. Technique, 231; and visions, 238; and the word, 56–57, 68, 266; and the Word of God, 52; and writing, 44–45. See also Falsehood; Hearing; Language; Meaning; Word

Uncertainty. See Certainty

Universalism. See Salvation, universal

Usefulness: of audiovisuals, 218–19; of images, 127–39; of language, 162–63

Utopia: and language, 176; and truth, 230

Vahanian, Gabriel, 95–96, 256n.3

Vain words, 108–9

Vergote, Antoine, 71, 75n.23

Viallaneix, Nelly, 37–39, 195–98

Violence: and images, 147; vs. language, 23; and propaganda, 147

Vision, visions, 237–41; and apocalyptic, 237–41; biblical, 74–79, 85–86; and eschatology, 238–41; and icons, 105; importance of, 237, 239, 241; interpretation of, 239–40; vs. language, 75, 76; and prophecy, 77–79, 239; vs. reality, 75; and revelation, 243; and sight, 8, 140; and truth, 238; and writing, 239–40. See also Evidence; Images; Reality; Sight; Spectacle

Western civilization and freedom, 59

Wiener, Norbert, 225

Witness, 10, 22, 36, 41–42, 106–11; certainty of, 243, 246, 251; and language, 107; and power, 199; and sight, 247; and truth, 45; and the word, 57

Word, words, 155–82; and action, 49–50, 54, 100, 110, 201, 267; and alienation, 254; in the Bible, 48–

71; and Creation, 53-54, 59, 60; vs. dissonance, 195-96; and faith, 80; and falsehood, 101-2; and freedom, 57, 58, 110-11, 267-69; hated, 108, 172-82, 204, 205-6; humiliated, 254; and icons, 103; vs. idols, 191; vs. image, 48n.1, 90-91, 97, 102-3, 111, 130-33, 143-44, 158-60, 185, 190, 192, 203, 210, 214-18, 220-21; importance of, 52, 254; and the Incarnation, 55-56; and language, 196, 260; and liturgy, 265; nature of, 268; needed, 229-30; and prophecy, 239; and reality, 100; vs. religion, 84-85; and revelation, 57; vs. sacrament, 70; and science, 266; and sight, 70, 78, 83, 87, 96-97, 102, 184, 195, 199, 230, 239-40, 251, 265; superabundant, 127, 156-57; and Technique, 148, 266; and time, 111; and truth, 56-57, 68, 266; vain, 155-57; and visions, 239-40; written, 111. *See also* Hearing; Language; Meaning; Truth

Word of God: and closure of language, 264; and freedom, 68; and human word, 51, 57, 63-65, 100, 107, 109-10, 110-11, 196, 197, 202-3; as invisible, 62-63; and mathematics, 107; as self-revelation, 57-58

Worship and images, 184-85, 188

Writing, 26n.8, 36, 42-47, 153; and abstraction, 45; ambiguity of, 240; and anonymity, 45-46; and art, 42-44; and certainty, 46; and closure, 47; and freedom, 107; vs. images, 116-17; and meaning, 46; and myth, 46, 106; origin of, 42-44; and the person speaking, 44, 45, 46-47; as pervasive, 126-27; picture writing, 42-44; and reality, 44; religious, 46-47; and repetition, 44; and sight vs. hearing, 42-45; and speech, 14, 15, 46, 160-61; and television, 46; and time, 44; and truth, 44-45; and visions, 239-40; and the word, 111

# INDEX
# OF SCRIPTURE REFERENCES

## OLD TESTAMENT

**Genesis**
| | |
|---|---|
| 1 | 64n.14, 73, 96, 152, 176, 233 |
| 1:3 | 51 |
| 1:3–5 | 96 |
| 1:28 | 67 |
| 1:28–29 | 68 |
| 2:19 | 52, 66 |
| 3:6 | 96, 101 |
| 3:7 | 97, 245 |
| 3:8–10 | 98 |
| 3:20 | 66 |
| 4:17–22 | 68 |
| 9:1–7 | 68 |
| 9:2 | 68 |
| 11 | 52, 100–102 |
| 11:3–4 | 100 |
| 15:1 | 75, 237 |
| 18 | 74 |
| 22 | 77 |
| 32:22–32 | 74 |
| 46:2 | 237 |

**Exodus**
| | |
|---|---|
| 3:1–6 | 73–74 |
| 3:6 | 71 |
| 3:14 | 53 |
| 19:21 | 74 |
| 20:4–5 | 91, 92n.30, 106, 231, 256n.3 |
| 20:17 | 101 |
| 24:10 | 76–77 |
| 32 | 62–63, 87–88 |

**Numbers**
| | |
|---|---|
| 32:1 | 228 |
| 32:4 | 88 |
| 33:11 | 74 |
| 33:19–20 | 93 |
| 33:20 | 71 |
| 12:6 | 237 |

**Deuteronomy**
| | |
|---|---|
| 4:15–19 | 74 |
| 6:8–9 | 63 |
| 7:25 | 89 |
| 8:3 | 230 |
| 27:15 | 89 |

**Judges**
| | |
|---|---|
| 13 | 74 |
| 13:22 | 71, 93 |

**1 Samuel**
| | |
|---|---|
| 3:1–18 | 75 |

**1 Kings**
| | |
|---|---|
| 8:27 | 55n.8 |

**Job**
| | |
|---|---|
| 19:26 | 238 |
| 22:14 | 73 |
| 36:30 | 73 |
| 37:21 | 73 |
| 38:9 | 73 |
| 42:5 | 269 |

**Psalms**
| | |
|---|---|
| 74:4 | 99 |
| 97:7 | 89 |
| 115 | 94 |
| 119 | 61 |
| 135 | 94 |
| 139:4 | 64 |
| 139:14 | 64n.14 |

**Isaiah**
| | |
|---|---|
| 6 | 76, 237, 239, 240 |
| 6:10 | 249 |
| 6:13 | 237 |
| 40:18–19 | 94 |
| 45:13–20 | 86 |
| 46:6–7 | 94 |
| 53:2 | 83 |

**Jeremiah**
| | |
|---|---|
| 1:9 | 63 |
| 1:11–12 | 78 |
| 1:13–14 | 78 |
| 10:3–4 | 94 |
| 18:1–11 | 78 |
| 28 | 239 |

**Ezekiel**
| | |
|---|---|
| 10 | 240 |
| 37 | 238 |

**Joel**
| | |
|---|---|
| 2:28 | 238 |

**Amos**
| | |
|---|---|
| 7–8 | 77 |

**Zechariah**
| | |
|---|---|
| 5:5–11 | 237 |

# NEW TESTAMENT

Matthew
3:16 — 75
3:17 — 57–58
5:8 — 238
5:14 — 234
5:37 — 109
7:21–22 — 108
12:36 — 108
12:37 — 108
13:24–30 — 255
16:17 — 248
23:15 — 202

Mark
1:10 — 57–58
1:10–11 — 83
2:5 — 56
2:11 — 56
6:30–44 — 108

Luke
17:21 — 82
24:13–35 — 84, 235–36, 237

John — 231, 242–54
1:1 — 48, 233
1:5 — 234
1:9 — 233
1:9–11 — 234
1:17 — 252
1:18 — 79, 243, 244, 246, 252
1:29 — 244
1:32 — 57–58, 83, 244, 247
1:34 — 247
1:42 — 245
1:47 — 245
1:51 — 251
3 — 248
3:11 — 247

5:30 — 108
6:2 — 247
6:26 — 80, 247
6:30 — 248
6:36 — 79, 248
6:40 — 79, 248
8:7 — 56
8:12 — 234
8:56 — 251
9 — 248
9:41 — 245
11:40 — 249, 251
12:40 — 249
12:45 — 79
14:6 — 56
14:7–9 — 247
14:9 — 79
14:17 — 245
14:19 — 245
15:24 — 248
16:16 — 80, 84n.26, 250
16:16–17 — 250
18:36 — 198
19:35 — 247
19:37 — 251
20 — 249, 250, 251
20:17 — 236, 237
20:18 — 250
20:29 — 80, 243, 244, 246, 250
21:1–14 — 84

Acts
7:55–60 — 85, 238
9:3–8 — 85
9:10–16 — 85
10:3–6 — 85
10:9–16 — 85
16:9 — 85
18:9–10 — 85

Romans
1:23 — 90, 92, 93
10:17 — 80

1 Corinthians
2:4 — 108
4:20 — 108
8:4–6 — 89
13:12 — 253, 269
14:1–19 — 260–61, 263
14:8 — 108
14:18 — 262
15:28 — 252, 256n.3
15:53 — 253

2 Corinthians
4 — 92
4:18 — 246
5:16 — 84, 243
12:2 — 77

Galatians
5:1 — 58

Philippians
2:5–8 — 81
2:6 — 101

Colossians
1:15–16 — 84

Hebrews
4:12 — 65
11:1 — 103, 246
11:3 — 246

James
1:23 — 52
2:12 — 58

1 John
1:5 — 231
2:16 — 81

Revelation
1:12–20 — 76
3:20 — 99